D0017517

MIND, SELF, and SOCIETY

FROM THE STANDPOINT OF
A SOCIAL BEHAVIORIST

GEORGE H. MEAD

EDITED AND WITH AN INTRODUCTION BY

CHARLES W. MORRIS

THE UNIVERSITY OF CHICAGO PRESS

CHICAGO AND LONDON

ISBN: 0–226–51667–9 (clothbound); 0–226–51668–7 (paperbound)

Library of Congress Catalog Card Number: 35–292

THE UNIVERSITY OF CHICAGO PRESS, CHICAGO 60637

The University of Chicago Press, Ltd., London

PREFACE

THE following pages present the larger outlines of George H. Mead's system of social psychology. His views were developed from 1900 on at the University of Chicago in the widely known and highly influential course, "Social Psychology." Year after year students with psychological, sociological, linguistic, educational, philanthropic, and philosophical interests attended the course—frequently for a number of years; and book after book has borne testimony to the impact of Mead's ideas on his numerous students. The present volume contains much that will be of value to those of similar interests. For many of his listeners Mead's point of view—at once humanistic and scholarly—came to function as a focus of orientation for their entire intellectual and valuational life. The course in social psychology gave the foundation of Mead's thought. It was in effect Mead as scientist; it was upon this foundation that his philosophical elaboration and social participation rested. It is hoped that the present volume will be followed by volumes on *Movements of Thought in the Nineteenth Century*, and *The Philosophy of the Act*. Together these three volumes would represent the three main fields of Mead's work: social psychology and social philosophy, the history of ideas, systematic pragmatism. They are supplemented by the already published volume, *The Philosophy of the Present*, edited by Arthur E. Murphy, and published in 1932 by the Open Court Publishing Company, Chicago.

Though he published many papers in the field of social psychology (as the bibliography at the end of this volume shows), Professor Mead never systematized his position and results in longer form. The present volume aims to do this task of systematization, partly by the arrangement of the material and partly through references at the appropriate places to the published writings. It provides the natural entrance into the intellectual world of George H. Mead.

None of the material here used has been previously published. The volume is in the main composed of two sets of excellent student notes on the course, together with excerpts from other such notes and selections from unpublished manuscripts left by Mr. Mead. A stenographic copy of the 1927 course in social psychology has been taken as basic. This set, together with a number of similar sets for other courses, owes its existence to the devotion and foresight of Mr. George Anagnos. Sensing, as a student, the importance of the material of Mr. Mead's lectures (always delivered without notes), he found in Mr. Alvin Carus a sympathetic fellow-worker who was able to provide the means necessary to employ persons to take down verbatim the various courses. The completeness of the material varies considerably, but the set basic to this volume was very full. The whole is by no means a court record, but it is certainly as adequate and as faithful a record as has been left of a great thinker's last years. This material can be utilized through the Department of Philosophy at the University of Chicago.

The basic manuscript has been greatly enriched by the faithful and full notes of another devoted student, Mr. Robert Page, notes especially valuable since they are for 1930, the last year in which the course was given in its complete form at Chicago. Into the 1927 material (when rearranged, pruned of superfluous repetitions, and stylistically corrected) were inserted portions of the 1930 material, both into the text and as footnotes. The same was done to a much lesser degree with material from other courses, and selections from other sets than 1927 and 1930 are indicated by giving the year after the selection. Insertion of material from manuscripts has been indicated by inserting MS after the selection. All titles have been added by the editor. Other editorial additions are inclosed in brackets.

Supplementary Essays I*a*, II, III taken together practically constitute one unpublished manuscript. Essay IV is a compilation made from a 1927 stenographic set of notes of an elemen-

PREFACE

tary ethics course. I am grateful to Mr. Anagnos, Mr. Carus, and Mr. Page for making available the bulk of the material used. Professor T. V. Smith and Professor Herbert Blumer have read and commented on portions of the manuscript. Mr. John M. Brewster and Professor Albert M. Dunham have given freely of their time and of their intimate knowledge of Mead's views. Students too numerous to mention have kindly put at my disposal their class notes, and I wish to express to them my sincere thanks. The main work on the bibliography was done by Professor Dunham, though Mr. Brewster, Mr. V. Lewis Bassie, and Professor Merritt H. Moore have contributed items. Mr. Arthur C. Bergholz is responsible for the final bibliography. A grant by the Committee on Humanistic Research of the University made possible valuable assistance in the preparation of the manuscript. Mrs. Rachel W. Stevenson had the task of turning a confusion of marks into ordered copy. Professor James H. Tufts graciously aided in the reading of proof. My wife assisted in the preparation of the Index. At every stage of the work the staff of the University Press has given its efficient assistance.

I am well aware that all of our combined efforts have not been able to produce the volume which we wish George H. Mead might have written. But there is no evidence that even an added grant of life would have seen the material brought to volume form by his hands. That he was not the writer of a system is due to the fact that he was always engaged in building one. His thought was too rich in internal development to allow him to set down his ideas in ordered array. His genius expressed itself best in the lecture room. Perhaps a volume like this one—suggestive, penetrating, incomplete, conversational in tone—is the most fitting form for his thoughts; the form most able to carry to a wider audience in time and space the adventures of ideas (to use Mr. Whitehead's phrase) which made notable to smaller audiences for over thirty years Mr. Mead's lectures on social psychology.

C. W. M.

INTRODUCTION

GEORGE H. MEAD AS SOCIAL PSYCHOLOGIST AND SOCIAL PHILOSOPHER

I

PHILOSOPHICALLY, Mead was a pragmatist; scientifically, he was a social psychologist. He belonged to an old tradition—the tradition of Aristotle, Descartes, Leibniz; of Russell, Whitehead, Dewey—which fails to see any sharp separation or any antagonism between the activities of science and philosophy, and whose members are themselves both scientists and philosophers. It would be difficult to overemphasize the contribution to philosophy made by those whose philosophy has been nourished in their own scientific activities. Mead stated in one of his lectures that "the philosophy of a period is always an attempt to interpret its most secure knowledge." While that remark may need qualification in terms of the place that value considerations play in philosophical generalization, it provides the clue to Mead's own development, and indeed to pragmatism in general.

By the end of the last century no item of knowledge seemed more secure than the doctrine of biological evolution. This doctrine had dramatically called attention to the factor of developmental change in the world, as physics and mathematics had previously exhibited the element of structural constancy. The implication seemed to be that not only the human organism but the entire life of mind as well had to be interpreted within the evolutionary development, sharing in its quality of change, and arising in the interactivity of organism and environment. Mind had to appear within, and presumably to stay within, conduct. Societies themselves had to be envisaged as complex biological entities and fitted into the evolutionary categories. It has been the philosophical task of pragmatism to reinterpret the concepts of mind and intelligence in the biological, psychological, and sociological terms which post-Darwinian currents of thought have made prominent, and to reconsider the problems and task of philosophy from this new standpoint. The task is by no means completed, as is evidenced by the fact that the system-forming period is hardly yet in evidence. But the outlines of an empirical naturalism erected on biological, psychological, and sociological data and attitudes are clearly discerned, a naturalism which sees thinking man in nature, and which aims to avoid the inherited dualisms of mind and matter, experience and nature, philosophy and science, teleology and mechanism, theory and practice. It is a philosophy which, in terms used by Mead, opposes "the otherworldliness of the reason . . . . of ancient philosophy, the otherworldliness of soul . . . . of Christian doctrine, and the otherworldliness of the mind . . . . of the Renaissance dualisms." Much, too, has been done in the way of tracing the implications of the accompanying attitudes for education, aesthetics, logic, ethics, religion, scientific method, and epistemology. The pragmatic reliance upon the experimental method, coupled with the moral and valuational relation of the movement to the democratic tradition, has resulted in a conception of philosophy as having a double concern with fact and value; and a conception of the contemporary moral problem as the redirection and reformulation of human goods in terms of the attitudes and results of the experimental method. Darwinism, the experimental method, and democracy are the headwaters of the pragmatic stream.

In many ways the most secure and imposing result of pragmatic activity to date has been its theory of intelligence and mind. Such a theory is, of course, basic to the whole structure. The development and elaboration of this theory defines the lifelong activity of George H. Mead. The work of Mead and Dewey is in many respects complementary, and so far as I know, never in significant opposition. They were close friends from the years at the University of Michigan, and constantly discussed their problems together during the years at the University of Chicago. A natural division of labor at a common task was the result. Neither stands to the other in the exclusive relation of teacher to student; both, in my opinion, were of equal though different intellectual stature; both shared in a mutual give-and-take according to their own particular genius.[1] If Dewey gives range and vision, Mead gave analytical depth and scientific precision. If Dewey is at once the rolling rim and many of the radiating spokes of the contemporary pragmatic wheel, Mead is the hub. And though in mileage the rim of the wheel travels farthest, it can go no farther as the crow flies than its hub can go. Mead's thought rests closely upon a few basic ideas which were refined and elaborated over many years. True to his own words, the philosophy upon which he was more and more engaged in his later years was an elaboration, a "descriptive generalization," of the basic ideas which, as scientist, represented the most secure relevant knowledge he could obtain. Our task, however, is not to consider that philosophy as a whole here,[2] but rather the scientific basis upon which it rests (a basis which Mead as scientist has done much to create), and something of its social and ethical dimensions.

II

Mead as scientist was a social psychologist. It is commonly recognized today that science walks on two legs—theory and observation; that the logical phase of science (the phase of the isolation and definition of basic categories, and of system building) is of equal importance with the activity of the fact-finder and verifier. Mead adds little or nothing to the corpus of the facts of the social sciences as determined by distinctive methods

[1] Dewey discusses Mead in the *Journal of Philosophy*, XXVIII (1931), 309-14; and in the *University of Chicago Record* (New Series), XVII (1931), 173-77. For Mead's discussion of Dewey see *International Journal of Ethics*, XL (1930), 211-31; and the article on "The Philosophy of John Dewey," to be published in the 1936 volume of this journal.

[2] See Mead's works, *The Philosophy of the Present* (ed. Arthur E. Murphy); *The Philosophy of the Act* (ed. John M. Brewster, Albert M. Dunham, Charles W. Morris); *Movements of Thought in the Nineteenth Century* (ed. Merritt H. Moore).

of investigation; to the ideational and conceptual structure he adds much. It is true that the two aspects of science are ultimately inseparable, and that scientific ideas cannot be developed or analyzed fruitfully without reference to fact; but the observations to which Mead appeals are for the most part open to anyone—they involve no special scientific technique. Not in figures and charts and instruments is his contribution to be found, but in insight as to the nature of minds and selves and society.

The terms "social" and "psychologist" have not long appeared together, nor in company with biological categories. Tradition has identified psychology with the study of the individual self or mind. Even the post-Darwinian influence of biological concepts did not for a long time break up the inherited individualistic presuppositions (as is evidenced by the difficulties of a Huxley to find a place for moral behavior in the evolutionary process), though it did formulate the problem as to how the human mind appeared in the history of animal conduct. Mead traces in the following pages the process by which biological considerations forced psychology through the stages of associationism, parallelism, functionalism, and behaviorism. While Mead's own position is behavioristic, it is a social behaviorism and not an individualistic and subcutaneous one; he did not find an answer in any of the stages or schools of psychology as to how mind—full-fledged, reflective, creative, responsible, self-conscious mind—appeared within the natural history of conduct. Another factor had to be brought into the account: society. It was nevertheless fortunate that Mead was at the University of Chicago when the heavily charged psychological air precipitated itself into functional and behavioristic forms.[3]

The entrance of the other factor, the social, into Mead's

[3] The atmosphere of those days, and the confidence that the functional psychology implied a complete philosophy, is caught in James R. Angell's "The Relations of Structural and Functional Psychology to Philosophy," *The Decennial Publications*, III, 55-73, University of Chicago, 1903.

thought is less easy to account for, since he himself has not traced this development. Mead again was fortunate in being in environments in which sociology and social psychology were beginning to take the form of sciences. Idealistic philosophies such as those of Hegel and Royce stressed the social nature of the self and morality—and Mead had studied under Royce. Tarde and Baldwin had made many contributions toward a social psychology by 1900. Giddings had done his major work, and Cooley had begun his sociological career at the University of Michigan; Mead was a friend of Cooley and taught for three years in that environment. Attention had gradually been paid, especially by the Germans, to the social aspects of language, to mythology, to religion—and Mead had studied in Germany. Although he was at Berlin, and not at Leipzig with Wundt, there can be no doubt but that the influence of Wundt must be given credit for helping to isolate the concept of the gesture by seeing the social context in which it functions; instead of being simply "expressions of emotions" in the Darwinian sense, gestures were well on the way to being regarded as early stages of the act of one organism responded to by another as indications of the later stages of the social act. Mead specifically thinks of the gesture in social terms, and from such gestures traces the development of genuine language communication. In one sense, then, Mead may be said to follow a path partially indicated by Wundt; and certainly Wundt helped him to correct the inadequacies of an individualistic psychology by the employment of social categories.[4]

Nevertheless, Mead was no bare follower of Royce or Tarde or Baldwin or Giddings or Cooley or Wundt. As the following pages make clear, he had one basic criticism which he applied to them all: they did not go the whole way in explaining how

---

[4] Wundt is given credit for his voluntarism and is said to have "brought in the vocal gesture" (1930). On the other hand, "Wundt has not analyzed the gesture as such as parts of acts. He has treated them as an anatomist and not as a physiologist." "Wundt makes the social functions of the expressions of the emotions a later matter; at first he considers them merely as parallels of psychological processes" (1912). Wundt's parallelism is rejected, and explained methodologically.

minds and selves arose within conduct. This criticism breaks into two parts: (1) they all in some sense presupposed antecedently existent minds or selves to get the social process under way; (2) even in respect to the phases of mind or the self which they did attempt to account for socially, they failed to isolate the mechanism involved. The magic hat of the social, out of which mind and the self were to be drawn, was in part loaded in advance; and for the rest there was merely a pious announcement that the trick could be done, while the performance itself never took place. Mead's endeavor is to show that mind and the self are without residue social emergents; and that language, in the form of the vocal gesture, provides the mechanism for their emergence.

It is my belief that Mead has been successful in these tasks, especially in the isolation of the language mechanism by which mind is socially constituted and through which the self that is conscious of itself as an object appears. There is a question whether in identifying mind with the operation of symbols it must be held that such symbols are all language symbols of a social-vocal origin. If this is not so there may be individual aspects of mind in men and animals that do not come within the scope of Mead's terminology. In current terms, the question is as to the genetic priority of sign-situations (non-language symbols) and symbol-situations (language symbols). The issue here is largely as to the denotation of the words "mind" and "symbol," since Mead in some places admits the facts of redintegration which Hollingworth stresses, and the facts of delayed reaction which Hunter emphasizes, but unlike these men, feels that such processes do not come under the classification of "significant symbol" or "mind." Mead admits that the individual organism must have certain physiological prerequisites for developing language symbols; those who wish to use mind and symbol in a wider sense might add that the individual could not develop language symbols without being able to respond to non-linguistic, and so non-social, signs, in which one event leads at some organic center to the expectation of and redintegration

of some other event.[5] However this may be, with the acceptance
of Mead's use of the terms "mind" and "self," it seems to me
that he has shown that mind and the self are, without remain-
der, generated in a social process, and that he has for the first
time isolated the mechanism of this genesis. It is hardly necessary to say that a much smaller achievement would be sufficient to serve as a milestone in science and philosophy. Mead's
work marks an early stage in the actual birth of social psychology as a science, since his basic ideas go back to the early years
of this century.[6]

So it is that the problem as to how the human mind and self
arise in the process of conduct is answered by Mead in biosocial
terms. He does not neglect with the traditional psychologist
the social process in which human development takes place; he
does not neglect with the traditional social scientist the biological level of the social process by falling back upon a mentalistic
and subjective conception of society as being lived in antecedent
minds.[7] Both extremes are avoided by an appeal to an ongoing
social process of interacting biological organisms, within which
process, through the internalization of the conversation of gestures (in the form of the vocal gesture), mind and selves arise.
And a third extreme of biologic individualism is avoided through
the recognition of the social nature of the underlying biological
process in which minds arise.

The individual act is seen within the social act; psychology

[5] H. L. Hollingworth, *Psychology;* W. S. Hunter, *The Delayed Reaction in Animals
and Children.* Also his articles in the 1924 *Psychological Review.* A position essentially
akin to Mead's is developed by John F. Markey, *The Symbolic Process and Its Integration in Children.* Mead remarked that he thought the account was, however, oversimplified. Mead's distinction between non-significant and significant symbols is not
the same as the foregoing distinction of sign and symbol, since the former two are both
social. Section 23 contains a hint of Mead's distinction and the nature of the difference.

[6] A stenographic copy of the 1912 lectures on social psychology shows that his root
ideas were already in a mature form.

[7] The criticism of Watson is made clear in this volume. The brief indications to the
divergence of Mead's views from Cooley's may be amplified by reference to his article,
"Cooley's Contribution to American Sociological Thought," *American Journal of
Sociology,* XXXV (1930), 693 ff.

and sociology are united upon a biological basis; social psychology is grounded upon a social behaviorism. It is in these terms that Mead endeavored to carry out a major problem posed by evolutionary conceptions: the problem of how to bridge the gap between impulse and rationality, of showing how certain biological organisms acquire the capacity of self-consciousness, of thinking, of abstract reasoning, of purposive behavior, of moral devotion; the problem in short of how man, the rational animal, arose.

III

Though not used by Mead, the term "social behaviorism" may serve to characterize the relation of Mead's position to that of John B. Watson. Mead considered Watson's views as oversimplified, as having abstracted the individual's segment of the act from the complete or social act. Though Watson talks much about language, the essence of language as found in a certain type of social interplay has escaped entirely, and hidden itself under the skin. And even there it hides in the movements of the vocal cords, or in the responses substituted for vocal responses, and is finally lost entirely among implicit responses. In contrast, for Mead language is an objective phenomenon of interaction within a social group, a complication of the gesture situation, and even when internalized to constitute the inner forum of the individual's mind, it remains social—a way of arousing in the individual by his own gestures the attitudes and rôles of others implicated in a common social activity.

A second difference lies in the treatment of the private. As Köhler has remarked in his *Gestalt Psychology*, Watson's position is essentially the preference for an epistemology; it says in effect that the private cannot fall within science even if it could be known to exist; hence we must write with the human animal in front of us. To describe what is so observable is perfectly proper, but as human animals we do in fact observe aspects of ourselves in our attitudes, our images, our thoughts, our emotions which we do not observe so completely in others; and that fact is communicable. Watsonism gave the impression of ruling out of court the very contents that a mature psychology must explain. Mead was keenly conscious of this situation, but clearly believed that his own version of behaviorism was adequate to the task. Not merely was it to include the neglected social aspects of the act, but also the internal aspects of the act open mainly, but not exclusively, to the observation of the acting individual himself. Mind was not to be reduced to non-mental behavior, but to be seen as a type of behavior genetically emerging out of non-mental types. Behaviorism accordingly meant for Mead not the denial of the private nor the neglect of consciousness, but the approach to all experience in terms of conduct. Some may feel that this wider use of the term is inadvisable, that the term is Watson's. However, the present use includes all that may be observed and quantified by the radical behaviorist, and where any confusion may result, behaviorism in this wider sense may be distinguished from Watsonism. The judgment of time will perhaps regard Watsonism as behaviorism methodologically simplified for purposes of initial laboratory investigation. Mead's (and Dewey's) use of the term "behaviorism" to suggest the approach to experience—reflective and non-reflective—in terms of conduct simply signalizes with an appropriate name the direction implicit in the evolutional approach of pragmatism, a direction established long before Watson appeared on the scene and continuing after he has professionally left it.

A third difference arises from the fact that Mead, in harmony with Dewey's 1896 paper on "The Reflex-Arc Concept in Psychology," stresses the correlativity of stimulus and response. Aspects of the world become parts of the psychological environment, become stimuli, only in so far as they effect the further release of an ongoing impulse.[8] Thus, the sensitivity and activity of the organism determine its effective environment as

---

[8] For a development of this position that owes much to Mead, see L. L. Thurstone's *The Nature of Intelligence*. Mead's behaviorism assimilates much of psychoanalysis, *Gestalt* psychology, and existential psychology.

genuinely as the physical environment affects the sensitivity of the form. The resulting view does more justice to the dynamic and aggressive aspects of behavior than does Watsonism, which gives the impression of regarding the organism as a puppet, whose wires are pulled by the physical environment. Thus, in the case of reflective thinking, which Watson treats quite on a par with the conditioning of the rat, Mead is able to give a penetrating analysis of such reflection in terms of the self-conditioning of the organism to future stimuli in virtue of being able to indicate to itself through symbols the consequences of certain types of response to such stimuli. This account is able to explain the behavior of Watson in conditioning the rat, and not merely the resulting behavior of the conditioned rat.

Finally, a basic difference is reflected in the circumstance that Watsonism has seemed to many not only to deny private experience, but to empty "experience" itself of any meaning not possessed by "response." Certain of the radical behaviorists have frankly identified "I see x" with "my ocular muscles have contracted"; and have as frankly admitted that this identification leads into a behavioristic form of solipsism. Such a situation is simply the appearance in psychology of the logical and methodological scandal which has long harassed scientific thought: on the one hand science has prided itself upon being empirical, on bringing its most subtle theories to the test of observation; on the other hand science has tended to accept a metaphysics which regards the data of observation as subjective and mental and which denies that the objects studied have the characters which as experienced they appear to have. The pragmatist of Mead's type cannot agree with the attempt of critical realism to make this situation palatable. Such a pragmatist holds that the world, as conceived by science, is found within the wider and richer world that is experienced; instead of being the "real" world in terms of which to depreciate the world as experienced, the world of science is something whose origin is to be traced in experiential terms. Thus, Mead held that the physical thing, though prior for science, is experientially a derivative from social objects, i.e., is in the order of experience socially derived. On Mead's view the world of science is composed of that which is common to and true for various observers—the world of common or social experience as symbolically formulated. Mead's suggestion for the solution of the riddle lies in an insistence that the basic datum for observation is a world in which other selves and objects have the same direct accessibility (though the completeness of the accessibility may vary) as the observer has of himself. The experienced world is conceived by Mead as a realm of natural events, emergent through the sensitivity of organisms, events no more a property of the organism than of the things observed. Philosophically the position is here an objective relativism: qualities of the object may yet be relative to a conditioning organism. A certain portion of the world, as experienced, is private; but a portion is social or common, and science formulates it. Private experience and common experience are polar concepts; the private can only be defined over against that which is common.

It is not possible here to go into the implications for epistemology and philosophy of science of this concept of social experience.[9] It is mentioned here to show that Mead's behaviorism does not reduce the experienced world to movements of nerves and muscles, even though it insists that the characters of this world are functions of impulses seeking expression. This view does not make experience mental nor individual. It is because experience has a social dimension, because the self or organism is given in a field with others, that Mead is empirically entitled to start with the social act and to ground his social psychology upon a social behaviorism. The resulting richer and more adequate conception of behaviorism makes his account of central importance in the development of psychology, while presenting for the first time a behaviorism that can claim to be adequate to the problems of philosophy.[10]

[9] It is clear that this conception challenges the individualistic basis of the traditionally conceived epistemology. See *The Philosophy of the Act*, Part I.

[10] Mead did not, perhaps, make the maximum use of his behaviorism, in failing to be

IV

The transformation of the biologic individual to the minded organism or self takes place, on Mead's account, through the agency of language, while language in turn presupposes the existence of a certain kind of society and certain physiological capacities in the individual organisms.

The minimal society must be composed of biologic individuals participating in a social act and using the early stages of each other's actions as gestures, that is, as guides to the completion of the act. In the "conversation of gestures" of the dog fight each dog determines his behavior in terms of what the other dog is beginning to do; and the same holds for the boxer, the fencer, and the chick which runs to the hen at the hen's cluck. Such action is a type of communication; in one sense the gestures are symbols, since they indicate, stand for, and cause action appropriate to the later stages of the act of which they are early fragments, and secondarily to the objects implicated in such acts.[11] In the same sense, the gestures may be said to have meaning, namely, they mean the later stages of the oncoming act and, secondarily, the objects implicated: the clenched fist means the blow, the outstretched hand means the object being

---

more definite as to the locus of the private. For a possible development see Sections 62 and 63 of my *Six Theories of Mind*. Mead at times is too content to regard behaviorism methodologically, as simply a technique of control. See Section 6 of the present volume.

[11] Mead frequently seems to neglect the reference to a non-social object, as in Section 11. Here it would seem that the reference is always to a later stage of the act. Apparently the position is that this is originally so, and only secondarily to things in so far as they become involved in and are given meaning through the social process. In Section 7 he speaks of reference as being to "some object or other within the field of social behavior." This interpretation is in harmony with his view of physical objects being isolated within a social process from social objects. It makes understandable the various confusing passages in which meaning is at times identified with the response of the second form to the gesture of the first, at times with later stages of the act of which the gesture is a part, and at times with objects referred to. A 1924 statement that meaning is "the presence of the response of the other in the animal giving the symbol" must be qualified by the recognition that on Mead's account the "other" may in time be the physical object. "The mechanism of putting content into the object is that of symbolism; the things which stand for a later stage of the act play into the earlier stage; the ultimate act of driving in a nail is for us the meaning of the hammer. Meanings of things are resultants that control the present act; ends of the act present in the ongoing process" (1927).

reached for. Such meanings are not subjective, not private, not mental, but are objectively there in the social situation.

Nevertheless, this type of communication is not language proper; the meanings are not yet "in mind"; the biologic individuals are not yet consciously communicating selves. For these results to transpire the symbols or gestures must become significant symbols or gestures. The individual must know what he is about; he himself, and not merely those who respond to him, must be able to interpret the meaning of his own gesture. Behavioristically, this is to say that the biologic individual must be able to call out in himself the response his gesture calls out in the other, and then utilize this response of the other for the control of his own further conduct. Such gestures are significant symbols. Through their use the individual is "taking the rôle of the other" in the regulation of his own conduct. Man is essentially the rôle-taking animal. The calling out of the same response in both the self and the other gives the common content necessary for community of meaning.

As an example of the significant symbol Mead uses the tendency to call out "Fire!" when smoke is seen in a crowded theater. The immediate utterance of the sound would simply be part of the initiated act, and would be at the best a non-significant symbol. But when the tendency to call out "Fire!" affects the individual as it affects others, and is itself controlled in terms of these effects, the vocal gesture has become a significant symbol; the individual is conscious[12] of what he is about; he has reached the stage of genuine language instead of unconscious communication; he may now be said to use symbols and not merely respond to signs; he has now acquired a mind.

In looking for gestures capable of becoming significant symbols, and so of transforming the biologic individual into a minded

[12] This use of consciousness is to be distinguished from that which denotes the field of the given ("experience"), and from a third use which makes it synonymous with private as distinct from social experience. On the present usage, "We are conscious when what we are going to do is controlling what we are doing" (1924). The same three distinctions are applicable to the term "mind." Mind as the presence of significant symbols is neither identical with experience in general nor with private experience.

organism, Mead comes upon the vocal gesture. No other gesture affects the individual himself so similarly as it affects others. We hear ourselves talk as others do, but we do not see our facial expressions, nor normally watch our own actions. For Mead, the vocal gesture is the actual fountainhead of language proper and all derivative forms of symbolism; and so of mind.

Mind is the presence in behavior of significant symbols. It is the internalization within the individual of the social process of communication in which meaning emerges. It is the ability to indicate to one's self the response (and implicated objects) that one's gesture indicates to others, and to control the response itself in these terms. The significant gesture, itself a part of a social process, internalizes and makes available to the component biologic individuals the meanings which have themselves emerged in the earlier, non-significant, stages of gestural communication. Instead of beginning with individual minds and working out to society, Mead starts with an objective social process and works inward through the importation of the social process of communication into the individual by the medium of the vocal gesture. The individual has then taken the social act into himself. Mind remains social; even in the inner forum so developed thought goes on by one's assuming the rôles of others and controlling one's behavior in terms of such rôle-taking. Since the isolation of the physical thing is for Mead dependent upon the ability to take the rôle of the other, and since thought about such objects involves taking their rôles, even the scientist's reflection about physical nature is a social process, though the objects thought about are no longer social.[13]

Not all animals which communicate at the level of the conversation of gestures pass to the level of the significant symbol. Indeed, Mead quite clearly believes that no animal but man has made the transition from impulse to rationality, although he generally adds the qualification that no evidence is at hand to

[13] Physical things are objects implicated in the social act, whose rôles we can take but which cannot in turn take our rôles. See Section 23; also *The Philosophy of the Present*, Supplementary Essay II; *The Philosophy of the Act*, Part II.

suggest otherwise. His position seems to be that only the human organism has the neurological makeup necessary for the significant symbol. Mead's neurological remarks are frequently made in terms congenial to the older and more static forms of behaviorism—in terms of the number of nerve cells, the possible combinations of cells, the breaking-up and reassociating of the elements of older associations—rather than in terms of the more congenial dynamical conceptions found in Child, Lashley, Köhler, and Pavlov. His basic points, however, are independent of these changes in biological categories. In discussing the neurological conditions of the significant symbol he stresses on the one hand the importance of the cortex and on the other what he calls the temporal dimension of the human nervous system—the ability of a slowly developing act to be controlled in its development by acts which it itself initiates. I take it that all control "by the future" rests on the possibility of such behavior. It is presumably the human cortex (whose place in the higher reflexes the reflexologists have made abundantly clear) and the temporal dimension of the nervous system (which allows the control of the gesture in terms of the consequences of making it) which permit the human animal alone to pass from the level of the conversation of gestures to that of the significant language symbol, and the absence of which prevent the talking birds from really talking. These two characteristics, coupled with the place of the human hand in the isolation of the physical object, are supposedly the organic bases which determine the biological differentiations of man and the animals.

V

It is the same agency of language which on this theory makes possible the appearance of the self. Indeed, the self, mind, "consciousness of," and the significant symbol are in a sense precipitated together. Mead finds the distinguishing trait of selfhood to reside in the capacity of the minded organism to be an object to itself. The mechanism by which this is possible on a behavioristic approach is found in the rôle-taking which is involved in the language symbol. In so far as one can take the rôle of the other, he can, as it were, look back at himself from (respond to himself from) that perspective, and so become an object to himself. Thus again, it is only in a social process that selves, as distinct from biological organisms, can arise—selves as beings that have become conscious of themselves.

Nor is it merely the process of being aware of one's self that is social: the self that one becomes conscious of in this manner is itself social in form, though not always in content. Mead stresses two stages in the development of the self: the stages of play and the game. In play the child simply assumes one rôle after another of persons and animals that have in some way or other entered into its life. One here sees, writ large as it were, the assumption of the attitudes of others through the self-stimulation of the vocal gesture, whereas later in life such attitudes are more abbreviated and harder to detect. In the game, however, one has become, as it were, all of the others implicated in the common activity—must have within one's self the whole organized activity in order to successfully play one's own part. The person here has not merely assumed the rôle of a specific other, but of any other participating in the common activity; he has generalized the attitude of rôle-taking. In one of Mead's happiest terms and most fertile concepts he has taken the attitude or rôle of the "generalized other."[14]

Now all of the attitudes of others organized and taken over into one's self—however specific or generalized they may be—constitute the "me." If this were all that there is to the self, the account would be an extreme and one-sided one, leaving no place for creative and reconstructive activity; the self would not merely reflect the social structure, but would be nothing beyond

[14] In his emphasis upon the concepts of rôle-taking and the generalized other, Mead might well have been influenced by the English associational school. Here, too, the problem was to discover the means by which the individual takes the position of the group, judges his own impulses, sanctions his interest in terms of social welfare, and even makes the happiness of others the object of his own desires. Hume sought the mechanism in sympathy, Adam Smith elaborated this in the notion of moral sentiments, while Mill and Bain sought the mechanism in the doctrine of the association of ideas.

that reflection. The complete self, however, is conceived by Mead as being both "I" and a "me." The "I" is the principle of action and of impulse; and in its action it changes the social structure. As Mead says of Dewey's views, "the individual is no thrall of society. He constitutes society as genuinely as society constitutes the individual." Indeed, every action of the individual at either the non-linguistic or linguistic levels of communication changes the social structure to some degree, slightly for the most part, greatly in the case of the genius and the leader.

Not merely is the self as a social being developed on the basis of the biological organism, but society itself, as an organic whole of a complex order, cannot be put into opposition with its distinguishable and recognizable components—biologic individuals at the simpler social levels, selves at the higher. This point is worth making since some readers have gained the impression that pragmatism has lost the individual in society. Certain phrases of Mead may suggest this at times, but the recognition of the biologic individual (the "I" over against the "me") and the fact that while selves presuppose a prior social process they in turn make possible the organization of a distinctively human society, should silence all doubt. Any other interpretation is incompatible with the stress which Mead's instrumentalism and ethical theory put upon thought as a reconstructive activity, and upon the individual thinker as—to use Dewey's phrase—"a reconstructive center of society."[15]

Through a social process, then, the biologic individual of proper organic stuff gets a mind and a self. Through society the impulsive animal becomes a rational animal, a man.[16] In vir-

---

[15] T. V. Smith's sympathetic but critical articles on Mead seem to me to neglect the place of the biologic individual in Mead's theory of the self. Because of these articles I have not felt it necessary to treat certain aspects of Mead's thought: "The Social Philosophy of George Herbert Mead," *American Journal of Sociology*, XXXVII (1931), 368–85; "George Herbert Mead and the Philosophy of Philanthropy," *Social Service Review*, VI (1932), 37–54; "The Religious Bearings of a Secular Mind: George Herbert Mead," *Journal of Religion*, XII (1932), 200–213. See also the article, "George Herbert Mead" in the *Encyclopaedia of the Social Sciences*, X, 241–42; Van Meter Ames, "George H. Mead, An Appreciation," *University of Chicago Magazine*, XXIII (1930–31), 370.

[16] The mind-body or soul-body problem is naturally explained in terms of the con-

tue of the internalization or importation of the social process of communication, the individual gains the mechanism of reflective thought (the ability to direct his action in terms of the foreseen consequences of alternative courses of action); acquires the ability to make himself an object to himself and to live in a common moral and scientific world; becomes a moral individual with impulsive ends transformed into the conscious pursuit of ends-in-view.

Because of the emergence of such an individual, society is in turn transformed. It receives through the reflective social self the organization distinctive of human society; instead of playing his social part through physiological differentiation (as in the case of the insect) or through the bare influence of gestures upon others, the human individual regulates his part in the social act through having within himself the rôles of the others implicated in the common activity. In attaining a new principle of social organization, society has gained a new technique of control, since it has now implanted itself within its component parts, and so regulates, to the degree that this is successfully done, the behavior of the individual in terms of the effect on others of his contemplated action. And finally, in the process, society has provided a technique for its own transformation. It can rationally wish to do no more than present to each of its members, through the "me," the social setting within which conduct is to take place, and to make each responsible for the social values affected through this action. Under the penalty of stagnation, society cannot but be grateful for the changes which the moral act of the creative "I" introduces upon the social stage.

VI

This is not the place to take up the multiplicity of insights which Mead weaves into his general framework; nor the impli-

---

trast of the biologic individual and the self. Just as the earlier levels of the social process remain after the higher levels are obtained, so the biologic individual remains even when organized into a self. Abnormal psychology reveals much concerning the failure to integrate adequately these basic phases of personality.

cations for education, psychopathology, sociology, psychology, and linguistics; nor the way in which his philosophy dovetails with his social psychology. But as an illustration of the fertility of his basic ideas I cannot avoid mentioning two related points —the theory of universals and the concept of the generalized other. The issue here is not narrowly philosophical, but concerns the possibility of doing justice on a pragmatic, relativistic, and empirical point of view to the factors of structure, stability, and universality. It is such factors that the mathematical and physical sciences have brought into prominence, while the post-Darwinian biological and social sciences have made prominent the categories of change and process. It would be a sign of the inadequacy of modern empiricism if it should merely again set a philosophy of Becoming alongside of the philosophies of Being, duplicating the impasse which beset Greek thought.

It is frequently stated that the pragmatist must be a nominalist and cannot do justice to the fact of universality. In reality, pragmatism is nearest at this point to medieval conceptualism. It is only when the symbol is a bare particular, standing indifferently for a number of other particulars, that nominalism is the result. As a fact, however, the significant symbol, as a gesture, is not arbitrary, but always a phase of an act, and so shares in whatever universality the act possesses. As Charles Peirce saw—and Ockham long before—universality is closely connected with habit. An act is universal in that many objects or aspects of objects can serve as appropriate stimuli: any object that one can sit on is a seat; any object that drives the nail is a hammer. Now the words "seat" and "hammer," as universals, are themselves segments of the involved attitudes, and not isolated particulars; the individual repetitions of the words, like a specific act of sitting or hammering, are instances (replicas, in Peirce's terms) of the universality of the attitude. It is in the attitude that the idea or concept as a universal lies. The concepts denote whatever objects fulfil the requirements of the act, that is, any objects that have the characteristics suitable to serve as stimuli for the ongoing act. Universality is thus not an entity but a functional relation of symbolization between a series of gestures and of objects, the individual members of which are "instances" of the universal.

This position, elaborated somewhat beyond Mead's brief references, is essentially an objective relativism in regard to universals. Just as objects have for Mead colors and values in certain situations involving organisms, so objects have the character of universality in relation to an act capable of being furthered by various objects or aspects of objects. The objects have universality in relation to the act which they indifferently support; the act has universality as the character of being supported indifferently by a range of objects. In such a situation the act or segment of the act that is the gesture may be regarded as the universal under which fall or in which participate the stimulus objects as particulars; while the universality of the objects is the character which they possess in common of serving as stimuli to the act. By making universality relative to the act it is brought within the scope of an empirical science and philosophy. All that is denied on this treatment is the necessity of hypostatizing such universals, thereby erecting the antithesis of Being and Becoming which has proved fatal from Plato to Whitehead.

A second element in the treatment of universality is the social factor. The generalized other, in terms of the account just given, may be regarded as the universalization of the process of rôle-taking: the generalized other is any and all others that stand or could stand as particulars over against the attitude of rôle-taking in the co-operative process at hand. Looked at from the standpoint of the act, the generalized other is the act of rôle-taking in its universality.

In so far as what the individual does or says is understandable by, accepted by, or true for any other individuals implicated in a common activity (and without common activity there would be no community of meaning), then what is done or said has a new type of universality—social universality. Such universality is in one sense of the term a synonym for objectivity. It is for the positivist the most important type of objectivity—some would say the only possible type. The individual transcends what is given to him alone when through communication he finds that his experience is shared by others, that is, that his experience and the experiences of others fall under the same universal (in the first sense of that term). Where the particulars or instances of this universal fall within different experiential perspectives, universality has taken on the social dimension. The individual has, as it were, gotten outside of his limited world by taking the rôles of others, being assured through communication empirically grounded and tested that in all these cases the world presents the same appearance. Where this is attained, experience is social, common, shared; it is only against this common world that the individual distinguishes his own private experience.

At the minimum, science is the record in verbalized form of the more universal aspects of such a common world. It attains an independence of the particular perspective of the observer by finding that which is common to many, and ideally to all, observers. Mead shows in his penetrating analysis of the social psychology of physical relativity (which thus becomes an instance of his general theory of rôle-taking) that the invariance sought and presumably found lies in the isolation of a formula that is true of the world whatever the point of observation. "Independence of experience" and "universal truth" may mean more than "independent of any particular experience" and "true for all observations," but they cannot mean less.

There are varying degrees of such social universality. While not absent in morality and aesthetics, it is wider in science, and there in proportion to the degree of formalism possible. It is the relational structure of the world that reveals the greatest universality; mathematics and logic are simply the end-results of the search for structural invariance. As the lowest common denominators of the world of discourse, and so of action and the world talked about, they are, as it were, common to all rational beings. While Mead himself gives no elaboration of his occasional references to logic, his account contains in implicit form the germs of a theory of logic and a philosophy of mathematics.

When it is realized that social universality is potentially extensible to the past and future, it can be realized that Mead's approach is compatible with the recognition that relatively to the most general co-operative acts there are highly invariant features of the world. The emergent and temporalistic aspects of the pragmatic position are not at odds with whatever constancy the world as experienced does in fact reveal, nor with whatever formalism logic and mathematics are able to attain. Pragmatism merely wishes to avoid fanaticism in these matters. It counsels sanity toward the mutual principles of being and becoming, by pointing out that empirically universality is a character of things over against the act, whether individual or social. And as such it is a matter of more or less, not of all or none.[17]

Did space permit it would be interesting to discuss other queries raised by the conception of the generalized other. How far, for instance, is the difference between Platonist and relativist dependent upon the degree to which one takes the rôle of the generalized other? Can the extension of the process of rôle-taking toward physical things permit one to transcend human observers altogether, so that one can meaningly pass from the social positivism, which at times Mead seems to regard as the limit of meaningful metaphysics,[18] to a philosophical realism?[19] What is the bearing of Mead's doctrine, when coupled with the concept of social experience, upon the nature of truth and knowledge? How far does the generalized other provide the psychological equivalent of the historical concept of God, and of the Absolute of the idealists, and so for the contrast of Reality and Appearance? It is only possible to raise such questions

---

[17] This account of the universal in functional terms gives Mead somewhat the status of a post-Darwinian Aristotle—an Aristotle freed by the growth of biology itself from the inadequacies of Platonism. Mead was a lifelong student of Aristotle.

[18] See especially pp. 117, 118 of *The Philosophy of the Present.*

[19] This issue is discussed in my article, "Pragmatism and Metaphysics," *Philosophical Review,* 1934.

here, and perhaps this digression and expansion of Mead's thought has been unfair to certain readers. It has been entered into in order to show the power of Mead's social psychology for the approach to problems which pragmatism has not sufficiently discussed, and where its critics have been most just in detecting lacunae.

VII

Mead, in common with all pragmatists since James, held an interest theory of value: that is good which satisfies an interest or impulse.[20] But once again Mead's statement of this is in objective relativistic terms: value is the character of an object in its capacity of satisfying an interest—it resides neither in the object alone nor in an emotional state of the subject. Interests or impulses clash, however, and so arises the problem of the standard of value and the need for evaluation.

The aesthetic object brings the emotionally toned impulses into a harmonious whole; the object capable of so stimulating and integrating the impulses has aesthetic character or value. Through an object of such a character one enjoys "the recovery of the sense of the final outcome in partial achievement," "savoring the end that he is fashioning."[21] The artist plays upon attitudes, arousing in himself, by the use of his medium, the emotional aspects of an attitude which his work in varying degrees communicates to others by calling out in them this attitude. In so far as this is done, the aesthetic exaltation is the fusion of the "I" and the "me" made possible by the object. Mead believed, without elaborating his views in detail, that his version of behavioristic psychology gives a fruitful basis for aesthetic theory.

Aesthetic value is, as it were, a consummatory gift offered to the self by nature or by the artist; the task of the moral life is

[20] At times Mead speaks of value as "the future character of the object in so far as it determines your action to it." Here reference is made only to his axiological usage. The present volume may be supplemented by the fuller discussion of value by Mead in *The Philosophy of the Act.*

[21] "The Nature of Aesthetic Experience," *International Journal of Ethics,* XXXVI (1926), 387, 385.

to create through reflective effort a similar integration of impulse at the level of interacting selves.[22]

In its essentials, Mead's ethical theory is the same as Dewey's, but the approach through the social psychology of the self throws the conception into new relief. Being social, there is no psychological problem as to how the self can take others into account in its reflective activity, just as there is no problem of surmounting hedonism on a view which takes an act directed upon objects as its basic unit. The self, as constituted by its impulses, is seeking the objects which allow the consummation of the impulses. As social, to the degree that the self has taken the attitudes of others into itself through the language process, it has become the others, and the values of others are its own; to the degree that the self assumes the rôle of the generalized other, its values are the values of the social process itself. The epistemological escape from the egocentric predicament by getting an ego which includes the standpoints of others is analogous in value theory to the getting of a self which includes within itself the values of others. This free construction of the implications of Mead's actual statements shows the fertility of the approach to the field of value. Certain it is that it gives a more precise way of formulating the breakdown of the alternatives of egoism and altruism, of self-assertion and self-sacrifice, than the psychological equipment of ethicists usually makes possible.

Stated in ethical terms, Mead is insisting that in the moral act the motive for action is the impulse itself as directed to a social end. A social self has social impulses that demand expression as imperatively as any other impulses. For Mead, moral ends are social ends because in the first place the only standard for impulse that impulse makes possible resides in the answer as to whether the impulse in question feeds or dies on its own satisfaction, and whether it expands and harmonizes, or narrows and defeats, other impulses; and second, because the self,

---

[22] A 1926 set of notes puts the matter in this way: "The aesthetic object stops life at one point. It is as if you cash in your life insurance policy. The ethical object is the organization of life so as to reach the fullest consummation. It is paying your life insurance premium."

as a social being, must be concerned within and without with a social harmony of impulses.

The moral task, it follows, is to be observant of all the values resident in the particular situations of life,[23] and to deal with these values reflectively in the endeavor to allow the maximum satisfaction and expansion—the maximum dynamic harmony—of the impulses concerned. Moral action is intelligent, socially directed action in which one acts with the interest of others as well as one's self in mind. The appeal is not from interest to reason, but from isolated interests to the interest in the social system of interests in which one's behavior is implicated. Such, as I read it, is the kernel of Mead's, and so pragmatism's, ethical theory. The right act, as relative to the situation, is nevertheless objective and universal in that it demands the assent of all rational beings. The right is neither subjective caprice nor a timeless essence; its universality is a social universality.

Such a view makes the moral life a strenuous and active life. Sustained by social ends and fed by all the knowledge that science can give, morality yet demands the creativity of the "I," of the self that is more than a "me." It is in a society of such selves that Mead sees the social ideal. This society would not have as its goal the bare sustenance and attainment of any set of existent or authoritatively defined values—this Mead calls the Augustinian philosophy of history. On the contrary its philosophy of history would be as experimental as the experimental method itself. It would be concerned with the technique for remaking values through the reinterpretation of the situation in terms of the best knowledge available, and that technique, it would appear, could be nothing but morality itself.

Such a society of moral beings would seem to be Mead's version of the democratic ideal. While an emergent universe can guarantee no future, Mead does believe that the agencies and institutions of human life—language, religion, the economic

[23] In one of the statements of this view Mead rather brusquely states that it is *not* the position that "the standard of morality is that which will do the most social good" (1927). Mead stresses the particular situation, not the vague and unmanageable utilitarian "society in general."

process—do in fact extend the very process of rôle-taking which they involve. The religious attitude, based upon the pattern of helpfulness in family relations,[24] and the economic attitude of offering to others some surplus for what one himself needs, are potentially universal, and language can extend as far as common activity extends. In this sense the capacity to take the rôle of the other in greater degree by more and more people would seem to move in the direction of the democratic ideal, provided that the selves become moral selves.[25] Such a democracy, as Mead clearly sees, has no undesirable leveling tendency, and puts no premium on mediocrity. Rather it is compatible with great differences of ability and contribution. The genuine implication of democracy is that each should realize himself through moral participation in a co-operative process. Ideally the individual "realizes himself in others through that which he does as peculiar to himself." The democratic society has no place for the superiority of class or possession or power as such: it must cherish deeply the superiorities and pride in superiority which arise in the performance of diverse social functions.

What applies to individuals here applies to nations. Mead is an internationalist, since the social attitude he describes can theoretically stop short of nothing less than conscious identification with and participation in the society of man as such. He

[24] The mystical character of the religious experience Mead finds in the extension of social attitudes to the universe at large. It is surprising that Mead nowhere expressly suggests the connection between the personalistic conceptions of God and the concept of the generalized other.

[25] In the non-moral sense of the term "social," wars and discord and disorganization are as social as their opposites. Mead's failure to stress the fact that the problem is one of getting moral selves, and not simply social selves, gives at times an impression of uncritical confidence in the future development of human society, even though at other times he is sufficiently sensitive to the socially disruptive aspects of behavior (see especially Section 39). The pragmatist's emphasis upon education is the logical corollary of his ethical theory: education is to provide the technique by which moral selves—intelligent and socialized selves—are to be developed. Mead's papers on education stress five points: (1) the importance of the school in giving common meanings, common linguistic tools; (2) the place of science in the curriculum; (3) the necessity of manipulatory activities, answering to the sense of reality in the contact phases of the act; (4) the significance of play as providing the material for assuming the rôles of others out of which the self is built up; (5) the duty of the school to build moral selves. For titles of papers, see Bibliography.

constantly refers to the League of Nations as a tentative reaching by nations for the wider society they feel themselves a part of, but which they are not yet able to enter in terms of a functional rôle—and so they are forced still to assert themselves in terms of power. Nations have not yet learned to take the rôle of the other, and to participate consciously and morally in the wider social processes which they are in fact engaged in. In analogy to the individual, nations are still at the level of the biologic individual; they have not yet attained moral selfhood; their "I" does not yet act on a stage set by an international "me." Just as within each social group a premium is put upon the contribution of the functionally differentiated self, so this internationalism calls for no obliteration of nations, but rather their self-affirmation at the moral level of social selves.

Mead's account does justice to both the factors of individual initiative and social concern. It organically unites within the nation and between nations both the principles of individualism and socialism, the attitude of the pioneer and the note of the brotherhood of man, which together characterize democracy.

Foreglow or afterglow? If the democratic ideal moves toward realization George H. Mead, together with John Dewey, will have been one of its major philosophical mouthpieces, a Walt Whitman in the realm of thought; if forces to the left or right make impossible this realization, Mead will have helped to write its epitaph.

Whatever be the fate of the democratic ideal, George H. Mead's extraordinarily fertile ideas have not merely given him a secure place among the creators of social psychology, led to social and ethical theories of intrinsic interest, and provided a matrix for a significant expansion of pragmatism in the form of "the philosophy of the act," but they give every indication of having within themselves the power to enrich the concepts of the social sciences, to suggest new avenues of empirical investigation, and to open new horizons for philosophical interpretation.

CHARLES W. MORRIS

TABLE OF CONTENTS

PART   PAGE

I. THE POINT OF VIEW OF SOCIAL BEHAVIORISM

    1. Social Psychology and Behaviorism 1
    2. The Behavioristic Significance of Attitudes 8
    3. The Behavioristic Significance of Gestures 13
    4. Rise of Parallelism in Psychology 18
    5. Parallelism and the Ambiguity of "Consciousness" . . . 27
    6. The Program of Behaviorism 33

II. MIND

    7. Wundt and the Concept of the Gesture 42
    8. Imitation and the Origin of Language 51
    9. The Vocal Gesture and the Significant Symbol 61
    10. Thought, Communication, and the Significant Symbol . . 68
    11. Meaning 75
    12. Universality 82
    13. The Nature of Reflective Intelligence 90
    14. Behaviorism, Watsonism, and Reflection 100
    15. Behaviorism and Psychological Parallelism 109
    16. Mind and the Symbol 117
    17. The Relation of Mind to Response and Environment . . . 125

III. THE SELF

    18. The Self and the Organism 135
    19. The Background of the Genesis of the Self 144
    20. Play, the Game, and the Generalized Other 152
    21. The Self and the Subjective 164
    22. The "I" and the "Me" 173
    23. Social Attitudes and the Physical World 178
    24. Mind as the Individual Importation of the Social Process . . 186
    25. The "I" and the "Me" as Phases of the Self 192

[xxxvii]

TABLE OF CONTENTS

PART   PAGE

26. The Realization of the Self in the Social Situation . . . 200

27. The Contributions of the "Me" and the "I" 209

28. The Social Creativity of the Emergent Self 214

29. A Contrast of Individualistic and Social Theories of the Self . 222

IV. SOCIETY

30. The Basis of Human Society: Man and the Insects . . . 227

31. The Basis of Human Society: Man and the Vertebrates . . 238

32. Organism, Community, and Environment 245

33. The Social Foundations and Functions of Thought and Communication 253

34. The Community and the Institution 260

35. The Fusion of the "I" and the "Me" in Social Activities . . 273

36. Democracy and Universality in Society 281

37. Further Consideration of Religious and Economic Attitudes . 289

38. The Nature of Sympathy 298

39. Conflict and Integration 303

40. The Functions of Personality and Reason in Social Organization 311

41. Obstacles and Promises in the Development of the Ideal Society 317

42. Summary and Conclusion 328

SUPPLEMENTARY ESSAYS

I. The Function of Imagery in Conduct 337

II. The Biologic Individual 347

III. The Self and the Process of Reflection 354

IV. Fragments on Ethics 379

BIBLIOGRAPHY 390

INDEX 393

PART I

THE POINT OF VIEW OF SOCIAL BEHAVIORISM

I. SOCIAL PSYCHOLOGY AND BEHAVIORISM

SOCIAL psychology has, as a rule, dealt with various phases of social experience from the psychological standpoint of individual experience. The point of approach which I wish to suggest is that of dealing with experience from the standpoint of society, at least from the standpoint of communication as essential to the social order. Social psychology, on this view, presupposes an approach to experience from the standpoint of the individual, but undertakes to determine in particular that which belongs to this experience because the individual himself belongs to a social structure, a social order.

No very sharp line can be drawn between social psychology and individual psychology. Social psychology is especially interested in the effect which the social group has in the determination of the experience and conduct of the individual member. If we abandon the conception of a substantive soul endowed with the self of the individual at birth, then we may regard the development of the individual's self, and of his self-consciousness within the field of his experience, as the social psychologist's special interest. There are, then, certain phases of psychology which are interested in studying the relation of the individual organism to the social group to which it belongs, and these phases constitute social psychology as a branch of general psychology. Thus, in the study of the experience and behavior of the individual organism or self in its dependence upon the social group to which it belongs, we find a definition of the field of social psychology.

While minds and selves are essentially social products, products or phenomena of the social side of human experience, the physiological mechanism underlying experience is far from irrelevant—indeed is indispensable—to their genesis and existence; for individual experience and behavior is, of course, physiologically basic to social experience and behavior: the processes and mechanisms of the latter (including those which are essential to the origin and existence of minds and selves) are dependent physiologically upon the processes and mechanisms of the former, and upon the social functioning of these. Individual psychology, nevertheless, definitely abstracts certain factors from the situation with which social psychology deals more nearly in its concrete totality. We shall approach this latter field from a behavioristic point of view.

The common psychological standpoint which is represented by behaviorism is found in John B. Watson. The behaviorism which we shall make use of is more adequate than that of which Watson makes use. Behaviorism in this wider sense is simply an approach to the study of the experience of the individual from the point of view of his conduct, particularly, but not exclusively, the conduct as it is observable by others. Historically, behaviorism entered psychology through the door of animal psychology. There it was found to be impossible to use what is termed introspection. One cannot appeal to the animal's introspection, but must study the animal in terms of external conduct. Earlier animal psychology added an inferential reference to consciousness, and even undertook to find the point in conduct at which consciousness appears. This inference had, perhaps, varying degrees of probability, but it was one which could not be tested experimentally. It could be then simply dropped as far as science was concerned. It was not necessary for the study of the conduct of the individual animal. Having taken that behavioristic standpoint for the lower animals, it was possible to carry it over to the human animal.

There remained, however, the field of introspection, of experiences which are private and belong to the individual himself—experiences commonly called subjective. What was to be done with these? John B. Watson's attitude was that of the

THE POINT OF VIEW OF SOCIAL BEHAVIORISM

Queen in *Alice in Wonderland*—"Off with their heads!"—there were no such things. There was no imagery, and no consciousness. The field of so-called introspection Watson explained by the use of language symbols.[1] These symbols were not necessarily uttered loudly enough to be heard by others, and often only involved the muscles of the throat without leading to audible speech. That was all there was to thought. One thinks, but one thinks in terms of language. In this way Watson explained the whole field of inner experience in terms of external behavior. Instead of calling such behavior subjective it was regarded as the field of behavior that was accessible only to the individual himself. One could observe his own movements, his own organs of articulation, where other persons could not normally observe them. Certain fields were accessible to the individual alone, but the observation was not different in kind; the difference lay only in the degree of accessibility of others to certain observations. One could be set up in a room by himself and observe something that no one else could observe. What a man observed in the room would be his own experience. Now, in this way something goes on in the throat or the body of the individual which no one else can observe. There are, of course, scientific instruments that can be attached to the throat or the body to reveal the tendency toward movement. There are some movements that are easily observable and others which can be detected only by the individual himself, but there is no qualitative difference in the two cases. It is simply recognized that the apparatus of observation is one that has various degrees of success. That, in brief, is the point of view of Watson's behavioristic psychology. It aims to observe conduct as it takes place, and to utilize that conduct to explain the experience of the individual without bringing in the observation of an inner experience, a consciousness as such.

There was another attack on consciousness, that of William James in his 1904 article entitled, "Does 'Consciousness' Ex-

[1] [Especially in *Behavior, an Introduction to Comparative Psychology*, chap. x; *Psychology from the Standpoint of a Behaviorist*, chap. ix; *Behaviorism*, chaps. x, xi.]

ist?"[2] James pointed out that if a person is in a room the objects of the interior can be looked at from two standpoints. The furniture, for instance, may be considered from the standpoint of the person who bought it and used it, from the point of view of its color values which attach to it in the minds of the persons who observe them, its aesthetic value, its economic value, its traditional value. All of these we can speak of in terms of psychology; they will be put into relationship with the experience of the individual. One man puts one value upon it and another gives it another value. But the same objects can be regarded as physical parts of a physical room. What James insisted upon was that the two cases differ only in an arrangement of certain contents in different series. The furniture, the walls, the house itself, belong to one historical series. We speak of the house as having been built, of the furniture as having been made. We put the house and furniture into another series when one comes in and assesses these objects from the point of view of his own experience. He is talking about the same chair, but the chair is for him now a matter of certain contours, certain colors, taken from his own experience. It involves the experience of the individual. Now one can take a cross-section of both of these two orders so that at a certain point there is a meeting of the two series. The statement in terms of consciousness simply means the recognition that the room lies not only in the historical series but also in the experience of the individual. There has been of late in philosophy a growing recognition of the importance of James's insistence that a great deal has been placed in consciousness that must be returned to the so-called objective world.[3]

Psychology itself cannot very well be made a study of the field of consciousness alone; it is necessarily a study of a more extensive field. It is, however, that science which does make use

[2] [Published in the *Journal of Philosophy, Psychology, and Scientific Method*. Reprinted in *Essays in Radical Empiricism*.]

[3] Modern philosophical realism has helped to free psychology from a concern with a philosophy of mental states (1924).

of introspection, in the sense that it looks within the experience of the individual for phenomena not dealt with in any other sciences—phenomena to which only the individual himself has experiential access. That which belongs (experientially) to the individual *qua* individual, and is accessible to him alone, is certainly included within the field of psychology, whatever else is or is not thus included. This is our best clue in attempting to isolate the field of psychology. The psychological datum is best defined, therefore, in terms of accessibility. That which is accessible, in the experience of the individual, only to the individual himself, is peculiarly psychological.

I want to point out, however, that even when we come to the discussion of such "inner" experience, we can approach it from the point of view of the behaviorist, provided that we do not too narrowly conceive this point of view. What one must insist upon is that objectively observable behavior finds expression within the individual, not in the sense of being in another world, a subjective world, but in the sense of being within his organism. Something of this behavior appears in what we may term "attitudes," the beginnings of acts. Now, if we come back to such attitudes we find them giving rise to all sorts of responses. The telescope in the hands of a novice is not a telescope in the sense that it is to those on top of Mount Wilson. If we want to trace the responses of the astronomer, we have to go back into his central nervous system, back to a whole series of neurons; and we find something there that answers to the exact way in which the astronomer approaches the instrument under certain conditions. That is the beginning of the act; it is a part of the act. The external act which we do observe is a part of the process which has started within; the values[4] which we say the instrument has are values through the relationship of the object to the person who has that sort of attitude. If a person did not have that particular nervous system, the instrument would be of no value. It would not be a telescope.

[4] Value: the future character of the object in so far as it determines your action to it (1924).

In both versions of behaviorism certain characteristics which things have and certain experiences which individuals have can be stated as occurrences inside of an act.[5] But part of the act lies within the organism and only comes to expression later; it is that side of behavior which I think Watson has passed over. There is a field within the act itself which is not external, but which belongs to the act, and there are characteristics of that inner organic conduct which do reveal themselves in our own attitudes, especially those connected with speech. Now, if our behavioristic point of view takes these attitudes into account we find that it can very well cover the field of psychology. In any case, this approach is one of particular importance because it is able to deal with the field of communication in a way which neither Watson nor the introspectionist can do. We want to approach language not from the standpoint of inner meanings to be expressed, but in its larger context of co-operation in the group taking place by means of signals and gestures.[6] Meaning appears within that process. Our behaviorism is a social behaviorism.

Social psychology studies the activity or behavior of the individual as it lies within the social process; the behavior of an individual can be understood only in terms of the behavior of the whole social group of which he is a member, since his indi-

---

[5] An act is an impulse that maintains the life-process by the selection of certain sorts of stimuli it needs. Thus, the organism creates its environment. The stimulus is the occasion for the expression of the impulse.

Stimuli are means, tendency is the real thing. Intelligence is the selection of stimuli that will set free and maintain life and aid in rebuilding it (1927).

The purpose need not be "in view," but the statement of the act includes the goal to which the act moves. This is a natural teleology, in harmony with a mechanical statement (1925).

[6] The study of the process of language or speech—its origins and development—is a branch of social psychology, because it can be understood only in terms of the social processes of behavior within a group of interacting organisms; because it is one of the activities of such a group. The philologist, however, has often taken the view of the prisoner in a cell. The prisoner knows that others are in a like position and he wants to get in communication with them. So he sets about some method of communication, some arbitrary affair, perhaps, such as tapping on the wall. Now, each of us, on this view, is shut up in his own cell of consciousness, and knowing that there are other people so shut up, develops ways to set up communication with them.

vidual acts are involved in larger, social acts which go beyond himself and which implicate the other members of that group.

We are not, in social psychology, building up the behavior of the social group in terms of the behavior of the separate individuals composing it; rather, we are starting out with a given social whole of complex group activity, into which we analyze (as elements) the behavior of each of the separate individuals composing it. We attempt, that is, to explain the conduct of the individual in terms of the organized conduct of the social group, rather than to account for the organized conduct of the social group in terms of the conduct of the separate individuals belonging to it. For social psychology, the whole (society) is prior to the part (the individual), not the part to the whole; and the part is explained in terms of the whole, not the whole in terms of the part or parts. The social act[7] is not explained by building it up out of stimulus plus response; it must be taken as a dynamic whole—as something going on—no part of which can be considered or understood by itself—a complex organic process implied by each individual stimulus and response involved in it.

In social psychology we get at the social process from the inside as well as from the outside. Social psychology is behavioristic in the sense of starting off with an observable activity—the dynamic, on-going social process, and the social acts which are its component elements—to be studied and analyzed scientifically. But it is not behavioristic in the sense of ignoring the inner experience of the individual—the inner phase of that process or activity. On the contrary, it is particularly concerned

[7] "A social act may be defined as one in which the occasion or stimulus which sets free an impulse is found in the character or conduct of a living form that belongs to the proper environment of the living form whose impulse it is. I wish, however, to restrict the social act to the class of acts which involve the co-operation of more than one individual, and whose object as defined by the act, in the sense of Bergson, is a social object. I mean by a social object one that answers to all the parts of the complex act, though these parts are found in the conduct of different individuals. The objective of the acts is then found in the life-process of the group, not in those of the separate individuals alone." [From "The Genesis of the Self and Social Control," *International Journal of Ethics*, XXXV (1925), 263-64.]

with the rise of such experience within the process as a whole. It simply works from the outside to the inside instead of from the inside to the outside, so to speak, in its endeavor to determine how such experience does arise within the process. The act, then, and not the tract, is the fundamental datum in both social and individual psychology when behavioristically conceived, and it has both an inner and an outer phase, an internal and an external aspect.

These general remarks have had to do with our point of approach. It is behavioristic, but unlike Watsonian behaviorism it recognizes the parts of the act which do not come to external observation, and it emphasizes the act of the human individual in its natural social situation.

2. THE BEHAVIORISTIC SIGNIFICANCE OF ATTITUDES

The problem that presents itself as crucial for human psychology concerns the field that is opened up by introspection; this field apparently could not be dealt with by a purely objective psychology which only studied conduct as it takes place for the observer. In order that this field could be brought within the range of objective psychology, the behaviorist, such as Watson, did what he could to cut down the field itself, to deny certain phenomena supposed to lie only in that field, such as "consciousness" as distinct from conduct without consciousness. The animal psychologist studied conduct without taking up the question as to whether it was conscious conduct or not.[8] But when we reach the field of human conduct we are in fact able to distinguish reflexes which take place without consciousness. There

[8] Comparative psychology freed psychology in general from being confined solely to the field of the central nervous system, which, through the physiological psychologists, had taken the place of consciousness as such, as the field of psychological investigation. It thus enabled psychology in general to consider the act as a whole, and as including or taking place within the entire social process of behavior. In other words, comparative psychology—and behaviorism as its outgrowth—has extended the field of general psychology beyond the central nervous system of the individual organism alone, and has caused psychologists to consider the individual act as a part of the larger social whole to which it in fact belongs, and from which, in a definite sense, it gets its meaning; though they do not, of course, lose interest thereby in the central nervous system and the physiological processes going on in it.

seems, then, to be a field which the behavioristic psychology cannot reach. The Watsonian behaviorist simply did what he could to minimize this difference.

The field of investigation of the behaviorist has been quite largely that of the young infant, where the methods employed are just the methods of animal psychology. He has endeavored to find out what the processes of behavior are, and to see how the activities of the infant may be used to explain the activities of the adult. It is here that the psychologist brings in the conditioned reflexes. He shows that by a mere association of certain stimuli he can get results which would not follow from these secondary stimuli alone. This conditioning of reflexes can be carried over into other fields, such as those of terror on the part of an infant. He can be made to fear something by associating the object with others producing terror. The same process can be used for explaining more elaborate conduct in which we associate elements with certain events which are not directly connected with them, and by elaborating this conditioning we can, it is believed, explain the more extended processes of reasoning and inference. In this way a method which belongs to objective psychology is carried over into the field which is dealt with ordinarily in terms of introspection. That is, instead of saying we have certain ideas when we have certain experiences, and that these ideas imply something else, we say that a certain experience has taken place at the same time that the first experience has taken place, so that now this secondary experience arouses the response which belongs to the primary experience.

There remain contents, such as those of imagery, which are more resistant to such analysis. What shall we say of responses that do not answer to any given experience? We can say, of course, that they are the results of past experiences. But take the contents themselves, the actual visual imagery that one has: it has outline; it has color; it has values; and other characters which are isolated with more difficulty. Such experience is one which plays a part, and a very large part, in our perception, our conduct; and yet it is an experience which can be revealed only by introspection. The behaviorist has to make a detour about this type of experience if he is going to stick to the Watsonian type of behavioristic psychology.

Such a behaviorist desires to analyze the act, whether individual or social, without any specific reference to consciousness whatever and without any attempt to locate it either within the field of organic behavior or within the larger field of reality in general. He wishes, in short, to deny its existence as such altogether. Watson insists that objectively observable behavior completely and exclusively constitutes the field of scientific psychology, individual and social. He pushes aside as erroneous the idea of "mind" or "consciousness," and attempts to reduce all "mental" phenomena to conditioned reflexes and similar physiological mechanisms—in short, to purely behavioristic terms. This attempt, of course, is misguided and unsuccessful, for the existence as such of mind or consciousness, in some sense or other, must be admitted—the denial of it leads inevitably to obvious absurdities. But though it is impossible to *reduce* mind or consciousness to purely behavioristic terms—in the sense of thus explaining it away and denying its existence as such entirely—yet it is not impossible to *explain* it in these terms, and to do so without explaining it away, or denying its existence as such, in the least. Watson apparently assumes that to deny the existence of mind or consciousness as a psychical stuff, substance, or entity is to deny its existence altogether, and that a naturalistic or behavioristic account of it as such is out of the question. But, on the contrary, we may deny its existence as a psychical entity without denying its existence in some other sense at all; and if we then conceive it functionally, and as a natural rather than a transcendental phenomenon, it becomes possible to deal with it in behavioristic terms. In short, it is not possible to deny the existence of mind or consciousness or mental phenomena, nor is it desirable to do so; but it is possible to account for them or deal with them in behavioristic terms which are precisely similar to those which Watson employs in dealing with non-mental psychological phenomena (phenomena which, according to his definition of the field of psychology, are all the psychological phenomena there are). Mental behavior is not reducible to non-mental behavior. But mental behavior or phenomena can be explained in terms of non-mental behavior or phenomena, as arising out of, and as resulting from complications in, the latter.

If we are going to use behavioristic psychology to explain conscious behavior we have to be much more thoroughgoing in our statement of the act than Watson was. We have to take into account not merely the complete or social act, but what goes on in the central nervous system as the beginning of the individual's act and as the organization of the act. Of course, that takes us beyond the field of our direct observation. It takes us beyond that field because we cannot get at the process itself. It is a field that is more or less shut off, seemingly because of the difficulty of the country itself that has to be investigated. The central nervous system is only partly explored. Present results, however, suggest the organization of the act in terms of attitudes. There is an organization of the various parts of the nervous system that are going to be responsible for acts, an organization which represents not only that which is immediately taking place, but also the later stages that are to take place. If one approaches a distant object he approaches it with reference to what he is going to do when he arrives there. If one is approaching a hammer he is muscularly all ready to seize the handle of the hammer. The later stages of the act are present in the early stages—not simply in the sense that they are all ready to go off, but in the sense that they serve to control the process itself. They determine how we are going to approach the object, and the steps in our early manipulation of it. We can recognize, then, that the innervation of certain groups of cells in the central nervous system can already initiate in advance the later stages of the act. The act as a whole can be there determining the process.

We can also recognize in such a general attitude toward an object an attitude that represents alternative responses, such as are involved when we talk about our ideas of an object. A person who is familiar with a horse approaches it as one who is going to ride it. He moves toward the proper side and is ready to swing himself into the saddle. His approach determines the success of the whole process. But the horse is not simply something that must be ridden. It is an animal that must eat, that belongs to somebody. It has certain economic values. The individual is ready to do a whole series of things with reference to the horse, and that readiness is involved in any one of the many phases of the various acts. It is a horse that he is going to mount; it is a biological animal; it is an economic animal. Those characters are involved in the ideas of a horse. If we seek this ideal character of a horse in the central nervous system we would have to find it in all those different parts of the initiated acts. One would have to think of each as associated with the other processes in which he uses the horse, so that no matter what the specific act is, there is a readiness to act in these different ways with reference to the horse. We can find in that sense in the beginning of the act just those characters which we assign to "horse" as an idea, or if you like, as a concept.

If we are going to look for this idea in a central nervous system we have to look for it in the neurons, particularly in the connection between the neurons. There are whole sets of connections there which are of such a character that we are able to act in a number of ways, and these possible actions have their effect on the way in which we do act. For example, if the horse belongs to the rider, the rider acts in a different way than if it belongs to someone else. These other processes involved determine the immediate action itself and particularly the later stages of the act, so that the temporal organization of the act may be present in the immediate process. We do not know how that temporal organization takes place in the central nervous system. In some sense these later processes which are going to take place, and are in some sense started, are worked into the immediate process. A behavioristic treatment, if it is made broad enough, if it makes use of the almost indefinite

complexities existing in the nervous system, can adjust itself
to many fields which were supposed to be confined to an introspective attack. Of course, a great deal of this must be hypothetical. We learn more day by day of what the connections
are, but they are largely hypothetical. However, they can at
least be stated in a behavioristic form. We can, therefore, in
principle, state behavioristically what we mean by an idea.

3. THE BEHAVIORISTIC SIGNIFICANCE OF GESTURES

The behaviorist of the Watsonian type has been prone to
carry his principle of conditioning over into the field of language. By a conditioning of reflexes the horse has become associated with the word "horse," and this in turn releases the set of
responses. We use the word, and the response may be that of
mounting, buying, selling, or trading. We are ready to do all
these different things. This statement, however, lacks the recognition that these different processes which the behaviorist says
are identified with the word "horse" must be worked into the
act itself, or the group of acts, which gather about the horse.
They go to make up that object in our experience, and the
function of the word is a function which has its place in that
organization; but it is not, however, the whole process. We find
that same sort of organization seemingly extended in the conduct of animals lower than\man: those processes which go to
make up our objects must be present in the animals themselves
who have not the use of language. It is, of course, the great
value, or one of the great values, of language that it does give
us control over this organization of the act. That is a point we
will have to consider in detail later, but it is important to recognize that that to which the word refers is something that can
lie in the experience of the individual without the use of language itself. Language does pick out and organize this content
in experience. It is an implement for that purpose.

Language is a part of social behavior.[9] There are an indefi-

---

[9] What is the basic mechanism whereby the social process goes on? It is the mechanism of gesture, which makes possible the appropriate responses to one another's be-

nite number of signs or symbols which may serve the purpose of what we term "language." We are reading the meaning of the conduct of other people when, perhaps, they are not aware of it. There is something that reveals to us what the purpose is—just the glance of an eye, the attitude of the body which leads to the response. The communication set up in this way between individuals may be very perfect. Conversation in gestures may be carried on which cannot be translated into articulate speech. This is also true of the lower animals. Dogs approaching each other in hostile attitude carry on such a language of gestures. They walk around each other, growling and snapping, and waiting for the opportunity to attack. Here is a process out of which language might arise, that is, a certain attitude of one individual that calls out a response in the other, which in turn calls out a different approach and a different response, and so on indefinitely. In fact, as we shall see, language does arise in just such a process as that. We are too prone, however, to approach language as the philologist does, from the standpoint of the symbol that is used.[10] We analyze that symbol and find out what is the intent in the mind of the individual in using that symbol, and then attempt to discover whether this symbol calls out this intent in the mind of the other. We assume that there are sets of ideas in persons' minds and that these individuals make use of certain arbitrary symbols which answer to the intent which the individuals had. But if we are going to broaden the concept of language in the sense I have

havior of the different individual organisms involved in the social process. Within any given social act, an adjustment is effected, by means of gestures, of the actions of one organism involved to the actions of another; the gestures are movements of the first organism which act as specific stimuli calling forth the (socially) appropriate responses of the second organism. The field of the operation of gestures is the field within which the rise and development of human intelligence has taken place through the process of the symbolization of experience which gestures—especially vocal gestures—have made possible. The specialization of the human animal within this field of the gesture has been responsible, ultimately, for the origin and growth of present human society and knowledge, with all the control over nature and over the human environment which science makes possible.

[10] ["The Relations of Psychology and Philology," *Psychological Bulletin*, I (1904), 375 ff.]

spoken of, so that it takes in the underlying attitudes, we can see that the so-called intent, the idea we are talking about, is one that is involved in the gesture or attitudes which we are using. The offering of a chair to a person who comes into the room is in itself a courteous act. We do not have to assume that a person says to himself that this person wants a chair. The offering of a chair by a person of good manners is something which is almost instinctive. This is the very attitude of the individual. From the point of view of the observer it is a gesture. Such early stages of social acts precede the symbol proper, and deliberate communication.

One of the important documents in the history of modern psychology, particularly for the psychology of language, is Darwin's *Expression of the Emotions in Man and Animals*. Here Darwin carried over his theory of evolution into the field of what we call "conscious experience." What Darwin did was to show that there was a whole series of acts or beginnings of acts which called out certain responses that do express emotions. If one animal attacks another, or is on the point of attacking, or of taking the bone of another dog, that action calls out violent responses which express the anger of the second dog. There we have a set of attitudes which express the emotional attitude of dogs; and we can carry this analysis into the human expression of emotion.

The part of our organism that most vividly and readily expresses the emotions is the face, and Darwin studied the face from this point of view. He took, naturally, the actor, the man whose business it is to express the emotions by the movements of the countenance, and studied the muscles themselves; and in studying them he undertook to show what the value of these changes of the face might be in the actual act. We speak of such expressions as those of anger, and note the way in which the blood may suffuse the face at one stage and then leave it at another. Darwin studied the blood flow in fear and in terror. In these emotions one can find changes taking place in the blood flow itself. These changes have their value. They represent, of course, changes in the circulation of blood in the acts. These actions are generally actions which are rapid and can only take place if the blood is flowing rapidly. There must be a change in the rhythm of circulation and this generally registers itself in the countenance.

Many of our acts of hostility exhibit themselves in attitudes of the face similar to animals which attack with their teeth. The attitude, or in a more generalized term, the gesture, has been preserved after the value of the act has disappeared. The title of Darwin's work indicates his point of approach. He was dealing with these gestures, these attitudes, as expressive of emotions and assuming at the time that the gesture has this function of expressing the emotions. That attitude has been preserved, on this view, after the value of the act has disappeared. This gesture seems to remain for the purpose of expressing emotions. One naturally assumed there an attitude in the experience of animals which answers in some sense to those of the human animal. One could apply the doctrine of the survival of the fittest here also. The implication in this particular case was that these gestures or attitudes had lost the value which they had in the original acts, and yet had survived. The indication was that they had survived because they served certain valuable functions, and the suggestion was that this was the expression of the emotions. That attitude on Darwin's part is reflected in the work of other psychologists, men who were interested, as Darwin was, in the study of the act, in the information that is conveyed by one individual to another by his attitude. They assume that these acts had a reason for existence because they expressed something in the mind of the individual. It is an approach like that of the philologist. They assume that language existed for the purpose of conveying certain ideas, certain feelings.

If one considers, he realizes that this is a false approach. It is quite impossible to assume that animals do undertake to express their emotions. They certainly do not undertake to express them for the benefit of other animals. The most that can be said is that the "expressions" did set free a certain emotion in the individual, an escape valve, so to speak, an emotional attitude which the animal needed, in some sense, to get rid of. They certainly could not exist in these lower animals as means of expressing emotions; we cannot approach them from the point of view of expressing a content in the mind of the individual. We can, of course, see how, for the actor, they may become definitely a language. An actor, for example, may undertake to express his rage, and he may do it by an expression of the countenance, and so convey to the audience the emotion he intended. However, he is not expressing his own emotion but simply conveying to the audience the evidence of anger, and if he is successful he may do it more effectively, as far as the audience is concerned, than a person who is in reality angered. There we have these gestures serving the purpose of expression of the emotions, but we cannot conceive that they arose as such a language in order to express emotion. Language, then, has to be studied from the point of view of the gestural type of conduct within which it existed without being as such a definite language. And we have to see how the communicative function could have arisen out of that prior sort of conduct.

The psychology of Darwin assumed that emotion was a psychological state, a state of consciousness, and that this state could not itself be formulated in terms of the attitude or the behavior of the form. It was assumed that the emotion is there and that certain movements might give evidence of it. The evidence would be received and acted upon by other forms that were fashioned like itself. That is, it presupposed the conscious state over against the biological organism. The conscious state was that which was to be expressed in the gesture or the attitude. It was to be expressed in behavior and to be recognized in some fashion as existent in the consciousness of the other form through this medium of expression. Such was the general psychological attitude which Darwin accepted.

Contrary to Darwin, however, we find no evidence for the prior existence of consciousness as something which brings about behavior on the part of one organism that is of such a sort as to call forth an adjustive response on the part of another organism, without itself being dependent on such behavior. We are rather forced to conclude that consciousness is an emergent from such behavior; that so far from being a precondition of the social act, the social act is the precondition of it. The mechanism of the social act can be traced out without introducing into it the conception of consciousness as a separable element within that act; hence the social act, in its more elementary stages or forms, is possible without, or apart from, some form of consciousness.

4. RISE OF PARALLELISM IN PSYCHOLOGY

The psychology which stresses parallelism has to be distinguished from the psychology which regards certain states of consciousness as existing in the mind of the individual, and succeeding each other in accordance with their own laws of association. The whole doctrine of the psychology which follows Hume was predominantly associationistic. Given certain states of consciousness they were supposed to be held together by other similar elements. Among these elements were those of pleasure and pain. Connected with this atomism of associated conscious states was a psychology of action grounded on the association of pleasure and pain with certain other sensations and experiences. The doctrine of association was the dominant psychological doctrine; it dealt with static rather than dynamic experience.

The pushing of the psychological side further and further into the central nervous system revealed that there were whole series of experiences which might be called sensations and yet were very different from those which could be regarded as static, such as sound, odor, taste, and color. Association belonged to this static world. It was increasingly recognized that there was a large part of our experience which was dynamic.[11] The form of actual doing was present in some of the sensations which

[11] The lines of association follow the lines of the act (1924).

answered to the innervation of sensory nerves. There was also the study of those tracts which went down to the viscera, and these certainly were aligned with the emotional experiences. The whole process of the circulation of the blood had been opened up, and the action which involved the sudden change of the circulation of the blood. Fear, hostility, anger, which called for sudden movement, or terror, which deprived the individual of the ability to move, reflected themselves in the visceral conditions; and also had their sensory aspects connected with the central nervous system. There was, then, a type of experience which did not fall into place in a static world. Wilhelm Wundt approached his problem from the standpoint of this sort of physiology which offered a clew by means of which one could follow out these various dynamic experiences into the mechanism of the organism itself.

The treatment which had been given to the central nervous system and its motor and sensory nerves had been that of bringing a nerve current to a central nervous system which was then in turn responsible for a sensation that happened in "consciousness." To get a complete statement of what we call the act one had to follow up the sensory side and then follow out the motor results that took place because of what happened in consciousness. The physiology to which I have referred in a certain sense separated itself from the field of consciousness. It was difficult to carry over such a mechanism as this into the lower animals. That, at least, took the psychologist out of the field of animal experience. Darwin regarded the animal as that out of which human conduct evolves, as well as the human form, and if this is true then it must be that in some sense consciousness evolves.

The resulting approach is from the point of view of conduct itself, and here the principle of parallelism is brought in. What takes place in consciousness runs parallel with what takes place in the central nervous system. It is necessary to study the content of the form as physiological and also as psychological. The center of consciousness, within which is registered that which affects the sensory nerves and out of which springs the conduct due to sensation and memory images, is to be taken out of the physiological mechanism; and yet one must find a parallel in what takes place in the nervous system for what the physiologist had placed in consciousness as such. What I have referred to in the matter of the emotions seemed to present a physiological counterpart for what takes place in consciousness, a field that seemed to belong peculiarly to the mental side of life. Hate, love, anger—these are seemingly states of mind. How could they be stated in physiological terms? The study of the acts themselves from an evolutionary standpoint, and also the study of the changes that take place in the organism itself when it is under the influence of what we call an emotion, present analogues to these emotional states. One could find something there that definitely answered to the emotions.

The further development of this lead occurred in James's theory of the emotions. Because we run away when we are afraid, and strike when we are angry, we can find something in the physiological organism that answers to fear and to anger. It is an attitude in the organism which answers to these emotional states, especially these visceral conditions to which I have referred, and the sudden changes in the circulation which are found associated with emotions. It becomes possible to relate the psychical conditions with physiological ones. The result was that one could make a much more complete statement of the conduct of the individual in physiological terms, could find a parallel for that which is stated in terms of consciousness in the mechanism of the body and in the operation of that mechanism. Such a psychology was called, naturally enough, a physiological psychology. It was a statement in terms of what went on in the organism of the content with which the psychologist had been dealing. What is there in the act of the animal which answers to these different so-called psychological categories? What is there that answers to the sensations, to the motor responses? When these questions were answered physiologically, they, of course, involved mechanisms located inside of the act, for all that takes place in the body is action. It may be delayed action, but there is nothing there that is itself simply a state, a physiological state that could be compared with a static state. We come then to the sensations and undertake to state them in terms of complete reflex action. We deal with the sensation from the standpoint of the stimulus, and when we come to deal with the various emotional states we deal with them in terms of the preparation for action and the act itself as it is going on.[12] That is, it becomes now essential to relate a set of psychical states with the different phases of the act. Parallelism, then, is an attempt to find analogues between action and experienced contents.

The inevitable result of this analysis was to carry psychology from a static to a dynamic form. It was not simply a question of relating what was found in introspection with what is found in the organism; it became a question of relating together those things which were found in introspection in the dynamic way in which the physiological elements were related to the life of the organism. Psychology became in turn associational, motor, functional, and finally behavioristic.

The historical transformation of psychology was a process which took place gradually. Consciousness was something which could not be simply dispensed with. In early psychology there was a crude attempt to account for consciousness as a certain secretion in the brain, but this was only a ridiculous phase of the transformation. Consciousness was something that was there, but it was something that could be brought into closer and closer relationship with what went on in the body. What went on there had a certain definite order. Everything that took place in the body was part of an act. The earlier conception of the central nervous system assumed that one could locate certain faculties of the mind in certain parts of the brain, but a study of the central nervous system did not reveal any such correlation. It became evident that there were nothing but

---

[12] Thus John Dewey added to James's doctrine the necessity of conflict in action in order for emotions to arise.

paths in the central nervous system.[13] The cells of the brain were seen to be parts of the nervous paths provided with material for carrying on the system, but nothing was found there to carry on the preservation of an idea as such. There was nothing in the central nervous system which would enable one to locate a tract given over to abstractions. There was a time when the frontal lobe was regarded as the locus of thought-processes—but the frontal lobe also represents nothing but paths. The paths make very complicated conduct possible, they complicate the act enormously through the mechanism of the brain; but they do not set up any structure which functionally answers to ideas. So the study of consciousness from the standpoint of the organism inevitably led men to look at consciousness itself from the point of view of action.

What, for example, is our experience that answers to clenching of the fist? Physiological psychology followed the action out through the nerves that came from the muscles of the arm and hand. The experience of the act would then be the sensation of what was going on; in consciousness as such there is an awareness of what the organ was doing; there is a parallelism between what goes on in the organ and what takes place in consciousness. This parallelism is, of course, not a complete parallelism. There seems to be consciousness corresponding only to the sensory nerves.[14] We are conscious of some things and not conscious of others, and attention seems to play a very great part in determining which is the case. The parallelism which we carry over does not seem to be complete, but one which occurs only at various points. The thing that is interesting here is that it is the organism that now provides the clew for the analysis. Only portions of the response appear in con-

[13] [Among philosophers, Henri Bergson especially stressed this point. See his *Matière et Mémoire*.]

[14] We are conscious always of what we have done, never of doing it. We are always conscious directly only of sensory processes, never of motor processes; hence we are conscious of motor processes only through sensory processes, which are their resultants. The contents of consciousness have, therefore, to be correlated with or fitted into a physiological system in dynamic terms, as processes going on.

sciousness as such. The organism has assumed the primary place. Experimental psychology started off from what it could get hold of in the physiological system, and then undertook to find out what in consciousness seemed to answer to it. The scientist felt that he had the same assurance that the physiologist had in identifying these facts in the nervous system, and given those facts he could look into consciousness. It was simpler to start off with the neurosis and then register what was found in the psychosis. Thus, the acceptance of some sort of a parallelism between the contents of consciousness and the physiological processes of the central nervous system led to a conception of those contents dynamically, in terms of acts, instead of statically, in terms of states. In this way the contents of consciousness were approached from below (that is, naturalistically) rather than from above (that is, transcendentally), by a study of the physiological processes of the central nervous system to determine what in the mind answers to the activities of the physiological organism.

There was a question as to the directive centers for unified action. We are apt to think of the central nervous system from the point of view of the telephone board, with calls coming in and responses going out. Certain centers come to be conceived as principal centers. If you go back to the base of the brain, to that portion which is the essence of the central nervous system of lower forms, you do find an organization there which controls in its activity other activities; but when you come to conduct in the human form, you fail to find any such system in which there is a single directive center or group of centers. One can see that the various processes which are involved in running away from danger can be processes which are so interrelated with other activities that the control comes in the organization. One sees the tree as a possible place of escape if a bull is after him; and in general, one sees things which will enable the ongoing activity to be carried out. A varying group of centers may be the determining factor in the whole activity of the individual. That is the concept which has also been carried over into the field of growth. Certain parts of the embryo start growing, and control the action of growth until some other process comes into control. In the cortex, that organ which in some sense answers to human intelligence, we fail to find any exclusive and unvarying control, that is, any evidence of it in the structure of the form itself. In some way we can assume that the cortex acts as a whole, but we cannot come back to certain centers and say that this is where the mind is lodged in thinking and in action. There are an indefinite number of cells connected with each other, and their innervation in some sense leads to a unitary action, but what that unity is in terms of the central nervous system it is almost impossible to state. All the different parts of the cortex seem to be involved in everything that happens. All the stimuli that reach the brain are reflected into all parts of the brain, and yet we do get a unitary action. There remains, then, a problem which is by no means definitely solved: the unity of the action of the central nervous system. Wundt undertook to find certain centers which would be responsible for this sort of unity, but there is nothing in the structure of the brain itself which isolated any parts of the brain as those which direct conduct as a whole. The unity is a unity of integration, though just how this integration takes place in detail we cannot say.

What I wanted to bring out is that the approach to psychological theory from the standpoint of the organism must inevitably be through an emphasis upon conduct, upon the dynamic rather than the static. It is, of course, possible to work in the other direction, that is, to look at experience from the point of view of the psychologist and to draw conclusions as to what must go on in the central nervous system. It is possible to recognize, for example, that we are not simply at the mercy of the different stimuli that play in the central nervous system—the natural view of the physiologist. We can see these organs adjust themselves to different types of stimuli. When air waves come in they affect the particular organs of the ear; when tastes and odors come in the stimuli get to tracts in the proper organs that respond. There may seem to be merely a response of the organism to the stimuli. This position is taken over into the psychology of Spencer, who accepted the Darwinian principle of evolution. The influence of environment is exercised over the form, and the adaptation of the form results from the influences of the environment on it. Spencer conceived of the central nervous system as being continually played upon by stimuli which set up certain paths, so that it was the environment which was fashioning the form.

The phenomena of attention, however, give a different picture of conduct. The human animal is an attentive animal, and his attention may be given to stimuli that are relatively faint. One can pick out sounds at a distance. Our whole intelligent process seems to lie in the attention which is selective of certain types of stimuli.[15] Other stimuli which are bombarding the system are in some fashion shunted off. We give our attention to one particular thing. Not only do we open the door to certain stimuli and close it to others, but our attention is an organizing process as well as a selective process. When giving attention to what we are going to do we are picking out the whole group of stimuli which represent successive activity. Our attention enables us to organize the field in which we are going to act. Here we have the organism as acting and determining its environment. It is not simply a set of passive senses played upon by the stimuli that come from without. The organism goes out and determines what it is going to respond to, and organizes that world. One organism picks out one thing and another picks out a different one, since it is going to act in a different way. Such is an approach to what goes on in the central nervous system which comes to the physiologist from the psychologist.

The physiology of attention is a field which is still. a dark continent. The organism itself fits itself to certain types of conduct, and this is of considerable importance in determining what the animal will do. There also lie back in the organism

[15] [See Sections 13 and 14.]

responses, such as those of escape from danger, that represent a peculiar sensitivity. A sound in some other direction would not have the same effect. The eye is very sensitive to motions that lie outside of the field of central vision, even though this area of the retina of the eye is not so sensitive to form and distinctions of color. You look for a book in a library and you carry a sort of mental image of the back of the book; you render yourself sensitive to a certain image of a friend you are going to meet. We can sensitize ourselves to certain types of stimuli and we can build up the sort of action we are going to take. In a chain set of responses the form carries out one instinctive response and then finds itself in the presence of another stimulus, and so forth; but as intelligent beings we build up such organized reactions ourselves. The field of attention is one in which there must be a mechanism in which we can organize the different stimuli with reference to others so that certain responses can take place. The description of this is something we can reach through a study of our own conduct, and at present that is the most that we can say.

Parallelism in psychology was very largely under the control of the study of the central nervous system, and that led on inevitably to functional, motor, voluntaristic, and finally behavioristic psychology. The more one could state of the processes of the individual in terms of the central nervous system, the more one would use the pattern which one found in the central nervous system to interpret conduct. What I am insisting upon is that the patterns which one finds in the central nervous system are patterns of action—not of contemplation, not of appreciation as such, but patterns of action. On the other hand I want to point out that one is able to approach the central nervous system from the psychologist's point of view and set certain problems to the physiologist. How is the physiologist to explain attention? When the physiologist attempts that he is bound to do so in terms of the various paths. If he is going to explain why one path is selected rather than another he must go back to these terms of paths and actions. You cannot set up in the central nervous system a selective principle which can be generally applied throughout; you cannot say there is a specific something in the central nervous system that is related to attention; you cannot say that there is a general power of attention. You have to state it specifically, so that even when you are directing your study of the central nervous system from the point of view of psychology, the type of explanation that you are going to get will have to be in terms of paths which represent action.

Such, in brief, is the history of the appearance of physiological psychology in its parallelistic form, a psychology which had moved to the next stage beyond that of associationalism. Attention is ordinarily stressed in tracing this transition, but the emphasis on attention is one which is derived largely from the study of the organism as such, and it accordingly should be seen in the larger context we have presented.

5. PARALLELISM AND THE AMBIGUITY OF "CONSCIOUSNESS"

"Consciousness" is a very ambiguous term. One often identifies consciousness with a certain something that is there under certain conditions and is not there under other conditions. One approaches this most naturally by assuming that it is something that happens under certain conditions of the organism, something, then, that can be conceived of as running parallel with certain phenomena in the nervous system, but not parallel with others. There seems to be no consciousness that answers to the motor processes as such; the consciousness we have of our action is that which is sensory in type and which answers to the current which comes from the sensory nerves which are affected by the contraction of the muscles. We are not conscious of the actual motor pocesses, but we have a sensory process that runs parallel to it. This is the situation out of which parallelistic psychology arises. It implies on the one side an organism which is a going concern, that seemingly can run without consciousness. A person continues to live when he is under a general anesthetic. Consciousness leaves and consciousness re-

turns, but the organism itself runs on. And the more completely one is able to state the psychological processes in terms of the
central nervous system the less important does this consciousness become.

The extreme statement of that sort was given by Hugo
Münsterberg.[16] He assumed the organism itself simply ran on,
but that answering to certain nervous changes there were conscious states. If one said that he did something, what that
amounted to was a consciousness of the movement of the muscles of his body in doing it; the consciousness of the beginning
of the act is that which he interpreted as his own volition to act.
There is only a consciousness of certain processes that are going
on. Parallelism in this extreme form, however, left out of account just such processes as those of attention and the selective
character of consciousness. If the physiologist had been able
to point out the mechanism of the central nervous system by
which we organize our action, there might be still dominant
such a statement in terms of this extreme parallelism which
would regard the individual as simply conscious of the selection which the organism made. But the process of selection itself is so complex that it becomes almost impossible to state it,
especially in such terms. Consciousness as such is peculiarly
selective, and the processes of selection, of sensitizing the organ
to stimuli, are something very difficult to isolate in the central
nervous system. William James points out that the amount of
difference which you have to give to a certain stimulus to make
it dominant is very slight, and he could conceive of an act of
volition which holds on to a certain stimulus, and just gives it
a little more emphasis than it otherwise would have. Wundt
tried to make parallelism possible by assuming the possibility
of certain centers which could perform this selective function.
But there was no satisfactory statement of the way in which
one could get this interaction between an organism and a consciousness, of the way in which consciousness could act upon a

[16] [See *Die Willenshandlung*.]

central nervous system. So that we get at this stage of the development of psychology parallelism rather than interactionism.

The parallelistic phase of psychology reveals itself not simply as one of the passing forms which has appeared in psychological investigation, but as one which has served a very evident purpose and met a very evident need.

We do distinguish, in some sense, the experiences that we call conscious from those going on in the world around us. We see a color and give it a certain name. We find that we are mistaken, due to a defect in our vision, and we go back to the spectral colors and analyze it. We say there is something that is independent of our immediate sensory process. We are trying to get hold of that part of experience that can be taken as independent of one's own immediate response. We want to get hold of that so that we can deal with the problem of error. Where no error is involved we do not draw the line. If we discover that a tree seen at a distance is not there when we reach the spot, we have mistaken something else for a tree. Thus, we have to have a field to which we can refer our own experience; and also we require objects which are recognized to be independent of our own vision. We want the mechanism which will make that distinction at any time, and we generalize it in this way. We work out the theory of sense perception in terms of the external stimulus, so that we can get hold of that which can be depended upon in order to distinguish it from that which cannot be depended upon in the same way. Even an object that is actually there can still be so resolved. In the laboratory we can distinguish between the stimulus and the sense experience. The experimenter turns on a certain light and he knows just what that light is. He can tell what takes place in the retina and in the central nervous system, and then he asks what the experiences are. He puts all sorts of elements in the process so that the subject will mistake what it is. He gets on the one side conscious data and on the other side the physical processes that are going on. He carries this analysis only into a field which is of importance for his investigation; and he himself has objects out there which could be analyzed in the same fashion.

We want to be able to distinguish what belongs to our own experience from that which can be stated, as we say, in scientific terms. We are sure of some processes, but we are not sure as to the reaction of people to these processes. We recognize that there are all sorts of differences among individuals. We have to make this distinction, so we have to set up a certain parallelism between things which are there and have a uniform value for everybody, and things which vary with certain individuals. We seem to get a field of consciousness and a field of physical things which are not conscious.

I want to distinguish the differences in the use of the term "consciousness" to stand for accessibility to certain contents, and as synonymous with certain contents themselves. When you shut your eyes you shut yourself off from certain stimuli. If one takes an anesthetic the world is inaccessible to him. Similarly, sleep renders one inaccessible to the world. Now I want to distinguish this use of consciousness, that of rendering one accessible and inaccessible to certain fields, from these contents themselves which are determined by the experience of the individual. We want to be able to deal with an experience which varies with the different individuals, to deal with the different contents which in some sense represent the same object. We want to be able to separate those contents which vary from contents which are in some sense common to all of us. Our psychologists undertake definitely to deal with experience as it varies with individuals. Some of these experiences are dependent upon the perspective of the individual and some are peculiar to a particular organ. If one is color-blind he has a different experience from a person with a normal eye.

When we use "consciousness," then, with reference to those conditions which are variable with the experience of the individual, this usage is a quite different one from that of rendering ourselves inaccessible to the world.[17] In one case we are dealing

[17] [And, incidentally, from a third use in which "consciousness" is restricted to the

with the situation of a person going to sleep, distracting his attention or centering his attention—a partial or complete exclusion of certain parts of a field. The other use is in application to the experience of the individual that is different from the experience of anybody else, and not only different in that way but different from his own experience at different times. Our experience varies not simply with our own organism but from moment to moment, and yet it is an experience which is of something which has not varied as our experiences vary, and we want to be able to study that experience in this variable form, so that some sort of parallelism has to be set up. One might attempt to set up the parallelism outside of the body, but the study of the stimuli inevitably takes us over into the study of the body itself.

Different positions will lead to different experiences in regard to such an object as a penny placed on a certain spot. There are other phenomena that are dependent upon the character of the eye, or the effect of past experiences. What the penny would be experienced as depends upon the past experiences that may have occurred to the different individuals. It is a different penny to one person from what it is to another; yet the penny is there as an entity by itself. We want to be able to deal with these spatially perspectival differences in individuals. Still more important from a psychological standpoint is the perspective of memory, by means of which one person sees one penny and another sees another penny. These are characters which we want to separate, and it is here that the legitimacy of our parallelism lies, namely, in that distinction between the object as it can be determined, physically and physiologically, as common to all, and the experience which is peculiar to a particular organism, a particular person.

Setting this distinction up as a psychological doctrine gives the sort of psychology that Wundt has most effectively and

level of the operation of symbols. On consciousness see "The Definition of the Psychical," *University of Chicago Decennial Publications,* III (1903), 77 ff.; "What Social Objects Must Psychology Presuppose?" *Journal of Philosophy,* VII (1910), 174 ff.]

exhaustively presented. He has tried to present the organism and its environment as identical physical objects for any experience, although the reflection of them in the different experiences are all different. Two persons studying the same central nervous system at the dissecting table will see it a little differently; yet they see the same central nervous system. Each of them has a different experience in that process. Now, put on one side the organism and its environment as a common object and then take what is left, so to speak, and put that into the experience of the separate individuals, and the result is a parallelism: on the one side the physical world, and on the other side consciousness.

The basis for this distinction is, as we have seen, a familiar and a justifiable one, but when put into the form of a psychology, as Wundt did, it reaches its limits; and if carried beyond leads into difficulty. The legitimate distinction is that which enables a person to identify that phase of an experience which is peculiar to himself, which has to be studied in terms of a moment in his biography. There are facts which are important only in so far as they lie in the biography of the individual. The technique of that sort of a separation comes back to the physiological environment on one side and to the experience on the other. In this way an experience of the object itself is contrasted with the individual's experience, consciousness on one side with the unconscious world on the other.

If we follow this distinction down to its limits we reach a physiological organism that is the same for all people, played upon by a set of stimuli which is the same to all. We want to follow the effects of such stimuli in the central nervous system up to the point where a particular individual has a specific experience. When we have done that for a particular case, we use this analysis as a basis for generalizing that distinction. We can say that there are physical things on one side and mental events on the other. We assume that the experienced world of each person is looked upon as a result of a causal series that lies inside of his brain. We follow stimuli into the brain, and there we say consciousness flashes out. In this way we have ultimately to locate all experience in the brain, and then old epistemological ghosts arise. Whose brain is it? How is the brain known? Where does that brain lie? The whole world comes to lie inside of the observer's brain; and his brain lies in everybody else's brain, and so on without end. All sorts of difficulties arise if one undertakes to erect this parallelistic division into a metaphysical one. The essentially practical nature of this division must now be pointed out.

6. THE PROGRAM OF BEHAVIORISM

We have seen that a certain sort of parallelism is involved in the attempt to state the experience of the individual in so far as it is peculiar to him as an individual. What is accessible only to that individual, what takes place only in the field of his own inner life, must be stated in its relationship to the situation within which it takes place. One individual has one experience and another has another experience, and both are stated in terms of their biographies; but there is in addition that which is common to the experience of all. And our scientific statement correlates that which the individual himself experiences, and which can ultimately be stated only in terms of his experience, with the experience which belongs to everyone. This is essential in order that we may interpret what is peculiar to the individual. We are always separating that which is peculiar to our own reaction, that which we can see that other persons cannot see, from that which is common to all. We are referring what belongs to the experience just of the individual to a common language, to a common world. And when we carry out this relationship, this correlation, into what takes place physically and physiologically, we get a parallelistic psychology.

The particular color or odor that any one of us experiences is a private affair. It differs from the experience of other individuals, and yet there is the common object to which it refers. It is the same light, the same rose, that is involved in these experiences. What we try to do is to follow these common stimuli in through the nervous system of each of these individuals. We aim to get the statement in universal terms which will answer to those particular conditions. We want to control them as far as we can, and it is that determination of the conditions under which the particular experience takes place that enables us to carry out that control.[18]

If one says that his experience of an object is made up of different sensations and then undertakes to state the conditions under which those sensations take place, he may say that he is stating those conditions in terms of his own experience. But they are conditions which are common to all. He measures, he determines just what is taking place, but this apparatus with which he measures is, after all, made up of his sensuous experience. Things that are hot or cold, rough or smooth, the objects themselves, are stated in terms of sensations; but they are stated in terms of sensations which we can make universal, and we take these common characters of experience and find in terms of them those experiences which are peculiar to the different individuals.

Psychology is interested in this correlation, in finding out what the relationship is between what goes on in the physical world and what goes on in the organism when a person has a sensory experience. That program was carried out by Hermann Helmholtz.[19] The world was there in terms which could be stated in the laws of science, i.e., the stimuli were stated in physical terms. What goes on in the nervous system could be stated more and more exactly, and this could be correlated with certain definite experiences which the individual found in his own life. And the psychologist is interested in getting the correlation between the conditions under which the experience takes place and that which is peculiar to the individual. He wishes to make these statements as universal as possible, and is scientific in that respect. He wants to state the ex-

---

[18] [The following methodological interpretation of parallelism is further discussed in Section 15.]

[19] [*Die Lehre von dem Tonempfindungen; Handbuch der physiologischen Optik.*]

perience of an individual just as closely as he can in terms of the field which he can control, those conditions under which it appears. He naturally tries to state the conduct of the individual in terms of his reflexes, and he carries back as far as he can the more complex reflexes of the individual to the simpler forms of action. He uses, as far as he is able to use, a behavioristic statement, because that can be formulated in terms of this same field over which he has control.

The motive back of modern psychology gets an expression in the field of mental testing, where one is getting correlations between certain situations and certain responses. It is characteristic of this psychology that not only is it as behavioristic as it can be (in that it states the experience of the individual as completely as it can in objective terms), but it also is interested in getting such statements and correlations so that it can control conduct as far as possible. We find modern psychology interested in practical problems, especially those of education. We have to lead the intelligences of infants and children into certain definite uses of media, and certain definite types of responses. How can we take the individual with his peculiarities and bring him over into a more nearly uniform type of response? He has to have the same language as others, and the same units of measurement; and he has to take over a certain definite culture as a background for his own experience. He has to fit himself into certain social structures and make them a part of himself. How is that to be accomplished? We are dealing with separate individuals and yet these individuals have to become a part of a common whole. We want to get the correlation between this world which is common and that which is peculiar to the individual. So we have psychology attacking the questions of learning, and the problems of the school, and trying to analyze different intelligences so that we can state them in terms which are as far as possible common; we want something which can correlate with the task which the child has to carry out. There are certain definite processes involved in speech. What is there that is uniform by means of which we are able to identify what the individual can do and what particular training he may have to take? Psychology also goes over into the field of business questions, of salesmanship, personnel questions; it goes over into the field of that which is abnormal and tries to get hold of that which is peculiar in the abnormal individual and to bring it into relation with the normal, and with the structures which get their expression in these abnormalities. It is interesting to see that psychology starts off with this problem of getting correlations between the experience of individuals and conditions under which it takes place, and undertakes to state this experience in terms of behavior; and that it at once endeavors to make a practical use of this correlation it finds for the purposes of training and control. It is becoming essentially a practical science, and has pushed to one side the psychological and philosophical problems which have been tied up with earlier dogma under associational psychology. Such are the influences which work in the behavioristic psychology.

This psychology is not, and should not be regarded as, a theory which is to be put over against an associational doctrine. What it is trying to do is to find out what the conditions are under which the experience of the individual arises. That experience is of the sort that takes us back to conduct in order that we may follow it. It is that which gives a distinctive mark to a psychological investigation. History and all the social sciences deal with human beings, but they are not primarily psychological. Psychology may be of great importance in dealing with, say, economics, the problem of value, of desire, the problems of political science, the relation of the individual to the state, personal relations which have to be considered in terms of individuals. All of the social sciences can be found to have a psychological phase. History is nothing but biography, a whole series of biographies; and yet all of these social sciences deal with individuals in their common characters; and where the individual stands out as different he is looked at from the point of view of that which he accomplishes in the whole society, or in terms of the destructive effect which he may have. But we are not primarily occupied as social scientists in studying his experience as such. Psychology does undertake to work out the technique which will enable it to deal with these experiences which any individual may have at any moment in his life, and which are peculiar to that individual. And the method of dealing with such an experience is in getting the conditions under which that experience of the individual takes place. We should undertake to state the experience of the individual just as far as we can in terms of the conditions under which it arises. It is essentially a control problem to which the psychologist is turning. It has, of course, its aspect of research for knowledge. We want to increase our knowledge, but there is back of that an attempt to get control through the knowledge which we obtain; and it is very interesting to see that our modern psychology is going farther and farther into those fields within which control can be so realized. It is successful in so far as it can work out correlations which can be tested. We want to get hold of those factors in the nature of the individual which can be recognized in the nature of all members of society but which can be identified in the particular individual. Those are problems which are forcing themselves more and more to the front.

There is another phase of recent psychology which I should refer to, namely, configuration or *gestalt* psychology, which has been of interest in recent years. There we have the recognition of elements or phases of experience which are common to the experience of the individual and to those conditions under which this experience arises.[20] There are certain general forms in the field of perception in the experience of the individual as well as in the objects themselves. They can be identified. One cannot take such a thing as a color and build it up out of certain sets of sensations. Experience, even that of the individual, must start with some whole. It must involve some whole in

[20] [W. Köhler, *Die physischen Gestalten in Ruhe und im stationaren Zustand; Gestalt Psychology.*]

order that we may get the elements we are after. What is of peculiar importance to us is this recognition of an element which is common in the perception of the individual and that which is regarded as a condition under which that perception arises—a position in opposition to an analysis of experience which proceeds on the assumption that the whole we have in our perception is simply an organization of these separate elements. *Gestalt* psychology gives us another element which is common to the experience of the individual and the world which determines the conditions under which that experience arises. Where before one had to do with the stimuli and what could be traced out in the central nervous system, and then correlated with the experience of the individual, now we have a certain structure that has to be recognized both in the experience of the individual and the conditioning world.

A behavioristic psychology represents a definite tendency rather than a system, a tendency to state as far as possible the conditions under which the experience of the individual arises. Correlation gets its expression in parallelism. The term is unfortunate in that it carries with it the distinction between mind and body, between the psychical and the physical. It is true that all the operations of stimuli can be traced through to the central nervous system, so we seem to be able to take the problem inside of our skins and get back to something in the organism, the central nervous system, which is representative of everything that happens outside. If we speak of a light as influencing us, it does not influence us until it strikes the retina of the eye. Sound does not exert influence until it reaches the ear, and so on, so that we can say the whole world can be stated in terms of what goes on inside of the organism itself. And we can say that what we are trying to correlate are the happenings in the central nervous system on the one side and the experience of the individual on the other.

But we have to recognize that we have made an arbitrary cut there. We cannot take the central nervous system by itself, nor the physical objects by themselves. The whole process is one which starts from a stimulus and involves everything that takes place. Thus, psychology correlates the difference of perceptions with the physical intensity of the stimulus. We could state the intensity of a weight we were lifting in terms of the central nervous system but that would be a difficult way of stating it. That is not what psychology is trying to do. It is not trying to relate a set of psychoses to a set of neuroses. What it is trying to do is to state the experiences of the individual in terms of the conditions under which they arise, and such conditions can very seldom be stated in terms of the neuroses. Occasionally we can follow the process right up into the central nervous system, but it is quite impossible to state most of the conditions in those terms. We control experiences in the intensity of the light which we have, in the noises that we produce, control them in terms of the effects which are produced on us by heat and cold. That is where we get our control. We may be able to change these by dealing with actual organisms, but in general we are trying to correlate the experience of the individual with the situation under which it arises. In order that we may get that sort of control we have to have a generalized statement. We want to know the conditions under which experience may appear. We are interested in finding the most general laws of correlation we can find. But the psychologist is interested in finding that sort of condition which can be correlated with the experience of the individual. We are trying to state the experience of the individual and situations in just as common terms as we can, and it is this which gives the importance to what we call behavioristic psychology. It is not a new psychology that comes in and takes the place of an old system.

An objective psychology is not trying to get rid of consciousness, but trying to state the intelligence of the individual in terms which will enable us to see how that intelligence is exercised, and how it may be improved. It is natural, then, that such a psychology as this should seek for a statement which would bring these two phases of the experience as close to each other as possible, or translate them into language which is common to both fields. We do not want two languages, one of certain physical facts and one of certain conscious facts. If you push that analysis to the limit you get such results as where you say that everything that takes place in consciousness in some way has to be located in the head, because you are following up a certain sort of causal relation which affects consciousness. The head you talk about is not stated in terms of the head you are observing. Bertrand Russell says the real head he is referring to is not the head that the physiologist is looking at, but the physiologist's own head. Whether that is the case or not, it is a matter of infinite indifference to psychologists. That is not a problem in the present psychology, and behaviorism is not to be regarded as legitimate up to a certain point and as then breaking down. Behavioristic psychology only undertakes to get a common statement that is significant and makes our correlation successful. The history of psychology has been a history which moved in this direction, and anyone who looks at what takes place in the psychological Associations at the present time, and the ways in which psychology is being carried over into other fields, sees that the interest, the impulse that lies behind it, is in getting just such a correlation which will enable science to get a control over the conditions of experience.

The term "parallelism" has an unfortunate implication: it is historically and philosophically bound up with the contrast of the physical over against the psychical, with consciousness over against the unconscious world. Actually, we simply state what an experience is over against those conditions under which it arises. That fact lies behind "parallelism," and to carry out the correlation one has to state both fields in as common a language as possible, and behaviorism is simply a movement in that direction. Psychology is not something that deals with consciousness; psychology deals with the experience of the individual in its relation to the conditions under which the experience goes on. It is social psychology where the conditions are social ones.

THE POINT OF VIEW OF SOCIAL BEHAVIORISM

It is behavioristic where the approach to experience is made through conduct.[21]

[21] By way of further avoiding certain metaphysical implications I wish to say that it does not follow that because we have on the one side experience which is individual, which may be perhaps private in the sense to which I have referred to privacy, and have on the other a common world, that we have two separate levels of existence or reality which are to be distinguished metaphysically from each other. A great deal that appears simply as the experience of an individual, as his own sensation or perception, becomes public later. Every discovery as such begins with experiences which have to be stated in terms of the biography of the discoverer. The man can note exceptions and implications which other people do not see and can only record them in terms of his own experience. He puts them in that form in order that other persons may get a like experience, and then he undertakes to find out what the explanation of these strange facts is. He works out hypotheses and tests them and they become common property thereafter. That is, there is a close relationship between these two fields of the psychical and the physical, the private and the public. We make distinctions between these, recognizing that the same factor may now be only private and yet later may become public. It is the work of the discoverer through his observations and through his hypotheses and experiments to be continually transforming what is his own private experience into a universal form. The same may be said of other fields, as in the work of the great artist who takes his own emotions and gives them a universal form so that others may enter into them.

PART II

MIND

7. WUNDT AND THE CONCEPT OF THE GESTURE

THE particular field of social science with which we are concerned is one which was opened up through the work of Darwin and the more elaborate presentation of Wundt.

If we take Wundt's parallelistic statement we get a point of view from which we can approach the problem of social experience. Wundt undertook to show the parallelism between what goes on in the body as represented by processes of the central nervous system, and what goes on in those experiences which the individual recognizes as his own. He had to find that which was common to these two fields—what in the psychical experience could be referred to in physical terms.[1]

Wundt isolated a very valuable conception of the gesture as that which becomes later a symbol, but which is to be found in its earlier stages as a part of a social act.[2] It is that part of the social act which serves as a stimulus to other forms involved in the same social act. I have given the illustration of the dog-fight as a method of presenting the gesture. The act of each dog becomes the stimulus to the other dog for his response. There is

[1] [Cf. *Grundzüge der physiologischen Psychologie.*]
The fundamental defect of Wundt's psychophysical parallelism is the fundamental defect of all psychophysical parallelism: the required parallelism is not in fact complete on the psychical side, since only the sensory and not the motor phase of the physiological process of experience has a psychic correlate; hence the psychical aspect of the required parallelism can be completed only physiologically, thus breaking it down. And this fundamental defect of his psychophysical parallelism vitiates the analysis of social experiences—and especially of communication—which he bases upon the assumption of that parallelism.

[2] [*Völkerpsychologie*, Vol. I. For Mead's treatment of Wundt compare "The Relations of Psychology and Philology," *Psychological Bulletin*, I (1904), 375 ff., with the more critical "The Imagination in Wundt's Treatment of Myth and Religion," *ibid.*, III (1906), 393 ff.]

then a relationship between these two; and as the act is responded to by the other dog, it, in turn, undergoes change. The very
fact that the dog is ready to attack another becomes a stimulus
to the other dog to change his own position or his own attitude.
He has no sooner done this than the change of attitude in the
second dog in turn causes the first dog to change his attitude.
We have here a conversation of gestures. They are not, however, gestures in the sense that they are significant. We do not
assume that the dog says to himself, "If the animal comes from
this direction he is going to spring at my throat and I will turn
in such a way." What does take place is an actual change in his
own position due to the direction of the approach of the other
dog.

We find a similar situation in boxing and in fencing, as in the
feint and the parry that is initiated on the part of the other.
And then the first one of the two in turn changes his attack;
there may be considerable play back and forth before actually
a stroke results. This is the same situation as in the dog-fight.
If the individual is successful a great deal of his attack and defense must be not considered, it must take place immediately.
He must adjust himself "instinctively" to the attitude of the
other individual. He may, of course, think it out. He may deliberately feint in order to open up a place of attack. But a great
deal has to be without deliberation.

In this case we have a situation in which certain parts of the
act become a stimulus to the other form to adjust itself to those
responses; and that adjustment in turn becomes a stimulus to
the first form to change his own act and start on a different one.
There are a series of attitudes, movements, on the part of these
forms which belong to the beginnings of acts that are the stimuli
for the responses that take place. The beginning of a response
becomes the stimulus to the first form to change his attitude, to
adopt a different act. The term "gesture" may be identified
with these beginnings of social acts which are stimuli for the response of other forms. Darwin was interested in such gestures
because they expressed emotions, and he dealt with them very

largely as if this were their sole function. He looked at them as serving the function with reference to the other forms which they served with reference to his own observation. The gestures expressed emotions of the animal to Darwin; he saw in the attitude of the dog the joy with which he accompanied his master in taking a walk. And he left his treatment of the gestures largely in these terms.

It was easy for Wundt to show that this was not a legitimate point of attack on the problem of these gestures. They did not at bottom serve the function of expression of the emotions: that was not the reason why they were stimuli, but rather because they were parts of complex acts in which different forms were involved. They became the tools through which the other forms responded. When they did give rise to a certain response, they were themselves changed in response to the change which took place in the other form. They are part of the organization of the social act, and highly important elements in that organization. To the human observer they are expressions of emotion, and that function of expressing emotion can legitimately become the field of the work of the artist and of the actor. The actor is in the same position as the poet: he is expressing emotions through his own attitude, his tones of voice, through his gestures, just as the poet through his poetry is expressing his emotions and arousing that emotion in others. We get in this way a function which is not found in the social act of these animals, or in a great deal of our own conduct, such as that of the boxer and the fencer. We have this interplay going on with the gestures serving their functions, calling out the responses of the others, these responses becoming themselves stimuli for readjustment, until the final social act itself can be carried out. Another illustration of this is in the relation of parent-form to the infant—the stimulating cry, the answering tone on the part of the parent-form, and the consequent change in the cry of the infant-form. Here we have a set of adjustments of the two forms carrying out a common social act involved in the care of the child. Thus we have, in all these instances, a social process in which one can isolate the gesture which has its function in the social process, and which can become an expression of emotions, or later can become the expression of a meaning, an idea.

The primitive situation is that of the social act which involves the interaction of different forms, which involves, therefore, the adjustment of the conduct of these different forms to each other, in carrying out the social process. Within that process one can find what we term the gestures, those phases of the act which bring about the adjustment of the response of the other form. These phases of the act carry with them the attitude as the observer recognizes it, and also what we call the inner attitude. The animal may be angry or afraid. There are such emotional attitudes which lie back of these acts, but these are only part of the whole process that is going on. Anger expresses itself in attack; fear expresses itself in flight. We can see, then, that the gestures mean these attitudes on the part of the form, that is, they have that meaning for us. We see that an animal is angry and that he is going to attack. We know that that is in the action of the animal, and is revealed by the attitude of the animal. We cannot say the animal means it in the sense that he has a reflective determination to attack. A man may strike another before he means it; a man may jump and run away from a loud sound behind his back before he knows what he is doing. If he has the idea in his mind, then the gesture not only means this to the observer but it also means the idea which the individual has. In one case the observer sees that the attitude of the dog means attack, but he does not say that it means a conscious determination to attack on the part of the dog. However, if somebody shakes his fist in your face you assume that he has not only a hostile attitude but that he has some idea behind it. You assume that it means not only a possible attack, but that the individual has an idea in his experience.

When, now, that gesture means this idea behind it and it arouses that idea in the other individual, then we have a significant symbol. In the case of the dog-fight we have a gesture which calls out appropriate response; in the present case we have a symbol which answers to a meaning in the experience of the first individual and which also calls out that meaning in the second individual. Where the gesture reaches that situation it has become what we call "language." It is now a significant symbol and it signifies a certain meaning.[3]

The gesture is that phase of the individual act to which adjustment takes place on the part of other individuals in the social process of behavior. The vocal gesture becomes a significant symbol (unimportant, as such, on the merely affective side of experience) when it has the same effect on the individual making it that it has on the individual to whom it is addressed or who explicitly responds to it, and thus involves a reference to the self of the individual making it. The gesture in general, and the vocal gesture in particular, indicates some object or other within the field of social behavior, an object of common interest to all the individuals involved in the given social act thus directed toward or upon that object. The function of the gesture is to make adjustment possible among the individuals implicated in any given social act with reference to the object or objects with which that act is concerned; and the significant gesture or significant symbol affords far greater facilities for such adjustment and readjustment than does the non-significant gesture, because it calls out in the individual making it the same attitude toward it (or toward its meaning) that it calls out in the other individuals participating with him in the given social act, and thus makes him conscious of their attitude toward it (as a component of his behavior) and enables him to adjust his subsequent behavior to theirs in the light of that attitude. In short, the conscious or significant conversation of gestures is a much more adequate and effective mechanism of mutual adjustment within the social act—involving, as it does, the taking, by each of the individuals carrying it on, of the attitudes of the others toward himself—than is the unconscious or non-significant conversation of gestures.

[3] [See "A Behavioristic Account of the Significant Symbol," *Journal of Philosophy*, XIX (1922), 157 ff.]

MIND

When, in any given social act or situation, one individual indicates by a gesture to another individual what this other individual is to do, the first individual is conscious of the meaning of his own gesture—or the meaning of his gesture appears in his own experience—in so far as he takes the attitude of the second individual toward that gesture, and tends to respond to it implicitly in the same way that the second individual responds to it explicitly. Gestures become significant symbols when they implicitly arouse in an individual making them the same responses which they explicitly arouse, or are supposed to arouse, in other individuals, the individuals to whom they are addressed; and in all conversations of gestures within the social process, whether external (between different individuals) or internal (between a given individual and himself), the individual's consciousness of the content and flow of meaning involved depends on his thus taking the attitude of the other toward his own gestures. In this way every gesture comes within a given social group or community to stand for a particular act or response, namely, the act or response which it calls forth explicitly in the individual to whom it is addressed, and implicitly in the individual who makes it; and this particular act or response for which it stands is its meaning as a significant symbol. Only in terms of gestures as significant symbols is the existence of mind or intelligence possible; for only in terms of gestures which are significant symbols can thinking—which is simply an internalized or implicit conversation of the individual with himself by means of such gestures—take place. The internalization in our experience of the external conversations of gestures which we carry on with other individuals in the social process is the essence of thinking; and the gestures thus internalized are significant symbols because they have the same meanings for all individual members of the given society or social group, i.e., they respectively arouse the same attitudes in the individuals making them that they arouse in the individuals responding to them: otherwise the individual could not internalize them or be conscious of them and their meanings. As we shall see, the same

[47]

procedure which is responsible for the genesis and existence of mind or consciousness—namely, the taking of the attitude of the other toward one's self, or toward one's own behavior—also necessarily involves the genesis and existence at the same time of significant symbols, or significant gestures.

In Wundt's doctrine, the parallelism between the gesture and the emotion or the intellectual attitude of the individual, makes it possible to set up a like parallelism in the other individual. The gesture calls out a gesture in the other form which will arouse or call out the same emotional attitude and the same idea. Where this has taken place the individuals have begun to talk to each other. What I referred to before was a conversation of gestures which did not involve significant symbols or gestures. The dogs are not talking to each other; there are no ideas in the minds of the dogs; nor do we assume that the dog is trying to convey an idea to the other dog. But if the gesture, in the case of the human individual, has parallel with it a certain psychical state which is the idea of what the person is going to do, and if this gesture calls out a like gesture in the other individual and calls out a similar idea, then it becomes a significant gesture. It stands for the ideas in the minds of both of them.

There is some difficulty in carrying out this analysis if we accept Wundt's parallelism. When a person shakes his fist in your face, that is a gesture in the sense in which we use the term, the beginning of an act that calls out a response on your part. Your response may vary: it may depend on the size of the man, it may mean shaking your fist, or it may mean flight. A whole series of different responses are possible. In order that Wundt's theory of the origin of language may be carried out, the gesture which the first individual makes use of must in some sense be reproduced in the experience of the individual in order that it may arouse the same idea in his mind. We must not confuse the beginning of language with its later stages. It is quite true that as soon as we see the attitude of the dog we say that it means an attack, or that when we see a person looking around for a chair that it means he would like to sit down. The gesture is one which means these processes, and that meaning is aroused by what we see. But we are supposed to be at the beginning of these developments of language. If we assume that there is a certain psychical state answering to a physical state how are we going to get to the point where the gesture will arouse the *same* gesture in the attitude of the other individual? In the very beginning the other person's gesture means what you are going to do about it. It does not mean what he is thinking about or even his emotion. Supposing his angry attack aroused fear in you, then you are not going to have anger in your mind, but fear. His gesture means fear as far as you are concerned. That is the primitive situation. Where the big dog attacks the little dog, the little dog puts his tail between his legs and runs away, but the gesture does not call out in the second individual what it did in the first. The response is generally of a different kind from the stimulus in the social act, a different action is aroused. If you assume that there is a certain idea answering to that act, then you want at a later stage to get the idea of the first form, but originally your idea will be your own idea which answers to a certain end. If we say that gesture "A" has idea "a" as answering to it, gesture "A" in the first form calls out gesture "B" and its related idea "b" in the second form. Here the idea that answers to gesture "A" is not idea "a" but idea "b." Such a process can never arouse in one mind just the idea which the other person has in his.

How, in terms of Wundt's psychological analysis of communication, does a responding organism get or experience the same idea or psychical correlate of any given gesture that the organism making this gesture has? The difficulty is that Wundt presupposes selves as antecedent to the social process in order to explain communication within that process, whereas, on the contrary, selves must be accounted for in terms of the social process, and in terms of communication; and individuals must be brought into essential relation within that process before communication, or the contact between the minds of different individuals, becomes possible. The body is not a self, as such; it becomes a self only when it has developed a mind within the context of social experience. It does not occur to Wundt to account for the existence and development of selves and minds within, or in terms of, the social process of experience; and his presupposition of them as making possible that process, and communication within it, invalidates his analysis of that process. For if, as Wundt does, you presuppose the existence of mind at the start, as explaining or making possible the social process of experience, then the origin of minds and the interaction among minds become mysteries. But if, on the other hand, you regard the social process of experience as prior (in a rudimentary form) to the existence of mind and explain the origin of minds in terms of the interaction among individuals within that process, then not only the origin of minds, but also the interaction among minds (which is thus seen to be internal to their very nature and presupposed by their existence or development at all) cease to seem mysterious or miraculous. Mind arises through communication by a conversation of gestures in a social process or context of experience—not communication through mind.

Wundt thus overlooks the important fact that communication is fundamental to the nature of what we term "mind"; and it is precisely in the recognition of this fact that the value and advantage of a behavioristic account of mind is chiefly to be found. Thus, Wundt's analysis of communication presupposes the existence of minds which are able to communicate, and this existence remains an inexplicable mystery on his psychological basis; whereas the behavioristic analysis of communication makes no such presupposition, but instead explains or accounts for the existence of minds in terms of communication and social experience; and by regarding minds as phenomena which have arisen and developed out of the process of communication and of social experience generally—phenomena which therefore presuppose that process, rather than being presupposed by it—this analysis is able to throw real light on their nature. Wundt preserves a dualism or separation between gesture (or symbol) and idea, between sensory process and psychic content, because his psychophysical parallelism commits him to this dualism; and though he recognizes the need for establishing a functional relationship between them in terms of the process of communication within the social act, yet the only relationship of this sort which can be established on his psychological basis is one which entirely fails to illuminate the bearing that the context of social experience has upon the existence and development of mind. Such illumination is provided only by the behavioristic analysis of communication, and by the statement of the nature of mind in terms of communication to which that analysis leads.

8. IMITATION AND THE ORIGIN OF LANGUAGE

Wundt's difficulty has been resolved in the past through the concept of imitation. Of course, if it were true that when a person shakes his fist in your face you just imitate him, you would be doing what he is doing and have the same idea as he has. There are, in fact, certain cases where the responses are like the stimuli in the social act, but as a rule they are different. And yet it has been generally assumed that certain forms imitate each other. There has been a good deal of study on this problem of imitation and the part it is supposed to play in conduct, especially in lower forms; but the result of this study has been to minimize imitation, even in the conduct of the higher animals. The monkey has been traditionally the most imitative animal, but under scientific study this was found to be a myth. The monkey learns very quickly but he does not imitate. Dogs and cats have been studied from this standpoint, and the conduct of one form has not been found to serve the purpose of arousing the same act in the other form.

In the human form there seems to be imitation in the case of a vocal gesture, the important gesture as far as language is concerned. So the philologist in particular, before the psychologist reached a more accurate analysis, went on the assumption that we imitate the sounds that we hear. There seemed to be a good deal of evidence for this also in certain animal forms, particularly those forms that utilize a richer phonetic articulation, such as birds. The sparrow can be taught to imitate the canary by close association with the canary. The parrot learns to "speak." It is not, we shall see, genuine speech, for he is not conveying ideas, but we commonly say the parrot imitates the sounds that appear about it.

Imitation as a general instinct is now discredited in human psychology. There was a time when people assumed that there was a definite impulse on the part of the human animal just to do what it saw other people do. There is a great deal of seeming imitation on the part of children. Also there is among undeveloped forms a speech that appears to be nothing but imitation. There are persons whom we consider unintelligent who say things over without having any idea of what is meant, a bare repetition of sounds they hear. But the question still remains why the form should so imitate. Is there any reason for imitation? We assume that all conduct has back of it some function. What is the function of imitation? Seemingly we get an answer in the development of young forms. The young fox goes about with the parents, hunts with them, learns to seize and avoid the right animals; it has no original objection to the odor of a man, but after it has been with the old fox the scent of man will cause it to run away. There is, in this case, a series of responses which become definitely associated with a particular stimulus; if the young form goes about with the parent, those responses which are all there in its nature become associated with certain definite stimuli. We can, in a very generalized sense, speak of the fox as imitating its parents and avoiding man. But that usage would not imply running away as an automatic act of imitation. The young fox has been put in a situation in which it does run away, and when the odor of man is present it becomes definitely associated with this flight response. No young forms in the lower animals ever merely imitate the acts of the adult form, but they do acquire during their period of infancy the association of a set of more or less instinctive responses to a certain set of stimuli.

The above observations and reservations do not, as we shall see, justify the questionable sense in which the notion of imitation has often been used. The term "imitation" became of great importance, for a time, in social psychology and in sociology. It was used as a basis for a whole theory of sociology by the French sociologist, Gabriel Tarde.[4] The psychologist at first, without adequate analysis, assumed on the part of the person a tendency to do what other persons do. One can see how difficult it would be to work out any mechanism of that sort. Why should a person wink because another person winks? What stimulus would cause another person to act in that way? The sight of another person acting in another way? This is an impossible assumption.

In the parallelism of Wundt we have the basis for his account of language. Wundt assumed a physical situation which has a certain import for the conduct of the form, and on the other hand he assumed a psychical complex of ideas which are in a certain sense the expression of physiological or biological values. His problem is to get out of this situation language as significant communication.

There are such situations as that represented by the conversation of gestures to which I have referred, situations in which certain phases of the act become stimuli to the forms involved in it to carry out their part in the act. Now these parts of the act which are stimuli for the other forms in their social activity are gestures. Gestures are then that part of the act which is responsible for its influence upon other forms. The gesture in some sense stands for the act as far as it affects the other form. The threat of violence, such as a clenched fist, is the stimulus to the other form for defense or flight. It carries with it the import of the act itself. I am not referring to import in terms of reflective consciousness, but in terms of behavior. For the observer the gesture means the danger and the response of the individual

4 [*Les lois de l'imitation.*]

to that danger. It calls out a certain sort of an act. If we assume a consciousness in which there is not only present the stimulus in the form of sensation but also an idea, then there is in the mind the sensation in which this stimulus appears, a vision of the clenched fist, and besides that the idea of the attack. The clenched fist in so far as it calls out that idea may be said to mean the danger.

Now the problem is to get this relationship between the idea and the symbol itself into the conversation of gestures. As I pointed out before, this relationship is not given in the immediate response of fighting or running. It may be present there, but as far as the conversation of gestures is concerned an act of one sort calls out an act of a different sort in the other form. That is, the threat which is involved leads, we will say, to flight. The idea of flight is not the idea of attack. In the conversation of gestures there is the preparation for the full social process involving the actions in different forms, and the gestures, which are the parts of the act, serve to stimulate the other forms. They call out acts different from themselves. While they may call out acts which are alike, as a rule the response is different from the stimulus itself. The cry of a child calls out the response of the care of the mother; the one is fear and the other protection, solicitude. The response is not in any sense identical with the other act. If there is an idea, in the Wundtian sense, the psychical content that answers to a certain particular stimulus, that will not get its reflection in the response.

What language seems to carry is a set of symbols answering to certain content which is measurably identical in the experience of the different individuals. If there is to be communication as such the symbol has to mean the same thing to all individuals involved. If a number of individuals respond in different ways to the stimulus, the stimulus means different things to them. If a number of persons are lifting a weight, one person takes one position and another a different position. If it is a co-operative process requiring different sorts of responses, then the call on the part of one individual to act calls out different responses in the others. The conversation of gestures does not carry with it a symbol which has a universal significance to all the different individuals. It may be quite effective without that, since the stimulus which one individual gives may be the proper stimulus to call out different responses in the individuals in the group. It is not essential that the individuals should give an identical meaning to the particular stimulus in order that each may properly respond. People get into a crowd and move this way, and that way; they adjust themselves to the people coming toward them, as we say, unconsciously. They move in an intelligent fashion with reference to each other, and perhaps all of them think of something entirely different, but they do find in the gestures of others, their attitudes and movements, adequate stimuli for different responses. This illustrates a conversation of gestures in which there is co-operative activity without any symbol that means the same thing to all. Of course, it is possible for intelligent individuals under such conditions to translate these gestures into significant symbols, but one need not stop to translate into terms of that sort. Such a universal discourse is not at all essential to the conversation of gestures in co-operative conduct.

Such co-operative conduct is presumably the only type of conduct which one finds among the ants and bees. In these very complex societies there is an interrelationship of different forms that seemingly is as complex as human conduct in many respects. There are societies of a million individuals in some of the large ant nests, and divided up into different groups with different functions. What is a stimulus to action for one leads to a different response in another. There is co-operative activity, but no evidence of any significant language in the conduct of these insects. It is, of course, a field in which a great deal of work has to be done, but still there has been no evidence found of any significant symbols.

I want to make clear the difference between those two situations. There can be a high degree of intelligence, as we use that term, in the conduct of animals without any significant symbols, without any presentation of meanings as such. What is essential is co-operative activity, so that the gesture of one form calls out the proper response to others. But the gesture of one may call out very different responses on the part of other forms, and yet there may be no common meaning which all the different forms give to any particular gesture. There is no common symbol that for the ants means food. Food means a great many things, things that have to be gathered, that have to be stored, that have to be carried by the workers and placed in the mouths of the fighters. There is no evidence that there is any symbol that means food as such. The sight, the odor of food, and its position lead to a certain response. An ant picks a food object up and staggers back to the nest with it. Later it means something to be eaten, it means a whole series of activities. The odor along the path is a stimulus to other insects following along the path, but there is no symbol that means "path" to such a group. The odor of a strange form in the nest means attack from other forms, but if a strange ant is dipped in liquid formed by crushing ants from the nest and then placed in the nest there is no attack, even though his form is very much larger. The odor does not mean an enemy as such. Contrast these two situations: in one there is a highly complex social activity in which the gestures are simply stimuli to the appropriate response of the whole group; in the human situation there is a different response which is mediated by means of particular symbols or particular gestures which have the same meaning for all members of a group. Here the cry of an enemy is not simply a stimulus to attack. It means that a person of a different race, of a different community, is present, and that there is warfare going on. It has the same meaning to all individuals and that meaning may mediate a whole series of different responses.

As I have said, the problem from Wundt's standpoint is to get this second character over into the more primitive conversation of gestures, or conduct which is mediated by a conversation of gestures. A mere intelligent response on the part of the different members of a group to a single stimulus (to what to the

observer is a single stimulus) does not carry with it any communication. Now how is one to reach genuine language? Wundt
starts off with the assumption that there are psychical conditions that answer to certain stimuli, and an association between
them. Certain sights, odors, and especially sounds are associated with certain ideas. If, when a person uses a certain
sound, he has that idea in his own mind, and the gesture that
he uses, say a vocal gesture, calls out the same gesture in the
other, then that gesture in the other person will call out the
same idea in him. Say the word "enemy" calls out a hostile response. Now, when I say "enemy" it calls out the same response in your mind that it calls out in mine. There we would
have a particular symbol that has a common meaning. If all
members of the group were so constituted that it has this meaning, then there would be a basis for communication by means of
significant symbols.

The difficulty in this analysis to which I have been referring
is to account for a particular gesture calling out the same gesture in another individual, even if we assume that this same
idea is associated with the same vocal gesture in another individual. Assuming that the word "enemy" means hostility, how
can the situation arise in which one person says "enemy," and
the other person says "enemy" too? Where one person says
"enemy" one individual will fight and another will run away.
There we have two different significations answering to the
sound. What we want to get is the one stimulus which has a
certain psychical content calling out the same stimulus in another form, and so the same content. We seem to have the beginnings of that process among the talking birds. One stimulus
seems to call out the same stimulus in the conduct of the other
form. What the psychical accompaniment is in the birds, of
course, we cannot tell, but we can record that they seem to have
no such signification as they have in our experience. The parrot
does not mean what the sentences mean to us. We have noted,
however, that the canary's melody can be taken over by the

sparrow, and this seemingly imitative process we must soon discuss in detail.

We argued that there is no evidence of any general tendency on the part of forms to imitate each other. If one attempts to state such a tendency it breaks down mechanically. It would mean that we have a tendency to do the same thing that other people are doing, and also that these tendencies are not only in our nature, but also that they are attached to certain specific stimuli which mean what the other people are doing. The sight of one person doing something would be a stimulus to another person to do the same thing. We should have to assume that what the person is doing is already a reaction that is in the nature of the imitating individual. It would mean that we have in our nature already all of these various activities, and that they are called out by the sight of other people doing the same thing. It is a perfectly impossible assumption.

When the psychologist came to analyze imitation he restricted it to the field in which people happened to be doing the same thing. If one person is running he may be said to arouse the stimulus for other people to run at the same time. We do assume that the sight of one animal actually running is the stimulus to other animals to run. That is very important for the preservation of animals that go in droves. Cattle grazing in a pasture all drift along together. One animal left by himself will be nervous and will not graze, but if put with other animals it is again normal. It does more readily what it is doing provided it is in a group. The tendency to drift together is not an impossible sort of an instinct, since we can conceive that the movement of animals in a certain direction should be a stimulus to other animals. That is about all that there is in the "herding" instinct, if reduced down to something concrete in the action of the form itself. The animal acts more normally when with others in the same group. He will feed better than otherwise. But when you come to some specific act about all you can find is that the animals do tend to move in the same direction. This may lead to a stampede in the herd. Something of that sort is involved in the so-called "sentinel." One animal, a little more sensitive than the others, lifts his head and starts to run away, and the other animals do tend to move with the sentinel form. It is not, of course, imitation in the sense of copying; for one animal is not copying the other animal. The one animal simply tends to run when the other does. If a cat is put in a puzzle box and the cat does get to the point where it opens the door by a lever action and does that often enough, it will strike that lever the first thing. Now, if another cat is put in, and where it can see the first cat, it will not imitate it. There is no evidence that what one animal does becomes a stimulus to the other animal to do the same thing. There is no direct imitative activity.

There does, however, seem to be a tendency to imitate among men, and in particular to reproduce vocal gestures. We find the latter tendency among birds as well as among men. If you go into a locality where there is a peculiar dialect and remain there for a length of time you find yourself speaking the same dialect, and it may be something which you did not want to do. The simplest way of stating it is to say that you unconsciously imitate. The same thing is also true of various other mannerisms. If you think of a certain person you are very apt to find yourself speaking as the other person spoke. Any mannerism which the individual has is one which you find yourself tending to carry out when the person comes to your mind. That is what we call "imitation," and what is curious is that there is practically no indication of such behavior on the part of lower forms. You can teach the sparrow to sing as a canary but you have to keep that sparrow constantly listening to a canary. It does not take place readily. The mocking bird does seem to take up the calls of other birds. It seems to be peculiarly endowed in this particular way. But in general the taking over of the processes of others is not natural to lower forms. Imitation seems to belong to the human form, where it has reached some sort of independent conscious existence.

But "imitation" gives no solution for the origin of language. We have to come back to some situation out of which we can reach some symbol that will have an identical meaning, and we cannot get it out of a mere instinct of imitation, as such. There is no evidence that the gesture generally tends to call out the same gesture in the other organism.

Imitation as the mere tendency on the part of an organism to reproduce what it sees or hears other organisms doing is mechanically impossible; one cannot conceive an organism as so constructed that all the sights and sounds which reach it would arouse in the organism tendencies to reproduce what it sees and hears in those fields of experience. Such an assumption is possible only in terms of an older psychology. If one assumed that the mind is made up out of ideas, that the character of our conscious experience is nothing but a set of impressions of objects, and if one adjusts to these impressions, so to speak, a motor tendency, one might conceive of that as being one which would seek to reproduce what was seen and heard. But as soon as you recognize in the organism a set of acts which carry out the processes which are essential to the life of the form, and undertake to put the sensitive or sensory experience into that scheme, the sensitive experience, as stimulus we will say to the response, cannot be a stimulus simply to reproduce what is seen and heard; it is rather a stimulus for the carrying out of the organic process. The animal sees or smells the food and hears the enemy, the parent form sees and hears the infant form—these are all stimuli to the forms to carry through the processes which are essential to the species to which they belong. They are acts which go beyond the organism taken by itself, but they belong to co-operative processes in which groups of animals act together, and they are the fulfilment of the processes which are essential to the life of the forms. One cannot fit into any such scheme as that a particular impulse of imitation, and if one undertakes to present the mechanism which would make intelligible that process, even the intricacies of the central nervous system would be inadequate. An individual would be in such a situation as one of Gulliver's figures who undertook to save his breath by not talking, and so carried a bagful of all the objects about which he would want to talk. One would have to carry about an enormous bagful, so to speak, of such possible actions if they were to be represented in the central nervous system. Imitation, however, cannot be taken as a primitive response.

9. THE VOCAL GESTURE AND THE SIGNIFICANT SYMBOL

The concept of imitation has been used very widely in the field of the vocal gesture. There we do seem to have a tendency on the part of certain organisms to reproduce sounds which are heard. Human beings and the talking birds provide illustrations. But even here "imitation" is hardly an immediate tendency, since it takes quite a while to get one bird to reproduce the song, or for the child to take over the phonetic gesture of the human form. The vocal gesture is a stimulus to some sort of response; it is not simply a stimulus to the calling out of the sound which the animal hears. Of course, the bird can be put into a situation where it may reach the mere repetition of that which it hears. If we assume that one sound that the bird makes calls out another sound, when the bird hears this first sound it responds by the second. If one asked why one note answers to another, one would have to go to some process where the vocal gesture would have a different pnysiological significance. An illustration is the cooing process of pigeons. There one note calls out another note in the other form. It is a conversation of gestures, where a certain attitude expressing itself in a certain note calls out another attitude with its corresponding note. If the form is to call out in itself the same note that it calls out in the other, it must act as the other acts, and use the note that the other makes use of in order to reproduce the particular note in question. So you find, if you put the sparrow and the canary together in neighboring cages, where the call of one calls out a series of notes in the other, that if the sparrow finds itself uttering a note such as a canary does, the vocal gesture here must be more or less of the same type. Where that situation exists, the sparrow in its own process of vocalization makes use of such notes as those which the canary makes use of. The sparrow is influencing not only the canary, but also in hearing itself it is influencing itself. The note that it is making use of, if it is identical with the note of the canary, calls out a response in itself that the canary's note would call out in itself. Those are the situations that have become emphasized and maintained where one has what we term "imitation." Where the sparrow is actually making use of a phonetic vocal gesture of the canary through a common note in the repertoire of both of them, then the sparrow would be tending to bring out in itself the same response that would be brought out by the note of the canary. That, then, would give an added weight in the experience of the sparrow to that particular response.

If the vocal gesture which the sparrow makes is identical with that which it hears when the canary makes use of the same note, then it is seen that its own response will be in that case identical with the response to the canary's note. It is this which gives such peculiar importance to the vocal gesture: it is one of those social stimuli which affect the form that makes it in the same fashion that it affects the form when made by another. That is, we can hear ourselves talking, and the import of what we say is the same to ourselves that it is to others. If the sparrow makes use of a canary's note it is calling out in itself the response that the canary's note calls out. In so far, then, as the sparrow does make use of the same note that the canary makes use of, it will emphasize the vocal responses to this note because they will be present not only when the canary makes use of it but also when the sparrow makes use of it. In such a case it is presupposed that the particular stimulus is present in the form itself, that is, that the vocal stimulus which calls out the particular note which is learned is present in the repertoire of the sparrow as well as in that of the canary. If one recognizes that, then one can see that those particular notes answering to this stimulus will be, so to speak, written in, underlined. They will become habitual. We are supposing that one note calls out another, a stimulus calls out a response. If this note which calls out this response is used not only by the canary but also by the sparrow, then whenever the sparrow hears the canary it makes use of that particular note, and if it has the same note in its own repertoire then there is a double tendency to bring about this particular response, so that it becomes more frequently made use of and becomes more definitely a part of the singing of the sparrow than otherwise. Such are the situations in which the sparrow does take the rôle of the canary in so far as there are certain notes to which it tends to react just as the canary does. There is a double weight, so to speak, upon this particular note or series of notes. It is in such a fashion that we can understand the learning by the sparrow of the canary's song. One has to assume a like tendency in the two forms if one is going to get any mechanism for imitation at all.

To illustrate this further let us go back to the conversation of gestures in the dog-fight. There the stimulus which one dog gets from the other is to a response which is different from the response of the stimulating form. One dog is attacking the other, and is ready to spring at the other dog's throat; the reply on the part of the second dog is to change its position, perhaps to spring at the throat of the first dog. There is a conversation of gestures, a reciprocal shifting of the dogs' positions and attitudes. In such a process there would be no mechanism for imitation. One dog does not imitate the other. The second dog assumes a different attitude to avoid the spring of the first dog. The stimulus in the attitude of one dog is not to call out the response in itself that it calls out in the other. The first dog is influenced by its own attitude, but it is simply carrying out the process of a prepared spring, so that the influence on the dog is simply in reinforcing the process which is going on. It is not a stimulus to the dog to take the attitude of the other dog.

When, however, one is making use of the vocal gesture, if we assume that one vocal element is a stimulus to a certain reply, then when the animal that makes use of that vocal gesture hears the resulting sound he will have aroused in himself at least a tendency to respond in the same way as the other animal responds. It may be a very slight tendency—the lion does not appreciably frighten itself by its roar. The roar has an effect of frightening the animal he is attacking, and it has also the character of a challenge under certain conditions. But when we come to such elaborate processes of vocalization as those of the song of birds, there one vocal gesture calls out another vocal gesture. These, of course, have their function in the intercourse of the birds, but the gestures themselves become of peculiar importance. The vocalization plays a very large part in such a process as wooing, and one call tends to call out another note. In the case of the lion's roar the response is not so much a vocal sound as it is a flight, or, if you like, a fight. The response is not primarily a vocal response. It is rather the action of the form itself. But in the song of birds, where vocalization is carried out in an elaborate fashion, the stimulus does definitely call out a certain response so that the bird when singing is influenced by its own stimulus to a response which will be like that which is produced in another form. That response which is produced in itself, since it is also produced by the influence of others, gets twice the emphasis that it would have if it were just called out by the note of others. It is called out more frequently than the response to other sounds. It is this that gives the seeming evidence of imitation in the case of sounds or vocal gestures.[5] The stimulus that calls out a particular sound may be found not only in the other forms of the group but also in the repertoire of the particular bird which uses the vocal gesture. This stimulus A calls out the response B. Now if this stimulus A is not like B, and if we assume that A calls out B, then if A is used by other forms these forms will respond in the fashion B. If this form also uses the vocal gesture A, it will be calling out in itself the response B, so that the response B will be emphasized over against other responses because it is called out not only by the

[5] An attempt was made by Baldwin to carry back imitation to a fundamental biological process—a tendency on the part of the organism to reinstate a pleasurable sensation. . . . . In the process of mastication the very process of chewing reinstates the stimulus, brings back the flavor. Baldwin would call this self-imitation. This process, if it takes place at all, does not by any means meet the situation with which we are dealing (1912).

vocal gestures of other forms but also by the form itself. This would never take place unless there were an identity represented by *A*, in this case an identity of stimuli.

In the case of the vocal gesture the form hears its own stimulus just as when this is used by other forms, so it tends to respond also to its own stimulus as it responds to the stimulus of other forms. That is, birds tend to sing to themselves, babies to talk to themselves. The sounds they make are stimuli to make other sounds. Where there is a specific sound that calls out a specific response, then if this sound is made by other forms it calls out this response in the form in question. If the sparrow makes use of this particular sound then the response to that sound will be one which will be heard more frequently than another response. In that way there will be selected out of the sparrow's repertoire those elements which are found in the song of the canary, and gradually such selection would build up in the song of the sparrow those elements which are common to both, without assuming a particular tendency of imitation. There is here a selective process by which is picked out what is common. "Imitation" depends upon the individual influencing himself as others influence him, so that he is under the influence not only of the other but also of himself in so far as he uses the same vocal gesture.

The vocal gesture, then, has an importance which no other gesture has. We cannot see ourselves when our face assumes a certain expression. If we hear ourselves speak we are more apt to pay attention. One hears himself when he is irritated using a tone that is of an irritable quality, and so catches himself. But in the facial expression of irritation the stimulus is not one that calls out an expression in the individual which it calls out in the other. One is more apt to catch himself up and control himself in the vocal gesture than in the expression of the countenance.

It is only the actor who uses bodily expressions as a means of looking as he wants others to feel. He gets a response which reveals to him how he looks by continually using a mirror. He registers anger, he registers love, he registers this, that, or the other attitude, and he examines himself in a glass to see how he does so. When he later makes use of the gesture it is present as a mental image. He realizes that that particular expression does call out fright. If we exclude vocal gestures, it is only by the use of the mirror that one could reach the position where he responds to his own gestures as other people respond. But the vocal gesture is one which does give one this capacity for answering to one's own stimulus as another would answer.

If there is any truth in the old axiom that the bully is always the coward, it will be found to rest on the fact that one arouses in himself that attitude of fear which his bullying attitude arouses in another, so that when put into a particular situation which calls his bluff, his own attitude is found to be that of the others. If one's own attitude of giving way to the bullying attitude of others is one that arouses the bullying attitude, he has in that degree aroused the attitude of bullying in himself. There is a certain amount of truth in this when we come back to the effect upon one's self of the gesture of which he makes use. In so far as one calls out the attitude in himself that one calls out in others, the response is picked out and strengthened. That is the only basis for what we call imitation. It is not imitation in the sense of simply doing what one sees another person doing. The mechanism is that of an individual calling out in himself the response which he calls out in another, consequently giving greater weight to those responses than to the other responses, and gradually building up those sets of responses into a dominant whole. That may be done, as we say, unconsciously. The sparrow does not know it is imitating the canary. It is just a gradual picking up of the notes which are common to both of them. And that is true wherever there is imitation.

So far as exclamatory sounds are concerned (and they would answer in our own vocal gestures to what is found in those of animals), the response to these does not enter into immediate conversation, and the influence of these responses on the individual are comparatively slight. It seems to be difficult to bring them into relationship with significant speech. We are not consciously frightened when we speak angrily to someone else, but the meaning of what we say is always present to us when we speak. The response in the individual to an exclamatory cry which is of the same sort as that in the other does not play any important part in the conduct of the form. The response of the lion to its roar is of very little importance in the response of the form itself, but our response to the meaning of what we say is constantly attached to our conversation. We must be constantly responding to the gesture we make if we are to carry on successful vocal conversation. The meaning of what we are saying is the tendency to respond to it. You ask somebody to bring a visitor a chair. You arouse the tendency to get the chair in the other, but if he is slow to act you get the chair yourself. The response to the vocal gesture is the doing of a certain thing, and you arouse that same tendency in yourself. You are always replying to yourself, just as other people reply. You assume that in some degree there must be identity in the reply. It is action on a common basis.

I have contrasted two situations to show what a long road speech or communication has to travel from the situation where there is nothing but vocal cries over to the situation in which significant symbols are utilized. What is peculiar to the latter is that the individual responds to his own stimulus in the same way as other people respond. Then the stimulus becomes significant; then one is saying something. As far as a parrot is concerned, its "speech" means nothing, but where one significantly says something with his own vocal process he is saying it to himself as well as to everybody else within reach of his voice. It is only the vocal gesture that is fitted for this sort of communication, because it is only the vocal gesture to which one responds or tends to respond as another person tends to respond to it. It is true that the language of the hands is of the same character. One sees one's self using the gestures which those who are deaf make use of. They influence one the same way as they influence others. Of course, the same is true of any form of script. But such symbols have all been developed out of the specific vocal gesture, for that is the basic gesture which does influence the individual as it influences others. Where it does not become significant is in the vocalization of the two birds.[6] Nevertheless, the same type of process is present, the stimulus of the one bird tending to call out the response in another bird which it tends to call out, however slightly, in the bird itself.

10. THOUGHT, COMMUNICATION, AND THE SIGNIFICANT SYMBOL

We have contended that there is no particular faculty of imitation in the sense that the sound or the sight of another's response is itself a stimulus to carry out the same reaction, but rather that if there is already present in the individual an action like the action of another, then there is a situation which makes imitation possible. What is necessary now to carry through that imitation is that the conduct and the gesture of the individual which calls out a response in the other should also tend to call out the same response in himself. In the dog-fight this is not present: the attitude in the one dog does not tend to call out the same attitude in the other. In some respects that actually may occur in the case of two boxers. The man who makes a feint is calling out a certain blow from his opponent, and that act of his own does have that meaning to him, that is, he has in some sense initiated the same act in himself. It does not go clear through, but he has stirred up the centers in his central nervous system which would lead to his making the same blow that his opponent is led to make, so that he calls out in himself, or tends to call out, the same response which he calls out in the other. There you have the basis for so-called imitation. Such is the process which is so widely recognized at present in manners of speech, of dress, and of attitudes.

We are more or less unconsciously seeing ourselves as others see us. We are unconsciously addressing ourselves as others address us; in the same way as the sparrow takes up the note of the canary we pick up the dialects about us. Of course, there must be these particular responses in our own mechanism. We are

[6] [See Supplementary Essay III for discussion.]

calling out in the other person something we are calling out in ourselves, so that unconsciously we take over these attitudes. We are unconsciously putting ourselves in the place of others and acting as others act. I want simply to isolate the general mechanism here, because it is of very fundamental importance in the development of what we call self-consciousness and the appearance of the self. We are, especially through the use of the vocal gestures, continually arousing in ourselves those responses which we call out in other persons, so that we are taking the attitudes of the other persons into our own conduct. The critical importance of language in the development of human experience lies in this fact that the stimulus is one that can react upon the speaking individual as it reacts upon the other.

A behaviorist, such as Watson, holds that all of our thinking is vocalization. In thinking we are simply starting to use certain words. That is in a sense true. However, Watson does not take into account all that is involved here, namely, that these stimuli are the essential elements in elaborate social processes and carry with them the value of those social processes. The vocal process as such has this great importance, and it is fair to assume that the vocal process, together with the intelligence and thought that go with it, is not simply a playing of particular vocal elements against each other. Such a view neglects the social context of language.[7]

The importance, then, of the vocal stimulus lies in this fact that the individual can hear what he says and in hearing what

[7] Gestures, if carried back to the matrix from which they spring, are always found to inhere in or involve a larger social act of which they are phases. In dealing with communication we have first to recognize its earliest origins in the unconscious conversation of gestures. Conscious communication—conscious conversation of gestures—arises when gestures become signs, that is, when they come to carry for the individuals making them and the individuals responding to them, definite meanings or significations in terms of the subsequent behavior of the individuals making them; so that, by serving as prior indications, to the individuals responding to them, of the subsequent behavior of the individuals making them, they make possible the mutual adjustment of the various individual components of the social act to one another, and also, by calling forth in the individuals making them the same responses implicitly that they call forth explicitly in the individuals to whom they are made, they render possible the rise of self-consciousness in connection with this mutual adjustment.

he says is tending to respond as the other person responds. When we speak now of this response on the part of the individual to the others we come back to the situation of asking some person to do something. We ordinarily express that by saying that one knows what he is asking you to do. Take the illustration of asking someone to do something, and then doing it one's self. Perhaps the person addressed does not hear you or acts slowly, and then you carry the action out yourself. You find in yourself, in this way, the same tendency which you are asking the other individual to carry out. Your request stirred up in you that same response which you stirred up in the other individual. How difficult it is to show someone else how to do something which you know how to do yourself! The slowness of the response makes it hard to restrain yourself from doing what you are teaching. You have aroused the same response in yourself as you arouse in the other individual.

In seeking for an explanation of this, we ordinarily assume a certain group of centers in the nervous system which are connected with each other, and which express themselves in the action. If we try to find in a central nervous system something that answers to our word "chair," what we should find would be presumably simply an organization of a whole group of possible reactions so connected that if one starts in one direction one will carry out one process, if in another direction one will carry out another process. The chair is primarily what one sits down in. It is a physical object at a distance. One may move toward an object at a distance and then enter upon the process of sitting down when one reaches it. There is a stimulus which excites certain paths which cause the individual to go toward that object and to sit down. Those centers are in some degree physical. There is, it is to be noted, an influence of the later act on the earlier act. The later process which is to go on has already been initiated and that later process has its influence on the earlier process (the one that takes place before this process, already initiated, can be completed). Now, such an organization of a great group of nervous elements as will lead to conduct with reference to the objects about us is what one would find in the central nervous system answering to what we call an object. The complications are very great, but the central nervous system has an almost infinite number of elements in it, and they can be organized not only in spatial connection with each other, but also from a temporal standpoint. In virtue of this last fact, our conduct is made up of a series of steps which follow each other, and the later steps may be already started and influence the earlier ones.[8] The thing we are going to do is playing back on what we are doing now. That organization in the neural elements in reference to what we call a physical object would be what we call a conceptual object stated in terms of the central nervous system.

In rough fashion it is the initiation of such a set of organized sets of responses that answers to what we call the idea or concept of a thing. If one asked what the idea of a dog is, and tried to find that idea in the central nervous system, one would find a whole group of responses which are more or less connected together by definite paths so that when one uses the term "dog" he does tend to call out this group of responses. A dog is a possible playmate, a possible enemy, one's own property or somebody else's. There is a whole series of possible responses. There are certain types of these responses which are in all of us, and there are others which vary with the individuals, but there is always an organization of the responses which can be called out by the term "dog." So if one is speaking of a dog to another person he is arousing in himself this set of responses which he is arousing in the other individual.

It is, of course, the relationship of this symbol, this vocal gesture, to such a set of responses in the individual himself as well as in the other that makes of that vocal gesture what I call a significant symbol. A symbol does tend to call out in the individual a group of reactions such as it calls out in the other, but there is something further that is involved in its being a significant symbol: this response within one's self to such a word as

[8] [See Sections 13, 16.]

"chair," or "dog," is one which is a stimulus to the individual as well as a response. This is what, of course, is involved in what we term the meaning of a thing, or its significance.[9] We often act with reference to objects in what we call an intelligent fashion, although we can act without the meaning of the object being present in our experience. One can start to dress for dinner, as they tell of the absent-minded college professor, and find himself in his pajamas in bed. A certain process of undressing was started and carried out mechanically; he did not recognize the meaning of what he was doing. He intended to go to dinner and found he had gone to bed. The meaning involved in his action was not present. The steps in this case were all intelligent steps which controlled his conduct with reference to later action, but he did not think about what he was doing. The later action was not a stimulus to his response, but just carried itself out when it was once started.

When we speak of the meaning of what we are doing we are making the response itself that we are on the point of carrying out a stimulus to our action. It becomes a stimulus to a later stage of action which is to take place from the point of view of this particular response. In the case of the boxer the blow that he is starting to direct toward his opponent is to call out a certain response which will open up the guard of his opponent so that he can strike. The meaning is a stimulus for the prepara-

[9] The inclusion of the matrix or complex of attitudes and responses constituting any given social situation or act, within the experience of any one of the individuals implicated in that situation or act (the inclusion within his experience of his attitudes toward other individuals, of their responses to his attitudes toward them, of their attitudes toward him, and of his responses to these attitudes) is all that an *idea* amounts to; or at any rate is the only basis for its occurrence or existence "in the mind" of the given individual.

In the case of the unconscious conversation of gestures, or in the case of the process of communication carried on by means of it, none of the individuals participating in it is conscious of the meaning of the conversation—that meaning does not appear in the experience of any one of the separate individuals involved in the conversation or carrying it on; whereas, in the case of the conscious conversation of gestures, or in the case of the process of communication carried on by means of it, each of the individuals participating in it is conscious of the meaning of the conversation, precisely because that meaning does appear in his experience, and because such appearance is what consciousness of that meaning implies.

tion of the real blow he expects to deliver. The response which he calls out in himself (the guarding reaction) is the stimulus to him to strike where an opening is given. This action which he has initiated already in himself thus becomes a stimulus for his later response. He knows what his opponent is going to do, since the guarding movement is one which is already aroused, and becomes a stimulus to strike where the opening is given. The meaning would not have been present in his conduct unless it became a stimulus to strike where the favorable opening appears.

Such is the difference between intelligent conduct on the part of animals and what we call a reflective individual.[10] We say the animal does not think. He does not put himself in a position for which he is responsible; he does not put himself in the place of the other person and say, in effect, "He will act in such a way and I will act in this way." If the individual can act in this way, and the attitude which he calls out in himself can become a stimulus to him for another act, we have meaningful conduct. Where the response of the other person is called out and becomes a stimulus to control his action, then he has the meaning of the other person's act in his own experience. That is the general mechanism of what we term "thought," for in order that thought may exist there must be symbols, vocal gestures generally, which arouse in the individual himself the response which he is calling out in the other, and such that from the point of view of that response he is able to direct his later conduct. It involves not only communication in the sense in which birds and animals communicate with each other, but also an arousal in the individual himself of the response which he is calling out in the other individual, a taking of the rôle of the other, a tendency to act as the other person acts. One participates in the same process the other person is carrying out and controls his action with reference to that participation. It is that which constitutes the meaning of an object, namely, the common response in

[10] [For the nature of animal conduct see "Concerning Animal Perception," *Psychological Review*, XIV (1907), 383 ff.]

one's self as well as in the other person, which becomes, in turn, a stimulus to one's self.

If you conceive of the mind as just a sort of conscious substance in which there are certain impressions and states, and hold that one of those states is a universal, then a word becomes purely arbitrary—it is just a symbol.[11] You can then take words and pronounce them backwards, as children do; there seems to be absolute freedom of arrangement and language seems to be an entirely mechanical thing that lies outside of the process of intelligence. If you recognize that language is, however, just a part of a co-operative process, that part which does lead to an adjustment to the response of the other so that the whole activity can go on, then language has only a limited range of arbitrariness. If you are talking to another person you are, perhaps, able to scent the change in his attitude by something that would not strike a third person at all. You may know his mannerism, and that becomes a gesture to you, a part of the response of the individual. There is a certain range possible within the gesture as to what is to serve as the symbol. We may say that a whole set of separate symbols with one meaning are acceptable; but they always are gestures, that is, they are always parts of the act of the individual which reveal what he is going to do to the other person so that when the person utilizes the clue he calls out in himself the attitude of the other. Language is not ever

[11] Müller attempts to put the values of thought into language; but this attempt is fallacious, because language has those values only as the most effective mechanism of thought merely because it carries the conscious or significant conversation of gestures to its highest and most perfect development. There must be some sort of an implicit attitude (that is, a response which is initiated without being fully carried out) in the organism making the gesture—an attitude which answers to the overt response to the gesture on the part of another individual, and which corresponds to the attitude called forth or aroused in this other organism by the gesture—if thought is to develop in the organism making the gesture. And it is the central nervous system which provides the mechanism for such implicit attitudes or responses.

The identification of language with reason is in one sense an absurdity, but in another sense it is valid. It is valid, namely, in the sense that the process of language brings the total social act into the experience of the given individual as himself involved in the act, and thus makes the process of reason possible. But though the process of reason is and must be carried on in terms of the process of language—in terms, that is, of words—it is not simply constituted by the latter.

arbitrary in the sense of simply denoting a bare state of consciousness by a word. What particular part of one's act will serve to direct co-operative activity is more or less arbitrary. Different phases of the act may do it. What seems unimportant in itself may be highly important in revealing what the attitude is. In that sense one can speak of the gesture itself as unimportant, but it is of great importance as to what the gesture is going to reveal. This is seen in the difference between the purely intellectual character of the symbol and its emotional character. A poet depends upon the latter; for him language is rich and full of values which we, perhaps, utterly ignore. In trying to express a message in something less than ten words, we merely want to convey a certain meaning, while the poet is dealing with what is really living tissue, the emotional throb in the expression itself. There is, then, a great range in our use of language; but whatever phase of this range is used is a part of a social process, and it is always that part by means of which we affect ourselves as we affect others and mediate the social situation through this understanding of what we are saying. That is fundamental for any language; if it is going to be language one has to understand what he is saying, has to affect himself as he affects others.

11. MEANING[12]

We are particularly concerned with intelligence on the human level, that is, with the adjustment to one another of the acts of different human individuals within the human social process; an adjustment which takes place through communication: by gestures on the lower planes of human evolution, and by significant symbols (gestures which possess meanings and are hence more than mere substitute stimuli) on the higher planes of human evolution.

The central factor in such adjustment is "meaning." Meaning arises and lies within the field of the relation between the

[12] [See also "Social Consciousness and the Consciousness of Meaning," *Psychological Bulletin*, VII (1910), 397 ff.; "The Mechanism of Social Consciousness," *Journal of Philosophy*, IX (1912), 401 ff.]

gesture of a given human organism and the subsequent behavior of this organism as indicated to another human organism by that gesture. If that gesture does so indicate to another
organism the subsequent (or resultant) behavior of the given
organism, then it has meaning. In other words, the relationship
between a given stimulus—as a gesture—and the later phases
of the social act of which it is an early (if not the initial) phase
constitutes the field within which meaning originates and exists. Meaning is thus a development of something objectively
there as a relation between certain phases of the social act; it is
not a psychical addition to that act and it is not an "idea" as
traditionally conceived. A gesture by one organism, the resultant of the social act in which the gesture is an early phase, and
the response of another organism to the gesture, are the relata
in a triple or threefold relationship of gesture to first organism,
of gesture to second organism, and of gesture to subsequent
phases of the given social act; and this threefold relationship
constitutes the matrix within which meaning arises, or which
develops into the field of meaning. The gesture stands for a
certain resultant of the social act, a resultant to which there is a
definite response on the part of the individuals involved therein;
so that meaning is given or stated in terms of response. Meaning is implicit—if not always explicit—in the relationship among
the various phases of the social act to which it refers, and out of
which it develops. And its development takes place in terms of
symbolization at the human evolutionary level.

We have been concerning ourselves, in general, with the social process of experience and behavior as it appears in the calling out by the act of one organism of an adjustment to that act
in the responsive act of another organism. We have seen that
the nature of meaning is intimately associated with the social
process as it thus appears, that meaning involves this three-fold
relation among phases of the social act as the context in which
it arises and develops: this relation of the gesture of one organism to the adjustive response of another organism (also implicated in the given act), and to the completion of the given act—

a relation such that the second organism responds to the gesture of the first as indicating or referring to the completion of the given act. For example, the chick's response to the cluck of the mother hen is a response to the meaning of the cluck; the cluck refers to danger or to food, as the case may be, and has this meaning or connotation for the chick.

The social process, as involving communication, is in a sense responsible for the appearance of new objects in the field of experience of the individual organisms implicated in that process. Organic processes or responses in a sense constitute the objects to which they are responses; that is to say, any given biological organism is in a way responsible for the existence (in the sense of the meanings they have for it) of the objects to which it physiologically and chemically responds. There would, for example, be no food—no edible objects—if there were no organisms which could digest it. And similarly, the social process in a sense constitutes the objects to which it responds, or to which it is an adjustment. That is to say, objects are constituted in terms of meanings within the social process of experience and behavior through the mutual adjustment to one another of the responses or actions of the various individual organisms involved in that process, an adjustment made possible by means of a communication which takes the form of a conversation of gestures in the earlier evolutionary stages of that process, and of language in its later stages.

Awareness or consciousness is not necessary to the presence of meaning in the process of social experience. A gesture on the part of one organism in any given social act calls out a response on the part of another organism which is directly related to the action of the first organism and its outcome; and a gesture is a symbol of the result of the given social act of one organism (the organism making it) in so far as it is responded to by another organism (thereby also involved in that act) as indicating that result. The mechanism of meaning is thus present in the social act before the emergence of consciousness or awareness of meaning occurs. The act or adjustive response of the second organism gives to the gesture of the first organism the meaning which it has.

Symbolization constitutes objects not constituted before, objects which would not exist except for the context of social relationships wherein symbolization occurs. Language does not simply symbolize a situation or object which is already there in advance; it makes possible the existence or the appearance of that situation or object, for it is a part of the mechanism whereby that situation or object is created. The social process relates the responses of one individual to the gestures of another, as the meanings of the latter, and is thus responsible for the rise and existence of new objects in the social situation, objects dependent upon or constituted by these meanings. Meaning is thus not to be conceived, fundamentally, as a state of consciousness, or as a set of organized relations existing or subsisting mentally outside the field of experience into which they enter; on the contrary, it should be conceived objectively, as having its existence entirely within this field itself.[13] The response of one organism to the gesture of another in any given social act is the meaning of that gesture, and also is in a sense responsible for the appearance or coming into being of the new object—or new content of an old object—to which that gesture refers through the outcome of the given social act in which it is an early phase. For, to repeat, objects are in a genuine sense constituted within the social process of experience, by the communication and mutual adjustment of behavior among the individual organisms which are involved in that process and which carry it on. Just as in fencing the parry is an interpretation of the thrust, so, in the social act, the adjustive response of one organism to the gesture of another is the interpretation of that gesture by that organism—it is the meaning of that gesture.

At the level of self-consciousness such a gesture becomes a symbol, a significant symbol. But the interpretation of gestures

[13] Nature has meaning and implication but not indication by symbols. The symbol is distinguishable from the meaning it refers to. Meanings are in nature, but symbols are the heritage of man (1924).

is not, basically, a process going on in a mind as such, or one necessarily involving a mind; it is an external, overt, physical, or physiological process going on in the actual field of social experience. Meaning can be described, accounted for, or stated in terms of symbols or language at its highest and most complex stage of development (the stage it reaches in human experience), but language simply lifts out of the social process a situation which is logically or implicitly there already. The language symbol is simply a significant or conscious gesture.

Two main points are being made here: (1) that the social process, through the communication which it makes possible among the individuals implicated in it, is responsible for the appearance of a whole set of new objects in nature, which exist in relation to it (objects, namely, of "common sense"); and (2) that the gesture of one organism and the adjustive response of another organism to that gesture within any given social act bring out the relationship that exists between the gesture as the beginning of the given act and the completion or resultant of the given act, to which the gesture refers. These are the two basic and complementary logical aspects of the social process.

The result of any given social act is definitely separated from the gesture indicating it by the response of another organism to that gesture, a response which points to the result of that act as indicated by that gesture. This situation is all there—is completely given—on the non-mental, non-conscious level, before the analysis of it on the mental or conscious level. Dewey says that meaning arises through communication.[14] It is to the content to which the social process gives rise that this statement refers; not to bare ideas or printed words as such, but to the social process which has been so largely responsible for the objects constituting the daily environment in which we live: a process in which communication plays the main part. That process can give rise to these new objects in nature only in so far as it makes possible communication among the individual organisms involved in it. And the sense in which it is responsible for their

[14] [See *Experience and Nature*, chap. v.]

existence—indeed for the existence of the whole world of common-sense objects—is the sense in which it determines, conditions, and makes possible their abstraction from the total structure of events, as identities which are relevant for everyday social behavior; and in that sense, or as having that meaning, they are existent only relative to that behavior. In the same way, at a later, more advanced stage of its development, communication is responsible for the existence of the whole realm of scientific objects as well as identities abstracted from the total structure of events by virtue of their relevance for scientific purposes.

The logical structure of meaning, we have seen, is to be found in the threefold relationship of gesture to adjustive response and to the resultant of the given social act. Response on the part of the second organism to the gesture of the first is the interpretation—and brings out the meaning—of that gesture, as indicating the resultant of the social act which it initiates, and in which both organisms are thus involved. This threefold or triadic relation between gesture, adjustive response, and resultant of the social act which the gesture initiates is the basis of meaning; for the existence of meaning depends upon the fact that the adjustive response of the second organism is directed toward the resultant of the given social act as initiated and indicated by the gesture of the first organism. The basis of meaning is thus objectively there in social conduct, or in nature in its relation to such conduct. Meaning is a content of an object which is dependent upon the relation of an organism or group of organisms to it. It is not essentially or primarily a psychical content (a content of mind or consciousness), for it need not be conscious at all, and is not in fact until significant symbols are evolved in the process of human social experience. Only when it becomes identified with such symbols does meaning become conscious. The meaning of a gesture on the part of one organism is the adjustive response of another organism to it, as indicating the resultant of the social act it initiates, the adjustive response of the second organism being itself directed toward or related to the completion of that act. In other words, meaning involves a reference of the gesture of one organism to the resultant of the social act it indicates or initiates, as adjustively responded to in this reference by another organism; and the adjustive response of the other organism is the meaning of the gesture.

Gestures may be either conscious (significant) or unconscious (non-significant). The conversation of gestures is not significant below the human level, because it is not conscious, that is, not *self*-conscious (though it is conscious in the sense of involving feelings or sensations). An animal as opposed to a human form, in indicating something to, or bringing out a meaning for, another form, is not at the same time indicating or bringing out the same thing or meaning to or for himself; for he has no mind, no thought, and hence there is no meaning here in the significant or self-conscious sense. A gesture is not significant when the response of another organism to it does not indicate to the organism making it what the other organism is responding to.[15]

Much subtlety has been wasted on the problem of the meaning of meaning. It is not necessary, in attempting to solve this problem, to have recourse to psychical states, for the nature of meaning, as we have seen, is found to be implicit in the structure of the social act, implicit in the relations among its three basic individual components: namely, in the triadic relation of a gesture of one individual, a response to that gesture by a second individual, and completion of the given social act initiated by the gesture of the first individual. And the fact that the nature of

[15] There are two characters which belong to that which we term "meanings," one is participation and the other is communicability. Meaning can arise only in so far as some phase of the act which the individual is arousing in the other can be aroused in himself. There is always to this extent participation. And the result of this participation is communicability, i.e., the individual can indicate to himself what he indicates to others. There is communication without significance where the gesture of the individual calls out the response in the other without calling out or tending to call out the same response in the individual himself. Significance from the standpoint of the observer may be said to be present in the gesture which calls out the appropriate response in the other or others within a co-operative act, but it does not become significant to the individuals who are involved in the act unless the tendency to the act is aroused within the individual who makes it, and unless the individual who is directly affected by the gesture puts himself in the attitude of the individual who makes the gesture (MS).

meaning is thus found to be implicit in the structure of the social act provides additional emphasis upon the necessity, in social psychology, of starting off with the initial assumption of an ongoing social process of experience and behavior in which any given group of human individuals is involved, and upon which the existence and development of their minds, selves, and self-consciousness depend.

12. UNIVERSALITY

Our experience does recognize or find that which is typical, and this is as essential for an adequate theory of meaning as is the element of particularity. There are not only facts of red, for example, but there is in the experience a red which is identical so far as experience has been concerned with some other red. One can isolate the red just as a sensation, and as such it is passing; but in addition to that passing character there is something that we call universal, something that gives a meaning to it. The event is a color, it is red, it is a certain kind of red—and that is something which does not have a passing character in the statement of color itself. If we go over from particular contents of this sort to other objects, such as a chair, a tree, a dog, we find there something that is distinguishable from the particular object, plant, or animal that we have about us. What we recognize in a dog is not the group of sensuous elements, but rather the character of being a dog, and unless we have some reason for interest in this particular dog, some problem as to its ownership or its likelihood to bite us, our relationship to the animal is to a universal—it is just a dog. If a person asks you what you saw you reply that it was a dog. You would not know the color of the dog; it was just a dog in general that you saw.

There is a meaning here that is given in the experience itself, and it is this meaning or universal character with which a behavioristic psychology is supposed to have difficulty in dealing. When there is a response to such an animal as a dog there is a response of recognition as well as a response toward an object in the landscape; and this response of recognition is something that is universal and not particular. Can this factor be stated in behavioristic terms? We are not, of course, interested in philosophical implications; we are not interested in the metaphysics of the dog; but we are interested in the recognition which would belong to any other animal of the same sort. Now, is there a response of such a universal character in our nature that it can be said to answer to this recognition of what we term the universal? It is the possibility of such a behavioristic statement that I endeavor to sketch.

What the central nervous system presents is not simply a set of automatisms, that is, certain inevitable reactions to certain specific stimuli, such as taking our hand away from a radiator that is touched, or jumping when a loud sound occurs behind us. The nervous system provides not only the mechanism for that sort of conduct but also for recognizing an object to which we are going to respond; and that recognition can be stated in terms of a response that may answer to any one of a certain group of stimuli. That is, one has a nail to drive, he reaches for the hammer and finds it gone, and he does not stop to look for it, but reaches for something else he can use, a brick or a stone, anything having the necessary weight to give momentum to the blow. Anything that he can get hold of that will serve the purpose will be a hammer. That sort of response which involves the grasping of a heavy object is a universal.[16] If the object does call out that response, no matter what its particular character may be, one can say that it has a universal character. It is something that can be recognized because of this character, notwithstanding the variations that are involved in the individual instances.

Now, can there be in the central nervous system a mechanism which can be aroused so that it will give rise to this response, however varied the conditions are otherwise? Can there be a mechanism of a sufficiently complicated character to represent

[16] Abstraction and universals are due to conflict and inhibition: a wall is something to be avoided and something to be jumped, and while both it is mental, a concept. Language makes it possible to hold on to these mental objects. Abstractions exist for lower animals but they cannot hold them (1924).

the objects with which we deal—objects that have not only spatial dimensions, but also temporal dimensions? An object such as a melody, a tune, is a unitary affair. We hear the first notes and we respond to it as a whole. There is such a unity in the lives presented by biographies which follow a man from his birth to his death, showing all that belongs to the growth of the individual and the changes that take place in his career. Now, is there something in the central nervous system that can answer to such characters of the object, so that we can give a behavioristic account of an object so complicated as a melody or a life? The mere complication does not present serious difficulty, because the central nervous system has an almost infinite number of elements and possible combinations, but can one find a structure there in the central nervous system that would answer to a certain type of response which represents for us the character of the object which we recognize, as distinct from the mere sensations?

Recognition always implies a something that can be discovered in an indefinite number of objects. One can only sense a color once, in so far as "color" means an immediate relationship of the light waves to the retina of a normal nervous system. That experience happens and is gone, and cannot be repeated. But something is recognized, there is a universal character given in the experience itself which is at least capable of an indefinite number of repetitions. It is this which has been supposed to be beyond the behavioristic explanation or statement. What a behavioristic psychology does is to state that character of the experience in terms of the response. It may be said that there cannot be a universal response, but only a response to a particular object. On the contrary, in so far as the response is one that can take place with reference to the brick, a stone, a hammer, there is a universal in the form of the response that answers to a whole set of particulars, and the particulars may be indefinite in number, provided only they have certain characters in relation to the response. The relationship of this response to an indefinite number of stimuli is just the relationship that is represented in what we call "recognition." When we use the term "recognition" we may mean no more than that we pick up an object that serves this particular purpose; what we generally mean is that the character of the object that is a stimulus to its recognition is present in our experience. We can have, in this way, something that is universal as over against various particulars. I think we can recognize in any habit that which answers to different stimuli; the response is universal and the stimulus is particular. As long as this element serves as a stimulus, calls out this response, one can say the particular comes under this universal. That is the statement of the behavioristic psychology of the universal form as over against the particular instance.

The next point is rather a matter of degree, illustrated by the more complex objects such as a symphony, or a life, with all their variations and harmonious contrasts. When a music critic discusses such a complex object as a symphony can we say that there is something in the central nervous system that answers to the object which the critic has before him? Or take the biography of a great man, a Lincoln or a Gladstone, where the historian, say Morley, has before him that entire life with all its indefinite number of elements. Can he be said to have in his central nervous system an object that answers to that attitude of recognizing Gladstone in all his changes as the same Gladstone? Could one, if he had the mechanism to do so, pick out in the historian's brain what answers to Gladstone? What would it be, supposing that it could be done? It would certainly not be just a single response to the name Gladstone. In some way it must represent all of the connections which took place in his experience, all those connections which were involved in his conduct in so far as their analogues took place in Gladstone's life. It must be some sort of a unity, such a unity that if this whole is touched at any point it may bring out any other element in the historian's experience of Gladstone. It may throw light on any phase of his character; it may bring out any of the situations in which Gladstone figures. All of this must be potentially present in such a mapping of Gladstone in Morley's central nervous system. It is indefinitely complex, but the central nervous system is also indefinitely complex. It does not represent merely spatial dimensions but temporal dimensions also. It can represent an action which is delayed, which is dependent upon an earlier reaction; and this later reaction can, in its inception, but before it takes place overtly, influence the earlier reaction.

We can conceive, then, in the structure of the central nervous system such a temporal dimension as that of the melody, or recognition of the notes and their distance from each other in the scale, and our appreciation of these as actually affected by the beginning of our response to the later notes, as when we are expecting a certain sort of an ending. If we ask how that expectation shows itself in our experience we should have difficulty in detailing it in terms of behavior, but we realize that this experience is determined by our readiness to respond to later notes and that such readiness can be there without the notes being themselves present. The way in which we are going to respond to a major or minor ending does determine the way in which we appreciate the notes that are occurring. It is that attitude that gives the character of our appreciation of all extended musical compositions. What is given at the outset is determined by the attitude to what is to come later. That is a phase of our experience which James has illustrated by his discussion of the sensory character of such conjunctions as "and," "but," "though." If you assert a proposition and add, "but," you determine the attitude of the hearer toward it. He does not know what you are going to introduce, but he does know there is some sort of an exception to it. His knowledge is not stated in reflective form, but is rather an attitude. There is a "but" attitude, an "if" attitude, a "though" attitude. It is such attitudes which we assume toward the beginning of a melody, toward the rhythm involved in poetry; it is these attitudes that give the import to the structure of what we are dealing with.

There are certain attitudes which we assume toward a rising

column or toward its supports, and we only have to have suggestions of the object to call out those attitudes. The artist and the sculptor play upon these attitudes just as the musician does. Through the indication of the stimuli each is able to bring in the reflection of the complexities of a response. Now, if one can bring in a number of these and get a multiform reflection of all of these attitudes into harmony, he calls out an aesthetic response which we consider beautiful. It is the harmonizing of these complexities of response that constitutes the beauty of the object. There are different stimuli calling out an indefinite number of responses and the natures of these are reflected back into our immediate experience, and brought into harmonious relationship with each other. The later stages of the experience itself can be present in the immediate experience which influences them. Given a sufficiently complicated central nervous system, we can then find an indefinite number of responses, and these responses can be not only immediate but delayed, and as delayed can be already influencing present conduct.

We can thus find, in some sense, in the central nervous system what would answer to complex objects, with their somewhat vague and indefinite meaning, as they lie in our actual experience—objects complex not only spatially but also temporally. When we respond to any phase of these objects all the other values are there ready to play into it, and give it its intellectual and emotional content. I see no reason why one should not find, then, in the organization of the attitude as presented in the central nervous system, what it is we refer to as the meaning of the object, that which is universal. The answering of the response to an indefinite number of stimuli which vary from each other is something that gives us the relation of the universal to the particular, and the complexity of the object may be as indefinitely great as are the elements in the central nervous system that represent possible temporal and spatial combinations of our own conduct. We can speak, then, legitimately of a certain sort of response which a Morley has to a Gladstone, a response that can find its expression in the central nervous system, taking into account all of its complexities.

[So far we have stressed the universality or generality of the response as standing over against the particularity of the stimulus which evokes it. I now wish to call attention to the social dimension of universality.]

Thinking takes place in terms of universals, and a universal is an entity that is distinguishable from the object by means of which we think it. When we think of a spade we are not confined in our thought to any particular spade. Now if we think of the universal spade there must be something that we think about, and that is confessedly not given in the particular occurrence which is the occasion of the thought. The thought transcends all the occurrences. Must we assume a realm of such entities, essences or subsistents, to account for our thinking? That is generally assumed by modern realists. Dewey's answer seems to be that we have isolated by our abstracting attention certain features of spades which are irrelevant to the particular different spades, though they have their existence or being in these particular spades. These characters which will occur in any spade that is a spade are therefore irrelevant to any one of them. We may go farther and say that these characters are irrelevant to the occurrence of the spades that arise and are worn out. In other words, they are irrelevant to time, and may be called eternal objects or entities. But, says Dewey, this irrelevancy of these characters to time in our thought does not abstract their being from the particular spades. . . . . Dewey quite agrees with the realists aforesaid that the meaning is not lodged in the word itself, that is, he is not a nominalist. He insists, however, that the meaning resides in the spade as a character which has arisen through the social nature of thinking. I suppose we can say in current terminology that meanings have emerged in social experience, just as colors emerged in the experience of organisms with the apparatus of vision.[17]

[17] [This paragraph is selected from a manuscript, "The Philosophy of John Dewey." To be published in the 1936 *International Journal of Ethics*.]

Meaning as such, i.e., the object of thought, arises in experience through the individual stimulating himself to take the attitude of the other in his reaction toward the object. Meaning is that which can be indicated to others while it is by the same process indicated to the indicating individual. In so far as the individual indicates it to himself in the rôle of the other, he is occupying his perspective, and as he is indicating it to the other from his own perspective, and as that which is so indicated is identical, it must be that which can be in different perspectives. It must therefore be a universal, at least in the identity which belongs to the different perspectives which are organized in the single perspective, and in so far as the principle of organization is one which admits of other perspectives than those actually present, the universality may be logically indefinitely extended. Its universality in conduct, however, amounts only to the irrelevance of the differences of the different perspectives to the characters which are indicated by the significant symbols in use, i.e., the gestures which indicate to the individual who uses them what they indicate to the others, for whom they serve as appropriate stimuli in the co-operative process.[18]

The significant gesture or symbol always presupposes for its significance the social process of experience and behavior in which it arises; or, as the logicians say, a universe of discourse is always implied as the context in terms of which, or as the field within which, significant gestures or symbols do in fact have significance. This universe of discourse is constituted by a group of individuals carrying on and participating in a common social process of experience[19] and behavior, within which these gestures or symbols have the same or common meanings for all members of that group, whether they make them or address them to other individuals, or whether they overtly respond to them as made or addressed to them by other individuals. A uni-

[18] [Paragraph selected from MS.]

[19] A common world exists . . . . only in so far as there is a common (group) experience (MS.)

verse of discourse is simply a system of common or social meanings.[20]

The very universality and impersonality of thought and reason is from the behavioristic standpoint the result of the given individual taking the attitudes of others toward himself, and of his finally crystallizing all these particular attitudes into a single attitude or standpoint which may be called that of the "generalized other."

Alternative ways of acting under an indefinite number of different particular conditions or in an indefinite number of different particular situations—ways which are more or less identical for an indefinite number of normal individuals—are all that universals (however treated in logic or metaphysics) really amount to; they are meaningless apart from the social acts in which they are implicated and from which they derive their significance.[21]

13. THE NATURE OF REFLECTIVE INTELLIGENCE

In the type of temporary inhibition of action which signifies thinking, or in which reflection arises, we have presented in the experience of the individual, tentatively and in advance and for his selection among them, the different possibilities or alternatives of future action open to him within the given social situa-

---

[20] Our so-called laws of thought are the abstractions of social intercourse. Our whole process of abstract thought, technique and method is essentially social (1912).

The organization of the social act answers to what we call the universal. Functionally it is the universal (1930).

[21] All the enduring relations have been subject to revision. There remain the logical constants, and the deductions from logical implications. To the same category belong the so-called universals or concepts. They are the elements and structure of a universe of discourse. In so far as in social conduct with others and with ourselves we indicate the characters that endure in the perspective of the group to which we belong and out of which we arise, we are indicating that which relative to our conduct is unchanged, to which, in other words, passage is irrelevant. A metaphysics which lifts these logical elements out of their experiential habitat and endows them with a subsistential being overlooks the fact that the irrelevance to passage is strictly relative to the situation in conduct within which the reflection arises, that while we can find in different situations a method of conversation and so of thought which proves irrelevant to the differences in the situations, and so provides a method of translation from one perspective to another, this irrelevance belongs only to the wider character which the problem in reflection assumes, and never transcends the social conduct within which the method arises (MS.).

tion—the different or alternative ways of completing the given social act wherein he is implicated, or which he has already initiated. Reflection or reflective behavior arises only under the conditions of self-consciousness, and makes possible the purposive control and organization by the individual organism of its conduct, with reference to its social and physical environment, i.e., with reference to the various social and physical situations in which it becomes involved and to which it reacts. The organization of the self is simply the organization, by the individual organism, of the set of attitudes toward its social environment—and toward itself from the standpoint of that environment, or as a functioning element in the process of social experience and behavior constituting that environment—which it is able to take. It is essential that such reflective intelligence be dealt with from the point of view of social behaviorism.

I said a moment ago that there is something involved in our statement of the meaning of an object which is more than the mere response, however complex that may be. We may respond to a musical phrase and there may be nothing in the experience beyond the response; we may not be able to say why we respond or what it is we respond to. Our attitude may simply be that we like some music and do not like other music. Most of our recognitions are of this sort. We pick out the book we want but could not say what the character of the book is. We probably could give a more detailed account of the countenance of a man we meet for the first time than of our most intimate friends. With our friends we are ready to start our conversation the moment they are there; we do not have to make sure who they are. But if we try to pick out a man who has been described to us we narrowly examine the person to make sure he answers to the account that is given to us. With a person with whom we are familiar we carry on our conversation without thinking of these things. Most of our processes of recognition do not involve this identification of the characters which enable us to identify the objects. We may have to describe a person and we find we cannot do it—we know him too well. We may have to pick those details out, and then if we are taking a critical attitude we have to find out what it is in the object that calls out this complex response. When we are doing that we are getting a statement of what the nature of the object is, or if you like, its meaning. We have to indicate to ourselves what it is that calls out this particular response. We recognize a person, say, because of the character of his physique. If one should come into the room greatly changed by a long attack of sickness, or by exposure to the tropical sun, one's friends would not be able to recognize him immediately. There are certain elements which enable us to recognize a friend. We may have to pick out the characters which make recognition successful, to indicate those characters to somebody or to ourselves. We may have to determine what the stimuli are that call out a response of this complex character. That is often a very difficult thing to do, as is evidenced by musical criticism. A whole audience may be swept away by a composition and perhaps not a person there will be able to state what it is in the production that calls out this particular response, or to tell what the various reactions are in these individuals. It is an unusual gift which can analyze that sort of an object and pick out what the stimulus is for so complex an action.

What I want to call attention to is the process by which there is an indication of those characters which do call out the response. Animals of a type lower than man respond to certain characters with a nicety that is beyond human capacity, such as odor in the case of a dog. But it would be beyond the capacity of a dog to indicate to another dog what the odor was. Another dog could not be sent out by the first dog to pick out this odor. A man may tell how to identify another man. He can indicate what the characters are that will bring about a certain response. That ability absolutely distinguishes the intelligence of such a reflective being as man from that of the lower animals, however intelligent they may be. We generally say that man is a rational animal and lower animals are not. What I wanted to show, at least in terms of behavioristic psychology, is that what we have in mind in this distinction is the indication of those characters which lead to the sort of response which we give to an object. Pointing out the characters which lead to the response is precisely that which distinguishes a detective office that sends out a man, from a bloodhound which runs down a man. Here are two types of intelligence, each one specialized; the detective could not do what the bloodhound does and the bloodhound could not do what the detective does. Now, the intelligence of the detective over against the intelligence of the bloodhound lies in this capacity to indicate what the particular characters are which will call out his response of taking the man.[22]

Such would be a behaviorist's account of what is involved in reason. When you are reasoning you are indicating to yourself the characters that call out certain responses—and that is all you are doing. If you have the angle and a side you can determine the area of a triangle; given certain characters there are certain responses indicated. There are other processes, not exactly rational, out of which you can build up new responses from old ones. You may pick out responses which are there in other reactions and put them together. A book of directions may provide a set of stimuli which lead to a certain set of responses, and you pick them out of your other complex responses, perhaps as they have not been picked out before. When you write on a typewriter you may be instructed as to the way in which to use it. You can build up a fairly good technique to start with, but even that is a process which still involves the indication of the stimuli to call out the various responses. You unite stimuli which have not been united in the past, and then these stimuli take with them the compound responses. It may be a crude response at first, and must be freed from the responses had in the past. The way in which you react toward the doubling of letters when you write is different from the way you react in writing the

---

[22] Intelligence and knowledge are inside the process of conduct. Thinking is an elaborate process of . . . . presenting the world so that it will be favorable for conduct, so that the ends of the life of the form may be reached (MS).

Thinking is pointing out—to think about a thing is to point it out before acting (1924).

letters on a typewriter. You make mistakes because the responses you utilize have been different, have been connected with a whole set of other responses. A drawing teacher will sometimes have pupils draw with the left hand rather than the right, because the habits of the right hand are very difficult to get rid of. This is what you are doing when you act in a rational fashion: you are indicating to yourself what the stimuli are that will call out a complex response, and by the order of the stimuli you are determining what the whole of the response will be. Now, to be able to indicate those stimuli to other persons or to yourself is what we call rational conduct as distinct from the unreasoning intelligence of the lower animals, and from a good deal of our own conduct.

Man is distinguished by that power of analysis of the field of stimulation which enables him to pick out one stimulus rather than another and so to hold on to the response that belongs to that stimulus, picking it out from others, and recombining it with others. You cannot get a lock to work. You notice certain elements, each of which brings out a certain sort of response; and what you are doing is holding on to these processes of response by giving attention to the stimuli. Man can combine not only the responses already there, which is the thing an animal lower than man can do, but the human individual can get into his activities and break them up, giving attention to specific elements, holding the responses that answer to these particular stimuli, and then combining them to build up another act. That is what we mean by learning or by teaching a person to do a thing. You indicate to him certain specific phases or characters of the object which call out certain sorts of responses. We state that generally by saying consciousness accompanies only the sensory process and not the motor process. We can directly control the sensory but not the motor processes; we can give our attention to a particular element in the field and by giving such attention and so holding on to the stimulus we can get control of the response. That is the way we get control of our action;

we do not directly control our response through the motor paths themselves.

There is no capacity in the lower forms to give attention to some analyzed element in the field of stimulation which would enable them to control the response. But one can say to a person "Look at this, just see this thing" and he can fasten his attention on the specific object. He can direct attention and so isolate the particular response that answers to it. That is the way in which we break up our complex activities and thereby make learning possible. What takes place is an analysis of the process by giving attention to the specific stimuli that call out a particular act, and this analysis makes possible a reconstruction of the act. An animal makes combinations, as we say, only by trial and error, and the combination that is successful simply maintains itself.

The gesture as worked out in the conduct of the human group serves definitely to indicate just these elements and thus to bring them within the field of voluntary attention. There is, of course, a fundamental likeness between voluntary attention and involuntary attention. A bright light, a peculiar odor, may be something which takes complete control of the organism and in so far inhibits other activity. A voluntary action, however, is dependent upon the indication of a certain character, pointing it out, holding on to it, and so holding on to the response that belongs to it. That sort of an analysis is essential to what we call human intelligence, and it is made possible by language.

The psychology of attention ousted the psychology of association. An indefinite number of associations were found which lie in our experience with reference to anything that comes before us, but associational psychology never explained why one association rather than another was the dominant one. It laid down rules that if a certain association had been intense, recent, and frequent it would be dominant, but often there are in fact situations in which what seems to be the weakest element in the situation occupies the mind. It was not until the psychologist took up the analysis of attention that he was able to deal with such situations, and to realize that voluntary attention is dependent upon indication of some character in the field of stimulation. Such indication makes possible the isolation and recombination of responses.

In the case of the vocal gesture there is a tendency to call out the response in one form that is called out in the other, so that the child plays the part of parent, of teacher, or preacher. The gesture under those conditions calls out certain responses in the individual which it calls out in the other person, and carrying it out in the individual isolates that particular character of the stimulus. The response of the other is there in the individual isolating the stimulus. If one calls out quickly to a person in danger, he himself is in the attitude of jumping away, though the act is not performed. He is not in danger, but he has those particular elements of the response in himself, and we speak of them as meanings. Stated in terms of the central nervous system, this means that he has stirred up its upper tracts which would lead to the actual jumping away. A person picks out the different responses involved in escape when he enters the theater and notices the signs on the program cautioning him to choose the nearest exit in case of fire. He has all the different responses, so to speak, listed before him, and he prepares what he is going to do by picking out the different elements and putting them together in the way required. The efficiency engineer comes in to pick out this, that, or the other thing, and chooses the order in which they should be carried out. One is doing the same himself in so far as he is self-conscious. Where we have to determine what will be the order of a set of responses, we are putting them together in a certain fashion, and we can do this because we can indicate the order of the stimuli which are going to act upon us. That is what is involved in the human intelligence as distinguished from the intelligence type of the lower forms. We cannot tell an elephant that he is to take hold of the other elephant's tail; the stimulus will not indicate the same thing to the elephant as to ourselves. We can create a situation which is a stimulus to the elephant but we cannot get the elephant to indicate to itself what this stimulus is so that he has the response to it in his own system.

The gesture provides a process by means of which one does arouse in himself the reaction that might be aroused in another, and this is not a part of his immediate reaction in so far as his immediate physical environment is concerned. When we tell a person to do something the response we have is not the doing of the actual thing, but the beginning of it. Communication gives to us those elements of response which can be held in the mental field. We do not carry them out, but they are there constituting the meanings of these objects which we indicate. Language is a process of indicating certain stimuli and changing the response to them in the system of behavior. Language as a social process has made it possible for us to pick out responses and hold them in the organism of the individual, so that they are there in relation to that which we indicate. The actual gesture is, within limits, arbitrary. Whether one points with his finger, or points with the glance of the eye, or motion of the head, or the attitude of the body, or by means of a vocal gesture in one language or another, is indifferent, provided it does call out the response that belongs to that thing which is indicated. That is the essential part of language. The gesture must be one that calls out the response in the individual, or tends to call out the response in the individual, which its utilization will bring out in another's response. Such is the material with which the mind works. However slight, there must be some sort of gesture. To have the response isolated without an indication of a stimulus is almost a contradiction in terms. I have been trying to point out what this process of communication does in the way of providing us with the material that exists in our mind. It does this by furnishing those gestures which in affecting us as they affect others call out the attitude which the other takes, and that we take in so far as we assume his rôle. We get the attitude, the meaning, within the field of our own control, and that control consists in combining all these various possible responses to furnish the newly constructed act demanded by the problem. In such a way we can state rational conduct in terms of a behavioristic psychology.

I wish to add one further factor to our account: the relation of the temporal character of the nervous system to foresight and choice.[23]

The central nervous system makes possible the implicit initiation of a number of possible alternative responses with reference to any given object or objects for the completion of any already initiated act, in advance of the actual completion of that act; and thus makes possible the exercise of intelligent or reflective choice in the acceptance of that one among these possible alternative responses which is to be carried into overt effect.[24]

Human intelligence, by means of the physiological mechanism of the human central nervous system, deliberately selects one from among the several alternative responses which are possible in the given problematic environmental situation; and if the given response which it selects is complex—i.e., is a set or chain or group or succession of simple responses—it can organize this set or chain of simple responses in such a way as to make possible the most adequate and harmonious solution by the individual of the given environmental problem.

It is the entrance of the alternative possibilities of future response into the determination of present conduct in any given environmental situation, and their operation, through the mechanism of the central nervous system, as part of the factors or conditions determining present behavior, which decisively contrasts intelligent conduct or behavior with reflex, instinctive, and habitual conduct or behavior—delayed reaction with immediate reaction. That which takes place in present organic behavior is always in some sense an emergent from the past, and

[23] [See also Section 16.]

[24] It is an advantage to have these responses ready before we get to the object. If our world were right on top of us, in contact with us, we would have no time for deliberation. There would be only one way of responding to that world.

Through his distance organs and his capacity for delayed responses the individual lives in the future with the possibility of planning his life with reference to that future (1931).

never could have been precisely predicted in advance—never could have been predicted on the basis of a knowledge, however complete, of the past, and of the conditions in the past which are relevant to its emergence; and in the case of organic behavior which is intelligently controlled, this element of spontaneity is especially prominent by virtue of the present influence exercised over such behavior by the possible future results or consequences which it may have. Our ideas of or about future conduct are our tendencies to act in several alternative ways in the presence of a given environmental situation—tendencies or attitudes which can appear, or be implicitly aroused, in the structure of the central nervous system in advance of the overt response or reaction to that situation, and which thus can enter as determining factors into the control or selection of this overt response. Ideas, as distinct from acts, or as failing to issue in overt behavior, are simply what we do not do; they are possibilities of overt responses which we test out implicitly in the central nervous system and then reject in favor of those which we do in fact act upon or carry into effect. The process of intelligent conduct is essentially a process of selection from among various alternatives; intelligence is largely a matter of selectivity.

Delayed reaction is necessary to intelligent conduct. The organization, implicit testing, and final selection by the individual of his overt responses or reactions to the social situations which confront him and which present him with problems of adjustment, would be impossible if his overt responses or reactions could not in such situations be delayed until this process of organizing, implicitly testing, and finally selecting is carried out; that is, would be impossible if some overt response or other to the given environmental stimuli had to be immediate. Without delayed reaction, or except in terms of it, no conscious or intelligent control over behavior could be exercised; for it is through this process of selective reaction—which can be selective only because it is delayed—that intelligence operates in the determination of behavior. Indeed, it is this process which constitutes intelligence. The central nervous system provides not only the necessary physiological mechanism for this process, but also the necessary physiological condition of delayed reaction which this process presupposes. Intelligence is essentially the ability to solve the problems of present behavior in terms of its possible future consequences as implicated on the basis of past experience—the ability, that is, to solve the problems of present behavior in the light of, or by reference to, both the past and the future; it involves both memory and foresight. And the process of exercising intelligence is the process of delaying, organizing, and selecting a response or reaction to the stimuli of the given environmental situation. The process is made possible by the mechanism of the central nervous system, which permits the individual's taking of the attitude of the other toward himself, and thus becoming an object to himself. This is the most effective means of adjustment to the social environment, and indeed to the environment in general, that the individual has at his disposal.

An attitude of any sort represents the beginning, or potential initiation, of some composite act or other, a social act in which, along with other individuals, the individual taking the given attitude is involved or implicated. The traditional supposition has been that the purposive element in behavior must ultimately be an idea, a conscious motive, and hence must imply or depend upon the presence of a mind. But the study of the nature of the central nervous system shows that in the form of physiological attitudes (expressed in specific physiological sets) different possible completions to the given act are there in advance of its actual completion, and that through them the earlier parts of the given act are affected or influenced (in present conduct) by its later phases; so that the purposive element in behavior has a physiological seat, a behavioristic basis, and is not fundamentally nor necessarily conscious or psychical.

14. BEHAVIORISM, WATSONISM, AND REFLECTION

I have been discussing the possibility of bringing the concept or idea into the range of behavioristic treatment, endeavoring in this way to relieve behaviorism as presented by Watson of what seems to be an inadequacy. In carrying back the thinking process to the talking process, Watson seems to identify thought simply with the word, with the symbol, with the vocal gesture. He does this by means of the transference of a reflex from one stimulus to another—conditioned reflex is the technical term for the process. The psychologist isolates a set of reflexes which answer to certain specific stimuli, and then allows these reflexes expression under different conditions so that the stimulus itself is accompanied by other stimuli. He finds that these reflexes can then be brought about by the new stimulus even in the absence of that which has been previously the necessary stimulus. The typical illustration is that of a child becoming afraid of a white rat because it was presented to him several times at the moment at which a loud sound was made behind him. The loud noise occasions fright. The presence of the white rat conditions this reaction of fright so that the child becomes afraid of the white rat. The fear reactions are then called out by the white rat even when no sound is made.[25]

The conditioned reflex of the objective psychologists is also used by Watson to explain the process of thinking. On this view we utilize vocal gestures in connection with things, and thereby condition our reflexes to the things in terms of the vocal process. If we have a tendency to sit down when the chair is there, we condition this reflex by the word "chair." Originally the chair is a stimulus that sets free this act of sitting, and by being conditioned the child may come to the point of setting free the act by the use of the word. No particular limit can be set up to such a process. The language process is peculiarly adapted to such a conditioning of reflexes. We have an indefinite number of responses to objects about us. If we can condition these responses by the vocal gesture so that whenever a certain reaction is carried out we at the same time utilize cer-

[25] The child's fear of the dark may have arisen out of his being awakened by loud thunder, so that he is frightened in the darkness. This has not been proven but it is a possible interpretation in terms of conditioning.

tain phonetic elements, then we can reach the point at which the response will be called out whenever this vocal gesture arises. Thinking would then be nothing but the use of these various vocal elements together with the responses which they call out. Psychologists would not need to look for anything more elaborate in the thinking process than the mere conditioning of reflexes by vocal gestures.

From the point of view of the analysis of the experience involved this account seems very inadequate. For certain types of experience it may perhaps be sufficient. A trained body of troops exhibits a set of conditioned reflexes. A certain formation is brought about by means of certain orders. Its success lies in an automatic response when these orders are given. There, of course, one has action without thought. If the soldier thinks under the circumstances he very likely will not act; his action is dependent in a certain sense on the absence of thought. There must be elaborate thinking done somewhere, but after that has been done by the officers higher up, then the process must become automatic. What we recognize is that this statement does not do justice to the thinking that has to be done higher up. It is true that the people below carry out the process without thinking. Now if the thinking is done higher up under the same conditions the behaviorist evidently fails to bring into account what is peculiar to planning. Something very definite goes on there which cannot be stated in terms of conditioned reflexes.

The unthinking conduct of the soldier in carrying out the order, so that the mere giving of the order involves its execution, is characteristic of the type of conduct in lower animals. We use this mechanism to explain the elaborate instincts of certain organisms. One set of responses follows another; the completion of one step brings the form into contact with certain stimuli which set another free, and so on. Great elaborations of this process are found, especially in the ants. That thought which belongs to the human community is presumably absent in these communities. The wasp that stores the paralyzed spider as food for larvae that it never will see and with which it never has come into contact, is not acting in terms of conscious foresight. The human community that stores away food in cold storage, and later makes use of it, is doing in a certain sense the same thing that the wasp is doing, but the important distinction is that the action is now consciously purposive. The individual arranging for the cold storage is actually presenting to himself a situation that is going to arise, and determining his methods of preservation with reference to future uses.

The statement which Watson gives of the conditioning of reflexes does not bring in these parts of experience. Such a treatment has been experimentally applied only in such experiences as those of the infant. Watson is trying to work out a simple mechanism which can be widely applied without taking into consideration all the complications involved in that application. It is, of course, legitimate for a new idea to find its widest application and then meet the specific difficulties later. Now, is it possible to recast our statement of behavioristic psychology so that it can do more justice to what we ordinarily term a consciousness of what we are doing? I have been suggesting that we could at least give a picture in the central nervous system of what answers to an idea. That seems to be what is left out of Watson's statement. He simply attaches a set of responses to certain stimuli and shows that the mechanism of the organism is able to change those stimuli, substitute one stimulus for another stimulus; but the ideas that accomplish such a process are not accounted for simply by this substitution.

In the illustration I gave of offering a chair and asking a person to sit down, the asking may take the place of the particular perception of the chair. One may be occupied entirely with something else, and then the stimulus is not the stimulus operative in the original reflex; one might come in and sit down without paying any attention to the chair. But such substitution does not give to us the picture of the mechanism which in some sense answers to the chair, or the idea of what the person is asking him to do. What I suggested was that we have such a mechanism in the central nervous system that answers to these elaborate reactions, and that the stimuli which call these out may set up a process there which is not fully carried out. We do not actually sit down when a person asks us to, yet the process is in some sense initiated; we are ready to sit down but we do not. We prepare for a certain process by thinking about it, mapping out a campaign of conduct, and then we are ready to carry out the different steps. The motor impulses which are already there have stirred up those different paths, and the reactions may take place more readily and more securely. This is particularly true of the relation of different acts to another. We can attach one process of response to another and we can build up from the lower instinctive form what is called a general reflex in our own conduct. Now that can be, in some sense, indicated by the structure of the nervous system. We can conceive of reactions arising with their different responses to these objects, to what, in other words, we call the meanings of these objects. The meaning of a chair is sitting down in it, the meaning of the hammer is to drive a nail—and these responses can be innervated even though not carried out. The innervation of these processes in the central nervous system is perhaps necessary for what we call meaning.

It may be asked at this point whether the actual nervous excitement in a certain area or over certain paths, is a legitimate substitute for what we call the idea. We come up against the parallelistic explanation of the seeming difference between ideas and bodily states, between that which we call psychical and the physical statement in terms of neuroses. It may be complained of the behavioristic psychology that it sets up a number of mechanisms, but still leaves what we term consciousness out of play. It may be said that such a connection of different processes as I have been describing, such an organization of different responses in the central nervous system, is after all not different from what Watson referred to. He, too, has a whole set of reactions that answer to the chair, and he conditions the response by the vocal gesture, "chair." It may be felt that that is all we have done. And yet, as I have said, we recognize there is something more to consciousness than such a conditioned response. The automatic response which the soldier gives is different from the conduct which involves thought in regard to it, and a consciousness of what we are doing.

The behavioristic psychology has tried to get rid of the more or less metaphysical complications involved in the setting-up of the psychical over against the world, mind over against body, consciousness over against matter. That was felt to lead into a blind alley. Such a parallelism had proved valuable, but after it had been utilized in the analysis of what goes on in the central nervous system it simply led into a blind alley. The opposition of the behaviorist to introspection is justified. It is not a fruitful undertaking from the point of view of psychological study. It may be illegitimate for Watson simply to wipe it out, and to say that all we are doing is listening to the words we are subjectively pronouncing; that certainly is an entirely inadequate way of dealing with what we term introspection. Yet it is true that introspection as a means of dealing with phenomena with which psychology must concern itself is pretty hopeless. What the behaviorist is occupied with, what we have to come back to, is the actual reaction itself, and it is only in so far as we can translate the content of introspection over into response that we can get any satisfactory psychological doctrine. It is not necessary for psychology to get into metaphysical questions, but it is of importance that it should try to get hold of the response that is used in the psychological analysis itself.

What I want to insist upon is that the process, by means of which these responses that are the ideas or meanings become associated with a certain vocal gesture, lies in the activity of the organism, while in the case of the dog, the child, the soldier, this process takes place, as it were, outside of the organism. The soldier is trained through a whole set of evolutions. He does not know why this particular set is given to him or the uses to which it will be put; he is just put through his drill, as an animal is trained in a circus. The child is similarly exposed to experiments without any thinking on his part. What thinking proper means is that this process of associating chair as object with the word "chair" is a process that human beings in society carry out, and then internalize. Such behavior certainly has to be considered just as much as conditioned behavior which takes place externally, and should be considered still more, because it is vastly more important that we should understand the process of thinking than the product of it.

Now, where does this thought process itself take place? If you like, I am here sidestepping the question as to just what consciousness is, or the question whether what is going on in the area of the brain is to be identified with consciousness. That is a question which is not psychological. What I am asking is, where does this process, by means of which, in Watson's sense, all of our reflexes or reactions are conditioned, take place? For this process is one which takes place in conduct and cannot be explained by the conditioned reflexes which result from it. You can explain the child's fear of the white rat by conditioning its reflexes, but you cannot explain the conduct of Mr. Watson in conditioning that stated reflex by means of a set of conditioned reflexes, unless you set up a super-Watson to condition his reflexes. That process of conditioning reflexes has to be taken into conduct itself, not in the metaphysical sense of setting up a mind in a spiritual fashion which acts on the body, but as an actual process with which the behavioristic psychology can deal. The metaphysical problems still remain, but the psychologist has to be able to state this very process of conditioning reflexes as it takes place in conduct itself.

We can find part of the necessary mechanism of such conduct in the central nervous system. We can identify some of the reflexes, such as that of the knee jerk, and follow the stimulus from the reflex up to the central nervous system and back again. Most of the reflexes we cannot follow out in detail. With such suitable elements we can carry out the analogy, and present to ourselves the elaborate organization to which I have referred, and which answers to the objects about us and the more complex objects such as a symphony or a biography. The question now is whether the mere excitement of the set of these groups of responses is what we mean by an idea. When we try to undertake to carry over, translate, such an idea in terms of behavior, instead of stopping with a bit of consciousness, can we take that idea over into conduct, and at least express in conduct just what we mean by saying that we have an idea? It may be simpler to assume that each one of us has a little bit of consciousness stored away and that impressions are made on consciousness, and as a result of the idea, consciousness in some unexplained way sets up the response in the system itself. But what must be asked of behaviorism is whether it can state in behavioristic terms what is meant by having an idea, or getting a concept.

I have just said that Watson's statement of the mere conditioning of the reflex, the setting off of a certain set of responses when the word is used, does not seem to answer to this process of getting an idea. It does answer to the result of having an idea, for having reached the idea, then one starts off to accomplish it, and we assume that the process follows. The getting of an idea is very different from the result of having an idea, for the former involves the setting-up or conditioning of reflexes, which cannot, themselves, be used to explain the process. Now, under what conditions does this take place? Can we indicate these conditions in terms of behavior? We can state in behavioristic terms what the result will be, but can we state in terms of behaviorism the process of getting and having ideas?

The process of getting an idea is, in the case of the infant, a process of intercourse with those about him, a social process. He can battle on by himself without getting any idea of what he is doing. There is no mechanism in his talking to himself for conditioning any reflex by means of vocal gestures, but in his intercourse with other individuals he can so condition them, and that takes place also in the conduct of lower animals. We can teach a dog to do certain things in answer to particular words. We condition his reflexes by means of certain vocal gestures. In the same way a child gets to refer to a chair by the word "chair." But the animal does not have an idea of what he is going to do, and if we stopped with the child here we could not attribute to him any idea. What is involved in the giving of an idea is what cannot be stated in terms of this conditioning of a reflex. I have suggested that involved in such giving is the fact that the stimulus not only calls out the response, but that the individual who receives the response also himself uses that stimulus, that vocal gesture, and calls out that response in himself. Such is, at least, the beginning of that which follows. It is the further complication that we do not find in the conduct of the dog. The dog only stands on its hind legs and walks when we use a particular word, but the dog cannot give to himself that stimulus which somebody else gives to him. He can respond to it but he cannot himself take a hand, so to speak, in conditioning his own reflexes; his reflexes can be conditioned by another but he cannot do it himself. Now, it is characteristic of significant speech that just this process of self-conditioning is going on all the time.

There are, of course, certain phases of our speech which do not come within the range of what we term self-consciousness. There are changes which have taken place in the speech of people through long centuries—changes which none of the individuals were aware of at all. But when we speak of significant speech we always imply that the individual that hears a word does in some sense use that word with reference to himself. That is what we call a personal understanding of what is said. He is not only ready to respond, but he also uses the same stimulus that he hears, and is tending to respond to it in turn. That is true of a person who makes use of significant speech to another. He knows and understands what he is asking the other person to do, and in some sense is inviting in himself the response to carry out the process. The process of addressing another person is a process of addressing himself as well, and of calling out the response he calls out in another; and the person who is addressed, in so far as he is conscious of what he is doing, does himself tend to make use of the same vocal gesture and so to call out in himself the response which the other calls out—at least to carry on the social process which involves that conduct. This is distinct from the action of the soldier; for in significant speech the person himself understands what he is asked to do, and consents to carry out something he makes himself a part of. If one gives to another directions as to how to proceed to a certain street he himself receives all of these detailed directions. He is identifying himself with the other individual. The hearer is not simply moving at an order, but is giving to himself the same directions that the other person gives to him. That, in behavioristic terms, is what we mean by the person being conscious of something. It is certainly always implied that the individual does tend to carry out the same process as the person addressed; he gives to himself the same stimulus, and so takes part in the same process. In so far as he is conditioning his own reflexes, that process enters into his own experience.

I think it is important to recognize that our behavioristic psychology in dealing with human intelligence must present the situation which I have just described, where a person knows the meaning of what is said to him. If the individual does himself make use of something answering to the same gesture he observes, saying it over again to himself, putting himself in the rôle of the person who is speaking to him, then he has the meaning of what he hears, he has the idea: the meaning has become his. It is that sort of a situation which seems to be involved in what we term mind, as such: this social process, in which one individual affects other individuals, is carried over into the experience of the individuals that are so affected.[26] The individual takes this attitude not simply as a matter of repetition, but as part of the elaborate social reaction which is going on. It is the necessity of stating that process in terms of behavior that is involved in an adequate behavioristic statement, as over against a mere account of the conditioned reflex.

15. BEHAVIORISM AND PSYCHOLOGICAL PARALLELISM

Behaviorism might seem to reach what could be called a parallelism in relation to the neuroses and psychoses, that is,

[26] [See Sections 16, 24.]

in the relationship of what is taking place in the central nervous system to the experience that parallels this, or answers to it. It might be argued, for instance, that there is an excitement in the retina due to the disturbance taking place outside, and that only when such excitement reaches a certain point in the central nervous system does a sensation of color, or an experience of a colored object, appear. We believe that we see the object at the point at which this disturbance takes place outside. That is, we see, say, an electric light. But we are told that light represents physical changes that are going on at enormous rates, and that are in some fashion transferred by the light waves to the retina and then to the central nervous system, so that we see the light at the point at which we assume these vibrations take place. Of course, this transmission involves some time, and during the course of this action a physical change in the object may take place. There is not only that possibility of error in perception, but we may be mistaken even in the object which we see before us, since the light is temporally later than the disturbance which it seems to reveal. The light has a finite velocity, and the process that goes on between the retina and the point in the central nervous system is a much longer process than that of the light. The situation is stretched out for us conveniently by the illustration of the light of the stars. We see light that left the sun some eight minutes ago; the sun that we see is eight minutes old —and there are stars that are so far away from us that they consume many light-years in reaching us. Thus, our perceptions have conditions which we locate in the central nervous system at a certain moment; if anything interferes with the nervous process, then this particular experience does not arise. In some such way we get the statement of what lies back of the parallelistic account; if we relate what takes place at that point as a neurosis to what takes place in our experience we have seemingly two entirely different things. The disturbance in the central nervous system is an electrical or chemical or mechanical process going on in the nervous elements, whereas that which we see is a colored light, and the most we can say is that the one is seemingly parallel to the other, since we cannot say that the two are identical.

Now behavioristic psychology, instead of setting up these events in the central nervous system as a causal series which is at least conditional to the sensory experience, takes the entire response to the environment as that which answers to the colored object we see, in this case the light. It does not locate the experience at any point in the nervous system; it does not put it, in the terms of Mr. Russell, inside of a head. Russell makes the experience the effect of what happens at that point where a causal process takes place in the head. He points out that, from his own point of view, the head inside of which you can place this experience exists empirically only in the heads of other people. The physiologist explains to you where this excitement is taking place. He sees the head he is demonstrating to you and he sees what is inside of the head in imagination, but, on this account, that which he sees must be inside of his own head. The way in which Russell gets out of this mess is by saying that the head which he is referring to is not the head we see, but the head which is implied in physiological analysis. Well, instead of assuming that the experienced world as such is inside of a head, located at that point at which certain nervous disturbances are going on, what the behaviorist does is to relate the world of experience to the whole act of the organism. It is true, as we have just said, that this experienced world does not appear except when the various excitements reach certain points in the central nervous system; it is also true that if you cut off any of those channels you wipe out so much of that world. What the behaviorist does, or ought to do, is to take the complete act, the whole process of conduct, as the unit in his account. In doing that he has to take into account not simply the nervous system but also the rest of the organism, for the nervous system is only a specialized part of the entire organism.

Consciousness as stuff, as experience, from the standpoint of behavioristic or dynamic psychology, is simply the environment of the human individual or social group in so far as constituted by or dependent upon or existentially relative to that individual or social group. (Another signification of the term "consciousness" arises in connection with reflective intelligence, and still another in connection with the private or subjective aspects of experience as contrasted with the common or social aspects.)

Our whole experiential world—nature as we experience it—is basically related to the social process of behavior, a process in which acts are initiated by gestures that function as such because they in turn call forth adjustive responses from other organisms, as indicating or having reference to the completion or resultant of the acts they initiate. That is to say, the content of the objective world, as we experience it, is in large measure constituted through the relations of the social process to it, and particularly through the triadic relation of meaning, which is created within that process. The whole content of mind and of nature, in so far as it takes on the character of meaning, is dependent upon this triadic relation within the social process and among the component phases of the social act, which the existence of meaning presupposes.

Consciousness or experience as thus explained or accounted for in terms of the social process cannot, however, be located in the brain—not only because such location of it implies a spatial conception of mind (a conception which is at least unwarranted as an uncritically accepted assumption), but also because such location leads to Russell's physiological solipsism, and to the insuperable difficulties of interactionism. Consciousness is functional, not substantive; and in either of the main senses of the term it must be located in the objective world rather than in the brain—it belongs to, or is a characteristic of, the environment in which we find ourselves. What is located, what does take place, in the brain, however, is the physiological process whereby we lose and regain consciousness: a process which is somewhat analogous to that of pulling down and raising a window shade.

Now, as we noticed earlier, if we want to control the process of experience or consciqusness we may go back to the various processes in the body, especially the central nervous system. When we are setting up a parallelism what we are trying to do is to state those elements in the world which enable us to control the processes of experience. Parallelism lies between the point at which conduct takes place and the experiential reaction, and we must determine those elements which will enable us to control the reaction itself. As a rule, we control this reaction by means of objects outside of the organism rather than by directing attention to the organism itself. If we want better light we put in a higher powered bulb. Our control, as a rule, consists in a reaction on the objects themselves, and from that point of view the parallelism is between the object and the percept, between the electric light and visibility. That is the sort of parallelism that the ordinary individual establishes; by setting up a parallelism between the things about him and his experience, he picks out those characters of the thing which will enable him to control the experience. His experience is that of keeping himself seeing things which help him, and consequently he picks out in the objects those characters which will express themselves in that sort of experience; but if the trouble he has is due to some disturbance in his central nervous system, then he will have to go back to it. In this case the parallelism will be between his experience and the excitements in the central nervous system. If he finds that he is not seeing well he may discover some trouble with the optic nerve, and the parallelism is then between his vision and the functioning of the optic nerve. If he is interested in certain mental images he has, he goes back to experiences which have affected the central nervous system in the past. Certain of the effects on the central nervous system of such experiences are still present, so that if he is setting up a parallelism he will find that it lies between that past event and the present condition of his central nervous system. Such a relationship becomes a matter of great importance in our whole perception. The traces of past experience are continually playing in upon our perceived world. Now, to get hold of that in the organism which answers to this stage of our conduct, to our remembering, to our intelligently responding to the present in terms of the past, we set up a parallelism between what is going on in the central nervous system and immediate experience. Our memory is dependent upon the condition of certain tracts in our head, and these conditions have to be picked out to get control of processes of that sort.

This type of correlation is increasingly noticeable when we go from the images as such over to the thinking process. The intelligence that is involved in perception is elaborated enormously in what we call "thought." One perceives an object in terms of his response to it. If you notice your conduct you find frequently that you are turning your head to one side to see something because of light rays which have reached the periphery of the retina. You turn your head to see what it was. You come to use the term "aware of something there." We may have the impression that someone is looking at us out of a crowd and find ourselves turning our head to see who is looking at us, and our tendency to turn reveals to us the fact that there are rays from other people's eyes. It is true of all of our experience that it is the response that interprets to us what comes to us in the stimulus, and it is such attention which makes the percept out of what we call "sensation." The interpretation of the response is what gives the content to it. Our thinking is simply an elaboration of that interpretation in terms of our own response. The sound is something that leads to a jumping-away; the light is something we are to look at. When the danger is something that is perhaps a long way off, the danger of loss of funds through a bad investment, the danger to some of our organs on account of injury, the interpretation is one which involves a very elaborate process of thinking. Instead of simply jumping aside, we can change our diet, take more exercise, or change our investments. This process of thinking, which is the elaboration of our responses to the stimulus, is a process which also necessarily goes on in the organism. Yet it is a mistake to assume that all that we call thought can be located in the organism or can be put inside of the head. The goodness or badness of the investment is in the investment, and the valuable or dangerous character of food is in the food, not in our heads. The relationship between these and the organism depends upon the sort of response we are going to make, and that is a relationship which is mapped out in the central nervous system. The way in which we are going to respond is found there, and in the possible connections there must be connections of past experiences with present responses in order that there may be thought. We connect up a whole set of things outside, especially those which are past, with our present condition in order that we may intelligently meet some distant danger. In the case of an investment or organic trouble the danger is a long way off, but still we have to react to it in the way of avoiding the danger. And the process is one which involves an elaborate connection which has to be found in the central nervous system, especially in so far as it represents the past. So, then, we set up what is taking place in the central nervous system as that which is parallel to what lies in experience. If called upon to make any change in the central nervous system, so far as that could be effected under present knowledge, we might assist what goes on in the processes of the central nervous system. We should have to apply our supposed remedies to the central nervous system itself, while in the previous cases we should have been changing our objects which affect the central nervous system. There is very little we can do directly at the present time, but we can conceive of such a response as would enable us to affect our memory and to affect our thought. We do, of course, try to select the time of the day and conditions when our heads are clear if we have a difficult piece of work to do. That is an indirect way of attempting to get favorable co-operation of the nervous elements in the brain to do a certain amount of thinking. It is the same sort of parallelism which lies between the lighting systems in our houses and the experience we have of visibility. In one case we have to attend to conditions outside and in the other to conditions inside the central nervous system in order to control our responses. There is no parallelism in general between the world and the brain. What a behavioristic psychology is trying to do is to find that in the responses, in our whole group of responses, which answers to those conditions in the world which we want to change, to improve, in order that our conduct may be successful.

The past that is in our present experience is there because of the central nervous system in relation to the rest of the organism. If one has acquired a certain facility in playing the violin, that past experience is registered in the nerves and muscles themselves, but mainly in connections found in the central nervous system, in the whole set of paths there which are kept open so that when the stimulus comes in there is released a complex set of elaborate responses. Our past stays with us in terms of those changes which have resulted from our experience and which are in some sense registered there. The peculiar intelligence of the human form lies in this elaborate control gained through the past. The human animal's past is constantly present in the facility with which he acts, but to say that that past is simply located in the central nervous system is not a correct statement. It is true such a mechanism must be present in order that the past may appear in our experience, but this is part of the conditions, not the only condition. If you recognize somebody it must be through the fact that you have seen that individual in the past, and when you see him again there are those tendencies to react as you have in the past, but the individual must be there, or somebody like him, in order that this may take place. The past must be found in the present world.[17] From the standpoint of behavioristic psychology we pick out the central nervous system only because it is that which is the immediate mechanism through which our organism operates in bringing the past to bear on the present. If we want to understand the way in which an organism responds to a certain situation which has a past, we have to get into the effects of the past actions on that organism which have been left in the central nervous system. There is no question about that fact. These effects ac-

[17] [For the implied theory of the past, see *The Philosophy of the Present*, pp. 1–31.]

cordingly become peculiarly important, but the "parallelism" is no different for a behavioristic psychology from the parallelism that lies between the warmth in the house and the heating apparatus installed there.

16. MIND AND THE SYMBOL

I have attempted to point out that the meanings of things, our ideas of them, answer to the structure of the organism in its conduct with reference to things. The structure which makes this possible was found primarily in the central nervous system. One of the peculiarities of this system is that it has, in a sense, a temporal dimension: the things we are going to do can be arranged in a temporal order so that the later processes can in their inception be present determining the earlier processes; what we are going to do can determine our immediate approach to the object.

The mechanism of the central nervous system enables us to have now present, in terms of attitudes or implicit responses, the alternative possible overt completions of any given act in which we are involved; and this fact must be realized and recognized, in virtue of the obvious control which later phases of any given act exert over its earlier phases. More specifically, the central nervous system provides a mechanism of implicit response which enables the individual to test out implicitly the various possible completions of an already initiated act in advance of the actual completion of the act—and thus to choose for himself, on the basis of this testing, the one which it is most desirable to perform explicitly or carry into overt effect. The central nervous system, in short, enables the individual to exercise conscious control over his behavior. It is the possibility of delayed response which principally differentiates reflective conduct from non-reflective conduct in which the response is always immediate. The higher centers of the central nervous system are involved in the former type of behavior by making possible the interposition, between stimulus and response in the simple stimulus-response arc, of a process of selecting one or another of a whole set of possible responses and combinations of responses to the given stimulus.

Mental processes take place in this field of attitudes as expressed by the central nervous system; and this field is hence the field of ideas: the field of the control of present behavior in terms of its future consequences, or in terms of future behavior; the field of that type of intelligent conduct which is peculiarly characteristic of the higher forms of life, and especially of human beings. The various attitudes expressible through the central nervous system can be organized into different types of subsequent acts; and the delayed reactions or responses thus made possible by the central nervous system are the distinctive feature of mentally controlled or intelligent behavior.[28]

What is the mind as such, if we are to think in behavioristic terms? Mind, of course, is a very ambiguous term, and I want to avoid ambiguities. What I suggested as characteristic of the mind is the reflective intelligence of the human animal which can be distinguished from the intelligence of lower forms. If we should try to regard reason as a specific faculty which deals with that which is universal we should find responses in lower forms which are universal. We can also point out that their conduct is purposive, and that types of conduct which do not lead up to certain ends are eliminated. This would seem to answer to what we term "mind" when we talk about the animal mind, but what we refer to as reflective intelligence we generally recognize as belonging only to the human organism. The nonhuman animal acts with reference to a future in the sense that it has impulses which are seeking expression that can only be sat-

[28] In considering the rôle or function of the central nervous system—important though it is—in intelligent human behavior, we must nevertheless keep in mind the fact that such behavior is essentially and fundamentally social; that it involves and presupposes an ever ongoing social life-process; and that the unity of this ongoing social process—or of any one of its component acts—is irreducible, and in particular cannot be adequately analyzed simply into a number of discrete nerve elements. This fact must be recognized by the social psychologist. These discrete nerve elements lie within the unity of this ongoing social process, or within the unity of any one of the social acts in which this process is expressed or embodied; and the analysis which isolates them—the analysis of which they are the results or end-products—does not and cannot destroy that unity.

isfied in later experience, and however this is to be explained, this later experience does determine what the present experience shall be. If one accepts a Darwinian explanation he says that only those forms survive whose conduct has a certain relationship to a specific future, such as belongs to the environment of the specific form. The forms whose conduct does insure the future will naturally survive. In such a statement, indirectly at least, one is making the future determine the conduct of the form through the structure of things as they now exist as a result of past happenings.

When, on the other hand, we speak of reflective conduct we very definitely refer to the presence of the future in terms of ideas. The intelligent man as distinguished from the intelligent animal presents to himself what is going to happen. The animal may act in such a way as to insure its food tomorrow. A squirrel hides nuts, but we do not hold that the squirrel has a picture of what is going to happen. The young squirrel is born in the summer time, and has no directions from other forms, but it will start off hiding nuts as well as the older ones. Such action shows that experience could not direct the activity of the specific form. The provident man, however, does definitely pursue a certain course, pictures a certain situation, and directs his own conduct with reference to it. The squirrel follows certain blind impulses, and the carrying-out of its impulses leads to the same result that the storing of grain does for the provident man. It is this picture, however, of what the future is to be as determining our present conduct that is the characteristic of human intelligence —the future as present in terms of ideas.

When we present such a picture it is in terms of our reactions, in terms of what we are going to do. There is some sort of a problem before us, and our statement of the problem is in terms of a future situation which will enable us to meet it by our present reactions. That sort of thinking characterizes the human form and we have endeavored to isolate its mechanism. What is essential to this mechanism is a way of indicating characters of things which control responses, and which have various values to the form itself, so that such characters will engage the attention of the organism and bring about a desired result. The odor of the victim engages the attention of the beast of prey, and by attention to that odor he does satisfy his hunger and insure his future. What is the difference between such a situation and the conduct of the man who acts, as we say, rationally? The fundamental difference is that the latter individual in some way indicates this character, whatever it may be, to another person and to himself; and the symbolization of it by means of this indicative gesture is what constitutes the mechanism that gives the implements, at least, for intelligent conduct. Thus, one points to a certain footprint, and says that it means bear. Now to identify that sort of a trace by means of some symbol so that it can be utilized by the different members of the group, but particularly by the individual himself later, is the characteristic thing about human intelligence. To be able to identify "this as leading to that," and to get some sort of a gesture, vocal or otherwise, which can be used to indicate the implication to others and to himself so as to make possible the control of conduct with reference to it, is the distinctive thing in human intelligence which is not found in animal intelligence.

What such symbols do is to pick out particular characteristics of the situation so that the response to them can be present in the experience of the individual. We may say they are present in ideal form, as in a tendency to run away, in a sinking of the stomach when we come on the fresh footprints of a bear. The indication that this is a bear calls out the response of avoiding the bear, or if one is on a bear hunt, it indicates the further progress of the hunt. One gets the response into experience before that response is overtly carried out through indicating and emphasizing the stimulus that instigates it. When this symbol is utilized for the thing itself one is, in Watson's terms, conditioning a reflex. The sight of the bear would lead one to run away, the footprint conditioned that reflex, and the word "bear" spoken by one's self or a friend can also condition the reflex, so that the sign comes to stand for the thing so far as action is concerned.

What I have been trying to bring out is the difference between the foregoing type of conduct and the type which I have illustrated by the experiment on the baby with the white rat and the noise behind its head. In the latter situation there is a conditioning of the reflex in which there is no holding apart of the different elements. But when there is a conditioning of the reflex which involves the word "bear," or the sight of the footprint, there is in the experience of the individual the separation of the stimulus and the response. Here the symbol means bear, and that in turn means getting out of the way, or furthering the hunt. Under those circumstances the person who stumbles on the footprints of the bear is not afraid of the footprints—he is afraid of the bear. The footprint means a bear. The child is afraid of the rat, so that the response of fear is to the sight of the white rat; the man is not afraid of the footprint, but of the bear. The footprint and the symbol which refers to the bear in some sense may be said to condition or set off the response, but the bear and not the sign is the object of the fear. The isolation of the symbol, as such, enables one to hold on to these given characters and to isolate them in their relationship to the object, and consequently in their relation to the response. It is that, I think, which characterizes our human intelligence to a peculiar degree. We have a set of symbols by means of which we indicate certain characters, and in indicating those characters hold them apart from their immediate environment, and keep simply one relationship clear. We isolate the footprint of the bear and keep only that relationship to the animal that made it. We are reacting to that, nothing else. One holds on to it as an indication of the bear and of the value that object has in experience as something to be avoided or to be hunted. The ability to isolate these important characters in their relationship to the object and to the response which belongs to the object is, I think, what we generally mean when we speak of a human being thinking a thing out, or having a mind. Such ability makes the world-wide difference between the conditioning of reflexes in the case of the white rat and the human process of thinking by means of symbols.[29]

What is there in conduct that makes this level of experience possible, this selection of certain characters with their relationship to other characters and to the responses which these call out? My own answer, it is clear, is in terms of such a set of symbols as arise in our social conduct, in the conversation of gestures—in a word, in terms of language. When we get into conduct these symbols which indicate certain characters and their relationship to things and to responses, they enable us to pick out these characters and hold them in so far as they determine our conduct.

A man walking across country comes upon a chasm which he cannot jump. He wants to go ahead but the chasm prevents this tendency from being carried out. In that kind of a situation there arises a sensitivity to all sorts of characters which he has not noticed before. When he stops, mind, we say, is freed. He does not simply look for the indication of the path going ahead. The dog and the man would both try to find a point where they could cross. But what the man could do that the dog could not would be to note that the sides of the chasm seem

[29] The meanings of things or objects are actual inherent properties or qualities of them; the locus of any given meaning is in the thing which, as we say, "has it." We refer to the meaning of a thing when we make use of the symbol. Symbols stand for the meanings of those things or objects which have meanings; they are given portions of experience which point to, indicate, or represent other portions of experience not directly present or given at the time when, and in the situation in which, any one of them is thus present (or is immediately experienced). The symbol is thus more than a mere substitute stimulus—more than a mere stimulus for a conditioned response or reflex. For the conditioned reflex—the response to a mere substitute stimulus—does not or need not involve consciousness; whereas the response to a symbol does and must involve consciousness. Conditioned reflexes plus consciousness of the attitudes and meanings they involve are what constitute language, and hence lay the basis, or comprise the mechanism for, thought and intelligent conduct. Language is the means whereby individuals can indicate to one another what their responses to objects will be, and hence what the meanings of objects are; it is not a mere system of conditioned reflexes. Rational conduct always involves a reflexive reference to self, that is, an indication to the individual of the significances which his actions or gestures have for other individuals. And the experiential or behavioristic basis for such conduct—the neuro-physiological mechanism of thinking—is to be found, as we have seen, in the central nervous system.

to be approaching each other in one direction. He picks out the best places to try, and that approach which he indicates to himself determines the way in which he is going to go. If the dog saw at a distance a narrow place he would run to it, but probably he would not be affected by the gradual approach which the human individual symbolically could indicate to himself.

The human individual would see other objects about him, and have other images appear in his experience. He sees a tree which might serve as a bridge across the space ahead of him. He might try various sorts of possible actions which would be suggested to him in such a situation, and present them to himself by means of the symbols he uses. He has not simply conditioned certain responses by certain stimuli. If he had, he would be bound to those. What he does·do by means of these symbols is to indicate certain characters which are present, so that he can have these responses there all ready to go off. He looks down the chasm and thinks he sees the edges drawing together, and he may run toward that point. Or he may stop and ask if there is not some other way in which he can hasten his crossing. What stops him is a variety of other things he may do. He notes all the possibilities of getting across. He can hold on to them by means of symbols, and relate them to each other so that he can get a final action. The beginning of the act is there in his experience. He already has a tendency to go in a certain direction and what he would do is already there determining him. And not only is that determination there in his attitude but he has that which is picked out by means of the term "that is narrow, I can jump it." He is ready to jump, and that reflex is ready to determine what he is doing. These symbols, instead of being a mere conditioning of reflexes, are ways of picking out the stimuli so that the various responses can organize themselves into a form of action.[30]

[30] The reflective act consists in a reconstruction of the perceptual field so that it becomes possible for impulses which were in conflict to inhibit action no longer. This may take place by such a temporal readjustment that one of the conflicting impulses finds a later expression. In this case there has entered into the perceptual field other impulses which postpone the expression of that which had inhibited action. Thus,

The situation in which one seeks conditioning responses is, I think, as far as effective intelligence is concerned, always present in the form of a problem. When a man is just going ahead he seeks the indications of the path but he does it unconsciously. He just sees the path ahead of him; he is not aware of looking for it under those conditions. But when he reaches the chasm, this onward movement is stopped by the very process of drawing back from the chasm. That conflict, so to speak, sets him free to see a whole set of other things. Now, the sort of things he will see will be the characters which represent various possibilities of action under the circumstances. The man holds on to these different possibilities of response in terms of the different stimuli which present themselves, and it is his ability to hold them there that constitutes his mind.

We have no evidence of such a situation in the case of the lower animals, as is made fairly clear by the fact that we do not find in any animal behavior that we can work out in detail any symbol, any method of communication, anything that will answer to these different responses so that they can all be held there in the experience of the individual. It is that which differentiates the action of the reflectively intelligent being from the conduct of the lower forms; and the mechanism that makes that possible is language. We have to recognize that language is a part of conduct. Mind involves, however, a relationship to the characters of things. Those characters are in the things,

---

the width of the ditch inhibits the impulse to jump. There enters into the perceptual field the image of a narrower stretch and the impulse to go ahead finds its place in a combination of impulses, including that of movement toward the narrower stretch.

The reconstruction may take place through the appearance of other sensory characters in the field ignored before. A board long enough to bridge the ditch is recognized. Because the individual has already the complex of impulses which lead to lifting it and placing it across the ditch it becomes a part of the organized group of impulses that carry the man along toward his destination. In neither case would he be ready to respond to the stimulus (in the one case the image of the narrower stretch of the ditch, in the other the sight of the board) if he had not reactions in his nature answering to these objects, nor would these tendencies to response sensitize him to their stimuli if they were not freed from firmly organized habits. It is this freedom, then, that is the prerequisite of reflection, and it is our social self-reflective conduct that gives this freedom to human individuals in their group life (MS).

and while the stimuli call out the response which is in one sense present in the organism, the responses are to things out there. The whole process is not a mental product and you cannot put it inside of the brain. Mentality is that relationship of the organism to the situation which is mediated by sets of symbols.

17. THE RELATION OF MIND TO RESPONSE AND ENVIRONMENT

We have seen that mental processes have to do with the meanings of things, and that these meanings can be stated in terms of highly organized attitudes of the individual. These attitudes involve not only situations in which the elements are simultaneous, but also ones which involve other temporal relationships, i.e., the adjustment of the present response to later responses which are in some sense already initiated. Such an organization of attitudes with reference to what we term objects is what constitutes for us the meanings of things. These meanings in logical terminology are considered as universals, and this universality, we have seen, attaches in a certain sense to a habitual response in contrast to the particular stimuli which elicit this response. The universality is reflected in behavioristic terms in the identity of the response, although the stimuli that call out this response are all different. We can throw this statement into a logical form and say that the response is universal while the stimuli are particulars which are brought under such a universal.

These relations of attitudes to each other throw light upon the relation of a "substance" to its attributes. We speak of a house as, in a certain sense, a substance to which the attribute of color may be applied. The color is an accident which inheres in a certain substance, as such. This relationship of the inherence of a certain character in a certain substance is a relationship of a specific response, such as that of ornamenting objects about us, to the group of actions involved in dwelling in a house. The house must protect us, it must provide for us when we are asleep and when we are awake, it must carry the requisites of a family life—these are essentials that stand for a set of responses in which one inevitably implies the other. There are other responses, however, that vary. We can satisfy not simply our taste, but also our whims in the ornaments we use. Those are not essential. There are certain responses that vary, whereas there is a certain body of more or less standardized responses that remain unchanged. The organized sets of responses answer to the meanings of things, answer to them in their universality, that is, in the habitual response that is called out by a great variety of stimuli. They answer to things in their logical relationships.

I have referred just now to the relationship of the substance as reflected in the body of habits, to the varied responses answering to the attributes. In the relationship of cause and effect there is the relation of the responses to each other in the sense of dependence, involving the adjustment of the steps to be taken with reference to the thing to be carried out. The arrangement which may appear at one time in terms of means and end appears at another time in terms of cause and effect. We have here a relationship of dependence of one response on another, a necessary relation that lies inside of a larger system.[31] It depends upon what we are going to do whether we select this means or another one, one causal series or another. Our habits are so adjusted that if we decide to take a journey, for instance, we have a body of related habits that begin to operate—packing our bags, getting our railroad tickets, drawing out money for use, selecting books to read on the journey, and so on. There are a whole set of organized responses which at once start to go off in their proper relationship to each other when a person makes up his mind that he will take a journey. There must be such an organization in our habits in order that man may have the sort of intelligence which he in fact has.

We have, then, in the behavioristic statement, a place for that which is supposed to be the peculiar content of mind, that

[31] Representation involves relation of earlier to later acts. This relation of responses gives implication (1924).

is, the meanings of things. I have referred to these factors as attitudes. There is, of course, that in the world which answers to the group of attitudes. We are here avoiding logical and metaphysical problems, just as modern psychology does. What this psychology is seeking to do is to get control; it is not seeking to settle metaphysical questions. Now, from the point of view of behavioristic psychology, we can state in terms of attitudes what we call the meanings of things; the organized attitude of the individual is that which the psychologist gets hold of in this situation. It is at least as legitimate for him to state meaning in terms of attitudes as it was for an earlier psychologist to state it in terms of a static concept that had its place in the mind.

What I have pointed out is that in the central nervous system one can find, or at least justifiably assume, just such complexities of responses, or the mechanism of just such complexities of response, as we have been discussing. If we speak of a person going through the steps to which I have referred, in preparing for a journey, we have to assume that not only are the nervous elements essential to the steps, but that the relation of those responses in the central nervous system is of a such sort that if the person carries out one response he is inevitably ready to find the stimulus which will set free another related response. There must be an organization in the central nervous system in the way of its elements, its neurons, for all the combinations which can possibly enter into a mind and for just such a relationship of responses which are interdependent upon each other. Some of these have been identified in the physiological study of the nervous system, while others have to be assumed on the basis of such study. As I have said before, it is not the specific physiological process which is going on inside of the neurons that as such is supposed to answer to meaning. Earlier physiological psychologists had spoken of a specific psychical process, but there is nothing in the mechanical, electrical, and physical activity that goes on in the nerve which answers to what we term an idea. What is going on in the nerve in a particular situation is the innervation of a certain response which means this, that, and the other thing, and here is where the specificity of a certain nervous organization is found. It is in the central nervous system that organization takes place. In a certain sense you can say that it is in the engineer's office that the organization of the concern is carried out. But what is found there in the blue-prints and body of statistics is not the actual production that is going on in the factory, even though that office does organize and co-ordinate those various branches of the concern. In the same way the central nervous system co-ordinates all the various processes that the body carries out. If there is anything in the organism as a purely physiological mechanism which answers to what we call experience, when that is ordinarily termed conscious, it is the total organic process for which these nervous elements stand. These processes are, as we have seen, attitudes of response, adjustments of the organism to a complex environment, attitudes which sensitize the form to the stimuli which will set the response free.

The point I want to emphasize is the way that these attitudes determine the environment. There is an organized set of responses which first send off certain telegrams, then select the means of transportation, then send us to the bank to get money, and then see to it that we get something to read on the train. As we advance from one set of responses to another we find ourselves picking out the environment which answers to this next set of responses. To finish one response is to put ourselves in a position where we see other things. The appearance of the retinal elements has given the world color; the development of the organs in the ear has given the world sound. We pick out an organized environment in relationship to our response, so that these attitudes, as such, not only represent our organized responses but they also represent what exists for us in the world; the particular phase of reality that is there for us is picked out for us by our response. We can recognize that it is the sensitizing of the organism to the stimuli which will set free its responses that is responsible for one's living in this sort of an environment rather than in another. We see things in their tem-

[128]

poral relationship which answer to the temporal organization which is found in the central nervous system. We see things as distant from us not only spatially but temporally; when we do this we can do that. Our world is definitely mapped out for us by the responses which are going to take place.[32]

It is a difficult matter to state just what we mean by dividing up a certain situation between the organism and its environment. Certain objects come to exist for us because of the character of the organism. Take the case of food. If an animal that can digest grass, such as an ox, comes into the world, then grass becomes food. That object did not exist before, that is, grass as food. The advent of the ox brings in a new object. In that sense, organisms are responsible for the appearance of whole sets of objects that did not exist before.[33] The distribution of meaning to the organism and the environment has its expression in the organism as well as in the thing, and that expression is not a matter of psychical or mental conditions. There is an expression of the reaction of the organized response of the organism to the environment, and that reaction is not simply a determination of the organism by the environment, since the organism determines the environment as fully as the environment determines the organs. The organic reaction is responsible for the appearance of a whole set of objects which did not exist before.

There is a definite and necessary structure or *gestalt* of sensitivity within the organism, which determines selectively and relatively the character of the external object it perceives. What we term consciousness needs to be brought inside just this relation between an organism and its environment. Our constructive selection of an environment—colors, emotional values, and the like—in terms of our physiological sensitivities, is essentially what we mean by consciousness. This consciousness we have tended historically to locate in the mind or in the

[32] The structure of the environment is a mapping out of organic responses to nature; any environment, whether social or individual, is a mapping out of the logical structure of the act to which it answers, an act seeking overt expression.

[33] It is objectionable to speak of the food-process in the animal as constituting the food-object. They are certainly relative to each other (MS).

brain. The eye and related processes endow objects with color in exactly the same sense that an ox endows grass with the character of food, that is, not in the sense of projecting sensations into objects, but rather of putting itself into a relation with the object which makes the appearance and existence of the color possible, as a quality of the object. Colors inhere in objects only by virtue of their relations to given percipient organisms. The physiological or sensory structure of the percipient organism determines the experienced content of the object.

The organism, then, is in a sense responsible for its environment. And since organism and environment determine each other and are mutually dependent for their existence, it follows that the life-process, to be adequately understood, must be considered in terms of their interrelations.

The social environment is endowed with meanings in terms of the process of social activity; it is an organization of objective relations which arises in relation to a group of organisms engaged in such activity, in processes of social experience and behavior. Certain characters of the external world are possessed by it only with reference to or in relation to an interacting social group of individual organisms; just as other characters of it are possessed by it only with reference to or in relation to individual organisms themselves. The relation of the social process of behavior—or the relation of the social organism—to the social environment is analogous to the relation of the processes of individual biological activity—or the relation of the individual organism—to the physical-biological environment.[34]

The parallelism I have been referring to is the parallelism of the set of the organism and the objects answering to it. In the ox there is hunger, and also the sight and odor which bring in the food. The whole process is not found simply in the stomach, but in all the activities of grazing, chewing the cud, and so on.

[34] A social organism—that is, a social group of individual organisms—constitutes or creates its own special environment of objects just as, and in the same sense as, an individual organism constitutes or creates its own special environment of objects (which, however, is much more rudimentary than the environment constructed by a social organism).

This process is one which is intimately related to the so-called food which exists out there. The organism sets up a bacteriological laboratory, such as the ox carries around to take care of the grass which then becomes food. Within that parallelism what we term the meaning of the object is found, specifically, in the organized attitude of response on the part of the organism to the characters and the things. The meanings are there, and the mind is occupied with these meanings. The organized stimuli answer to the organized responses.

It is the organization of the different responses to each other in their relationship to the stimuli they are setting free that is the peculiar subject matter of psychology in dealing with what we term "mind." We generally confine the term "mental," and so "mind," to the human organism, because there we find that body of symbols that enables us to isolate these characters, these meanings. We try to distinguish the meaning of a house from the stone, the cement, the bricks that make it up as a physical object, and in doing so we are referring to the use of it. That is what makes the house a mental affair.[35] We are isolating, if you like, the building materials from the standpoint of the physicist and the architect. There are various standpoints from which one can look at a house. The burrow in which some animal lives is in one sense the house of the animal, but when the human being lives in a house it takes on what we term a mental character for him which it presumably has not for the mole that lives in the burrow. The human individual has the ability to pick out the elements in a house which answer to his responses so that he can control them. He reads the advertisement of a new

[35] Nature—the external world—is objectively there, in opposition to our experience of it, or in opposition to the individual thinker himself. Although external objects are there independent of the experiencing individual, nevertheless they possess certain characteristics by virtue of their relations to his experiencing or to his mind, which they would not possess otherwise or apart from those relations. These characteristics are their meanings for him, or in general, for us. The distinction between physical objects or physical reality and the mental or self-conscious experience of those objects or that reality—the distinction between external and internal experience—lies in the fact that the latter is concerned with or constituted by meanings. Experienced objects have definite meanings for the individuals thinking about them.

form of a boiler and can then have more warmth, have a more comfortable dressing-room than before. Man is able to control the process from the standpoint of his own responses. He gets meanings and so controls his responses. His ability to pick those out is what makes the house a mental affair. The mole, too, has to find his food, meet his enemies, and avoid them, but we do not assume that the mole is able to indicate to himself the peculiar advantages of his burrow over against another one. His house has no mental characteristics. Mentality resides in the ability of the organism to indicate that in the environment which answers to his responses, so that he can control those responses in various ways. That, from the point of view of behavioristic psychology, is what mentality consists in. There are in the mole and other animals complex elements of behavior related to the environment, but the human animal is able to indicate to itself and to others what the characters are in the environment which call out these complex, highly organized responses, and by such indication is able to control the responses. The human animal has the ability over and above the adjustment which belongs to the lower animal to pick out and isolate the stimulus. The biologist recognizes that food has certain values, and while the human animal responds to these values as other animals do, it can also indicate certain characters in the food which mean certain things in his digestive responses to these foods. Mentality consists in indicating these values to others and to one's self so that one can control one's responses.

Mentality on our approach simply comes in when the organism is able to point out meanings to others and to himself. This is the point at which mind appears, or if you like, emerges. What we need to recognize is that we are dealing with the relationship of the organism to the environment selected by its own sensitivity. The psychologist is interested in the mechanism which the human species has evolved to get control over these relationships. The relationships have been there before the indications are made, but the organism has not in its own conduct controlled that relationship. It originally has no mechanism by means of which it can control it. The human animal, however, has worked out a mechanism of language communication by means of which it can get this control. Now, it is evident that much of that mechanism does not lie in the central nervous system, but in the relation of things to the organism. The ability to pick these meanings out and to indicate them to others and to the organism is an ability which gives peculiar power to the human individual. The control has been made possible by language. It is that mechanism of control over meaning in this sense which has, I say, constituted what we term "mind." The mental processes do not, however, lie in words any more than the intelligence of the organism lies in the elements of the central nervous system. Both are part of a process that is going on between organism and environment. The symbols serve their part in this process, and it is that which makes communication so important. Out of language emerges the field of mind.

It is absurd to look at the mind simply from the standpoint of the individual human organism; for, although it has its focus there, it is essentially a social phenomenon; even its biological functions are primarily social. The subjective experience of the individual must be brought into relation with the natural, sociobiological activities of the brain in order to render an acceptable account of mind possible at all; and this can be done only if the social nature of mind is recognized. The meagerness of individual experience in isolation from the processes of social experience—in isolation from its social environment—should, moreover, be apparent. We must regard mind, then, as arising and developing within the social process, within the empirical matrix of social interactions. We must, that is, get an inner individual experience from the standpoint of social acts which include the experiences of separate individuals in a social context wherein those individuals interact. The processes of experience which the human brain makes possible are made possible only for a group of interacting individuals: only for individual organisms which are members of a society; not for the individual organism in isolation from other individual organisms.

Mind arises in the social process only when that process as a whole enters into, or is present in, the experience of any one of the given individuals involved in that process. When this occurs the individual becomes self-conscious and has a mind; he becomes aware of his relations to that process as a whole, and to the other individuals participating in it with him; he becomes aware of that process as modified by the reactions and interactions of the individuals—including himself—who are carrying it on. The evolutionary appearance of mind or intelligence takes place when the whole social process of experience and behavior is brought within the experience of any one of the separate individuals implicated therein, and when the individual's adjustment to the process is modified and refined by the awareness or consciousness which he thus has of it. It is by means of reflexiveness—the turning-back of the experience of the individual upon himself—that the whole social process is thus brought into the experience of the individuals involved in it; it is by such means, which enable the individual to take the attitude of the other toward himself, that the individual is able consciously to adjust himself to that process, and to modify the resultant of that process in any given social act in terms of his adjustment to it. Reflexiveness, then, is the essential condition, within the social process, for the development of mind.

PART III

THE SELF

18. THE SELF AND THE ORGANISM

In our statement of the development of intelligence we have already suggested that the language process is essential for the development of the self. The self has a character which is different from that of the physiological organism proper. The self is something which has a development; it is not initially there, at birth, but arises in the process of social experience and activity, that is, develops in the given individual as a result of his relations to that process as a whole and to other individuals within that process. The intelligence of the lower forms of animal life, like a great deal of human intelligence, does not involve a self. In our habitual actions, for example, in our moving about in a world that is simply there and to which we are so adjusted that no thinking is involved, there is a certain amount of sensuous experience such as persons have when they are just waking up, a bare thereness of the world. Such characters about us may exist in experience without taking their place in relationship to the self. One must, of course, under those conditions, distinguish between the experience that immediately takes place and our own organization of it into the experience of the self. One says upon analysis that a certain item had its place in his experience, in the experience of his self. We do inevitably tend at a certain level of sophistication to organize all experience into that of a self. We do so intimately identify our experiences, especially our affective experiences, with the self that it takes a moment's abstraction to realize that pain and pleasure can be there without being the experience of the self. Similarly, we normally organize our memories upon the string of our self. If we date things we always date them from the point of view of our past experiences. We frequently have memories that we cannot date, that we cannot place. A picture comes before us suddenly and we are at a loss to explain when that experience originally took place. We remember perfectly distinctly the picture, but we do not have it definitely placed, and until we can place it in terms of our past experience we are not satisfied. Nevertheless, I think it is obvious when one comes to consider it that the self is not necessarily involved in the life of the organism, nor involved in what we term our sensuous experience, that is, experience in a world about us for which we have habitual reactions.

We can distinguish very definitely between the self and the body. The body can be there and can operate in a very intelligent fashion without there being a self involved in the experience. The self has the characteristic that it is an object to itself, and that characteristic distinguishes it from other objects and from the body. It is perfectly true that the eye can see the foot, but it does not see the body as a whole. We cannot see our backs; we can feel certain portions of them, if we are agile, but we cannot get an experience of our whole body. There are, of course, experiences which are somewhat vague and difficult of location, but the bodily experiences are for us organized about a self. The foot and hand belong to the self. We can see our feet, especially if we look at them from the wrong end of an opera glass, as strange things which we have difficulty in recognizing as our own. The parts of the body are quite distinguishable from the self. We can lose parts of the body without any serious invasion of the self. The mere ability to experience different parts of the body is not different from the experience of a table. The table presents a different feel from what the hand does when one hand feels another, but it is an experience of something with which we come definitely into contact. The body does not experience itself as a whole, in the sense in which the self in some way enters into the experience of the self.

It is the characteristic of the self as an object to itself that I want to bring out. This characteristic is represented in the word "self," which is a reflexive, and indicates that which can be both subject and object. This type of object is essentially different from other objects, and in the past it has been distinguished as conscious, a term which indicates an experience with, an experience of, one's self. It was assumed that consciousness in some way carried this capacity of being an object to itself. In giving a behavioristic statement of consciousness we have to look for some sort of experience in which the physical organism can become an object to itself.[1]

When one is running to get away from someone who is chasing him, he is entirely occupied in this action, and his experience may be swallowed up in the objects about him, so that he has, at the time being, no consciousness of self at all. We must be, of course, very completely occupied to have that take place, but we can, I think, recognize that sort of a possible experience in which the self does not enter. We can, perhaps, get some light on that situation through those experiences in which in very intense action there appear in the experience of the individual, back of this intense action, memories and anticipations. Tolstoi as an officer in the war gives an account of having pictures of his past experience in the midst of his most intense action. There are also the pictures that flash into a person's mind when he is drowning. In such instances there is a contrast between an experience that is absolutely wound up in outside activity in which the self as an object does not enter, and an activity of memory and imagination in which the self is the principal object. The self is then entirely distinguishable from an organism that is surrounded by things and acts with reference to things, including parts of its own body. These latter may be objects like other objects, but they are just objects out there in the field, and they do not involve a self that is an object to the organism. This is, I think, frequently overlooked. It is that

[1] Man's behavior is such in his social group that he is able to become an object to himself, a fact which constitutes him a more advanced product of evolutionary development than are the lower animals. Fundamentally it is this social fact—and not his alleged possession of a soul or mind with which he, as an individual, has been mysteriously and supernaturally endowed, and with which the lower animals have not been endowed—that differentiates him from them.

fact which makes our anthropomorphic reconstructions of animal life so fallacious. How can an individual get outside himself (experientially) in such a way as to become an object to himself? This is the essential psychological problem of selfhood or of self-consciousness; and its solution is to be found by referring to the process of social conduct or activity in which the given person or individual is implicated. The apparatus of reason would not be complete unless it swept itself into its own analysis of the field of experience; or unless the individual brought himself into the same experiential field as that of the other individual selves in relation to whom he acts in any given social situation. Reason cannot become impersonal unless it takes an objective, non-affective attitude toward itself; otherwise we have just consciousness, not *self*-consciousness. And it is necessary to rational conduct that the individual should thus take an objective, impersonal attitude toward himself, that he should become an object to himself. For the individual organism is obviously an essential and important fact or constituent element of the empirical situation in which it acts; and without taking objective account of itself as such, it cannot act intelligently, or rationally.

The individual experiences himself as such, not directly, but only indirectly, from the particular standpoints of other individual members of the same social group, or from the generalized standpoint of the social group as a whole to which he belongs. For he enters his own experience as a self or individual, not directly or immediately, not by becoming a subject to himself, but only in so far as he first becomes an object to himself just as other individuals are objects to him or in his experience; and he becomes an object to himself only by taking the attitudes of other individuals toward himself within a social environment or context of experience and behavior in which both he and they are involved.

The importance of what we term "communication" lies in the fact that it provides a form of behavior in which the organism or the individual may become an object to himself. It is that sort of communication which we have been discussing—not communication in the sense of the cluck of the hen to the chickens, or the bark of a wolf to the pack, or the lowing of a cow, but communication in the sense of significant symbols, communication which is directed not only to others but also to the individual himself. So far as that type of communication is a part of behavior it at least introduces a self. Of course, one may hear without listening; one may see things that he does not realize; do things that he is not really aware of. But it is where one does respond to that which he addresses to another and where that response of his own becomes a part of his conduct, where he not only hears himself but responds to himself, talks and replies to himself as truly as the other person replies to him, that we have behavior in which the individuals become objects to themselves.

Such a self is not, I would say, primarily the physiological organism. The physiological organism is essential to it,[2] but we

[2] a) All social interrelations and interactions are rooted in a certain common socio-physiological endowment of every individual involved in them. These physiological bases of social behavior—which have their ultimate seat or locus in the lower part of the individual's central nervous system—are the bases of such behavior, precisely because they in themselves are also social; that is, because they consist in drives or instincts or behavior tendencies, on the part of the given individual, which he cannot carry out or give overt expression and satisfaction to without the co-operative aid of one or more other individuals. The physiological processes of behavior of which they are the mechanisms are processes which necessarily involve more than one individual, processes in which other individuals besides the given individual are perforce implicated. Examples of the fundamental social relations to which these physiological bases of social behavior give rise are those between the sexes (expressing the reproductive instinct), between parent and child (expressing the parental instinct), and between neighbors (expressing the gregarious instinct). These relatively simple and rudimentary physiological mechanisms or tendencies of individual human behavior, besides constituting the physiological bases of all human social behavior, are also the fundamental biological materials of human nature; so that when we refer to human nature, we are referring to something which is essentially social.

b) Sexually and parentally, as well as in its attacks and defenses, the activities of the physiological organism are social in that the acts begun within the organism require their completion in the actions of others. . . . . But while the pattern of the individual act may be said to be in these cases social, it is only so in so far as the organism seeks for the stimuli in the attitudes and characters of other forms for the completion of its own responses, and by its behavior tends to maintain the other as a part of its own environment. The actual behavior of the other or the others is not initiated in the individual form as a part of its own pattern of behavior (MS).

are at least able to think of a self without it. Persons who believe in immortality, or believe in ghosts, or in the possibility
of the self leaving the body, assume a self which is quite distinguishable from the body. How successfully they can hold
these conceptions is an open question, but we do, as a fact,
separate the self and the organism. It is fair to say that the
beginning of the self as an object, so far as we can see, is to be
found in the experiences of people that lead to the conception
of a "double." Primitive people assume that there is a double,
located presumably in the diaphragm, that leaves the body
temporarily in sleep and completely in death. It can be enticed
out of the body of one's enemy and perhaps killed. It is represented in infancy by the imaginary playmates which children
set up, and through which they come to control their experiences
in their play.

The self, as that which can be an object to itself, is essentially
a social structure, and it arises in social experience. After a self
has arisen, it in a certain sense provides for itself its social experiences, and so we can conceive of an absolutely solitary self.
But it is impossible to conceive of a self arising outside of social
experience. When it has arisen we can think of a person in solitary confinement for the rest of his life, but who still has himself
as a companion, and is able to think and to converse with himself as he had communicated with others. That process to which
I have just referred, of responding to one's self as another responds to it, taking part in one's own conversation with others,
being aware of what one is saying and using that awareness of
what one is saying to determine what one is going to say thereafter—that is a process with which we are all familiar. We are
continually following up our own address to other persons by an
understanding of what we are saying, and using that understanding in the direction of our continued speech. We are finding out what we are going to say, what we are going to do, by
saying and doing, and in the process we are continually controlling the process itself. In the conversation of gestures what
we say calls out a certain response in another and that in turn

changes our own action, so that we shift from what we started to do because of the reply the other makes. The conversation of gestures is the beginning of communication. The individual comes to carry on a conversation of gestures with himself. He says something, and that calls out a certain reply in himself which makes him change what he was going to say. One starts to say something, we will presume an unpleasant something, but when he starts to say it he realizes it is cruel. The effect on himself of what he is saying checks him; there is here a conversation of gestures between the individual and himself. We mean by significant speech that the action is one that affects the individual himself, and that the effect upon the individual himself is part of the intelligent carrying-out of the conversation with others. Now we, so to speak, amputate that social phase and dispense with it for the time being, so that one is talking to one's self as one would talk to another person.[3]

This process of abstraction cannot be carried on indefinitely. One inevitably seeks an audience, has to pour himself out to somebody. In reflective intelligence one thinks to act, and to act solely so that this action remains a part of a social process. Thinking becomes preparatory to social action. The very process of thinking is, of course, simply an inner conversation that goes on, but it is a conversation of gestures which in its completion implies the expression of that which one thinks to

---

[3] It is generally recognized that the specifically social expressions of intelligence, or the exercise of what is often called "social intelligence," depend upon the given individual's ability to take the rôles of, or "put himself in the place of," the other individuals implicated with him in given social situations; and upon his consequent sensitivity to their attitudes toward himself and toward one another. These specifically social expressions of intelligence, of course, acquire unique significance in terms of our view that the whole nature of intelligence is social to the very core—that this putting of one's self in the places of others, this taking by one's self of their rôles or attitudes, is not merely one of the various aspects or expressions of intelligence or of intelligent behavior, but is the very essence of its character. Spearman's "X factor" in intelligence— the unknown factor which, according to him, intelligence contains—is simply (if our social theory of intelligence is correct) this ability of the intelligent individual to take the attitude of the other, or the attitudes of others, thus realizing the significations or grasping the meanings of the symbols or gestures in terms of which thinking proceeds; and thus being able to carry on with himself the internal conversation with these symbols or gestures which thinking involves.

an audience. One separates the significance of what he is saying
to others from the actual speech and gets it ready before saying
it. He thinks it out, and perhaps writes it in the form of a book;
but it is still a part of social intercourse in which one is addressing other persons and at the same time addressing one's
self, and in which one controls the address to other persons by
the response made to one's own gesture. That the person should
be responding to himself is necessary to the self, and it is this
sort of social conduct which provides behavior within which that
self appears. I know of no other form of behavior than the linguistic in which the individual is an object to himself, and, so
far as I can see, the individual is not a self in the reflexive sense
unless he is an object to himself. It is this fact that gives a
critical importance to communication, since this is a type of behavior in which the individual does so respond to himself.

We realize in everyday conduct and experience that an individual does not mean a great deal of what he is doing and saying. We frequently say that such an individual is not himself.
We come away from an interview with a realization that we
have left out important things, that there are parts of the self
that did not get into what was said. What determines the
amount of the self that gets into communication is the social
experience itself. Of course, a good deal of the self does not need
to get expression. We carry on a whole series of different relationships to different people. We are one thing to one man and
another thing to another. There are parts of the self which
exist only for the self in relationship to itself. We divide ourselves up in all sorts of different selves with reference to our
acquaintances. We discuss politics with one and religion with
another. There are all sorts of different selves answering to all
sorts of different social reactions. It is the social process itself
that is responsible for the appearance of the self; it is not there
as a self apart from this type of experience.

A multiple personality is in a certain sense normal, as I have
just pointed out. There is usually an organization of the whole
self with reference to the community to which we belong, and

the situation in which we find ourselves. What the society is, whether we are living with people of the present, people of our own imaginations, people of the past, varies, of cóurse, with different individuals. Normally, within the sort of community as a whole to which we belong, there is a unified self, but that may be broken up. To a person who is somewhat unstable nervously and in whom there is a line of cleavage, certain activities become impossible, and that set of activities may separate and evolve another self. Two separate "me's" and "I's," two different selves, result, and that is the condition under which there is a tendency to break up the personality. There is an account of a professor of education who disappeared, was lost to the community, and later turned up in a logging camp in the West. He freed himself of his occupation and turned to the woods where he felt, if you like, more at home. The pathological side of it was the forgetting, the leaving out of the rest of the self. This result involved getting rid of certain bodily memories which would identify the individual to himself. We often recognize the lines of cleavage that run through us. We would be glad to forget certain things, get rid of things the self is bound up with in past experiences. What we have here is a situation in which there can be different selves, and it is dependent upon the set of social reactions that is involved as to which self we are going to be. If we can forget everything involved in one set of activities, obviously we relinquish that part of the self. Take a person who is unstable, get him occupied by speech, and at the same time get his eye on something you are writing so that he is carrying on two separate lines of communication, and if you go about it in the right way you can get those two currents going so that they do not run into each other. You can get two entirely different sets of activities going on. You can bring about in that way the dissociation of a person's self. It is a process of setting up two sorts of communication which separate the behavior of the individual. For one individual it is this thing said and heard, and for the other individual there exists only that which he sees written. You must, of course, keep one experience out of the field of the other. Dissociations are apt to take place when an event leads to emotional upheavals. That which is separated goes on in its own way.

The unity and structure of the complete self reflects the unity and structure of the social process as a whole; and each of the elementary selves of which it is composed reflects the unity and structure of one of the various aspects of that process in which the individual is implicated. In other words, the various elementary selves which constitute, or are organized into, a complete self are the various aspects of the structure of that complete self answering to the various aspects of the structure of the social process as a whole; the structure of the complete self is thus a reflection of the complete social process. The organization and unification of a social group is identical with the organization and unification of any one of the selves arising within the social process in which that group is engaged, or which it is carrying on.[4]

The phenomenon of dissociation of personality is caused by a breaking up of the complete, unitary self into the component selves of which it is composed, and which respectively correspond to different aspects of the social process in which the person is involved, and within which his complete or unitary self has arisen; these aspects being the different social groups to which he belongs within that process.

19. THE BACKGROUND OF THE GENESIS OF THE SELF

The problem now presents itself as to how, in detail, a self arises. We have to note something of the background of its genesis. First of all there is the conversation of gestures between animals involving some sort of co-operative activity. There the beginning of the act of one is a stimulus to the other to respond

[4] The unity of the mind is not identical with the unity of the self. The unity of the self is constituted by the unity of the entire relational pattern of social behavior and experience in which the individual is implicated, and which is reflected in the structure of the self; but many of the aspects or features of this entire pattern do not enter into consciousness, so that the unity of the mind is in a sense an abstraction from the more inclusive unity of the self.

in a certain way, while the beginning of this response becomes again a stimulus to the first to adjust his action to the oncoming response. Such is the preparation for the completed act, and ultimately it leads up to the conduct which is the outcome of this preparation. The conversation of gestures, however, does not carry with it the reference of the individual, the animal, the organism, to itself. It is not acting in a fashion which calls for a response from the form itself, although it is conduct with reference to the conduct of others. We have seen, however, that there are certain gestures that do affect the organism as they affect other organisms and may, therefore, arouse in the organism responses of the same character as aroused in the other. Here, then, we have a situation in which the individual may at least arouse responses in himself and reply to these responses, the condition being that the social stimuli have an effect on the individual which is like that which they have on the other. That, for example, is what is implied in language; otherwise language as significant symbol would disappear, since the individual would not get the meaning of that which he says.

The peculiar character possessed by our human social environment belongs to it by virtue of the peculiar character of human social activity; and that character, as we have seen, is to be found in the process of communication, and more particularly in the triadic relation on which the existence of meaning is based: the relation of the gesture of one organism to the adjustive response made to it by another organism, in its indicative capacity as pointing to the completion or resultant of the act it initiates (the meaning of the gesture being thus the response of the second organism to it as such, or as a gesture). What, as it were, takes the gesture out of the social act and isolates it as such—what makes it something more than just an early phase of an individual act—is the response of another organism, or of other organisms, to it. Such a response is its meaning, or gives it its meaning. The social situation and process of behavior are here presupposed by the acts of the individual organisms implicated therein. The gesture arises as a separable element in the social act, by virtue of the fact that it is selected out by the sensitivities of other organisms to it; it does not exist as a gesture merely in the experience of the single individual. The meaning of a gesture by one organism, to repeat, is found in the response of another organism to what would be the completion of the act of the first organism which that gesture initiates and indicates.

We sometimes speak as if a person could build up an entire argument in his mind, and then put it into words to convey it to someone else. Actually, our thinking always takes place by means of some sort of symbols. It is possible that one could have the meaning of "chair" in his experience without there being a symbol, but we would not be thinking about it in that case. We may sit down in a chair without thinking about what we are doing, that is, the approach to the chair is presumably already aroused in our experience, so that the meaning is there. But if one is thinking about the chair he must have some sort of a symbol for it. It may be the form of the chair, it may be the attitude that somebody else takes in sitting down, but it is more apt to be some language symbol that arouses this response. In a thought process there has to be some sort of a symbol that can refer to this meaning, that is, tend to call out this response, and also serve this purpose for other persons as well. It would not be a thought process if that were not the case.

Our symbols are all universal.⁵ You cannot say anything that is absolutely particular; anything you say that has any meaning at all is universal. You are saying something that calls out a specific response in anybody else provided that the symbol

⁵ Thinking proceeds in terms of or by means of universals. A universal may be interpreted behavioristically as simply the social act as a whole, involving the organization and interrelation of the attitudes of all the individuals implicated in the act, as controlling their overt responses. This organization of the different individual attitudes and interactions in a given social act, with reference to their interrelations as realized by the individuals themselves, is what we mean by a universal; and it determines what the actual overt responses of the individuals involved in the given social act will be, whether that act be concerned with a concrete project of some sort (such as the relation of physical and social means to ends desired) or with some purely abstract discussion, say the theory of relativity or the Platonic ideas.

exists for him in his experience as it does for you. There is the language of speech and the language of hands, and there may be the language of the expression of the countenance. One can register grief or joy and call out certain responses. There are primitive people who can carry on elaborate conversations just by expressions of the countenance. Even in these cases the person who communicates is affected by that expression just as he expects somebody else to be affected. Thinking always implies a symbol which will call out the same response in another that it calls out in the thinker. Such a symbol is a universal of discourse; it is universal in its character. We always assume that the symbol we use is one which will call out in the other person the same response, provided it is a part of his mechanism of conduct. A person who is saying something is saying to himself what he says to others; otherwise he does not know what he is talking about.

There is, of course, a great deal in one's conversation with others that does not arouse in one's self the same response it arouses in others. That is particularly true in the case of emotional attitudes. One tries to bully somebody else; he is not trying to bully himself. There is, further, a whole set of values given in speech which are not of a symbolic character. The actor is conscious of these values; that is, if he assumes a certain attitude he is, as we say, aware that this attitude represents grief. If it does he is able to respond to his own gesture in some sense as his audience does. It is not a natural situation; one is not an actor all of the time. We do at times act and consider just what the effect of our attitude is going to be, and we may deliberately use a certain tone of voice to bring about a certain result. Such a tone arouses the same response in ourselves that we want to arouse in somebody else. But a very large part of what goes on in speech has not this symbolic status.

It is the task not only of the actor but of the artist as well to find the sort of expression that will arouse in others what is going on in himself. The lyric poet has an experience of beauty with an emotional thrill to it, and as an artist using words he is seeking for those words which will answer to his emotional attitude, and which will call out in others the attitude he himself has. He can only test his results in himself by seeing whether these words do call out in him the response he wants to call out in others. He is in somewhat the same position as that of the actor. The first direct and immediate experience is not in the form of communication. We have an interesting light on this from such a poet as Wordsworth, who was very much interested in the technique of the poet's expression; and he has told us in his prefaces and also in his own poetry how his poems, as poems, arose—and uniformly the experience itself was not the immediate stimulus to the poetic expression. A period of ten years might lie between the original experience and the expression of it. This process of finding the expression in language which will call out the emotion once had is more easily accomplished when one is dealing with the memory of it than when one is in the midst of the trance-like experiences through which Wordsworth passed in his contact with nature. One has to experiment and see how the expression that is given does answer to the responses which are now had in the fainter memories of experience. Someone once said that he had very great difficulty in writing poetry; he had plenty of ideas but could not get the language he needed. He was rightly told that poetry was written in words, not in ideas.

A great deal of our speech is not of this genuinely aesthetic character; in most of it we do not deliberately feel the emotions which we arouse. We do not normally use language stimuli to call out in ourselves the emotional response which we are calling out in others. One does, of course, have sympathy in emotional situations; but what one is seeking for there is something which is, after all, that in the other which supports the individual in his own experience. In the case of the poet and actor, the stimulus calls out in the artist that which it calls out in the other, but this is not the natural function of language; we do not assume that the person who is angry is calling out the fear in himself that he is calling out in someone else. The emotional part of our act does not directly call out in us the response it calls out in the other. If a person is hostile the attitude of the other that he is interested in, an attitude which flows naturally from his angered tones, is not one that he definitely recognizes in himself. We are not frightened by a tone which we may use to frighten somebody else. On the emotional side, which is a very large part of the vocal gesture, we do not call out in ourselves in any such degree the response we call out in others as we do in the case of significant speech. Here we should call out in ourselves the type of response we are calling out in others; we must know what we are saying, and the attitude of the other which we arouse in ourselves should control what we do say. Rationality means that the type of the response which we call out in others should be so called out in ourselves, and that this response should in turn take its place in determining what further thing we are going to say and do.

What is essential to communication is that the symbol should arouse in one's self what it arouses in the other individual. It must have that sort of universality to any person who finds himself in the same situation. There is a possibility of language whenever a stimulus can affect the individual as it affects the other. With a blind person such as Helen Keller, it is a contact experience that could be given to another as it is given to herself. It is out of that sort of language that the mind of Helen Keller was built up. As she has recognized, it was not until she could get into communication with other persons through symbols which could arouse in herself the responses they arouse in other people that she could get what we term a mental content, or a self.

Another set of background factors in the genesis of the self is represented in the activities of play and the game.

Among primitive people, as I have said, the necessity of distinguishing the self and the organism was recognized in what we term the "double": the individual has a thing-like self that is affected by the individual as it affects other people and which is distinguished from the immediate organism in that it can leave the body and come back to it. This is the basis for the concept of the soul as a separate entity.

We find in children something that answers to this double, namely, the invisible, imaginary companions which a good many children produce in their own experience. They organize in this way the responses which they call out in other persons and call out also in themselves. Of course, this playing with an imaginary companion is only a peculiarly interesting phase of ordinary play. Play in this sense, especially the stage which precedes the organized games, is a play at something. A child plays at being a mother, at being a teacher, at being a policeman; that is, it is taking different rôles, as we say. We have something that suggests this in what we call the play of animals: a cat will play with her kittens, and dogs play with each other. Two dogs playing with each other will attack and defend, in a process which if carried through would amount to an actual fight. There is a combination of responses which checks the depth of the bite. But we do not have in such a situation the dogs taking a definite rôle in the sense that a child deliberately takes the rôle of another. This tendency on the part of the children is what we are working with in the kindergarten where the rôles which the children assume are made the basis for training. When a child does assume a rôle he has in himself the stimuli which call out that particular response or group of responses. He may, of course, run away when he is chased, as the dog does, or he may turn around and strike back just as the dog does in his play. But that is not the same as playing at something. Children get together to "play Indian." This means that the child has a certain set of stimuli which call out in itself the responses that they would call out in others, and which answer to an Indian. In the play period the child utilizes his own responses to these stimuli which he makes use of in building a self. The response which he has a tendency to make to these stimuli organizes them. He plays that he is, for instance, offering himself something, and he buys it; he gives a letter to himself and takes it away; he addresses himself as a parent, as a teacher; he arrests himself as a policeman. He has a set of stimuli which call out in himself the sort of responses they call out in others. He takes this group of responses and organizes them into a certain whole. Such is the simplest form of being another to one's self. It involves a temporal situation. The child says something in one character and responds in another character, and then his responding in another character is a stimulus to himself in the first character, and so the conversation goes on. A certain organized structure arises in him and in his other which replies to it, and these carry on the conversation of gestures between themselves.

If we contrast play with the situation in an organized game, we note the essential difference that the child who plays in a game must be ready to take the attitude of everyone else involved in that game, and that these different rôles must have a definite relationship to each other. Taking a very simple game such as hide-and-seek, everyone with the exception of the one who is hiding is a person who is hunting. A child does not require more than the person who is hunted and the one who is hunting. If a child is playing in the first sense he just goes on playing, but there is no basic organization gained. In that early stage he passes from one rôle to another just as a whim takes him. But in a game where a number of individuals are involved, then the child taking one rôle must be ready to take the rôle of everyone else. If he gets in a ball nine he must have the responses of each position involved in his own position. He must know what everyone else is going to do in order to carry out his own play. He has to take all of these rôles. They do not all have to be present in consciousness at the same time, but at some moments he has to have three or four individuals present in his own attitude, such as the one who is going to throw the ball, the one who is going to catch it, and so on. These responses must be, in some degree, present in his own make-up. In the game, then, there is a set of responses of such others so organized that the attitude of one calls out the appropriate attitudes of the other.

This organization is put in the form of the rules of the game. Children take a great interest in rules. They make rules on the spot in order to help themselves out of difficulties. Part of the enjoyment of the game is to get these rules. Now, the rules are the set of responses which a particular attitude calls out. You can demand a certain response in others if you take a certain attitude. These responses are all in yourself as well. There you get an organized set of such responses as that to which I have referred, which is something more elaborate than the rôles found in play. Here there is just a set of responses that follow on each other indefinitely. At such a stage we speak of a child as not yet having a fully developed self. The child responds in a fairly intelligent fashion to the immediate stimuli that come to him, but they are not organized. He does not organize his life as we would like to have him do, namely, as a whole. There is just a set of responses of the type of play. The child reacts to a certain stimulus, and the reaction is in himself that is called out in others, but he is not a whole self. In his game he has to have an organization of these rôles; otherwise he cannot play the game. The game represents the passage in the life of the child from taking the rôle of others in play to the organized part that is essential to self-consciousness in the full sense of the term.

20. PLAY, THE GAME, AND THE GENERALIZED OTHER

We were speaking of the social conditions under which the self arises as an object. In addition to language we found two illustrations, one in play and the other in the game, and I wish to summarize and expand my account on these points. I have spoken of these from the point of view of children. We can, of course, refer also to the attitudes of more primitive people out of which our civilization has arisen. A striking illustration of play as distinct from the game is found in the myths and various of the plays which primitive people carry out, especially in religious pageants. The pure play attitude which we find in the case of little children may not be found here, since the participants are adults, and undoubtedly the relationship of these play processes to that which they interpret is more or less in the minds of even the most primitive people. In the process of interpretation of such rituals, there is an organization of play which perhaps might be compared to that which is taking place in the kindergarten in dealing with the plays of little children, where these are made into a set that will have a definite structure or relationship. At least something of the same sort is found in the play of primitive people. This type of activity belongs, of course, not to the everyday life of the people in their dealing with the objects about them—there we have a more or less definitely developed self-consciousness—but in their attitudes toward the forces about them, the nature upon which they depend; in their attitude toward this nature which is vague and uncertain, there we have a much more primitive response; and that response finds its expression in taking the rôle of the other, playing at the expression of their gods and their heroes, going through certain rites which are the representation of what these individuals are supposed to be doing. The process is one which develops, to be sure, into a more or less definite technique and is controlled; and yet we can say that it has arisen out of situations similar to those in which little children play at being a parent, at being a teacher—vague personalities that are about them and which affect them and on which they depend. These are personalities which they take, rôles they play, and in so far control the development of their own personality. This outcome is just what the kindergarten works toward. It takes the characters of these various vague beings and gets them into such an organized social relationship to each other that they build up the character of the little child.[6] The very introduction of organization from outside supposes a lack of organization at this period in the child's experience. Over against such a situation of the little child and primitive people, we have the game as such.

The fundamental difference between the game and play is

[6] ["The Relation of Play to Education," *University of Chicago Record*, I (1896–97), 140 ff.]

that in the latter the child must have the attitude of all the others involved in that game. The attitudes of the other players which the participant assumes organize into a sort of unit, and it is that organization which controls the response of the individual. The illustration used was of a person playing baseball. Each one of his own acts is determined by his assumption of the action of the others who are playing the game. What he does is controlled by his being everyone else on that team, at least in so far as those attitudes affect his own particular response. We get then an "other" which is an organization of the attitudes of those involved in the same process.

The organized community or social group which gives to the individual his unity of self may be called "the generalized other." The attitude of the generalized other is the attitude of the whole community.[7] Thus, for example, in the case of such a social group as a ball team, the team is the generalized other in so far as it enters—as an organized process or social activity—into the experience of any one of the individual members of it.

If the given human individual is to develop a self in the fullest sense, it is not sufficient for him merely to take the attitudes of other human individuals toward himself and toward one another within the human social process, and to bring that social process as a whole into his individual experience merely in these terms: he must also, in the same way that he takes the attitudes of other individuals toward himself and toward one another,

[7] It is possible for inanimate objects, no less than for other human organisms, to form parts of the generalized and organized—the completely socialized—other for any given human individual, in so far as he responds to such objects socially or in a social fashion (by means of the mechanism of thought, the internalized conversation of gestures). Any thing—any object or set of objects, whether animate or inanimate, human or animal, or merely physical—toward which he acts, or to which he responds, socially, is an element in what for him is the generalized other; by taking the attitudes of which toward himself he becomes conscious of himself as an object or individual, and thus develops a self or personality. Thus, for example, the cult, in its primitive form, is merely the social embodiment of the relation between the given social group or community and its physical environment—an organized social means, adopted by the individual members of that group or community, of entering into social relations with that environment, or (in a sense) of carrying on conversations with it; and in this way that environment becomes part of the total generalized other for each of the individual members of the given social group or community.

take their attitudes toward the various phases or aspects of the common social activity or set of social undertakings in which, as members of an organized society or social group, they are all engaged; and he must then, by generalizing these individual attitudes of that organized society or social group itself, as a whole, act toward different social projects which at any given time it is carrying out, or toward the various larger phases of the general social process which constitutes its life and of which these projects are specific manifestations. This getting of the broad activities of any given social whole or organized society as such within the experiential field of any one of the individuals involved or included in that whole is, in other words, the essential basis and prerequisite of the fullest development of that individual's self: only in so far as he takes the attitudes of the organized social group to which he belongs toward the organized, co-operative social activity or set of such activities in which that group as such is engaged, does he develop a complete self or possess the sort of complete self he has developed. And on the other hand, the complex co-operative processes and activities and institutional functionings of organized human society are also possible only in so far as every individual involved in them or belonging to that society can take the general attitudes of all other such individuals with reference to these processes and activities and institutional functionings, and to the organized social whole of experiential relations and interactions thereby constituted—and can direct his own behavior accordingly.

It is in the form of the generalized other that the social process influences the behavior of the individuals involved in it and carrying it on, i.e., that the community exercises control over the conduct of its individual members; for it is in this form that the social process or community enters as a determining factor into the individual's thinking. In abstract thought the individual takes the attitude of the generalized other[8]

---

[8] We have said that the internal conversation of the individual with himself in terms of words or significant gestures—the conversation which constitutes the process or activity of thinking—is carried on by the individual from the standpoint of the "generalized other." And the more abstract that conversation is, the more abstract thinking happens

toward himself, without reference to its expression in any particular other individuals; and in concrete thought he takes that attitude in so far as it is expressed in the attitudes toward his behavior of those other individuals with whom he is involved in the given social situation or act. But only by taking the attitude of the generalized other toward himself, in one or another of these ways, can he think at all; for only thus can thinking—or the internalized conversation of gestures which constitutes thinking—occur. And only through the taking by individuals of the attitude or attitudes of the generalized other toward themselves is the existence of a universe of discourse, as that system of common or social meanings which thinking presupposes at its context, rendered possible.

The self-conscious human individual, then, takes or assumes the organized social attitudes of the given social group or community (or of some one section thereof) to which he belongs, toward the social problems of various kinds which confront that group or community at any given time, and which arise in connection with the correspondingly different social projects or organized co-operative enterprises in which that group or community as such is engaged; and as an individual participant in these social projects or co-operative enterprises, he governs his own conduct accordingly. In politics, for example, the individual identifies himself with an entire political party and takes the organized attitudes of that entire party toward the rest of the given social community and toward the problems which confront the party within the given social situation; and he consequently reacts or responds in terms of the organized attitudes of the party as a whole. He thus enters into a special set of

---

to be, the further removed is the generalized other from any connection with particular individuals. It is especially in abstract thinking, that is to say, that the conversation involved is carried on by the individual with the generalized other, rather than with any particular individuals. Thus it is, for example, that abstract concepts are concepts stated in terms of the attitudes of the entire social group or community; they are stated on the basis of the individual's consciousness of the attitudes of the generalized other toward them, as a result of his taking these attitudes of the generalized other and then responding to them. And thus it is also that abstract propositions are stated in a form which anyone—any other intelligent individual—will accept.

social relations with all the other individuals who belong to that political party; and in the same way he enters into various other special sets of social relations, with various other classes of individuals respectively, the individuals of each of these classes being the other members of some one of the particular organized subgroups (determined in socially functional terms) of which he himself is a member within the entire given society or social community. In the most highly developed, organized, and complicated human social communities—those evolved by civilized man—these various socially functional classes or subgroups of individuals to which any given individual belongs (and with the other individual members of which he thus enters into a special set of social relations) are of two kinds. Some of them are concrete social classes or subgroups, such as political parties, clubs, corporations, which are all actually functional social units, in terms of which their individual members are directly related to one another. The others are abstract social classes or subgroups, such as the class of debtors and the class of creditors, in terms of which their individual members are related to one another only more or less indirectly, and which only more or less indirectly function as social units, but which afford or represent unlimited possibilities for the widening and ramifying and enriching of the social relations among all the individual members of the given society as an organized and unified whole. The given individual's membership in several of these abstract social classes or subgroups makes possible his entrance into definite social relations (however indirect) with an almost infinite number of other individuals who also belong to or are included within one or another of these abstract social classes or subgroups cutting across functional lines of demarcation which divide different human social communities from one another, and including individual members from several (in some cases from all) such communities. Of these abstract social classes or subgroups of human individuals the one which is most inclusive and extensive is, of course, the one defined by the logical universe of discourse (or system of universally signifi-

cant symbols) determined by the participation and communicative interaction of individuals; for of all such classes or subgroups, it is the one which claims the largest number of individual members, and which enables the largest conceivable
number of human individuals to enter into some sort of social
relation, however indirect or abstract it may be, with one another—a relation arising from the universal functioning of gestures as significant symbols in the general human social process
of communication.

I have pointed out, then, that there are two general stages in
the full development of the self. At the first of these stages, the
individual's self is constituted simply by an organization of the
particular attitudes of other individuals toward himself and
toward one another in the specific social acts in which he participates with them. But at the second stage in the full development of the individual's self that self is constituted not only by
an organization of these particular individual attitudes, but also
by an organization of the social attitudes of the generalized
other or the social group as a whole to which he belongs. These
social or group attitudes are brought within the individual's
field of direct experience, and are included as elements in the
structure or constitution of his self, in the same way that the
attitudes of particular other individuals are; and the individual
arrives at them, or succeeds in taking them, by means of further organizing, and then generalizing, the attitudes of particular other individuals in terms of their organized social bearings
and implications. So the self reaches its full development by
organizing these individual attitudes of others into the organized social or group attitudes, and by thus becoming an individual reflection of the general systematic pattern of social or
group behavior in which it and the others are all involved—a
pattern which enters as a whole into the individual's experience
in terms of these organized group attitudes which, through the
mechanism of his central nervous system, he takes toward himself, just as he takes the individual attitudes of others.

The game has a logic, so that such an organization of the self is rendered possible: there is a definite end to be obtained; the actions of the different individuals are all related to each other with reference to that end so that they do not conflict; one is not in conflict with himself in the attitude of another man on the team. If one has the attitude of the person throwing the ball he can also have the response of catching the ball. The two are related so that they further the purpose of the game itself. They are interrelated in a unitary, organic fashion. There is a definite unity, then, which is introduced into the organization of other selves when we reach such a stage as that of the game, as over against the situation of play where there is a simple succession of one rôle after another, a situation which is, of course, characteristic of the child's own personality. The child is one thing at one time and another at another, and what he is at one moment does not determine what he is at another. That is both the charm of childhood as well as its inadequacy. You cannot count on the child; you cannot assume that all the things he does are going to determine what he will do at any moment. He is not organized into a whole. The child has no definite character, no definite personality.

The game is then an illustration of the situation out of which an organized personality arises. In so far as the child does take the attitude of the other and allows that attitude of the other to determine the thing he is going to do with reference to a common end, he is becoming an organic member of society. He is taking over the morale of that society and is becoming an essential member of it. He belongs to it in so far as he does allow the attitude of the other that he takes to control his own immediate expression. What is involved here is some sort of an organized process. That which is expressed in terms of the game is, of course, being continually expressed in the social life of the child, but this wider process goes beyond the immediate experience of the child himself. The importance of the game is that it lies entirely inside of the child's own experience, and the importance of our modern type of education is that it is brought as far as possible within this realm. The different attitudes that a child assumes are so organized that they exercise a definite control over his response, as the attitudes in a game control his own immediate response. In the game we get an organized other, a generalized other, which is found in the nature of the child itself, and finds its expression in the immediate experience of the child. And it is that organized activity in the child's own nature controlling the particular response which gives unity, and which builds up his own self.

What goes on in the game goes on in the life of the child all the time. He is continually taking the attitudes of those about him, especially the rôles of those who in some sense control him and on whom he depends. He gets the function of the process in an abstract sort of a way at first. It goes over from the play into the game in a real sense. He has to play the game. The morale of the game takes hold of the child more than the larger morale of the whole community. The child passes into the game and the game expresses a social situation in which he can completely enter; its morale may have a greater hold on him than that of the family to which he belongs or the community in which he lives. There are all sorts of social organizations, some of which are fairly lasting, some temporary, into which the child is entering, and he is playing a sort of social game in them. It is a period in which he likes "to belong," and he gets into organizations which come into existence and pass out of existence. He becomes a something which can function in the organized whole, and thus tends to determine himself in his relationship with the group to which he belongs. That process is one which is a striking stage in the development of the child's morale. It constitutes him a self-conscious member of the community to which he belongs.

Such is the process by which a personality arises. I have spoken of this as a process in which a child takes the rôle of the other, and said that it takes place essentially through the use of language. Language is predominantly based on the vocal gesture by means of which co-operative activities in a community are carried out. Language in its significant sense is that vocal gesture which tends to arouse in the individual the attitude which it arouses in others, and it is this perfecting of the self by the gesture which mediates the social activities that gives rise to the process of taking the rôle of the other. The latter phrase is a little unfortunate because it suggests an actor's attitude which is actually more sophisticated than that which is involved in our own experience. To this degree it does not correctly describe that which I have in mind. We see the process most definitely in a primitive form in those situations where the child's play takes different rôles. Here the very fact that he is ready to pay out money, for instance, arouses the attitude of the person who receives money; the very process is calling out in him the corresponding activities of the other person involved. The individual stimulates himself to the response which he is calling out in the other person, and then acts in some degree in response to that situation. In play the child does definitely act out the rôle which he himself has aroused in himself. It is that which gives, as I have said, a definite content in the individual which answers to the stimulus that affects him as it affects somebody else. The content of the other that enters into one personality is the response in the individual which his gesture calls out in the other.

We may illustrate our basic concept by a reference to the notion of property. If we say "This is my property, I shall control it," that affirmation calls out a certain set of responses which must be the same in any community in which property exists. It involves an organized attitude with reference to property which is common to all the members of the community. One must have a definite attitude of control of his own property and respect for the property of others. Those attitudes (as organized sets of responses) must be there on the part of all, so that when one says such a thing he calls out in himself the response of the others. He is calling out the response of what I have called a generalized other. That which makes society possible is such common responses, such organized attitudes, with reference to what we term property, the cults of religion, the process of education, and the relations of the family. Of course, the wider the society the more definitely universal these objects must be. In any case there must be a definite set of responses, which we may speak of as abstract, and which can belong to a very large group. Property is in itself a very abstract concept. It is that which the individual himself can control and nobody else can control. The attitude is different from that of a dog toward a bone. A dog will fight any other dog trying to take the bone. The dog is not taking the attitude of the other dog. A man who says "This is my property" is taking an attitude of the other person. The man is appealing to his rights because he is able to take the attitude which everybody else in the group has with reference to property, thus arousing in himself the attitude of others.

What goes to make up the organized self is the organization of the attitudes which are common to the group. A person is a personality because he belongs to a community, because he takes over the institutions of that community into his own conduct. He takes its language as a medium by which he gets his personality, and then through a process of taking the different rôles that all the others furnish he comes to get the attitude of the members of the community. Such, in a certain sense, is the structure of a man's personality. There are certain common responses which each individual has toward certain common things, and in so far as those common responses are awakened in the individual when he is affecting other persons he arouses his own self. The structure, then, on which the self is built is this response which is common to all, for one has to be a member of a community to be a self. Such responses are abstract attitudes, but they constitute just what we term a man's character. They give him what we term his principles, the acknowledged attitudes of all members of the community toward what are the values of that community. He is putting himself in the place of the generalized other, which represents the organized responses of all the members of the group. It is that which guides conduct controlled by principles, and a person who has such an organized group of responses is a man whom we say has character, in the moral sense.

It is a structure of attitudes, then, which goes to make up a self, as distinct from a group of habits. We all of us have, for example, certain groups of habits, such as the particular intonations which a person uses in his speech. This is a set of habits of vocal expression which one has but which one does not know about. The sets of habits which we have of that sort mean nothing to us; we do not hear the intonations of our speech that others hear unless we are paying particular attention to them. The habits of emotional expression which belong to our speech are of the same sort. We may know that we have expressed ourselves in a joyous fashion but the detailed process is one which does not come back to our conscious selves. There are whole bundles of such habits which do not enter into a conscious self, but which help to make up what is termed the unconscious self.

After all, what we mean by self-consciousness is an awakening in ourselves of the group of attitudes which we are arousing in others, especially when it is an important set of responses which go to make up the members of the community. It is unfortunate to fuse or mix up consciousness, as we ordinarily use that term, and self-consciousness. Consciousness, as frequently used, simply has reference to the field of experience, but self-consciousness refers to the ability to call out in ourselves a set of definite responses which belong to the others of the group. Consciousness and self-consciousness are not on the same level. A man alone has, fortunately or unfortunately, access to his own toothache, but that is not what we mean by self-consciousness.

I have so far emphasized what I have called the structures upon which the self is constructed, the framework of the self, as it were. Of course we are not only what is common to all: each one of the selves is different from everyone else; but there has to be such a common structure as I have sketched in order that we may be members of a community at all. We cannot be ourselves unless we are also members in whom there is a community of attitudes which control the attitudes of all. We cannot have rights unless we have common attitudes. That which we have acquired as self-conscious persons makes us such members of society and gives us selves. Selves can only exist in definite relationships to other selves. No hard-and-fast line can be drawn between our own selves and the selves of others, since our own selves exist and enter as such into our experience only in so far as the selves of others exist and enter as such into our experience also. The individual possesses a self only in relation to the selves of the other members of his social group; and the structure of his self expresses or reflects the general behavior pattern of this social group to which he belongs, just as does the structure of the self of every other individual belonging to this social group.

21. THE SELF AND THE SUBJECTIVE

The process out of which the self arises is a social process which implies interaction of individuals in the group, implies the pre-existence of the group.[9] It implies also certain co-operative activities in which the different members of the group are involved. It implies, further, that out of this process there may in turn develop a more elaborate organization than that out of which the self has arisen, and that the selves may be the organs, the essential parts at least, of this more elaborate social organization within which these selves arise and exist. Thus, there is a social process out of which selves arise and within which further differentiation, further evolution, further organization, take place.

It has been the tendency of psychology to deal with the self as a more or less isolated and independent element, a sort of entity that could conceivably exist by itself. It is possible that there might be a single self in the universe if we start off by identifying the self with a certain feeling-consciousness. If we

[9] The relation of individual organisms to the social whole of which they are members is analogous to the relation of the individual cells of a multi-cellular organism to the organism as a whole.

speak of this feeling as objective, then we can think of that self as existing by itself. We can think of a separate physical body existing by itself, we can assume that it has these feelings or conscious states in question, and so we can set up that sort of a self in thought as existing simply by itself.

Then there is another use of "consciousness" with which we have been particularly occupied, denoting that which we term thinking or reflective intelligence, a use of consciousness which always has, implicitly at least, the reference to an "I" in it. This use of consciousness has no necessary connection with the other; it is an entirely different conception. One usage has to do with a certain mechanism, a certain way in which an organism acts. If an organism is endowed with sense organs then there are objects in its environment, and among those objects will be parts of its own body.[10] It is true that if the organism did not have a retina and a central nervous system there would not be any objects of vision. For such objects to exist there have to be certain physiological conditions, but these objects are not in themselves necessarily related to a self. When we reach a self we reach a certain sort of conduct, a certain type of social process which involves the interaction of different individuals and yet implies individuals engaged in some sort of co-operative activity. In that process a self, as such, can arise.

We want to distinguish the self as a certain sort of structural process in the conduct of the form, from what we term consciousness of objects that are experienced. The two have no necessary relationship. The aching tooth is a very important

[10] Our constructive selection of our environment is what we term "consciousness," in the first sense of the term. The organism does not project sensuous qualities—colors, for example—into the environment to which it responds; but it endows this environment with such qualities, in a sense similar to that in which an ox endows grass with the quality of being food, or in which—speaking more generally—the relation between biological organisms and certain environmental contents give rise to food objects. If there were no organisms with particular sense organs there would be no environment, in the proper or usual sense of the term. An organism constructs (in the selective sense) its environment; and consciousness often refers to the character of the environment in so far as it is determined or constructively selected by our human organisms, and depends upon the relationship between the former (as thus selected or constructed) and the latter.

element. We have to pay attention to it. It is identified in a certain sense with the self in order that we may control that sort of experience. Occasionally we have experiences which we say belong to the atmosphere. The whole world seems to be depressed, the sky is dark, the weather is unpleasant, values that we are interested in are sinking. We do not necessarily identify such a situation with the self; we simply feel a certain atmosphere about us. We come to remember that we are subject to such sorts of depression, and find that kind of an experience in our past. And then we get some sort of relief, we take aspirin, or we take a rest, and the result is that the world changes its character. There are other experiences which we may at all times identify with selves. We can distinguish, I think, very clearly between certain types of experience, which we call subjective because we alone have access to them, and that experience which we call reflective.

It is true that reflection taken by itself is something to which we alone have access. One thinks out his own demonstration of a proposition, we will say in Euclid, and the thinking is something that takes place within his own conduct. For the time being it is a demonstration which exists only in his thought. Then he publishes it and it becomes common property. For the time being it was accessible only to him. There are other contents of this sort, such as memory images and the play of the imagination, which are accessible only to the individual. There is a common character that belongs to these types of objects which we generally identify with consciousness and this process which we call that of thinking, in that both are, at least in certain phases, accessible only to the individual. But, as I have said, the two sets of phenomena stand on entirely different levels. This common feature of accessibility does not necessarily give them the same metaphysical status. I do not now want to discuss metaphysical problems, but I do want to insist that the self has a sort of structure that arises in social conduct that is entirely distinguishable from this so-called subjective experience of these particular sets of objects to which the organism alone has access—the common character of privacy of access does not fuse them together.

The self to which we have been referring arises when the conversation of gestures is taken over into the conduct of the individual form. When this conversation of gestures can be taken over into the individual's conduct so that the attitude of the other forms can affect the organism, and the organism can reply with its corresponding gesture and thus arouse the attitude of the other in its own process, then a self arises. Even the bare conversation of gestures that can be carried out in lower forms is to be explained by the fact that this conversation of gestures has an intelligent function. Even there it is a part of social process. If it is taken over into the conduct of the individual it not only maintains that function but acquires still greater capacity. If I can take the attitude of a friend with whom I am going to carry on a discussion, in taking that attitude I can apply it to myself and reply as he replies, and I can have things in very much better shape than if I had not employed that conversation of gestures in my own conduct. The same is true of him. It is good for both to think out the situation in advance. Each individual has to take also the attitude of the community, the generalized attitude. He has to be ready to act with reference to his own conditions just as any individual in the community would act.

One of the greatest advances in the development of the community arises when this reaction of the community on the individual takes on what we call an institutional form. What we mean by that is that the whole community acts toward the individual under certain circumstances in an identical way. It makes no difference, over against a person who is stealing your property, whether it is Tom, Dick, or Harry. There is an identical response on the part of the whole community under these conditions. We call that the formation of the institution.

There is one other matter which I wish briefly to refer to now. The only way in which we can react against the disapproval of the entire community is by setting up a higher sort of community which in a certain sense out-votes the one we find. A person may reach a point of going against the whole world about him; he may stand out by himself over against it. But to do that he has to speak with the voice of reason to himself. He has to comprehend the voices of the past and of the future. That is the only way in which the self can get a voice which is more than the voice of the community. As a rule we assume that this general voice of the community is identical with the larger community of the past and the future; we assume that an organized custom represents what we call morality. The things one cannot do are those which everybody would condemn. If we take the attitude of the community over against our own responses, that is a true statement, but we must not forget this other capacity, that of replying to the community and insisting on the gesture· of the community changing. We can reform the order of things; we can insist on making the community standards better standards. We are not simply bound by the community. We are engaged in a conversation in which what we say is listened to by the community and its response is one which is affected by what we have to say. This is especially true in critical situations. A man rises up and defends himself for what he does; he has his "day in court"; he can present his views. He can perhaps change the attitude of the community toward himself. The process of conversation is one in which the individual has not only the right but the duty of talking to the community of which he is a part, and bringing about those changes which take place through the interaction of individuals. That is the way, of course, in which society gets ahead, by just such interactions as those in which some person thinks a thing out. We are continually changing our social system in some respects, and we are able to do that intelligently because we can think.

Such is the reflective process within which a self arises; and what I have been trying to do is to distinguish this kind of consciousness from consciousness as a set of characters determined by the accessibility to the organism of certain sorts of objects. It is true that our thinking is also, while it is just thinking, accessible only to the organism. But that common character of being accessible only to the organism does not make either thought or the self something which we are to identify with a group of objects which simply are accessible. We cannot identify the self with what is commonly called consciousness, that is, with the private or subjective thereness of the characters of objects.

There is, of course, a current distinction between consciousness and self-consciousness: consciousness answering to certain experiences such as those of pain or pleasure, self-consciousness referring to a recognition or appearance of a self as an object. It is, however, very generally assumed that these other conscious contents carry with them also a self-consciousness—that a pain is always somebody's pain, and that if there were not this reference to some individual it would not be pain. There is a very definite element of truth in this, but it is far from the whole story. The pain does have to belong to an individual; it has to be your pain if it is going to belong to you. Pain can belong to anybody, but if it did belong to everybody it would be comparatively unimportant. I suppose it is conceivable that under an anesthetic what takes place is the dissociation of experiences so that the suffering, so to speak, is no longer your suffering. We have illustrations of that, short of the anesthetic dissociation, in an experience of a disagreeable thing which loses its power over us because we give our attention to something else. If we can get, so to speak, outside of the thing, dissociating it from the eye that is regarding it, we may find that it has lost a great deal of its unendurable character. The unendurableness of pain is a reaction against it. If you can actually keep yourself from reacting against suffering you get rid of a certain content in the suffering itself. What takes place in effect is that it ceases to be your pain. You simply regard it objectively. Such is the point of view we are continually impressing on a person when he is apt to be swept away by emotion. In that case what we get rid of is not the offense itself, but the reaction against the offense. The objective character of the judge is that of a person who is neutral, who can simply stand outside of a situation and assess it. If we can get that judicial attitude in regard to the offenses of a person against ourselves, we reach the point where we do not resent them but understand them, we get the situation where to understand is to forgive. We remove much of experience outside of our own self by this attitude. The distinctive and natural attitude against another is a resentment of an offense, but we now have in a certain sense passed beyond that self and become a self with other attitudes. There is a certain technique, then, to which we subject ourselves in enduring suffering or any emotional situation, and which consists in partially separating one's self from the experience so that it is no longer the experience of the individual in question.

If, now, we could separate the experience entirely, so that we should not remember it, so that we should not have to take it up continually into the self from day to day, from moment to moment, then it would not exist any longer so far as we are concerned. If we had no memory which identifies experiences with the self, then they would certainly disappear so far as their relation to the self is concerned, and yet they might continue as sensuous or sensible experiences without being taken up into a self. That sort of a situation is presented in the pathological case of a multiple personality in which an individual loses the memory of a certain phase of his existence. Everything connected with that phase of his existence is gone and he becomes a different personality. The past has a reality whether in the experience or not, but here it is not identified with the self—it does not go to make up the self. We take an attitude of that sort, for example, with reference to others when a person has committed some sort of an offense which leads to a statement of the situation, an admission, and perhaps regret, and then is dropped. A person who forgives but does not forget is an unpleasant companion; what goes with forgiving is forgetting, getting rid of the memory of it.

There are many illustrations which can be brought up of the loose relationship of given contents to a self in defense of our recognition of them as having a certain value outside of the self. At the least, it must be granted that we can approach the point where something which we recognize as a content is less and less essential to the self, is held off from the present self, and no longer has the value for that self which it had for the former self. Extreme cases seem to support the view that a certain portion of such contents can be entirely cut off from the self. While in some sense it is there ready to appear under specific conditions, for the time being it is dissociated and does not get in above the threshold of our self-consciousness.

Self-consciousness, on the other hand, is definitely organized about the social individual, and that, as we have seen, is not simply because one is in a social group and affected by others and affects them, but because (and this is a point I have been emphasizing) his own experience as a self is one which he takes over from his action upon others. He becomes a self in so far as he can take the attitude of another and act toward himself as others act. In so far as the conversation of gestures can become part of conduct in the direction and control of experience, then a self can arise. It is the social process of influencing others in a social act and then taking the attitude of the others aroused by the stimulus, and then reacting in turn to this response, which constitutes a self.

Our bodies are parts of our environment; and it is possible for the individual to experience and be conscious of his body, and of bodily sensations, without being conscious or aware of himself—without, in other words, taking the attitude of the other toward himself. According to the social theory of consciousness, what we mean by consciousness is that peculiar character and aspect of the environment of individual human experience which is due to human society, a society of other individual selves who take the attitude of the other toward themselves. The physiological conception or theory of consciousness is by itself inadequate; it requires supplementation from the socio-psychological point of view. The taking or feeling of the attitude of the other toward yourself is what constitutes self-consciousness, and not mere organic sensations of which the individual is aware and which he experiences. Until the rise of his self-consciousness in the process of social experience, the individual experiences his body—its feelings and sensations—merely as an immediate part of his environment, not as his own, not in terms of self-consciousness. The self and self-consciousness have first to arise, and then these experiences can be identified peculiarly with the self, or appropriated by the self; to enter, so to speak, into this heritage of experience, the self has first to develop within the social process in which this heritage is involved.

Through self-consciousness the individual organism enters in some sense into its own environmental field; its own body becomes a part of the set of environmental stimuli to which it responds or reacts. Apart from the context of the social process at its higher levels—those at which it involves conscious communication, conscious conversations of gestures, among the individual organisms interacting with it—the individual organism does not set itself as a whole over against its environment; it does not as a whole become an object to itself (and hence is not self-conscious); it is not as a whole a stimulus to which it reacts. On the contrary, it responds only to parts or separate aspects of itself, and regards them, not as parts or aspects of itself at all, but simply as parts or aspects of its environment in general. Only within the social process at its higher levels, only in terms of the more developed forms of the social environment or social situation, does the total individual organism become an object to itself, and hence self-conscious; in the social process at its lower, non-conscious levels, and also in the merely psychophysiological environment or situation which is logically antecedent to and presupposed by the social process of experience and behavior, it does not thus become an object to itself. In such experience or behavior as may be called self-conscious, we act and react particularly with reference to ourselves, though also with reference to other individuals; and to be self-conscious is essentially to become an object to one's self in virtue of one's social relations to other individuals.

Emphasis should be laid on the central position of thinking when considering the nature of the self. Self-consciousness, rather than affective experience with its motor accompaniments, provides the core and primary structure of the self, which is thus essentially a cognitive rather than an emotional phenomenon. The thinking or intellectual process—the internalization and inner dramatization, by the individual, of the external conversation of significant gestures which constitutes his chief mode of interaction with other individuals belonging to the same society —is the earliest experiential phase in the genesis and development of the self. Cooley and James, it is true, endeavor to find the basis of the self in reflexive affective experiences, i.e., experiences involving "self-feeling"; but the theory that the nature of the self is to be found in such experiences does not account for the origin of the self, or of the self-feeling which is supposed to characterize such experiences. The individual need not take the attitudes of others toward himself in these experiences, since these experiences merely in themselves do not necessitate his doing so, and unless he does so, he cannot develop a self; and he will not do so in these experiences unless his self has already originated otherwise, namely, in the way we have been describing. The essence of the self, as we have said, is cognitive: it lies in the internalized conversation of gestures which constitutes thinking, or in terms of which thought or reflection proceeds. And hence the origin and foundations of the self, like those of thinking, are social.

22. THE "I" AND THE "ME"

We have discussed at length the social foundations of the self, and hinted that the self does not consist simply in the bare organization of social attitudes. We may now explicitly raise the question as to the nature of the "I" which is aware of the social "me." I do not mean to raise the metaphysical question of how a person can be both "I" and "me," but to ask for the significance of this distinction from the point of view of conduct itself. Where in conduct does the "I" come in as over against

[173]

the "me"? If one determines what his position is in society and feels himself as having a certain function and privilege, these are all defined with reference to an "I," but the "I" is not a "me" and cannot become a "me." We may have a better self and a worse self, but that again is not the "I" as over against the "me," because they are both selves. We approve of one and disapprove of the other, but when we bring up one or the other they are there for such approval as "me's." The "I" does not get into the limelight; we talk to ourselves, but do not see ourselves. The "I" reacts to the self which arises through the taking of the attitudes of others. Through taking those attitudes we have introduced the "me" and we react to it as an "I."

The simplest way of handling the problem would be in terms of memory. I talk to myself, and I remember what I said and perhaps the emotional content that went with it. The "I" of this moment is present in the "me" of the next moment. There again I cannot turn around quick enough to catch myself. I become a "me" in so far as I remember what I said. The "I" can be given, however, this functional relationship. It is because of the "I" that we say that we are never fully aware of what we are, that we surprise ourselves by our own action. It is as we act that we are aware of ourselves. It is in memory that the "I" is constantly present in experience. We can go back directly a few moments in our experience, and then we are dependent upon memory images for the rest. So that the "I" in memory is there as the spokesman of the self of the second, or minute, or day ago. As given, it is a "me," but it is a "me" which was the "I" at the earlier time. If you ask, then, where directly in your own experience the "I" comes in, the answer is that it comes in as a historical figure. It is what you were a second ago that is the "I" of the "me." It is another "me" that has to take that rôle. You cannot get the immediate response of the "I" in the process.[11] The "I" is in a certain sense that with which we do

[11] The sensitivity of the organism brings parts of itself into the environment. It does not, however, bring the life-process itself into the environment, and the complete imaginative presentation of the organism is unable to present the living of the organ-

identify ourselves. The getting of it into experience constitutes one of the problems of most of our conscious experience; it is not directly given in experience.

The "I" is the response of the organism to the attitudes of the others;[12] the "me" is the organized set of attitudes of others which one himself assumes. The attitudes of the others constitute the organized "me," and then one reacts toward that as an "I." I now wish to examine these concepts in greater detail.

There is neither "I" nor "me" in the conversation of gestures; the whole act is not yet carried out, but the preparation takes place in this field of gesture. Now, in so far as the individual arouses in himself the attitudes of the others, there arises an organized group of responses. And it is due to the individual's ability to take the attitudes of these others in so far as they can be organized that he gets self-consciousness. The taking of all of those organized sets of attitudes gives him his "me"; that is the self he is aware of. He can throw the ball to some other member because of the demand made upon him from other members of the team. That is the self that immediately exists for him in his consciousness. He has their attitudes, knows what they want and what the consequence of any act of his will be, and he has assumed responsibility for the situation. Now, it is the presence of those organized sets of attitudes that constitutes that "me" to which he as an "I" is responding. But what that response will be he does not know and nobody else knows. Perhaps he will make a brilliant play or an error. The response to that situation as it appears in his immediate experience is uncertain, and it is that which constitutes the "I."

The "I" is his action over against that social situation within his own conduct, and it gets into his experience only after he has carried out the act. Then he is aware of it. He had to do such a thing and he did it. He fulfils his duty and he may look with

---

ism. It can conceivably present the conditions under which living takes place but not the unitary life-process. The physical organism in the environment always remains a thing (MS).

[12] [For the "I" viewed as the biologic individual, see Supplementary Essays II, III.]

pride at the throw which he made. The "me" arises to do that duty—that is the way in which it arises in his experience. He had in him all the attitudes of others, calling for a certain response; that was the "me" of that situation, and his response is the "I."

I want to call attention particularly to the fact that this response of the "I" is something that is more or less uncertain. The attitudes of others which one assumes as affecting his own conduct constitute the "me," and that is something that is there, but the response to it is as yet not given. When one sits down to think anything out, he has certain data that are there. Suppose that it is a social situation which he has to straighten out. He sees himself from the point of view of one individual or another in the group. These individuals, related all together, give him a certain self. Well, what is he going to do? He does not know and nobody else knows. He can get the situation into his experience because he can assume the attitudes of the various individuals involved in it. He knows how they feel about it by the assumption of their attitudes. He says, in effect, "I have done certain things that seem to commit me to a certain course of conduct." Perhaps if he does so act it will place him in a false position with another group. The "I" as a response to this situation, in contrast to the "me" which is involved in the attitudes which he takes, is uncertain. And when the response takes place, then it appears in the field of experience largely as a memory image.

Our specious present as such is very short. We do, however, experience passing events; part of the process of the passage of events is directly there in our experience, including some of the past and some of the future. We see a ball falling as it passes, and as it does pass part of the ball is covered and part is being uncovered. We remember where the ball was a moment ago and we anticipate where it will be beyond what is given in our experience. So of ourselves; we are doing something, but to look back and see what we are doing involves getting memory images. So the "I" really appears experientially as a part of a "me." But on the basis of this experience we distinguish that individual who is doing something from the "me" who puts the problem up to him. The response enters into his experience only when it takes place. If he says he knows what he is going to do, even there he may be mistaken. He starts out to do something and something happens to interfere. The resulting action is always a little different from anything which he could anticipate. This is true even if he is simply carrying out the process of walking. The very taking of his expected steps puts him in a certain situation which has a slightly different aspect from what is expected, which is in a certain sense novel. That movement into the future is the step, so to speak, of the ego, of the "I." It is something that is not given in the "me."

Take the situation of a scientist solving a problem, where he has certain data which call for certain responses. Some of this set of data call for his applying such and such a law, while others call for another law. Data are there with their implications. He knows what such and such coloration means, and when he has these data before him they stand for certain responses on his part; but now they are in conflict with each other. If he makes one response he cannot make another. What he is going to do he does not know, nor does anybody else. The action of the self is in response to these conflicting sets of data in the form of a problem, with conflicting demands upon him as a scientist. He has to look at it in different ways. That action of the "I" is something the nature of which we cannot tell in advance.

The "I," then, in this relation of the "I" and the "me," is something that is, so to speak, responding to a social situation which is within the experience of the individual. It is the answer which the individual makes to the attitude which others take toward him when he assumes an attitude toward them. Now, the attitudes he is taking toward them are present in his own experience, but his response to them will contain a novel element. The "I" gives the sense of freedom, of initiative. The situation is there for us to act in a self-conscious fashion. We are aware of ourselves, and of what the situation is, but exactly how we will act never gets into experience until after the action takes place.

Such is the basis for the fact that the "I" does not appear in the same sense in experience as does the "me." The "me" represents a definite organization of the community there in our own attitudes, and calling for a response, but the response that takes place is something that just happens. There is no certainty in regard to it. There is a moral necessity but no mechanical necessity for the act. When it does take place then we find what has been done. The above account gives us, I think, the relative position of the "I" and "me" in the situation, and the grounds for the separation of the two in behavior. The two are separated in the process but they belong together in the sense of being parts of a whole. They are separated and yet they belong together. The separation of the "I" and the "me" is not fictitious. They are not identical, for, as I have said, the "I" is something that is never entirely calculable. The "me" does call for a certain sort of an "I" in so far as we meet the obligations that are given in conduct itself, but the "I" is always something different from what the situation itself calls for. So there is always that distinction, if you like, between the "I" and the "me." The "I" both calls out the "me" and responds to it. Taken together they constitute a personality as it appears in social experience. The self is essentially a social process going on with these two distinguishable phases. If it did not have these two phases there could not be conscious responsibility, and there would be nothing novel in experience.

23. SOCIAL ATTITUDES AND THE PHYSICAL WORLD

The self is not so much a substance as a process in which the conversation of gestures has been internalized within an organic form. This process does not exist for itself, but is simply a phase of the whole social organization of which the individual is a part. The organization of the social act has been imported into the organism and becomes then the mind of the individual. It still includes the attitudes of others, but now highly organized, so that they become what we call social attitudes rather than rôles of separate individuals. This process of relating one's own organism to the others in the interactions that are going on, in so far as it is imported into the conduct of the individual with the conversation of the "I" and the "me," constitutes the self.[13] The value of this importation of the conversation of gestures into the conduct of the individual lies in the superior co-ordination gained for society as a whole, and in the increased efficiency of the individual as a member of the group. It is the difference between the process which can take place in a group of rats or ants or bees, and that which can take place in a human community. The social process with its various implications is actually taken up into the experience of the individual so that that which is going on takes place more effectively, because in a certain sense it has been rehearsed in the individual. He not only plays his part better under those conditions but he also reacts back on the organization of which he is a part.

The very nature of this conversation of gestures requires that the attitude of the other is changed through the attitude of the individual to the other's stimulus. In the conversation of gestures of the lower forms the play back and forth is noticeable, since the individual not only adjusts himself to the attitude of others, but also changes the attitudes of the others. The reaction of the individual in this conversation of gestures is one that in some degree is continually modifying the social process itself. It is this modification of the process which is of greatest interest in the experience of the individual. He takes the attitude of the other toward his own stimulus, and in taking that he finds it modified in that his response becomes a different one, and leads in turn to further change.

Fundamental attitudes are presumably those that are only changed gradually, and no one individual can reorganize the

[13] According to this view, conscious communication develops out of unconscious communication within the social process; conversation in terms of significant gestures out of conversation in terms of non-significant gestures; and the development in such fashion of conscious communication is coincident with the development of minds and selves within the social process.

whole society; but one is continually affecting society by his own attitude because he does bring up the attitude of the group toward himself, responds to it, and through that response changes the attitude of the group. This is, of course, what we are constantly doing in our imagination, in our thought; we are utilizing our own attitude to bring about a different situation in the community of which we are a part; we are exerting ourselves, bringing forward our own opinion, criticizing the attitudes of others, and approving or disapproving. But we can do that only in so far as we can call out in ourselves the response of the community; we only have ideas in so far as we are able to take the attitude of the community and then respond to it.

In the case of lower animals the response of the individual to the social situation, its gesture as over against the social situation, is what answers to the idea in the human animal. It is not, however, an idea. We use the vocal gesture to call out the response which answers to that of the community. We have, then, in our own stimulus, a reply to that response, and it is that reply which is an idea. You say that "it is my idea that such and such a thing should be done." Your idea is the reply which you make to the social demand made upon you. The social demand, we will say, is that you should pay taxes of a certain sort. You consider those taxes illegitimate. Now, your reply to the demand of the community, specifically to the tax assessor, as it takes place in your own experience, is an idea. To the extent that you have in your own conduct symbols which are the expression of your reply to the demand, you have an idea of what your assessment ought to be. It is an ideal situation in so far as you are taking the rôle of the tax assessor over against yourself, and replying to it. It is not like the situation in the dog-fight where the dog is actually preparing to spring and another dog takes another attitude which defeats that spring. The difference is that the conversation of gestures is a part of the actual realized fight, whereas in the other case you are taking the attitude of the tax authorities in advance and working or calling out your own response to it. When that takes place in your experience you have ideas.

A person threatens you, and you knock him down on the spot. There has been no ideal element in the situation. If you count ten and consider what the threat means, you are having an idea, are bringing the situation into an ideal setting. It is that, we have seen, which constitutes what we term mind. We are taking the attitude of the community and we are responding to it in this conversation of gestures. The gestures in this case are vocal gestures. They are significant symbols, and by symbol we do not mean something that lies outside of the field of conduct. A symbol is nothing but the stimulus whose response is given in advance. That is all we mean by a symbol. There is a word, and a blow. The blow is the historical antecedent of the word, but if the word means an insult, the response is one now involved in the word, something given in the very stimulus itself. That is all that is meant by a symbol. Now, if that response can be given in terms of an attitude utilized for the further control of action, then the relation of that stimulus and attitude is what we mean by a significant symbol.

Our thinking that goes on, as we say, inside of us, is a play of symbols in the above sense. Through gestures responses are called out in our own attitudes, and as soon as they are called out they evoke, in turn, other attitudes. What was the meaning now becomes a symbol which has another meaning. The meaning has itself become a stimulus to another response. In the dog-fight the attitude of the one has the meaning of changing the attitude of the other dog, but the change of attitude now becomes a symbol (though not a language or significant symbol) to the first dog and he, too, changes his attitude. What was a meaning now becomes a stimulus. Conversation is continually going on, and what was response becomes in the field of gesture a stimulus, and the response to that is the meaning. Responses are meanings in so far as they lie inside of such a conversation of gestures. Our thinking is just such a continual change of a situation by our capacity to take it over into our own action; to change it so that it calls for a different attitude on our own part, and to carry it on to the point where the social act may be completed.

The "me" and the "I" lie in the process of thinking and they indicate the give-and-take which characterizes it. There would not be an "I" in the sense in which we use that term if there were not a "me"; there would not be a "me" without a response in the form of the "I." These two, as they appear in our experience, constitute the personality. We are individuals born into a certain nationality, located at a certain spot geographically, with such and such family relations, and such and such political relations. All of these represent a certain situation which constitutes the "me"; but this necessarily involves a continued action of the organism toward the "me" in the process within which that lies. The self is not something that exists first and then enters into relationship with others, but it is, so to speak, an eddy in the social current and so still a part of the current. It is a process in which the individual is continually adjusting himself in advance to the situation to which he belongs, and reacting back on it. So that the "I" and the "me," this thinking, this conscious adjustment, becomes then a part of the whole social process and makes a much more highly organized society possible.

The "I" and the "me" belong to the conversation of gestures. If there were simply "a word and a blow," if one answered to a social situation immediately without reflection, there would be no personality in the foregoing sense any more than there is personality in the nature of the dog or the horse. We, of course, tend to endow our domestic animals with personality, but as we get insight into their conditions we see there is no place for this sort of importation of the social process into the conduct of the individual. They do not have the mechanism for it—language. So we say that they have no personality; they are not responsible for the social situation in which they find themselves. The human individual, on the other hand, identifies himself with that social situation. He responds to it, and although his re-

[182]

sponse to it may be in the nature of criticism as well as support, it involves an acceptance of the responsibility presented by the situation. Such an acceptance does not exist in the case of the lower animals. We put personalities into the animals, but they do not belong to them; and ultimately we realize that those animals have no rights. We are at liberty to cut off their lives; there is no wrong committed when an animal's life is taken away. He has not lost anything because the future does not exist for the animal; he has not the "me" in his experience which by the response of the "I" is in some sense under his control, so that the future can exist for him. He has no conscious past since there is no self of the sort we have been describing that can be extended into the past by memories. There are presumably images in the experience of lower animals, but no ideas or memories in the required sense.[14] They have not the personality that looks before or after. They have not that future and past which gives them, so to speak, any rights as such. And yet the common attitude is that of giving them just such personalities as our own. We talk to them and in our talking to them we act as if they had the sort of inner world that we have.

A similar attribution is present in the immediate attitude which we take toward inanimate physical objects about us. We take the attitude of social beings toward them. This is most elaborately true, of course, in those whom we term nature poets. The poet is in a social relation with the things about him, a fact perhaps most vividly presented in Wordsworth. The "Lines on Tintern Abbey" gives us, I believe, the social relationships of Wordsworth when he was a child and their continuation through his life. His statement of the relationship of man to nature is essentially the relationship of love, a social relation. This social attitude of the individual toward the physical thing is just the attitude which one has toward other objects; it is a social attitude. The man kicks the chair he stumbles over, and he has an affection for an object connected with him in his work or

[14] There is no evidence of animals being able to recognize that one thing is a sign of something else and so make use of that sign . . . . (1912).

play. The immediate reaction of children to things about them is social. There is an evident basis for the particular response which we make to little things, since there is something that calls out a parental response in any small thing; such a thing calls out a parental response which is universal. This holds for physical things, as well as for animals.

The physical object is an abstraction which we make from the social response to nature. We talk to nature; we address the clouds, the sea, the tree, and objects about us. We later abstract from that type of response because of what we come to know of such objects.[15] The immediate response is, however, social; where we carry over a thinking process into nature we are making nature rational. It acts as it is expected to act. We are taking the attitude of the physical things about us, and when we change the situation nature responds in a different way.

The hand is responsible for what I term physical things, distinguishing the physical thing from what I call the consummation of the act. If we took our food as dogs do by the very organs by which we masticate it, we should not have any ground for distinguishing the food as a physical thing from the actual consummation of the act, the consumption of the food. We should reach it and seize it with the teeth, and the very act of taking hold of it would be the act of eating it. But with the human animal the hand is interposed between the consummation and the getting of the object to the mouth. In that case we are manipulating a physical thing. Such a thing comes in between the beginning of the act and its final consummation. It is in that sense a universal. When we speak of a thing we have in mind a physical thing, something we can get hold of. There are, of course, "things" you cannot get hold of, such as property rights and the imaginations of a poet; but when we ordinarily

---

[15] The physical object is found to be that object to which there is no social response which calls out again a social response in the individual. The objects with which we cannot carry on social intercourse are the physical objects of the world (MS).

We have carried our attitude in physical science over into psychology, so that we have lost sight of the social nature of our early consciousness. The child forms social objects before he forms physical objects (1912).

speak of things about us we refer to physical things. The characters that go to make these up are primarily determined by the hand. Contact constitutes what we call the substance of such a thing. It has color and odor, of course, but we think of these as inherent in the something which we can manipulate, the physical thing. Such a thing is of very great importance in the development of human intelligence. It is universal in the sense that it is a physical thing, whether the consummation is that of eating, or of listening to a concert. There is a whole set of physical things that come in between the beginning of an act and its consummation, but they are universal in the sense that they belong to the experience of all of us. The consummation that we get out of a concert is very different for all of us, but the physical things we are dealing with are common, universal in that sense. The actual enjoyments may take on forms which represent an experience that is accessible only to separate individuals, but what the hand handles is something that is universal. We isolate a particular locality to which any person may come. We have a set of apparatus which any person may use. We have a certain set of weights and measures by means of which we can define these physical things. In this sense the physical thing comes in to make possible a common quality within which the selves can operate.[16]

An engineer who is constructing a bridge is talking to nature in the same sense that we talk to an engineer. There are stresses and strains there which he meets, and nature comes back with other responses that have to be met in another way. In his thinking he is taking the attitude of physical things. He is talking to nature and nature is replying to him. Nature is intelligent in the sense that there are certain responses of nature toward our action which we can present and which we can reply to, and which become different when we have replied. It is a change we then can answer to, and we finally reach a point at which we can co-operate with nature.

[16] [On the social genesis and nature of the physical thing, see Section 35; also *The Philosophy of the Present*, pp. 119–39.]

Such is the development of modern science out of what we term magic. Magic is just this same response, but with the further assumption that physical things do think and act as we do. It is preserved in the attitude which we have toward an offending object or the trustworthy object upon which we depend. We all carry about a certain amount of this sort of magic. We avoid something because we feel it is in some way dangerous; we all respect certain omens to which we pay some attention. We keep up some social response to nature about us, even though we do not allow this to affect us in important decisions. These are attitudes which perhaps we normally cover up, but which are revealed to us in numerous situations. In so far as we are rational, as we reason and think, we are taking a social attitude toward the world about us, critically in the case of science, uncritically in the case of magic.

24. MIND AS THE INDIVIDUAL IMPORTATION OF THE SOCIAL PROCESS

I have been presenting the self and the mind in terms of a social process, as the importation of the conversation of gestures into the conduct of the individual organism, so that the individual organism takes these organized attitudes of the others called out by its own attitude, in the form of its gestures, and in reacting to that response calls out other organized attitudes in the others in the community to which the individual belongs. This process can be characterized in a certain sense in terms of the "I" and the "me," the "me" being that group of organized attitudes to which the individual responds as an "I."

What I want particularly to emphasize is the temporal and logical pre-existence of the social process to the self-conscious individual that arises in it.[17] The conversation of gestures is a

[17] The relation of mind and body is that lying between the organization of the self in its behavior as a member of a rational community and the bodily organism as a physical thing.

The rational attitude which characterizes the human being is then the relationship of the whole process in which the individual is engaged to himself as reflected in his assumption of the organized rôles of the others in stimulating himself to his response. This self as distinguished from the others lies within the field of communication, and

part of the social process which is going on. It is not something that the individual alone makes possible. What the development of language, especially the significant symbol, has rendered possible is just the taking over of this external social situation into the conduct of the individual himself. There follows from this the enormous development which belongs to human society, the possibility of the prevision of what is going to take place in the response of other individuals, and a preliminary adjustment to this by the individual. These, in turn, produce a different social situation which is again reflected in what I have termed the "me," so that the individual himself takes a different attitude.

Consider a politician or a statesman putting through some project in which he has the attitude of the community in himself. He knows how the community reacts to this proposal. He reacts to this expression of the community in his own experience—he feels with it. He has a set of organized attitudes which are those of the community. His own contribution, the "I" in this case, is a project of reorganization, a project which he brings forward to the community as it is reflected in himself. He himself changes, of course, in so far as he brings this project forward and makes it a political issue. There has now arisen a new social situation as a result of the project which he is presenting. The whole procedure takes place in his own experience as well as in the general experience of the community. He is successful to the degree that the final "me" reflects the attitude of all in the community. What I am pointing out is that what

---

they lie also within this field. What may be indicated to others or one's self and does not respond to such gestures of indication is, in the field of perception, what we call a physical thing. The human body is, especially in its analysis, regarded as a physical thing.

The line of demarcation between the self and the body is found, then, first of all in the social organization of the act within which the self arises, in its contrast with the activity of the physiological organism (MS).

The legitimate basis of distinction between mind and body is between the social patterns and the patterns of the organism itself. Education must bring the two closely together. We have, as yet, no comprehending category. This does not mean to say that there is anything logically against it; it is merely a lack of our apparatus or knowledge (1927).

occurs takes place not simply in his own mind, but rather that his mind is the expression in his own conduct of this social situation, this great co-operative community process which is going on.

I want to avoid the implication that the individual is taking something that is objective and making it subjective. There is an actual process of living together on the part of all members of the community which takes place by means of gestures. The gestures are certain stages in the co-operative activities which mediate the whole process. Now, all that has taken place in the appearance of the mind is that this process has been in some degree taken over into the conduct of the particular individual. There is a certain symbol, such as the policeman uses when he directs traffic. That is something that is out there. It does not become subjective when the engineer, who is engaged by the city to examine its traffic regulations, takes the same attitude the policeman takes with reference to traffic, and takes the attitude also of the drivers of machines. We do imply that he has the driver's organization; he knows that stopping means slowing down, putting on the brakes. There is a definite set of parts of his organism so trained that under certain circumstances he brings the machine to a stop. The raising of the policeman's hand is the gesture which calls out the various acts by means of which the machine is checked. Those various acts are in the expert's own organization; he can take the attitude of both the policeman and the driver. Only in this sense has the social process been made "subjective." If the expert just did it as a child does, it would be play; but if it is done for the actual regulation of traffic, then there is the operation of what we term mind. Mind is nothing but the importation of this external process into the conduct of the individual so as to meet the problems that arise.

This peculiar organization arises out of a social process that is logically its antecedent. A community within which the organism acts in such a co-operative fashion that the action of one is the stimulus to the other to respond, and so on, is the antecedent of the peculiar type of organization we term a mind, or a self. Take the simple family relation, where there is the male and the female and the child which has to be cared for. Here is a process which can only go on through interactions within this group. It cannot be said that the individuals come first and the community later, for the individuals arise in the very process itself, just as much as the human body or any multi-cellular form is one in which differentiated cells arise. There has to be a life-process going on in order to have the differentiated cells; in the same way there has to be a social process going on in order that there may be individuals. It is just as true in society as it is in the physiological situation that there could not be the individual if there was not the process of which he is a part. Given such a social process, there is the possibility of human intelligence when this social process, in terms of the conversation of gestures, is taken over into the conduct of the individual—and then there arises, of course, a different type of individual in terms of the responses now possible. There might conceivably be an individual who simply plays as the child does, without getting into a social game; but the human individual is possible because there is a social process in which it can function responsibly. The attitudes are parts of the social reaction; the cries would not maintain themselves as vocal gestures unless they did call out certain responses in the others; the attitude itself could only exist as such in this inter-play of gestures.

The mind is simply the interplay of such gestures in the form of significant symbols. We must remember that the gesture is there only in its relationship to the response, to the attitude. One would not have words unless there were such responses. Language would never have arisen as a set of bare arbitrary terms which were attached to certain stimuli. Words have arisen out of a social interrelationship. One of Gulliver's tales was of a community in which a machine was created into which the letters of the alphabet could be mechanically fed in an end-less number of combinations, and then the members of the community gathered around to see how the letters arranged after each rotation, on the theory that they might come in the form of an Iliad or one of Shakespeare's plays, or some other great work. The assumption back of this would be that symbols are entirely independent of what we term their meaning. The assumption is baseless: there cannot be symbols unless there are responses. There would not be a call for assistance if there was not a tendency to respond to the cry of distress. It is such significant symbols, in the sense of a sub-set of social stimuli initiating a co-operative response, that do in a certain sense constitute our mind, provided that not only the symbol but also the responses are in our own nature. What the human being has succeeded in doing is in organizing the response to a certain symbol which is a part of the social act, so that he takes the attitude of the other person who co-operates with him. It is that which gives him a mind.

The sentinel of a herd is that member of the herd which is more sensitive to odor or sound than the others. At the approach of danger, he starts to run earlier than the others, who then follow along, in virtue of a herding tendency to run together. There is a social stimulus, a gesture, if you like, to which the other forms respond. The first form gets the odor earlier and starts to run, and its starting to run is a stimulus to the others to run also. It is all external; there is no mental process involved. The sentinel does not regard itself as the individual who is to give a signal; it just runs at a certain moment and so starts the others to run. But with a mind, the animal that gives the signal also takes the attitude of the others who respond to it. He knows what his signal means. A man who calls "fire" would be able to call out in himself the reaction he calls out in the other. In so far as the man can take the attitude of the other—his attitude of response to fire, his sense of terror—that response to his own cry is something that makes of his conduct a mental affair, as over against the conduct of the others.[18] But the only thing that has hap-

[18] Language as made up of significant symbols is what we mean by mind. The content of our minds is (1) inner conversation, 'the importation of conversation from the

pened here is that what takes place externally in the herd has been imported into the conduct of the man. There is the same signal and the same tendency to respond, but the man not only can give the signal but also can arouse in himself the attitude of the terrified escape, and through calling that out he can come back upon his own tendency to call out and can check it. He can react upon himself in taking the organized attitude of the whole group in trying to escape from danger. There is nothing more subjective about it than that the response to his own stimulus can be found in his own conduct, and that he can utilize the conversation of gestures that takes place to determine his own conduct. If he can so act, he can set up a rational control, and thus make possible a far more highly organized society than otherwise. The process is one which does not utilize a man endowed with a consciousness where there was no consciousness before, but rather an individual who takes over the whole social process into his own conduct. That ability, of course, is dependent first of all on the symbol being one to which he can respond; and so far as we know, the vocal gesture has been the condition for the development of that type of symbol. Whether it can develop without the vocal gesture I cannot tell.

I want to be sure that we see that the content put into the mind is only a development and product of social interaction. It is a development which is of enormous importance, and which leads to complexities and complications of society which go almost beyond our power to trace, but originally it is nothing but the taking over of the attitude of the other. To the extent that the animal can take the attitude of the other and utilize that attitude for the control of his own conduct, we have what is termed mind; and that is the only apparatus involved in the appearance of the mind.

I know of no way in which intelligence or mind could arise or

---

social group to the individual (2) . . . . imagery. Imagery should be regarded in relation to the behavior in which its functions (1931).

Imagery plays just the part in the act that hunger does in the food process (1912). [See Supplementary Essay I.]

could have arisen, other than through the internalization by the individual of social processes of experience and behavior, that is, through this internalization of the conversation of significant gestures, as made possible by the individual's taking the attitudes of other individuals toward himself and toward what is being thought about. And if mind or thought has arisen in this way, then there neither can be nor could have been any mind or thought without language; and the early stages of the development of language must have been prior to the development of mind or thought.

25. THE "I" AND THE "ME" AS PHASES OF THE SELF[19]

We come now to the position of the self-conscious self or mind in the community. Such a self finds its expression in self-assertion, or in the devotion of itself to the cause of the community. The self appears as a new type of individual in the social whole. There is a new social whole because of the appearance of the type of individual mind I have described, and because of the self with its own assertion of itself or its own identification with the community. The self is the important phase in the development because it is in the possibility of the importation of this social attitude into the responses of the whole community that such a society could arise. The change that takes place through this importation of the conversation of gestures into the conduct of the individual is one that takes place in the experience of all of the component individuals.

These, of course, are not the only changes that take place in the community. In speech definite changes take place that nobody is aware of at all. It requires the investigation of scientists to discover that such processes have taken place. This is also true of other phases of human organization. They change, we say, unconsciously, as is illustrated in such a study of the myth as Wundt has carried out in his *Völkerpsychologie*. The myth

---

[19] [See also "The Definition of the Psychical," *University of Chicago Decennial Publications*, 1903, pp. 104 ff.; "The Mechanism of Social Consciousness," *Journal of Philosophy*, IX (1912), 401 ff.; "The Social Self," *ibid.*, X (1913), 374 ff.]

carries an account of the way in which organization has taken place while largely without any conscious direction—and that sort of change is going on all the time. Take a person's attitude toward a new fashion. It may at first be one of objection. After a while he gets to the point of thinking of himself in this changed fashion, noticing the clothes in the window and seeing himself in them. The change has taken place in him without his being aware of it. There is, then, a process by means of which the individual in interaction with others inevitably becomes like others in doing the same thing, without that process appearing in what we term consciousness. We become conscious of the process when we do definitely take the attitude of the others, and this situation must be distinguished from the previous one. Perhaps one says that he does not care to dress in a certain fashion, but prefers to be different; then he is taking the attitude of others toward himself into his own conduct. When an ant from another nest is introduced into the nest of other forms, these turn on it and tear it to pieces. The attitude in the human community may be that of the individual himself, refusing to submit himself because he does take that common attitude. The ant case is an entirely external affair, but in the human individual it is a matter of taking the attitudes of the others and adjusting one's self or fighting it out. It is this recognition of the individual as a self in the process of using his self-consciousness which gives him the attitude of self-assertion or the attitude of devotion to the community. He has become, then, a definite self. In such a case of self-assertion there is an entirely different situation from that of the member of the pack who perhaps dominates it, and may turn savagely on different members of it. There an individual is just acting instinctively, we say, in a certain situation. In the human society we have an individual who not only takes his own attitude but takes the attitude in a certain sense of his subjects; in so far as he is dominating he knows what to expect. When that occurs in the experience of the individual a different response results with different emotional accompaniments, from that in the case of the leader of the pack. In the latter case there is simple anger or hostility, and in the other case there is the experience of the self asserting itself consciously over against other selves, with the sense of power, of domination. In general, when the community reaction has been imported into the individual there is a new value in experience and a new order of response.

We have discussed the self from the point of view of the "I" and the "me," the "me" representing that group of attitudes which stands for others in the community, especially that organized group of responses which we have detailed in discussing the game on the one hand and social institutions on the other. In these situations there is a certain organized group of attitudes which answer to any social act on the part of the individual organism. In any co-operative process, such as the family, the individual calls out a response from the other members of the group. Now, to the extent that those responses can be called out in the individual so that he can answer to them, we have both those contents which go to make up the self, the "other" and the "I." The distinction expresses itself in our experience in what we call the recognition of others and the recognition of ourselves in the others. We cannot realize ourselves except in so far as we can recognize the other in his relationship to us. It is as he takes the attitude of the other that the individual is able to realize himself as a self.

We are referring, of course, to a social situation as distinct from such bare organic responses as reflexes of the organism, some of which we have already discussed, as in the case where a person adjusts himself unconsciously to those about him. In such an experience there is no self-consciousness. One attains self-consciousness only as he takes, or finds himself stimulated to take, the attitude of the other. Then he is in a position of reacting in himself to that attitude of the other. Suppose we find ourselves in an economic situation. It is when we take the attitude of the other in making an offer to us that we can express ourselves in accepting or declining such an offer. That is a different response of the self from a distinctly automatic offering that can take place without self-consciousness. A small boy thrusts an advertising bill into our hand and we take it without any definite consciousness of him or of ourselves. Our thought may be elsewhere but the process still goes on. The same thing is true, of course, in the care of infants. Young children experience that which comes to them, they adjust themselves to it in an immediate fashion, without there being present in their experience a self.

When a self does appear it always involves an experience of another; there could not be an experience of a self simply by itself. The plant or the lower animal reacts to its environment, but there is no experience of a self. When a self does appear in experience it appears over against the other, and we have been delineating the condition under which this other does appear in the experience of the human animal, namely in the presence of that sort of stimulation in the co-operative activity which arouses in the individual himself the same response it arouses in the other. When the response of the other becomes an essential part in the experience or conduct of the individual; when taking the attitude of the other becomes an essential part in his behavior—then the individual appears in his own experience as a self; and until this happens he does not appear as a self.

Rational society, of course, is not limited to any specific set of individuals. Any person who is rational can become a part of it. The attitude of the community toward our own response is imported into ourselves in terms of the meaning of what we are doing. This occurs in its widest extent in universal discourse, in the reply which the rational world makes to our remark. The meaning is as universal as the community; it is necessarily involved in the rational character of that community; it is the response that the world made up out of rational beings inevitably makes to our own statement. We both get the object and ourselves into experience in terms of such a process; the other appears in our own experience in so far as we do take such an organized and generalized attitude.

If one meets a person on the street whom he fails to recognize, one's reaction toward him is that toward any other who is a member of the same community. He is the other, the organized, generalized other, if you like. One takes his attitude over against one's self. If he turns in one direction one is to go in another direction. One has his response as an attitude within himself. It is having that attitude within himself that makes it possible for one to be a self. That involves something beyond the mere turning to the right, as we say, instinctively, without self-consciousness. To have self-consciousness one must have the attitude of the other in one's own organism as controlling the thing that he is going to do. What appears in the immediate experience of one's self in taking that attitude is what we term the "me." It is that self which is able to maintain itself in the community, that is recognized in the community in so far as it recognizes the others. Such is the phase of the self which I have referred to as that of the "me."

Over against the "me" is the "I." The individual not only has rights, but he has duties; he is not only a citizen, a member of the community, but he is one who reacts to this community and in his reaction to it, as we have seen in the conversation of gestures, changes it. The "I" is the response of the individual to the attitude of the community as this appears in his own experience. His response to that organized attitude in turn changes it. As we have pointed out, this is a change which is not present in his own experience until after it takes place. The "I" appears in our experience in memory. It is only after we have acted that we know what we have done; it is only after we have spoken that we know what we have said. The adjustment to that organized world which is present in our own nature is one that represents the "me" and is constantly there. But if the response to it is a response which is of the nature of the conversation of gestures, if it creates a situation which is in some sense novel, if one puts up his side of the case, asserts himself over against others and insists that they take a different attitude toward himself, then there is something important occurring that is not previously present in experience.

The general conditions under which one is going to act may be present in one's experience, but he is as ignorant of just how he is going to respond as is the scientist of the particular hypothesis he will evolve out of the consideration of a problem. Such and such things are happening that are contrary to the theory that has been held. How are they to be explained? Take the discovery that a gram of radium would keep a pot of water boiling, and seemingly lead to no expenditure of energy. Here something is happening that runs contrary to the theory of physics up to the conception of radium activity. The scientist who has these facts before him has to pick out some explanation. He suggests that the radium atom is breaking down, and is consequently setting free energy. On the previous theory an atom was a permanent affair out of which one could not get energy. But now if it is assumed that the atom itself is a system involving an interrelationship of energies, then the breaking down of such a system sets free what is relatively an enormous amount of energy. The point I am making is that the idea of the scientist comes to him, it is not as yet there in his own mind. His mind, rather, is the process of the appearance of that idea. A person asserting his rights on a certain occasion has rehearsed the situation in his own mind; he has reacted toward the community and when the situation arises he arouses himself and says something already in his mind. But when he said it to himself in the first place he did not know what he was going to say. He then said something that was novel to himself, just as the scientist's hypothesis is a novelty when it flashes upon him.

Such a novel reply to the social situation involved in the organized set of attitudes constitutes the "I" as over against the "me." The "me" is a conventional, habitual individual. It is always there. It has to have those habits, those responses which everybody has; otherwise the individual could not be a member of the community. But an individual is constantly reacting to such an organized community in the way of expressing himself, not necessarily asserting himself in the offensive sense but expressing himself, being himself in such a co-operative process as belongs to any community. The attitudes involved are gathered from the group, but the individual in whom they are organized has the opportunity of giving them an expression which perhaps has never taken place before.

This brings out the general question as to whether anything novel can appear.[20] Practically, of course, the novel is constantly happening and the recognition of this gets its expression in more general terms in the concept of emergence. Emergence involves a reorganization, but the reorganization brings in something that was not there before. The first time oxygen and hydrogen come together, water appears. Now water is a combination of hydrogen and oxygen, but water was not there before in the separate elements. The conception of emergence is a concept which recent philosophy has made much of. If you look at the world simply from the point of view of a mathematical equation in which there is absolute equality of the different sides, then, of course, there is no novelty. The world is simply a satisfaction of that equation. Put in any values for X and Y and the same equation holds. The equations do hold, it is true, but in their holding something else in fact arises that was not there before. For instance, there is a group of individuals that have to work together. In a society there must be a set of common organized habits of response found in all, but the way in which individuals act under specific circumstances gives rise to all of the individual differences which characterize the different persons. The fact that they have to act in a certain common fashion does not deprive them of originality. The common language is there, but a different use of it is made in every new contact between persons; the element of novelty in the reconstruction takes place through the reaction of the individuals to the group to which they belong. That reconstruction is no more given in advance than is the particular hypothesis which the scientist brings forward given in the statement of the problem. Now, it is that reaction of the individual to the organized "me," the "me" that is in a certain sense simply a member of the

[20] [Cf. *The Philosophy of the Act*, Part III.]

community, which represents the "I" in the experience of the self.

The relative values of the "me" and the "I" depend very much on the situation. If one is maintaining his property in the community, it is of primary importance that he is a member of that community, for it is his taking of the attitude of the others that guarantees to him the recognition of his own rights. To be a "me" under those circumstances is the important thing. It gives him his position, gives him the dignity of being a member in the community, it is the source of his emotional response to the values that belong to him as a member of the community. It is the basis for his entering into the experience of others.

At times it is the response of the ego or "I" to a situation, the way in which one expresses himself, that brings to one a feeling of prime importance. One now asserts himself against a certain situation, and the emphasis is on the response. The demand is freedom from conventions, from given laws. Of course, such a situation is only possible where the individual appeals, so to speak, from a narrow and restricted community to a larger one, that is, larger in the logical sense of having rights which are not so restricted. One appeals from fixed conventions which no longer have any meaning to a community in which the rights shall be publicly recognized, and one appeals to others on the assumption that there is a group of organized others that answer to one's own appeal—even if the appeal be made to posterity. In that case there is the attitude of the "I" as over against the "me."

Both aspects of the "I" and "me" are essential to the self in its full expression. One must take the attitude of the others in a group in order to belong to a community; he has to employ that outer social world taken within himself in order to carry on thought. It is through his relationship to others in that community, because of the rational social processes that obtain in that community, that he has being as a citizen. On the other hand, the individual is constantly reacting to the social attitudes, and changing in this co-operative process the very community to which he belongs. Those changes may be humble and trivial ones. One may not have anything to say, although he takes a long time to say it. And yet a certain amount of adjustment and readjustment takes place. We speak of a person as a conventional individual; his ideas are exactly the same as those of his neighbors; he is hardly more than a "me" under the circumstances; his adjustments are only the slight adjustments that take place, as we say, unconsciously. Over against that there is the person who has a definite personality, who replies to the organized attitude in a way which makes a significant difference. With such a person it is the "I" that is the more important phase of the experience. Those two constantly appearing phases are the important phases in the self.[21]

26. THE REALIZATION OF THE SELF IN THE SOCIAL SITUATION

There is still one phase in the development of the self that needs to be presented in more detail: the realization of the self in the social situation in which it arises.

I have argued that the self appears in experience essentially as a "me" with the organization of the community to which it belongs. This organization is, of course, expressed in the particular endowment and particular social situation of the individual. He is a member of the community, but he is a particular part of the community, with a particular heredity and position which distinguishes him from anybody else. He is what he is in so far as he is a member of this community, and the raw materials out of which this particular individual is born would not be a self but for his relationship to others in the community of which he is a part. Thus is he aware of himself as such, and

[21] Psychologists deal as a rule with the processes which are involved in what we term "perception," but have very largely left out of account the character of the self. It has been largely through the pathologist that the importance of the self has entered into psychology. Dissociations have centered attention on the self, and have shown how absolutely fundamental is this social character of the mind. That which constitutes the personality lies in this sort of give-and-take between members in a group that engage in a co-operative process. It is this activity that has led to the humanly intelligent animal.

this not only in political citizenship, or in membership in groups of which he is a part, but also from the point of view of reflective thought. He is a member of the community of the thinkers whose literature he reads and to which he may contribute by his own published thought. He belongs to a society of all rational beings, and the rationality that he identifies with himself involves a continued social interchange. The widest community in which the individual finds himself, that which is everywhere, through and for everybody, is the thought world as such. He is a member of such a community and he is what he is as such a member.

The fact that all selves are constituted by or in terms of the social process, and are individual reflections of it—or rather of this organized behavior pattern which it exhibits, and which they prehend in their respective structures—is not in the least incompatible with, or destructive of, the fact that every individual self has its own peculiar individuality, its own unique pattern; because each individual self within that process, while it reflects in its organized structure the behavior pattern of that process as a whole, does so from its own particular and unique standpoint within that process, and thus reflects in its organized structure a different aspect or perspective of this whole social behavior pattern from that which is reflected in the organized structure of any other individual self within that process (just as every monad in the Leibnizian universe mirrors that universe from a different point of view, and thus mirrors a different aspect or perspective of that universe). In other words, the organized structure of every individual self within the human social process of experience and behavior reflects, and is constituted by, the organized relational pattern of that process as a whole; but each individual self-structure reflects, and is constituted by, a different aspect or perspective of this relational pattern, because each reflects this relational pattern from its own unique standpoint; so that the common social origin and constitution of individual selves and their structures does not preclude wide individual differences and variations among them, or contradict the peculiar and more or less distinctive individuality which each of them in fact possesses. Every individual self within a given society or social community reflects in its organized structure the whole relational pattern of organized social behavior which that society or community exhibits or is carrying on, and its organized structure is constituted by this pattern; but since each of these individual selves reflects a uniquely different aspect or perspective of this pattern in its structure, from its own particular and unique place or standpoint within the whole process of organized social behavior which exhibits this pattern—since, that is, each is differently or uniquely related to that whole process, and occupies its own essentially unique focus of relations therein—the structure of each is differently constituted by this pattern from the way in which the structure of any other is so constituted.

The individual, as we have seen, is continually reacting back against this society. Every adjustment involves some sort of change in the community to which the individual adjusts himself. And this change, of course, may be very important. Take even the widest community which we can present, the rational community that is represented in the so-called universal discourse. Up to a comparatively recent time the form of this was that of an Aristotelian world. But men in America, England, Italy, Germany, France, have very considerably changed the structure of that world, introducing a logic of multiple relations in place of the Aristotelian relation of substance and attribute. Another fundamental change has taken place in the form of the world through the reaction of an individual—Einstein. Great figures in history bring about very fundamental changes. These profound changes which take place through the action of individual minds are only the extreme expression of the sort of changes that take place steadily through reactions which are not simply those of a "me" but of an "I." These changes are changes that take place gradually and more or less imperceptibly. We know that as we pass from one historical period to another there have been fundamental changes, and we know these changes are due to the reactions of different individuals. It is only the ultimate effect that we can recognize, but the differences are due to the gestures of these countless individuals actually changing the situation in which they find themselves, although the specific changes are too minute for us to identify. As I have pointed out, the ego or "I" that is responsible for changes of that sort appears in experience only after its reaction has taken place. It is only after we have said the word we are saying that we recognize ourselves as the person that has said it, as this particular self that says this particular thing; it is only after we have done the thing that we are going to do that we are aware of what we are doing. However carefully we plan the future it always is different from that which we can previse, and this something that we are continually bringing in and adding to is what we identify with the self that comes into the level of our experience only in the completion of the act.

In some respects, of course, we can determine what that self is going to do. We can accept certain responsibilities in advance. One makes contracts and promises, and one is bound by them. The situation may change, the act may be different from that which the individual himself expected to carry out, but he is held to the contract which he has made. He must do certain things in order to remain a member of the community. In the duties of what we call rational conduct, in adjusting ourselves to a world in which the laws of nature and of economics and of political systems obtain, we can state what is going to happen and take over the responsibility for the thing we are going to do, and yet the real self that appears in that act awaits the completion of the act itself. Now, it is this living act which never gets directly into reflective experience. It is only after the act has taken place that we can catch it in our memory and place it in terms of that which we have done. It is that "I" which we may be said to be continually trying to realize, and to realize through the actual conduct itself. One does not ever get it fully before himself. Sometimes somebody else can tell him something about himself that he is not aware of. He is never sure about himself, and he astonishes himself by his conduct as much as he astonishes other people.

The possibilities in our nature, those sorts of energy which William James took so much pleasure in indicating, are possibilities of the self that lie beyond our own immediate presentation. We do not know just what they are. They are in a certain sense the most fascinating contents that we can contemplate, so far as we can get hold of them. We get a great deal of our enjoyment of romance, of moving pictures, of art, in setting free, at least in imagination, capacities which belong to ourselves, or which we want to belong to ourselves. Inferiority complexes arise from those wants of a self which we should like to carry out but which we cannot—we adjust ourselves to these by the so-called inferiority complexes. The possibilities of the "I" belong to that which is actually going on, taking place, and it is in some sense the most fascinating part of our experience. It is there that novelty arises and it is there that our most important values are located. It is the realization in some sense of this self that we are continually seeking.

There are various ways in which we can realize that self. Since it is a social self, it is a self that is realized in its relationship to others. It must be recognized by others to have the very values which we want to have belong to it. It realizes itself in some sense through its superiority to others, as it recognizes its inferiorities in comparison with others. The inferiority complexes are the reverse situations to those feelings of superiority which we entertain with reference to ourselves as over against people about us. It is interesting to go back into one's inner consciousness and pick out what it is that we are apt to depend upon in maintaining our self-respect. There are, of course, profound and solid foundations. One does keep his word, meet his obligations; and that provides a basis for self-respect. But those are characters which obtain in most of the members of the community with whom we have to do. We all fall down at certain points, but on the whole we always are people of our words. We do belong to the community and our self-respect depends on our recognition of ourselves as such self-respecting individuals. But that is not enough for us, since we want to recognize ourselves in our differences from other persons. We have, of course, a specific economic and social status that enables us to so distinguish ourselves. We also have to some extent positions in various groups which give a means of self-identification, but there is back of all these matters a sense of things which on the whole we do better than other people do. It is very interesting to get back to these superiorities, many of them of a very trivial character, but of great importance to us. We may come back to manners of speech and dress, to a capacity for remembering, to this, that, and the other thing—but always to something in which we stand out above people. We are careful, of course, not directly to plume ourselves. It would seem childish to intimate that we take satisfaction in showing that we can do something better than others. We take a great deal of pains to cover up such a situation; but actually we are vastly gratified. Among children and among primitive communities these superiorities are vaunted and a person glories in them; but even among our more advanced groups they are there as essential ways of realizing one's self, and they are not to be identified with what we term the expression of the egoistic or self-centered person. A person may be as genuine as you like in matters of dollars and cents or efforts, and he may be genuine in recognizing other people's successes and enjoy them, but that does not keep him from enjoying his own abilities and getting peculiar satisfaction out of his own successes.

This sense of superiority does not represent necessarily the disagreeable type of assertive character, and it does not mean that the person wants to lower other people in order to get himself into a higher standing. That is the form such self-realization is apt to appear to take, to say the least, and all of us recognize such a form as not simply unfortunate but as morally more or less despicable. But there is a demand, a constant demand, to realize one's self in some sort of superiority over those about us. It appears, perhaps, more definitely in such situations as those to which I have referred, and which are the hardest things to explain. There is a certain enjoyableness about the misfortunes of other people, especially those gathered about their personality. It finds its expression in what we term gossip, even mischievous gossip. We have to be on our guard against it. We may relate an event with real sorrow, and yet there is a certain satisfaction in something that has happened to somebody else but has not happened to us.

This is the same attitude that is involved in the humor of somebody else tumbling down. In such laughter there is a certain release from the effort which we do not have to make to get up again. It is a direct response, one that lies back of what we term self-consciousness, and the humor of it does not go along with the enjoyment of the other person's suffering. If a person does actually break a leg we can sympathize with him, but it was funny, after all, to see him sprawling out. This is a situation in which there is a more or less identification of the individual with the other. We do, so to speak, start to fall with him, and to rise up after he has fallen, and our theory of laughter is that it is a release from that immediate tendency to catch ourselves under those conditions. We have identified ourselves with the other person, taken his attitude. That attitude involves a strenuous effort which we do not have to carry out, and the release from that effort expresses itself in laughter. Laughter is the way in which the "I," so to speak, responds under those conditions. The individual probably sets to work helping the other person to get up, but there was an element in the response which expressed itself in the sense of the superiority of the person standing toward the person on the sidewalk. Now, that general situation is not simply found under physical situations, but is equally evident in the community in which a person commits a *faux pas*; we have here the same sense of amusement and of superiority.

I want to bring out in these instances the difference between the naïve attitude of the "I" and the more sophisticated attitude of the "me." One behaves perfectly properly, suppresses his laughter, is very prompt to get the fallen person on his feet again. There is the social attitude of the "me" over against the "I" that does enjoy the situation; but enjoys it, we will say, in a certain harmless way. There is nothing vicious about it, and even in those situations where one has a certain sort of satisfaction in following out the scandals and difficulties of a more serious sort, there is an attitude which involves the sense of superiority and at the same time does not carry with it anything that is vicious. We may be very careful about what we say, but there is still that attitude of the self which is in some sense superior under such conditions; we have not done this particular untoward thing, we have kept out of it.

The sense of superiority is magnified when it belongs to a self that identifies itself with the group. It is aggravated in our patriotism, where we legitimize an assertion of superiority which we would not admit in the situations to which I have been referring. It seems to be perfectly legitimate to assert the superiority of the nation to which one belongs over other nations, to brand the conduct of other nationalities in black colors in order that we may bring out values in the conduct of those that make up our own nation. It is just as true in politics and religion in the putting of one sect over against the others. This took the place of the exclusive expressions of nationalism in the early period, the period of religious wars. One belonged to one group that was superior to other groups and could assert himself confidently because he had God on his side. There we find a situation under which it seemed to be perfectly legitimate to assert this sort of superiority which goes with self-consciousness and which in some sense seems to be essential to self-consciousness. It is not, of course, confined to nationalism and patriotism. We all believe that the group we are in is superior to other groups. We can get together with the members in a bit of gossip that with anyone else or any other group would be impossible. Leadership, of course, plays its part, since the enthusiasm for those who have a high standing among us aids in the organization of the group; but on the whole we depend upon a common recognition that other people are not quite as good as we are.

The feeling of group superiority is generally explained in terms of the organization of the group. Groups have survived in the past in so far as they have organized against a common enemy. They maintain themselves because they have acted as one against the common enemy—such is the explanation, from the standpoint of the survival of the fittest, of the community which is most satisfactorily organized. It certainly is the easiest way of getting together, and it may be that it is an adequate explanation.

If one does have a genuine superiority it is a superiority which rests on the performance of definite functions. One is a good surgeon, a good lawyer, and he can pride himself on his superiority—but it is a superiority which he makes use of. And when he does actually make use of it in the very community to which he belongs it loses that element of egoism which we think of when we think of a person simply pluming himself on his superiority over somebody else. I have been emphasizing the other aspect because we do sometimes cover it up in our own experience. But when the sense of superiority goes over into a functional expression, then it becomes not only entirely legitimate, but it is the way in which the individuals do change the situations in which they live. We change things by the capacities which we have that other people do not have. Such capacity is what makes us effective. The immediate attitude is one which carries with it a sense of superiority, of maintaining one's self. The superiority is not the end in view. It is a means for the preservation of the self. We have to distinguish ourselves from other people and this is accomplished by doing something which other people cannot do, or cannot do as well.

Now, to be able to hold on to ourselves in our peculiarities is something which is lovable. If it is taken simply in the crude fashion of the person who boasts of himself, then a cheap and ugly side of this process is exhibited. But if it is an expression which goes out into the functions which it sustains, then it loses that character. We assume this will be the ultimate outcome of the expressions of nationalism. Nations ought to be able to express themselves in the functional fashion that the professional man does. There is the beginning of such an organization in the League of Nations. One nation recognizes certain things it has to do as a member of the community of nations. Even the mandate system at least puts a functional aspect on the action of the directing nation and not one which is simply an expression of power.

27. THE CONTRIBUTIONS OF THE "ME" AND THE "I"

I have been undertaking to distinguish between the "I" and the "me" as different phases of the self, the "me" answering to the organized attitudes of the others which we definitely assume and which determine consequently our own conduct so far as it is of a self-conscious character. Now the "me" may be regarded as giving the form of the "I." The novelty comes in the action of the "I," but the structure, the form of the self is one which is conventional.

This conventional form may be reduced to a minimum. In the artist's attitude, where there is artistic creation, the emphasis upon the element of novelty is carried to the limit. This demand for the unconventional is especially noticeable in modern art. Here the artist is supposed to break away from convention; a part of his artistic expression is thought to be in the breakdown of convention. That attitude is, of course, not essential to the artistic function, and it probably never occurs in the extreme form in which it is often proclaimed. Take certain of the artists of the past. In the Greek world the artists were, in a certain sense, the supreme artisans. What they were to do was more or less set by the community, and accepted by themselves, as the expression of heroic figures, certain deities, the erection of temples. Definite rules were accepted as essential to the expression. And yet the artist introduced an originality into it which distinguishes one artist from another. In the case of the artist the emphasis upon that which is unconventional, that which is not in the structure of the "me," is carried as far, perhaps, as it can be carried.

This same emphasis also appears in certain types of conduct which are impulsive. Impulsive conduct is uncontrolled conduct. The structure of the "me" does not there determine the expression of the "I." If we use a Freudian expression, the "me" is in a certain sense a censor. It determines the sort of expression which can take place, sets the stage, and gives the cue. In the case of impulsive conduct this structure of the "me" involved in the situation does not furnish to any such degree this control. Take the situation of self-assertion where the self simply asserts itself over against others, and suppose that the emotional stress is such that the forms of polite society in the performance of legitimate conduct are overthrown, so that the person expresses himself violently. There the "me" is determined by the situation. There are certain recognized fields within which an individual can assert himself, certain rights which he has within these limits. But let the stress become too great, these limits are not observed, and an individual asserts himself in perhaps a violent fashion. Then the "I" is the dominant element over against the "me." Under what we consider normal conditions the way in which an individual acts is determined by his taking the attitude of the others in the group, but if the individual is not given the opportunity to come up against people, as a child is not who is held out of intercourse with other people, then there results a situation in which the reaction is uncontrolled.

Social control[22] is the expression of the "me" over against the expression of the "I." It sets the limits, it gives the determination that enables the "I," so to speak, to use the "me" as the means of carrying out what is the undertaking that all are interested in. Where persons are held outside or beyond that sort of

[22] [On the topic of social control see "The Genesis of the Self and Social Control," *International Journal of Ethics*, XXXV (1924–25), 251 ff.; "The Working Hypothesis in Social Reform," *American Journal of Sociology*, V (1899–1900), 367 ff.; "The Psychology of Punitive Justice," *ibid.*, XXIII (1917–18), 577 ff.]

organized expression there arises a situation in which social control is absent. In the more or less fantastic psychology of the Freudian group, thinkers are dealing with the sexual life and with self-assertion in its violent form. The normal situation, however, is one which involves a reaction of the individual in a situation which is socially determined, but to which he brings his own responses as an "I." The response is, in the experience of the individual, an expression with which the self is identified. It is such a response which raises him above the institutionalized individual.

As I have said before, an institution is, after all, nothing but an organization of attitudes which we all carry in us, the organized attitudes of the others that control and determine conduct. Now, this institutionalized individual is, or should be, the means by which the individual expresses himself in his own way, for such individual expression is that which is identified with the self in those values which are essential to the self, and which arise from the self. To speak of them as arising from the self does not attach to them the character of the selfish egoist, for under the normal conditions to which we were referring the individual is making his contribution to a common undertaking. The baseball player who makes a brilliant play is making the play called for by the nine to which he belongs. He is playing for his side. A man may, of course, play the gallery, be more interested in making a brilliant play than in helping the nine to win, just as a surgeon may carry out a brilliant operation and sacrifice the patient. But under normal conditions the contribution of the individual gets its expression in the social processes that are involved in the act, so that the attachment of the values to the self does not involve egoism or selfishness. The other situation in which the self in its expression does in some sense exploit the group or society to which it belongs is one which sets up, so to speak, a narrow self which takes advantage of the whole group in satisfying itself. Even such a self is still a social affair. We distinguish very definitely between the selfish man and the impulsive man. The man who may lose his temper and knock another down may be a very unselfish man. He is not necessarily a person who would utilize a certain situation for the sake of his own interests. The latter case involves the narrow self that does not relate itself to the whole social group of which it is a part.

Values do definitely attach to this expression of the self which is peculiar to the self; and what is peculiar to the self is what it calls its own. And yet this value lies in the social situation, and would not be apart from that social situation. It is the contribution of the individual to the situation, even though it is only in the social situation that the value obtains.

We seek certainly for that sort of expression which is self-expression. When an individual feels himself hedged in he recognizes the necessity of getting a situation in which there shall be an opportunity for him to make his addition to the undertaking, and not simply to be the conventionalized "me." In a person who carries out the routine job, it leads to the reaction against the machine, and to the demand that that type of routine work shall fall into its place in the whole social process. There is, of course, a certain amount of real mental and physical health, a very essential part of one's life, that is involved in doing routine work. One can very well just carry out certain processes in which his contribution is very slight, in a more or less mechanical fashion, and find himself in a better position because of it. Such men as John Stuart Mill have been able to carry on routine occupations during a certain part of the day, and then give themselves to original work for the rest of the day. A person who cannot do a certain amount of stereotyped work is not a healthy individual. Both the health of the individual and the stability of society call for a very considerable amount of such work. The reaction to machine industry simply calls for the restriction of the amount of time given to it, but it does not involve its total abolition. Nevertheless, and granting this point, there must be some way in which the individual can express himself. It is the situations in which it is possible to get this sort of expression that seem to be particularly precious, namely, those situations in which the individual is able to do something on his own, where he can take over responsibility and carry out things in his own way, with an opportunity to think his own thoughts. Those social situations in which the structure of the "me" for the time being is one in which the individual gets an opportunity for that sort of expression of the self bring some of the most exciting and gratifying experiences.

These experiences may take place in a form which involves degradation, or in a form which involves the emergence of higher values. The mob furnishes a situation in which the "me" is one which simply supports and emphasizes the more violent sort of impulsive expression. This tendency is deeply imbedded in human nature. It is astonishing what part of the "I" of the sick is constituted by murder stories. Of course, in the story itself, it is the tracking-down of the murderer that is the focal point of interest; but that tracking-down of the murderer takes one back to the vengeance attitude of the primitive community. In the murder story one gets a real villain, runs him down, and brings him to justice. Such expressions may involve degradation of the self. In situations involving the defense of the country a mob attitude or a very high moral attitude may prevail, depending upon the individual. The situation in which one can let himself go, in which the very structure of the "me" opens the door for the "I," is favorable to self-expression. I have referred to the situation in which a person can sit down with a friend and say just what he is thinking about someone else. There is a satisfaction in letting one's self go in this way. The sort of thing that under other circumstances you would not say and would not even let yourself think is now naturally uttered. If you get in a group which thinks as you do then one can go to lengths which may surprise the person himself. The "me" in the above situations is definitely constituted by the social relations. Now if this situation is such that it opens the door to impulsive expression one gets a peculiar satisfaction, high or low, the source of which is the value that attaches to the expression of the "I" in the social process.

28. THE SOCIAL CREATIVITY OF THE EMERGENT SELF

We have been discussing the value which gathers about the self, especially that which is involved in the "I" as over against that involved in the "me." The "me" is essentially a member of a social group, and represents, therefore, the value of the group, that sort of experience which the group makes possible. Its values are the values that belong to society. In a sense these values are supreme. They are values which under certain extreme moral and religious conditions call out the sacrifice of the self for the whole. Without this structure of things, the life of the self would become impossible. These are the conditions under which that seeming paradox arises, that the individual sacrifices himself for the whole which makes his own life as a self possible. Just as there could not be individual consciousness except in a social group, so the individual in a certain sense is not willing to live under certain conditions which would involve a sort of suicide of the self in its process of realization. Over against that situation we referred to those values which attach particularly to the "I" rather than to the "me," those values which are found in the immediate attitude of the artist, the inventor, the scientist in his discovery, in general in the action of the "I" which cannot be calculated and which involves a reconstruction of the society, and so of the "me" which belongs to that society. It is that phase of experience which is found in the "I" and the values that attach to it are the values belonging to this type of experience as such. These values are not peculiar to the artist, the inventor, and the scientific discoverer, but belong to the experience of all selves where there is an "I" that answers to the "me."

The response of the "I" involves adaptation, but an adaptation which affects not only the self but also the social environment which helps to constitute the self; that is, it implies a view of evolution in which the individual affects its own environment as well as being affected by it. A statement of evolution that was common in an earlier period assumed simply the effect of an environment on organized living protoplasm, molding it in some sense to the world in which it had to live. On this view the individual is really passive as over against the influences which are affecting it all the time. But what needs now to be recognized is that the character of the organism is a determinant of its environment. We speak of bare sensitivity as existent by itself, forgetting it is always a sensitivity to certain types of stimuli. In terms of its sensitivity the form selects an environment, not selecting exactly in the sense in which a person selects a city or a country or a particular climate in which to live, but selects in the sense that it finds those characteristics to which it can respond, and uses the resulting experiences to gain certain organic results that are essential to its continued life-process. In a sense, therefore, the organism states its environment in terms of means and ends. That sort of a determination of the environment is as real, of course, as the effect of the environment on the form. When a form develops a capacity, however this takes place, to deal with parts of the environment which its progenitors could not deal with, it has to this degree created a new environment for itself. The ox that has a digestive organ capable of treating grass as a food adds a new food, and in adding this it adds a new object. The substance which was not food before becomes food now. The environment of the form has increased. The organism in a real sense is determinative of its environment. The situation is one in which there is action and reaction, and adaptation that changes the form must also change the environment.

As a man adjusts himself to a certain environment he becomes a different individual; but in becoming a different individual he has affected the community in which he lives. It may be a slight effect, but in so far as he has adjusted himself, the adjustments have changed the type of the environment to which he can respond and the world is accordingly a different world. There is always a mutual relationship of the individual and the community in which the individual lives. Our recognition of this under ordinary conditions is confined to relatively small social groups, for here an individual cannot come into the group without in some degree changing the character of the organization. People have to adjust themselves to him as much as he adjusts himself to them. It may seem to be a molding of the individual by the forces about him, but the society likewise changes in this process, and becomes to some degree a different society. The change may be desirable or it may be undesirable, but it inevitably takes place.

This relationship of the individual to the community becomes striking when we get minds that by their advent make the wider society a noticeably different society. Persons of great mind and great character have strikingly changed the communities to which they have responded. We call them leaders, as such, but they are simply carrying to the nth power this change in the community by the individual who makes himself a part of it, who belongs to it.[23] The great characters have been those who, by being what they were in the community, made that community a different one. They have enlarged and enriched the community. Such figures as great religious characters in history have, through their membership, indefinitely increased the possible size of the community itself. Jesus generalized the conception of the community in terms of the family in such a statement as that of the neighbor in the parables. Even the man outside of the community will now take that generalized family attitude toward it, and he makes those that are so brought into relationship with him members of the community to which he belongs, the community of a universal religion. The change of the community through the attitude of

[23] The behavior of a genius is socially conditioned, just as that of an ordinary individual is; and his achievements are the results of, or are responses to, social stimuli, just as those of an ordinary individual are. The genius, like the ordinary individual, comes back at himself from the standpoint of the organized social group to which he belongs, and the attitudes of that group toward any given project in which he becomes involved; and he responds to this generalized attitude of the group with a definite attitude of his own toward the given project, just as the ordinary individual does. But this definite attitude of his own with which he responds to the generalized attitude of the group is unique and original in the case of the genius, whereas it is not so in the case of the ordinary individual; and it is this uniqueness and originality of his response to a given social situation or problem or project—which nevertheless conditions his behavior no less than it does that of the ordinary individual—that distinguishes the genius from the ordinary individual.

the individual becomes, of course, peculiarly impressive and effective in history. It makes separate individuals stand out as symbolic. They represent, in their personal relationships, a new order, and then become representative of the community as it might exist if it were fully developed along the lines that they had started. New conceptions have brought with them, through great individuals, attitudes which enormously enlarge the environment within which these individuals lived. A man who is a neighbor of anybody else in the group is a member of a larger society, and to the extent that he lives in such a community he has helped to create that society.

It is in such reactions of the individual, the "I," over against the situation in which the "I" finds itself, that important social changes take place. We frequently speak of them as expressions of the individual genius of certain persons. We do not know when the great artist, scientist, statesman, religious leader will come—persons who will have a formative effect upon the society to which they belong. The very definition of genius would come back to something of the sort to which I have been referring, to this incalculable quality, this change of the environment on the part of an individual by himself becoming a member of the community.

An individual of the type to which we are referring arises always with reference to a form of society or social order which is implied but not adequately expressed. Take the religious genius, such as Jesus or Buddha, or the reflective type, such as Socrates. What has given them their unique importance is that they have taken the attitude of living with reference to a larger society. That larger state was one which was already more or less implied in the institutions of the community in which they lived. Such an individual is divergent from the point of view of what we would call the prejudices of the community; but in another sense he expresses the principles of the community more completely than any other. Thus arises the situation of an Athenian or a Hebrew stoning the genius who expresses the principles of his own society, one the principle of rationality and the other the principle of complete neighborliness. The type we refer to as the genius is of that sort. There is an analogous situation in the field of artistic creation: the artists also reveal contents which represent a wider emotional expression answering to a wider society. To the degree that we make the community in which we live different we all have what is essential to genius, and which becomes genius when the effects are profound.

The response of the "I" may be a process which involves a degradation of the social state as well as one which involves higher integration. Take the case of the mob in its various expressions. A mob is an organization which has eliminated certain values which have obtained in the interrelation of individuals with each other, has simplified itself, and in doing that has made it possible to allow the individual, especially the repressed individual, to get an expression which otherwise would not be allowed. The individual's response is made possible by the actual degradation of the social structure itself, but that does not take away the immediate value to the individual which arises under those conditions. He gets his emotional response out of that situation because in his expression of violence he is doing what everyone else is doing. The whole community is doing the same thing. The repression which existed has disappeared and he is at one with the community and the community is at one with him. An illustration of a more trivial character is found in our personal relations with those about us. Our manners are methods of not only mediated intercourse between persons but also ways of protecting ourselves against each other. A person may, by manners, isolate himself so that he cannot be touched by anyone else. Manners provide a way in which we keep people at a distance, people that we do not know and do not want to know. We all make use of processes of that sort. But there are occasions in which we can drop off the type of manner which holds people at arm's length. We meet the man in some distant country whom perhaps we would seek to avoid meeting at home, and we almost tear our arms off embracing him. There is a great deal of exhilaration in situations involved in the hostility of other nations; we all seem at one against a common enemy; the barriers drop, and we have a social sense of comradeship to those standing with us in a common undertaking. The same thing takes place in a political campaign. For the time being we extend the glad hand—and a cigar—to anyone who is a member of the particular group to which we belong. We get rid of certain restrictions under those circumstances, restrictions which really keep us from intense social experiences. A person may be a victim of his good manners; they may incase him as well as protect him. But under the conditions to which I have referred, a person does get outside of himself, and by doing so makes himself a definite member of a larger community than that to which he previously belonged.

This enlarged experience has a profound influence. It is the sort of experience which the neophyte has in conversion. It is the sense of belonging to the community, of having an intimate relationship with an indefinite number of individuals who belong to the same group. That is the experience which lies back of the sometimes hysterical extremes which belong to conversions. The person has entered into the universal community of the church, and the resulting experience is the expression of that sense of identification of one's self with everyone else in the community. The sense of love is shown by such proceedings as washing the feet of lepers; in general, by finding a person who is most distant from the community, and by making a seemingly servile offering, identifying one's self completely with this individual. This is a process of breaking down the walls so that the individual is a brother of everyone. The medieval saint worked out that method of identifying himself with all living beings, as did the religious technique of India. This breakdown of barriers is something that arouses a flood of emotions, because it sets free an indefinite number of possible contacts to other people which have been checked, held repressed. The individual, by entering into that new community, has, by his step in making himself a member, by his experience of identification, taken on the value that belongs to all members of that community.

Such experiences are, of course, of immense importance. We make use of them all the time in the community. We decry the attitude of hostility as a means of carrying on the interrelations between nations. We feel we should get beyond the methods of warfare and diplomacy, and reach some sort of political relation of nations to each other in which they could be regarded as members of a common community, and so be able to express themselves, not in the attitude of hostility, but in terms of their common values. That is what we set up as the ideal of the League of Nations. We have to remember, however, that we are not able to work out our own political institutions without introducing the hostilities of parties. Without parties we could not get a fraction of the voters to come to the polls to express themselves on issues of great public importance, but we can enrol a considerable part of the community in a political party that is fighting some other party. It is the element of the fight that keeps up the interest. We can enlist the interest of a number of people who want to defeat the opposing party, and get them to the polls to do that. The party platform is an abstraction, of course, and does not mean much to us, since we are actually depending psychologically upon the operation of these more barbarous impulses in order to keep our ordinary institutions running. When we object to the organization of corrupt political machines we ought to remember to feel a certain gratitude to people who are able to enlist the interest of people in public affairs.

We are normally dependent upon those situations in which the self is able to express itself in a direct fashion, and there is no situation in which the self can express itself so easily as it can over against the common enemy of the groups to which it is united. The hymn that comes to our minds most frequently as expressive of Christendom is "Onward Christian Soldiers"; Paul organized the church of his time against the world of heathens; and "Revelation" represents the community over against the world of darkness. The idea of Satan has been as essential to the organization of the church as politics has been to the organization of democracy. There has to be something to fight against because the self is most easily able to express itself in joining a definite group.

The value of an ordered society is essential to our existence, but there also has to be room for an expression of the individual himself if there is to be a satisfactorily developed society. A means for such expression must be provided. Until we have such a social structure in which an individual can express himself as the artist and the scientist does, we are thrown back on the sort of structure found in the mob, in which everybody is free to express himself against some hated object of the group.

One difference between primitive human society and civilized human society is that in primitive human society the individual self is much more completely determined, with regard to his thinking and his behavior, by the general pattern of the organized social activity carried on by the particular social group to which he belongs, than he is in civilized human society. In other words, primitive human society offers much less scope for individuality—for original, unique, or creative thinking and behavior on the part of the individual self within it or belonging to it—than does civilized human society; and indeed the evolution of civilized human society from primitive human society has largely depended upon or resulted from a progressive social liberation of the individual self and his conduct, with the modifications and elaborations of the human social process which have followed from and been made possible by that liberation. In primitive society, to a far greater extent than in civilized society, individuality is constituted by the more or less perfect achievement of a given social type—a type already given, indicated, or exemplified in the organized pattern of social conduct, in the integrated relational structure of the social process of experience and behavior which the given social group exhibits and is carrying on; in civilized society individuality is constituted rather by the individual's departure from, or modified realization of, any given social type than by his conformity, and tends to be something much more distinctive and singular and peculiar than it is in primitive human society. But even in the most modern and highly-evolved forms of human civilization the individual, however original and creative he may be in his thinking or behavior, always and necessarily assumes a definite relation to, and reflects in the structure of his self or personality, the general organized pattern of experience and activity exhibited in or characterizing the social life-process in which he is involved, and of which his self or personality is essentially a creative expression or embodiment. No individual has a mind which operates simply in itself, in isolation from the social life-process in which it has arisen or out of which it has emerged, and in which the pattern of organized social behavior has consequently been basically impressed upon it.

29. A CONTRAST OF INDIVIDUALISTIC AND SOCIAL THEORIES OF THE SELF

The differences between the type of social psychology which derives the selves of individuals from the social process in which they are implicated and in which they empirically interact with one another, and the type of social psychology which instead derives that process from the selves of the individuals involved in it, are clear. The first type assumes a social process or social order as the logical and biological precondition of the appearance of the selves of the individual organisms involved in that process or belonging to that order. The other type, on the contrary, assumes individual selves as the presuppositions, logically and biologically, of the social process or order within which they interact.

The difference between the social and the individual theories of the development of mind, self, and the social process of experience or behavior is analogous to the difference between the evolutionary and the contract theories of the state as held in the past by both rationalists and empiricists.[24] The latter theory

[24] Historically, both the rationalist and the empiricist are committed to the interpretation of experience in terms of the individual (1931).

[Footnote continued on opposite page]

takes individuals and their individual experiencing—individual minds and selves—as logically prior to the social process in which they are involved, and explains the existence of that social process in terms of them; whereas the former takes the social process of experience or behavior as logically prior to the individuals and their individual experiencing which are involved in it, and explains their existence in terms of that social process. But the latter type of theory cannot explain that which is taken as logically prior at all, cannot explain the existence of minds and selves; whereas the former type of theory can explain that which it takes as logically prior, namely, the existence of the social process of behavior, in terms of such fundamental biological or physiological relations and interactions as reproduction, or the co-operation of individuals for mutual protection or for the securing of food.

Our contention is that mind can never find expression, and could never have come into existence at all, except in terms of a social environment; that an organized set or pattern of social relations and interactions (especially those of communication by means of gestures functioning as significant symbols and thus creating a universe of discourse) is necessarily presupposed by it and involved in its nature. And this entirely social theory or interpretation of mind[25]—this contention that mind develops and has its being only in and by virtue of the social process of

---

Other people are there as much as we are there; to be a self requires other selves (1924).

In our experience the thing is there as much as we are here. Our experience is in the thing as much as it is in us (MS).

[25] In defending a social theory of mind we are defending a functional, as opposed to any form of substantive or entitive, view as to its nature. And in particular, we are opposing all intracranial or intra-epidermal views as to its character and locus. For it follows from our social theory of mind that the field of mind must be co-extensive with, and include all the components of, the field of the social process of experience and behavior, i.e., the matrix of social relations and interactions among individuals, which is presupposed by it, and out of which it arises or comes into being. If mind is socially constituted, then the field or locus of any given individual mind must extend as far as the social activity or apparatus of social relations which constitutes it extends; and hence that field cannot be bounded by the skin of the individual organism to which it belongs.

experience and activity, which it hence presupposes, and that in no other way can it develop and have its being—must be clearly distinguished from the partially (but only partially) social view of mind. On this view, though mind can get expression only within or in terms of the environment of an organized social group, yet it is nevertheless in some sense a native endowment— a congenital or hereditary biological attribute—of the individual organism, and could not otherwise exist or manifest itself in the social process at all; so that it is not itself essentially a social phenomenon, but rather is biological both in its nature and in its origin, and is social only in its characteristic manifestations or expressions. According to this latter view, moreover, the social process presupposes, and in a sense is a product of, mind; in direct contrast is our opposite view that mind presupposes, and is a product of, the social process. The advantage of our view is that it enables us to give a detailed account and actually to explain the genesis and development of mind; whereas the view that mind is a congenital biological endowment of the individual organism does not really enable us to explain its nature and origin at all: neither what sort of biological endowment it is, nor how organisms at a certain level of evolutionary progress come to possess it.[26] Furthermore, the supposition that the social process presupposes, and is in some sense a product of, mind seems to be contradicted by the existence of the social communities of certain of the lower animals, especially the high-

[26] According to the traditional assumption of psychology, the content of experience is entirely individual and not in any measure to be primarily accounted for in social terms, even though its setting or context is a social one. And for a social psychology like Cooley's—which is founded on precisely this same assumption—all social interactions depend upon the imaginations of the individuals involved, and take place in terms of their direct conscious influences upon one another in the processes of social experience. Cooley's social psychology, as found in his *Human Nature and the Social Order*, is hence inevitably introspective, and his psychological method carries with it the implication of complete solipsism: society really has no existence except in the individual's mind, and the concept of the self as in any sense intrinsically social is a product of imagination. Even for Cooley the self presupposes experience, and experience is a process within which selves arise; but since that process is for him primarily internal and individual rather than external and social, he is committed in his psychology to a subjectivistic and idealistic, rather than an objectivistic and naturalistic, metaphysical position.

ly complex social organizations of bees and ants, which apparently operate on a purely instinctive or reflex basis, and do not in the least involve the existence of mind or consciousness in the individual organisms which form or constitute them. And even if this contradiction is avoided by the admission that only at its higher levels—only at the levels represented by the social relations and interactions of human beings—does the social process of experience and behavior presuppose the existence of mind or become necessarily a product of mind, still it is hardly plausible to suppose that this already ongoing and developing process should suddenly, at a particular stage in its evolution, become dependent for its further continuance upon an entirely extraneous factor, introduced into it, so to speak, from without.

The individual enters as such into his own experience only as an object, not as a subject; and he can enter as an object only on the basis of social relations and interactions, only by means of his experiential transactions with other individuals in an organized social environment. It is true that certain contents of experience (particularly kinaesthetic) are accessible only to the given individual organism and not to any others; and that these private or "subjective," as opposed to public or "objective," contents of experience are usually regarded as being peculiarly and intimately connected with the individual's self, or as being in a special sense self-experiences. But this accessibility solely to the given individual organism of certain contents of its experience does not affect, nor in any way conflict with, the theory as to the social nature and origin of the self that we are presenting; the existence of private or "subjective" contents of experience does not alter the fact that self-consciousness involves the individual's becoming an object to himself by taking the attitudes of other individuals toward himself within an organized setting of social relationships, and that unless the individual had thus become an object to himself he would not be self-conscious or have a self at all. Apart from his social interactions with other individuals, he would not relate the private or "subjective" contents of his experience to himself, and he could not become aware of himself as such, that is, as an individual, a person, merely by means or in terms of these contents of his experience; for in order to become aware of himself as such he must, to repeat, become an object to himself, or enter his own experience as an object, and only by social means—only by taking the attitudes of others toward himself—is he able to become an object to himself.[27]

It is true, of course, that once mind has arisen in the social process it makes possible the development of that process into much more complex forms of social interaction among the component individuals than was possible before it had arisen. But there is nothing odd about a product of a given process contributing to, or becoming an essential factor in, the further development of that process. The social process, then, does not depend for its origin or initial existence upon the existence and interactions of selves; though it does depend upon the latter for the higher stages of complexity and organization which it reaches after selves have arisen within it.

[27] The human being's physiological capacity for developing mind or intelligence is a product of the process of biological evolution, just as is his whole organism; but the actual development of his mind or intelligence itself, given that capacity, must proceed in terms of the social situations wherein it gets its expression and import; and hence it itself is a product of the process of social evolution, the process of social experience and behavior.

PART IV

SOCIETY

30. THE BASIS OF HUMAN SOCIETY: MAN AND THE INSECTS

In the earlier parts of our discussion we have followed out the development of the self in the experience of the human organism, and now we are to consider something of the social organism within which this self arises.

Human society as we know it could not exist without minds and selves, since all its most characteristic features presuppose the possession of minds and selves by its individual members; but its individual members would not possess minds and selves if these had not arisen within or emerged out of the human social process in its lower stages of development—those stages at which it was merely a resultant of, and wholly dependent upon, the physiological differentiations and demands of the individual organisms implicated in it. There must have been such lower stages of the human social process, not only for physiological reasons, but also (if our social theory of the origin and nature of minds and selves is correct) because minds and selves, consciousness and intelligence, could not otherwise have emerged; because, that is, some sort of an ongoing social process in which human beings were implicated must have been there in advance of the existence of minds and selves in human beings, in order to make possible the development, by human beings, of minds and selves within or in terms of that process.[1]

The behavior of all living organisms has a basically social aspect: the fundamental biological or physiological impulses

---

[1] On the other hand, the rate of development or evolution of human society, since the emergence of minds and selves out of the human social processes of experience and behavior, has been tremendously accelerated as a result of that emergence.

Social evolution or development and self-evolution or development are correlative and interdependent, once the self has arisen out of the social life-process.

and needs which lie at the basis of all such behavior—especially those of hunger and sex, those connected with nutrition and reproduction—are impulses and needs which, in the broadest sense, are social in character or have social implications, since they involve or require social situations and relations for their satisfaction by any given individual organism; and they thus constitute the foundation of all types or forms of social behavior, however simple or complex, crude or highly organized, rudimentary or well developed. The experience and behavior of the individual organism are always components of a larger social whole or process of experience and behavior in which the individual organism—by virtue of the social character of the fundamental physiological impulses ahd needs which motivate and are expressed in its experience and behavior—is necessarily implicated, even at the lowest evolutionary levels. There is no living organism of any kind whose nature or constitution is such that it could exist or maintain itself in complete isolation from all other living organisms, or such that certain relations to other living organisms (whether of its own or of other species)—relations which in the strict sense are social—do not play a necessary and indispensable part in its life. All living organisms are bound up in a general social environment or situation, in a complex of social interrelations and interactions upon which their continued existence depends.

Among these fundamental socio-physiological impulses or needs (and consequent attitudes) which are basic to social behavior and social organization in all species of living organisms, the one which is most important in the case of human social behavior, and which most decisively or determinately expresses itself in the whole general form of human social organization (both primitive and civilized), is the sex or reproductive impulse; though hardly less important are the parental impulse or attitude, which is of course closely connected or associated with the sex impulse, and the impulse or attitude of neighborliness, which is a kind of generalization of the parental impulse or attitude and upon which all co-operative social behavior is more or less dependent. Thus the family is the fundamental unit of reproduction and of maintenance of the species: it is the unit of human social organization in terms of which these vital biological activities or functions are performed or carried on. And all such larger units or forms of human social organization as the clan or the state are ultimately based upon, and (whether directly or indirectly) are developments from or extensions of, the family. Clan or tribal organization is a direct generalization of family organization; and state or national organization is a direct generalization of clan or tribal organization—hence ultimately, though indirectly, of family organization also. In short, all organized human society—even in its most complex and highly developed forms—is in a sense merely an extension and ramification of those simple and basic socio-physiological relations among its individual members (relations between the sexes resulting from their physiological differentiation, and relations between parents and children) upon which it is founded, and from which it originates.

These socio-physiological impulses on which all social organizations are based constitute, moreover, one of the two poles in the general process of social differentiation and evolution, by expressing themselves in all the complexities of social relations and interactions, social responses and activities. They are the essential physiological materials from which human nature is socially formed; so that human nature is something social through and through, and always presupposes the truly social individual. Indeed, any psychological or philosophical treatment of human nature involves the assumption that the human individual belongs to an organized social community, and derives his human nature from his social interactions and relations with that community as a whole and with the other individual members of it. The other pole of the general process of social differentiation and evolution is constituted by the responses of individuals to the identical responses of others, that is, to class or social responses, or to responses of whole organized social groups of other individuals with reference to given sets of social stimuli, these class or social responses being the sources and bases and stuff of social institutions. Thus we may call the former pole of the general process of social differentiation and evolution the individual or physiological pole, and the latter pole of this process the institutional pole.[2]

I have pointed out that the social organism is used by individuals whose co-operative activity is essential to the life of the whole. Such social organisms exist outside of the human society. The insects reveal a very curious development. We are tempted to be anthropomorphic in our accounts of the life of bees and ants, since it seems comparatively easy to trace the organization of the human community in their organizations. There are different types of individuals with corresponding functions, and a life-process which seems to determine the life of the different individuals. It is tempting to refer to such a life-process as analogous to a human society. We have not, however, any basis as yet for carrying out the analogy in this fashion because we are unable to identify any system of communication in insect societies, and also because the principle of organization in these communities is a different one from that found in the human community.

The principle of organization among these insects is that of physiological plasticity, giving rise to an actual development in the physiological process of a different type of form adjusted to certain functions. Thus, the whole process of reproduction is carried on for the entire community by a single queen bee or queen ant, a single form with an enormous development of the reproductive organs, with the corresponding degeneration of the

[2] The selfish versus the unselfish aspects or sides of the self are to be accounted for in terms of the content versus the structure of the self. We may say, in a sense, that the content of the self is individual (selfish, therefore, or the source of selfishness), whereas the structure of the self is social—hence unselfish, or the basis of unselfishness.

The relation between the rational or primarily social side of the self and its impulsive or emotional or primarily anti-social and individual side is such that the latter is, for the most part, controlled with respect to its behavioristic expressions by the former; and that the conflicts which occur from time to time among its different impulses—or among the various components of its impulsive side—are settled and reconciled by its rational side.

reproductive organs in other insects in the community. There is the development of a single group of fighters, a differentiation carried so far that they cannot feed themselves. This process of physiological development that makes an individual an organ in the social whole is quite comparable to the development of different tissues in a physiological organism. In a sense, all of the functions which are to be found in a multicellular form may be found in a single cell. Unicellular forms may carry out the entire vital process; they move, get rid of their waste products, reproduce. But in a multicellular form there is a differentiation of tissue forming muscle cells for movement, cells which take in oxygen and pass out waste products, cells set aside for the process of reproduction. Thus, there results tissue made up of cells which are differentiated. Likewise there is in a community of ants, or of bees, a physiological differentiation among different forms which is comparable to the differentiation of different cells in the tissue of a multicellular form.

Now, such differentiation is not the principle of organization in human society. There is, of course, the fundamental distinction of sex which remains a physiological difference, and in the main the distinctions between the parent-forms and child-forms are physiological distinctions, but apart from these there is practically no physiological distinction between the different individuals that go to make up the human community. Hence, organization cannot take place, as it does in the community of ants or bees, through physiological differentiation of certain forms into social organs. On the contrary, all of the individuals have essentially the same physiological structures, and the process of organization among such forms has to be an entirely different process from that found among the insects.

The degree to which insect differentiation can be carried is astonishing. Many of the products of a high social organization are carried on by these communities. They capture other minute forms whose exudations they delight in, and keep them much as we keep milk cows. They have warrior classes and they seem to carry on raids, and carry off slaves, making later use of them. They can do what the human society cannot do: they can determine the sex of the next generation, pick out and determine who the parent in the next generation will be. We get astonishing developments which parallel our own undertakings that we try to carry on in society, but the manner in which they are carried on is essentially different. It is carried on through physiological differentiation, and we fail to find in the study of these animals any medium of communication like that through which human organization takes place. Although we are still very largely in the dark with reference to this social entity of the beehive or the ant's nest, and although we note an obvious likeness between them and human society, there is an entirely different system of organization in the two cases.

In both cases there is an organization within which the particular individuals arise and which is a condition for the appearance of the different individuals. There could not be the peculiar development found in the beehive except in a bee community. We can in some degree get a suggestion for understanding the evolution of such a social group. We can find solitary forms such as the bumble-bee, and can more or less profitably speculate as to other forms out of which the development of an insect society might take place. Presumably the finding of a surplus of food which these forms could carry over from one generation to another would be a determining factor. In the life of the solitary form the first generation disappears and the larvae are left behind, so that there is a complete disappearance of the adults with each appearance of the new generation. In such organizations as the beehive there arise the conditions under which, due to the abundance of food, the forms carry over from one generation to another. Under those conditions a complex social development is possible, but dependent still upon physiological differentiation. We have no evidence of the accruing of an experience which is passed on by means of communication from one generation to another. Nevertheless, under those conditions of surplus food this physiological development flowers out in an astonishing fashion. Such a differentiation as this could only take place in a community. The queen bee and the fighter among the ants could only arise out of an insect society. One could not bring together these different individuals and constitute an insect society; there has to be an insect society first in order that these individuals might arise.

In the human community we might not seem to have such disparate intelligences of separate individuals and the development of the individuals out of the social matrix, such as is responsible for the development of the insects. The human individuals are to a large degree identical; there is no essential difference of intelligence from the point of view of physiological differentiation between the sexes. There are physiological organisms which are essentially identical, so we do not seem to have there a social matrix that is responsible for the appearance of the individual. It is because of such considerations that a theory has developed that human societies have arisen out of individuals, not individuals out of society. Thus, the contract theory of society assumes that the individuals are first all there as intelligent individuals, as selves, and that these individuals get together and form society. On this view societies have arisen like business corporations, by the deliberate coming-together of a group of investors, who elect their officers and constitute themselves a society. The individuals come first and the societies arise out of the mastery of certain individuals. The theory is an old one and in some of its phases is still current. If, however, the position to which I have been referring is a correct one, if the individual reaches his self only through communication with others, only through the elaboration of social processes by means of significant communication, then the self could not antedate the social organism. The latter would have to be there first.

A social process is involved in the relation of parents and children among the mammals. There we start off with the only physical differentiation (except sex) which exists among human individuals, and these physiological differences give a basis for the social process. Such families can exist among animals lower than man. Their organization is on a physiological basis, that is, one form acts in a certain way on account of its physiological structure and another responds on account of its own physiological structure. There must be in that process a gesture which calls out the response, but the conversation of gestures is not at this early stage significant. The beginning of communication is nevertheless there in the process of organization dependent upon the physiological differences; there is also the conflict of individuals with each other, which is not based necessarily on physiological conditions.

A fight takes place between individuals. There may be a physiological background such as hunger, sex rivalry, rivalry in leadership. We can perhaps always find some physiological background, but the contest is between individuals that stand practically on the same level, and in such conflicts there is the same conversation of gestures which I have illustrated in the dog-fight. Thus, we get the beginnings of the process of communication in the co-operative process, whether of reproduction, caring for the young, or fighting. The gestures are not yet significant symbols, but they do allow of communication. Back of it lies a social process, and a certain part of it is dependent upon physiological differentiation, but the process is one which in addition involves gestures.

It is seemingly out of this process that there arises significant communication. It is in the process of communication that there appears another type of individual. This process is, of course, dependent upon a certain physiological structure: if the individual was not sensitive to his own stimuli which are essential to the carrying-out of the response to the other form, such communication could not take place. In fact we find that in the case of the deaf and dumb, if no care is given to the development of language, the child does not develop normal human intelligence, but remains on the level of lower animals. There is then a physiological background for language, but it is not one of physiological differentiation between the various forms. We all have vocal organs and auditory organs, and in so far as our development is a normal development, we are all capable of influencing ourselves as we influence others. It is out of this capacity for being influenced by our own gesture as we influence others that has arisen the peculiar form of the human social organism, made up out of beings that to that degree are physiologically identical. Certain of the social processes within which this communication takes place are dependent upon physiological differences, but the individual is not in the social process differentiated physiologically from other individuals. That, I am insisting, constitutes the fundamental difference between the societies of the insects and human society.[3] It is a distinction which still has to be made with reservations, because it may be that there will be some way of discovering in the future a language among the ants and bees. We do find, as I have said, a differentiation of physiological characters which so far explain the peculiar organization of these insect societies. Human society, then, is dependent upon the development of language for its own distinctive form of organization.

It is tempting to look at the physiology of the insect as over against the physiology of the human form and note its differences. But while it is tempting to speculate on such differences, there is as yet no adequate basis for generalization in that field. The human form is different from the insect form. Of course,

[3] The socialized human animal takes the attitude of the other toward himself and toward any given social situation in which he and other individuals may happen to be placed or implicated; and he thus identifies himself with the other in that given situation, responding implicitly as the other does or would respond explicitly, and governing his own explicit reaction accordingly. The socialized non-human animal, on the other hand, does not take the attitude of the other toward himself and toward the given social situation in which they are both involved because he is physiologically incapable of doing so; and hence, also, he cannot adjustively and co-operatively control his own explicit response to the given social situation in terms of an awareness of that attitude of the other, as the socialized human animal can.

All communication, all conversations of gestures, among the lower animals, and even among the members of the more highly developed insect societies, is presumably unconscious. Hence, it is only in human society—only within the peculiarly complex context of social relations and interactions which the human central nervous system makes physiologically possible—that minds arise or can arise; and thus also human beings are evidently the only biological organisms which are or can be self-conscious or possessed of selves.

the ants and bees have brains but they have not anything that answers to the cortex. We do recognize that just as we have a type of society built up on this principle of physiological differentiation, so we must have a different physiological organization. We get unity into the varied structures of the human form by means of an additional organ, the brain and the cortex. There is unity in the insect form by actual collaboration of physiological parts. There is some physiological basis back of this, obscure though the details are.[4] It is important to recognize that the intelligent form does attain the development of intelligence through such an organ as the central nervous system with its peculiar development of the brain and the cortex. The spinal column represents sets of more or less fixed responses. It is the development of the cortex that brings about all sorts of possible combinations of these numerous but relatively fixed responses. By means, then, of an organ which is superimposed on the central nervous system, connections can be set up between the different types of responses which arise through the lower system. There thus arises the almost indefinite multiplicity of the responses of the human organism.

While it is in the development of the brain as such that we get the possibility of the appearance of distinctively human conduct, human conduct, if put simply in terms of the stem of the brain and column, would be very restricted, and the human animal would be a feeble and unimportant animal. There would not be much he could do. He could run and climb, and eat what he could bring to his mouth with his hands, in virtue of those

[4] The individual members of even the most advanced invertebrate societies do not possess sufficient physiological capacities for developing minds or selves, consciousness or intelligence, out of their social relations and interactions with one another; and hence these societies cannot attain either the degree of complexity which would be presupposed by the emergence of minds and selves within them, or the further degree of complexity which would be possible only if minds and selves had emerged or arisen within them. Only the individual members of human societies possess the required physiological capacities for such social development of minds and selves; and hence only human societies are able to reach the level of complexity, in their structure and organization, which becomes possible as a result of the emergence of minds and selves in their individual members.

reflexes which go back to the original central nervous system. But a set of combinations of all the different processes found there gives an indefinite number of possible reactions in the activities of the human animal. It is because of the variety of combinations in the connections of the responses to stimuli, which take place in the paths that run into the cortex, that one can make any sort of combination of all the different ways in which a human being can use his arms, his legs, and the rest of his body.[5]

There is, as we have seen, another very important phase in the development of the human animal which is perhaps quite as essential as speech for the development of man's peculiar intelligence, and that is the use of the hand for the isolation of physical things. Speech and the hand go along together in the development of the social human being. There has to arise self-consciousness for the whole flowering-out of intelligence. But there has to be some phase of the act which stops short of consummation if that act is to develop intelligently, and language and the hand provide the necessary mechanisms. We all have hands and speech, and are all, as social beings, identical, intelligent beings. We all have what we term "consciousness" and we all live in a world of things. It is in such media that human society develops, media entirely different from those within which the insect society develops.

[5] We have said in general that the limit of possible social development in any species of animal organism—the degree of complexity of social organization which individuals of that species are capable of attaining—is determined by the nature and extent of their relevant physiological equipment, their physiological capacities for social behavior; and this limit of possible social development in the particular case of the human species is determined, theoretically at least, by the number of nerve cells or neural elements in the human brain, and by the consequent number and diversity of their possible combinations and interrelations with reference to their effect upon, or control of, overt individual behavior.

All that is innate or hereditary in connection with minds and selves is the physiological mechanism of the human central nervous system, by means of which the genesis of minds and selves out of the human social process of experience and behavior—out of the human matrix of social relations and interactions—is made biologically possible in human individuals.

31. THE BASIS OF HUMAN SOCIETY: MAN AND THE
VERTEBRATES

We have seen that human society is organized on a principle different from the insect societies, which are based on physiological differentiation. Human individuals are identical in large respects with each other and physiologically differentiated relatively slightly. The self-conscious individual that goes to constitute such a society is not dependent upon the physiological differentiations, even where they exist, while in the insect community the very existence of the communities is dependent upon such physiological differentiation. The organization of social attitudes constituting the structure and content of the human individual self is effected both in terms of the organization of neural elements and their interconnections in the individual's central nervous system, and in terms of the general ordered pattern of social or group behavior or conduct in which the individual—as a member of the society or group of individuals carrying on that behavior—is involved.

It is true, also, that many vertebrate forms with the beginnings of a society do not depend on physiological differentiation. Such societies lower than man are relatively insignificant. The family, of course, is significant, and we can say that the family exists lower than man. There is not only the necessary relationship of parent and child which is due to the period of infancy, but also the relationship between the sexes, which may be relatively permanent, and which leads to an organization of the family. But there is not found an organization of a larger group on the basis solely of the family organization. The herd, the school of fishes, groups of birds, so far as they form loose aggregations, do not arise out of the development of a physiological function which belongs to the family. Such herds exhibit what we may call "instinctive relationships," in the sense that the forms keep together and seem to find in each other a stimulus for carrying on their own activity. Animals in a group will perform the grazing functions better than when alone. There seem to be instinctive tendencies on the part of these forms to move in the direction which other animals are moving, such as is found in any group of cattle drifting across the prairie together as they graze. The movement of one form is a stimulus to the other form to move on in the direction in which the other form is moving. That seems to be about the limit of that phase of herding. There are also forms huddled together in defense or in attack, as the herd which defends itself against the attack of the wolves, or the wolves running together in attacking the herd. But such mechanisms give relatively slight bases for organization, and they do not enter into the life of the individual so as to determine that life throughout. The individual is not determined through his relationship to the herd. The herd comes in as a new sort of organization and makes the life of the individual possible from the point of view of the defense from an attack, but the actual processes of eating and of propagation are not dependent on the herding itself. It does not represent such an organization of all the members as to determine the life of the separate members. Still more fundamentally, the family, so far as it exists among the lower forms, does not come in as that which makes possible the structure of the herd as such. It is true that in this massing together of cattle against the attack from outside the young form is put inside of the circle, and this is a development of the family relation, of that general attitude of parental care toward the young. But it is not an instinct which is here developed definitely into a process of defense or into a process of attack.

In the case of the human group, on the other hand, there is a development in which the complex phases of society have arisen out of the organization which the appearance of the self made possible. One perhaps finds in the relationship of the different members of the most primitive group attitudes of mutual defense and attack. It is likely that such co-operative attitudes, combined with the attitudes of the family, supply the situations out of which selves arise. Given the self, there is then the possibility of the further development of the society on this self-conscious basis, which is so distinct from the loose organization of the herd or from the complex society of the insects. It is the self as such that makes the distinctively human society possible. It is true that some sort of co-operative activity antedates the self. There must be some loose organization in which the different organisms work together, and that sort of co-operation in which the gesture of the individual may become a stimulus to himself of the same type as the stimulus to the other form, so that the conversation of gestures can pass over into the conduct of the individual. Such conditions are presupposed in the development of the self. But when the self has developed, then a basis is obtained for the development of a society which is different in its character from these other societies to which I have referred.

The family relation, you might say, gives us some suggestion of the sort of organization which belongs to the insect, for here we have physiological differentiation between the different members, the parents and the child. And in the mob we have a reversion to the society of a herd of cattle. A group of individuals can be stampeded like cattle. But in those two expressions, taken by themselves and apart from the self, you do not have the structure of a human society; you could not make up a human society out of the family as it exists in forms lower than man; you could not make up human society out of a herd. To suggest this would be to leave out of account the fundamental organization of human society about a self or selves.

There is, of course, in one sense, a physiological basis for human society, namely, in the development of the central nervous system, such as belongs to the vertebrates, and which reaches its highest development in man. Through the organization of the central nervous system the different reactions of the form may be combined in all sorts of orders, spatial and temporal, the spinal column representing a whole series of different possible reactions which, when excited, go off by themselves, while the cortical levels of the central nervous system provide all sorts of combinations of these various possible reactions. These higher levels of the brain make possible the variety of activities of the higher vertebrates. Such is the raw stuff, stated in physiological terms, from which the intelligence of the human social being arises.

The human being is social in a distinguishing fashion. Physiologically he is social in relatively few responses. There are, of course, fundamental processes of propagation and of the care of the young which have been recognized as a part of the social development of human intelligence. Not only is there a physiological period of infancy, but it is so lengthened that it represents about one-third of the individual's expectation of life. Corresponding to that period, the parental relation to the individual has been increased far beyond the family; the development of schools, and of institutions, such as those involved in the church and the government, is an extension of the parental relation. That is an external illustration of the indefinite complication of simple physiological processes. We take the care of an infant form and look at it from the standpoint of the mother; we see the care that is given to the mother before the birth of the child, the consideration that is given for providing proper food; we see the way in which the school is carried on so that the beginning of the education of the child starts with the first year of its life in the formation of habits which are of primary importance to it; we take into account education in the form of recreation, which comes one way or another into public control; in all these ways we can see what an elaboration there is of the immediate care which parents give to children under the most primitive conditions, and yet it is nothing but a continued complication of sets of processes which belong to the original care of the child.

This, I say, is an external picture of the sort of development that takes place in a central nervous system. There are groups of relatively simple reactions which can be made indefinitely complex by uniting them with each other in all sorts of orders, and by breaking up a complex reaction, reconstructing it in a different fashion, and uniting it with other processes. Consider the playing of musical instruments. There is an immediate tendency to rhythmic processes, to use the rhythm of the body to emphasize certain sounds, movements which can be found among the gorillas. Then comes the possibility of picking to pieces the action of the whole body, the construction of elaborate dances, the relation of the dance to sound which appears in song, phenomena which get their expression in the great Greek dramas. These results are then externalized in musical instruments, which are in a way replicas of various organs of the body. All these external complications are nothing but an externalization in society of the sort of complication that exists in the higher levels of the central nervous system. We take the primitive reactions, analyze them, and reconstruct them under different conditions. That kind of reconstruction takes place through the development of the sort of intelligence which is identified with the appearance of the self. The institutions of society, such as libraries, systems of transportation, the complex interrelationship of individuals reached in political organizations, are nothing but ways of throwing on the social screen, so to speak, in enlarged fashion the complexities existing inside of the central nervous system, and they must, of course, express functionally the operation of this system.

The possibility of carrying this elaboration to the extent which has appeared in the human animal and the corresponding human society, is to be found in the development of communication in the conduct of the self. The arousing of the attitude which would lead to the same sort of action as that which is called out in the other individual makes possible the process of analysis, the breaking-up of the act itself. In the case of the fencer or boxer, where a man makes a certain feint to call out a certain response on the part of his opponent, he is at the same time calling out, in so far as he is aware of what he is doing, the beginning of the same response in himself. When he is doing that he is stimulating a certain area in the central nervous system which, if allowed to be the dominant area, would lead to the individual doing the same thing that his opponent does. He has taken his activity and isolated that particular phase of it, and in isolating that he has also broken up his response so that the different things he can do are within himself. He has stimulated those areas which answer to the different parts of the complex process. He can now combine them in various ways, and his combination of them is a process of reflective intelligence. It is a process which is illustrated most fully in a chess player. A good chess player has the response of the other person in his system. He can carry four or five moves ahead in his mind. What he is doing is stimulating another person to do a thing while he stimulates himself to do the same thing. That enables him to analyze his mode of attack into its different elements in terms of the responses coming from his opponent and then to reconstruct his own activity on that basis.

I have stressed the point that the process of communication is nothing but an elaboration of the peculiar intelligence with which the vertebrate form is endowed. The mechanism which can analyze the responses, take them to pieces, and reconstruct them, is made possible by the brain as such, and the process of communication is the means by which this is brought under the control of the individual himself. He can take his response to pieces and present it to himself as a set of different things he can do under conditions more or less controllable. The process of communication simply puts the intelligence of the individual at his own disposal. But the individual that has this ability is a social individual. He does not develop it by himself and then enter into society on the basis of this capacity. He becomes such a self and gets such control by being a social individual, and it is only in society that he can attain this sort of a self which will make it possible for him to turn back on himself and indicate to himself the different things he can do.

The elaboration, then, of the intelligence of the vertebrate form in human society is dependent upon the development of this sort of social reaction in which the individual can influence himself as he influences others. It is this that makes it possible for him to take over and elaborate the attitudes of the other individuals. He does it in terms of the higher levels of the central nervous system that are representative of the reactions that take place. The reaction of walking, striking, or any simple reaction, belongs to the column at the stem of the brain. What takes place beyond this is simply the combinations of reactions of this type. When a person goes across the room to take up a book, what has taken place in his brain has been the connection of the processes involved in going across the room with those in taking up the book. When you take the attitude of another you are simply arousing the above responses which combine a reaction with different reactions to effect the necessary response. The centers involved in the combining of the responses of the lower forms answer to the higher mental processes, and make possible the elaboration of responses in these complex forms.

The human form has a mechanism for making these combinations within itself. A human individual is able to indicate to himself what the other person is going to do, and then to take his attitude on the basis of that indication. He can analyze his act and reconstruct it by means of this process. The sort of intelligence he has is not based on physiological differentiation, nor based upon herd instinct, but upon the development through the social process which enables him to carry out his part in the social reaction by indicating to himself the different possible reactions, analyzing them, and recombining them. It is that sort of an individual which makes human society possible. The preceding considerations are to be opposed to the utterly illogical type of analysis which deals with the human individual as if he were physiologically differentiated, simply because one can find a differentiation of individuals in the human society which can be compared with the differentiation in a nest of ants. In man the functional differentiation through language gives an entirely different principle of organization which produces not only a different type of individual but also a different society.

32. ORGANISM, COMMUNITY, AND ENVIRONMENT

I want to take up next the relationship of the organism to the environment as this gets expression in the relation of the community and its environment.

We have seen that the individual organism determines in some sense its own environment by its sensitivity. The only environment to which the organism can react is one that its sensitivity reveals. The sort of environment that can exist for the organism, then, is one that the organism in some sense determines. If in the development of the form there is an increase in the diversity of sensitivity there will be an increase in the responses of the organism to its environment, that is, the organism will have a correspondingly larger environment. There is a direct reaction of the organism upon the environment which leads to some measure of control. In the matter of food, in the matter of protection against the rain and cold and against enemies, the form does in some sense directly control the environment through its response. Such direct control, however, is very slight as compared with the determination of the environment dependent upon the sensitivity of the form. There may be, of course, influences which affect the form as a whole which do not answer to this type of determination, such as great cataclysms like earthquakes, events which lift the organism into different environments without the sensitivity of the form being itself immediately involved. Great geological changes, such as the gradual advance and disappearance of the glacial epoch, are just superinduced on the organism. The organism cannot control them; they just take place. In that sense the environment controls the form rather than being controlled by it. Nevertheless, in so far as the form does respond it does so in virtue of its sensitivity. In this sense it selects and picks out what constitutes its environment. It selects that to which it responds and makes use of it for its own purposes, purposes involved in its life-processes. It utilizes the earth on which it treads and through which it burrows, and the trees that it climbs; but only when it is sensitive to them. There must be a relation of stimulus and response; the environment must lie in some sense inside of the act if the form is to respond to it.

This intimate relationship of environment and form is something that we need to impress on ourselves, for we are apt to approach the situation from the standpoint of a pre-existent environment just there, into which the living form enters or within which it happens, and then to think of this environment affecting the form, setting the conditions under which the form can live. In that way there is set up the problem of an environment within which adjustment is supposed to take place. This is a natural enough approach from the scientific point of view of the history of life on the earth. The earth was there before life appeared, and it remains while different forms pass away and others come on. We regard the forms that appear in the geological record as incidents, and more or less accidental. We can point to a number of critical periods in the history of the earth in which the appearance of life is dependent upon things that happen, or appear. The forms seem to be quite at the mercy of the environment. So we state the environment not in terms of the form but the form in terms of the environment.

Nevertheless, the only environment to which the form responds is the environment which is predetermined by the sensitivity of the form and its response to it. It is true that the response may be one which is unfavorable to the form, but the changes that we are interested in are those changes of the form in an environment which it itself does select and which it itself organizes in terms of its own conduct. It exists at a distance from objects which are favorable or unfavorable to it, and it measures the distance in terms of its own movements toward or away from the objects. That which affects it in its distant experience is a promise of what will happen after contact takes place. It may be favorable contact with food, or contact with the jaws of its enemies. It is such resultants which the distant experience is indicating; this is the way in which an environment exists.

The things we see at a distance are the contacts that we shall get after we move toward the thing. Our environment exists in a certain sense as hypotheses. "The wall is over there," means "We have certain visual experiences which promise to us certain contacts of hardness, roughness, coolness." Everything that exists about us exists for us in this hypothetical fashion. Of course, the hypotheses are supported by conduct, by experiment, if you like. We put our feet down with an assurance born out of past experience, and we expect the customary result. We are occasionally subject to illusions, and then we realize that the world that exists about us does exist in a hypothetical fashion. What comes to us through distant experience is a sort of language which reveals to us the probable experience we should get if we were actually to traverse the distance between us and those objects. The form which has no distant experience, such as an amoeba, or which has such distant experience involved only functionally, has not the sort of environment that other forms have. I want to bring this out to emphasize the fact that the environment is in a very real sense determined by the character of the form. It is possible for us, from the standpoint of our scientific account of the world, to get outside of these environments of the different forms and relate them to each other. We there have a study of environments in their relationship to the forms themselves, and we state our environments first and then relate them to the form. But as far as environments exist for the form itself they exist in this selected character and as constructed in terms of possible responses.[6]

Over against this control which the form exercises on its environment (expressible in terms of selection and organization), there is a further control which I have referred to in a form which does actually determine by its responses the objects that exist about it. In so far as an animal digs a hole or builds a nest, it does get things together so that it makes a house for itself. These actual constructions are of a different character from that sort of control to which I previously referred. The

[6] [For the relation of the world of common experience and of science, see *The Philosophy of the Act*, Part II.]

ants, for example, actually keep certain forms of vegetation in their galleries upon which they feed. This gives a control of the environment that goes beyond those to which we have yet referred, since it necessitates active responses by the animals determining what the vegetable growth will be. Such actions make up a very slight part of the lives of these insects, but they do occur. That sort of control goes beyond the building of the burrow or the nest, since there is an actual construction of the environment within which the animal carries on its life-process. The striking thing about the human organism is the elaborate extension of control of the type I have just referred to in the case of the insects.

The environment, I have said, is our environment. We see what we can reach, what we can manipulate, and then deal with it as we come in contact with it. I have emphasized the importance of the hand in the building-up of this environment. The acts of the living form are those which lead up to consummations such as that of eating food. The hand comes in between the beginning and the end of this process. We get hold of the food, we handle it, and so far as our statement of the environment is concerned, we can say that we present it to ourselves in terms of the manipulated object. The fruit that we can have is a thing that we can handle. It may be fruit which we can eat or a representation of it in wax. The object, however, is a physical thing. The world of physical things we have about us is not simply the goal of our movement but a world which permits the consummation of the act. A dog can, of course, pick up sticks and bring them back. He can utilize his jaws for carrying, but that is the only extension possible beyond their actual utilization for the process of devouring. The act is quickly carried through to its consummation. The human animal, however, has this implemental stage that comes between the actual consummation and the beginning of the act, and the thing appears in that phase of the act. Our environment as such is made up out of physical things. Our conduct translates the objects to which we respond over into physical things which lie beyond our actual consummation of the immediate act. The things that we can get hold of, that we can break up into minute parts, are the things which we reach short of the consummation of the act, and which we can in some sense manipulate with reference to further activity. If we speak now of the animal as constituting its environment by its sensitivity, by its movements toward the objects, by its reactions, we can see that the human form constitutes its environment in terms of these physical things which are in a real sense the products of our own hands. They, of course, have the further advantage from the point of view of intelligence that they are implements, things we can use. They come betwixt and between the beginning of the act and its consummation, so that we have objects in terms of which we can express the relation of means to ends. We can analyze our ends in terms of the means at our disposal. The human hand, backed up, of course, by the indefinite number of actions which the central nervous system makes possible, is of critical importance in the development of human intelligence. It is important that a man should be able to descend from a tree (providing his ancestors lived in a tree), but it is of greater importance that he should have a thumb opposite the fingers to grasp and utilize the objects that he needs. We thus break up our world into physical objects, into an environment of things that we can manipulate and can utilize for our final ends and purposes.

Beyond this individual function lies the uses to which we put such physical objects in facilitating the control which the organized group gets over its world. Reduce this group to its lowest terms—such as we find in our romances about the cave man—and the things with which it operates are hardly anything more than clubs or stones. Its environment is not so different from the environment of the animals. But the development of human society on a larger scale has led to a very complete control of its environment. The human form establishes its own home where it wishes; builds cities; brings its water from great distances; establishes the vegetation which shall grow about it; determines the animals that will exist; gets into that struggle which is going on now with insect life, determining what insects shall continue to live; is attempting to determine what micro-organisms shall remain in its environment. It determines, by means of its clothing and housing, what the temperature shall be about it; it regulates the extent of its environment by means of its methods of locomotion. The whole onward struggle of mankind on the face of the earth is such a determination of the life that shall exist about it and such a control of physical objects as determine and affect its own life. The community as such creates its environment by being sensitive to it.

We speak of Darwinian evolution, of the conflict of different forms with each other, as being the essential part of the problem of development; but if we leave out some of the insects and micro-organisms, there are no living forms with which the human form in its social capacity is in basic conflict. We determine what wild life we will keep; we can wipe out all the forms of animal or vegetable life that exist; we can sow what seed we want, and kill or breed what animals we want. There is no longer a biological environment in the Darwinian sense to set our problem. Of course, we cannot control the geological forces, the so-called "acts of God." They come in and wipe out what man has created. Changes in the solar system can simply annihilate the planet on which we live; such forces lie outside our control. But if we take those forces which we look upon as important in the development of this species on the face of the globe, they are to a great extent under the control of human society. The problem of the pressure of population has always played a large part in the selection of forms that survive. Nature has to select on the principle of overproduction in order that there may be, speaking in an anthropomorphic fashion, variations, some of which may possess advantages over the others. Just as Burrows used numerous varieties in his plant experiments in the hope that some would be of advantage, so, speaking anthropomorphically, nature uses variety, producing more forms that can survive in the hope that some superior form will survive. The death-rate of a certain insect is 99.8, and those forms that survive are of a diminishing number. There remain problems of population for the human form, but man could determine the population which is to exist in terms of knowledge he already possesses. The problem is in the hands of the community as far as it reacts intelligently upon its problems. Thus, even those problems which come from within the community itself can be definitely controlled by the community. It is this control of its own evolution which is the goal of the development of human society.

It has been legitimately said that there is not any goal presented in biological evolution, that the theory of evolution is part of a mechanical theory of nature. Such evolution works, so to speak, from behind. The explanation is in terms of forces already there, and in this process the particular forms appear which do fit certain situations and so survive in the struggle for existence. Such a process of adaptation is not necessarily a process which picks out what we consider the more desirable form. The parasite is definitely a result of evolutionary process. It loses various organs because they are no longer necessary, but it has adapted itself to the life of feeding on the host. We can explain that from the point of view of evolution. From such a point of view we do not have to regard nature as producing more and more highly complicated, more perfect forms. The changes are simply explained by variations and adaptation to the situations that arise. There is no necessity of bringing in an end toward which all creation moves.

Nevertheless, the human situation which I have just presented does in a certain sense present an end, not, if you like, in the physiological sense, but as a determination of the process of life on the surface of the earth. The human society that can itself determine what the conditions are within which it lives is no longer in a situation of simply trying to meet the problems that the environment presents. If humanity can control its environment, it will in a certain sense stabilize itself and reach the end of a process of development, except in so far as the society goes on developing in this process of controlling its own environment. We do not have to develop a new form with hairy covering to live in cold climates; we can simply produce clothes which enable the explorers to go to the North Pole. We can determine the conditions under which the heat of the tropics shall be made endurable. We can, by putting a wire into the wall of a room, raise or lower the temperature. Even in the case of the micro-organisms, if we can control these, as human society in part does, we have determined not only what the environment is in its immediate relation to us, but also what the physical environment is in its influence on the form; and that would produce a terminus as a goal of evolution.

We are so far away from any actual final adjustment of this sort that we correctly say that the evolution of the social organism has a long road ahead of it. But supposing it had attained this goal, had determined the conditions within which it could live and reproduce itself, then the further changes in the human form would no longer take place in terms of the principles that have determined biological evolution. The human situation is a development of the control which all living forms exercise over their environment in selection and in organization, but the human society has reached an end which no other form has reached, that of actually determining, within certain limits, what its inorganic environment will be. We cannot transport ourselves to other planets, or determine what the movements of the solar system will be (possible changes of that sort lie beyond any conceivable control of the human organism); but apart from such limits, those forces which affect the life of the form and can conceivably change it in the Darwinian sense have come under the control of the society itself, and, in so far as they come under the exercised control of the society, human society presents an end of the process of organic evolution. It is needless to add that, so far as the development of human society is concerned, the process itself is a long way from its goal.

SOCIETY

33. THE SOCIAL FOUNDATIONS AND FUNCTIONS OF THOUGHT AND COMMUNICATION

In the same socio-physiological way that the human individual becomes conscious of himself he also becomes conscious of other individuals; and his consciousness both of himself and of other individuals is equally important for his own self-development and for the development of the organized society or social group to which he belongs.

The principle which I have suggested as basic to human social organization is that of communication involving participation in the other. This requires the appearance of the other in the self, the identification of the other with the self, the reaching of self-consciousness through the other. This participation is made possible through the type of communication which the human animal is able to carry out—a type of communication distinguished from that which takes place among other forms which have not this principle in their societies. I discussed the sentinel, so-called, that may be said to communicate his discovery of the danger to the other members, as the clucking of the hen may be said to communicate to the chick. There are conditions under which the gesture of one form serves to place the other forms in the proper attitude toward external conditions. In one sense we may say the one form communicates with the other, but the difference between that and self-conscious communication is evident. One form does not know that communication is taking place with the other. We get illustrations of that in what we term mob-consciousness, the attitude which an audience will take when under the influence of a great speaker. One is influenced by the attitudes of those about him, which are reflected back into the different members of the audience so that they come to respond as a whole. One feels the general attitude of the whole audience. There is then communication in a real sense, that is, one form communicates to the other an attitude which the other assumes toward a certain part of the environment that is of importance to them both. That level of communication is found in forms of society which are of lower type than the social organization of the human group.

In the human group, on the other hand, there is not only this kind of communication but also that in which the person who uses this gesture and so communicates assumes the attitude of the other individual as well as calling it out in the other. He himself is in the rôle of the other person whom he is so exciting and influencing. It is through taking this rôle of the other that he is able to come back on himself and so direct his own process of communication. This taking the rôle of the other, an expression I have so often used, is not simply of passing importance. It is not something that just happens as an incidental result of the gesture, but it is of importance in the development of co-operative activity. The immediate effect of such rôle-taking lies in the control which the individual is able to exercise over his own response.[7] The control of the action of the individual in a co-operative process can take place in the conduct of the individual himself if he can take the rôle of the other. It is this control of the response of the individual himself through taking the rôle of the other that leads to the value of this type of communication from the point of view of the organization of the conduct in the group. It carries the process of co-operative

---

[7] From the standpoint of social evolution, it is this bringing of any given social act, or of the total social process in which that act is a constituent, directly and as an organized whole into the experience of each of the individual organisms implicated in that act, with reference to which he may consequently regulate and govern his individual conduct, that constitutes the peculiar value and significance of self-consciousness in these individual organisms.

We have seen that the process or activity of thinking is a conversation carried on by the individual between himself and the generalized other; and that the general form and subject matter of this conversation is given and determined by the appearance in experience of some sort of problem to be solved. Human intelligence, which expresses itself in thought, is recognized to have this character of facing and dealing with any problem of environmental adjustment which confronts an organism possessing it. And thus, as we have also seen, the essential characteristic of intelligent behavior is delayed responses—a halt in behavior while thinking is going on; this delayed response and the thinking for the purposes of which it is delayed (including the final selection, as the result of the thinking, of the best or most expedient among the several responses possible in the given environmental situation) being made possible physiologically through the mechanism of the central nervous system, and socially through the mechanism of language.

activity farther than it can be carried in the herd as such, or in the insect society.

And thus it is that social control, as operating in terms of self-criticism, exerts itself so intimately and extensively over individual behavior or conduct, serving to integrate the individual and his actions with reference to the organized social process of experience and behavior in which he is implicated. The physiological mechanism of the human individual's central nervous system makes it possible for him to take the attitudes of other individuals, and the attitudes of the organized social group of which he and they are members, toward himself, in terms of his integrated social relations to them and to the group as a whole; so that the general social process of experience and behavior which the group is carrying on is directly presented to him in his own experience, and so that he is thereby able to govern and direct his conduct consciously and critically, with reference to his relations both to the social group as a whole and to its other individual members, in terms of this social process. Thus he becomes not only self-conscious but also self-critical; and thus, through self-criticism, social control over individual behavior or conduct operates by virtue of the social origin and basis of such criticism. That is to say, self-criticism is essentially social criticism, and behavior controlled by self-criticism is essentially behavior controlled socially.[8] Hence social control, so far from tending to crush out the human individual or to obliterate his self-conscious individuality, is, on the contrary, actually constitutive of and inextricably associated with that individuality; for the individual is what he is, as a conscious and individual personality, just in as far as he is a member of society, involved in the social process of experience and activity, and thereby socially controlled in his conduct.

[8] Freud's conception of the psychological "censor" represents a partial recognition of this operation of social control in terms of self-criticism, a recognition, namely, of its operation with reference to sexual experience and conduct. But this same sort of censorship or criticism of himself by the individual is reflected also in all other aspects of his social experience, behavior, and relations—a fact which follows naturally and inevitably from our social theory of the self.

The very organization of the self-conscious community is dependent upon individuals taking the attitude of the other individuals. The development of this process, as I have indicated, is dependent upon getting the attitude of the group as distinct from that of a separate individual—getting what I have termed a "generalized other." I have illustrated this by the ball game, in which the attitudes of a set of individuals are involved in a co-operative response in which the different rôles involve each other. In so far as a man takes the attitude of one individual in the group, he must take it in its relationship to the action of the other members of the group; and if he is fully to adjust himself, he would have to take the attitudes of all involved in the process. The degree, of course, to which he can do that is restrained by his capacity, but still in all intelligent processes we are able sufficiently to take the rôles of those involved in the activity to make our own action intelligent. The degree to which the life of the whole community can get into the self-conscious life of the separate individuals varies enormously. History is largely occupied in tracing out the development which could not have been present in the actual experience of the members of the community at the time the historian is writing about. Such an account explains the importance of history. One can look back over that which took place, and bring out changes, forces, and interests which nobody at the time was conscious of. We have to wait for the historian to give the picture because the actual process was one which transcended the experience of the separate individuals.

Occasionally a person arises who is able to take in more than others of an act in process, who can put himself into relation with whole groups in the community whose attitudes have not entered into the lives of the others in the community. He becomes a leader. Classes under a feudal order may be so separate from each other that, while they can act in certain traditional circumstances, they cannot understand each other; and then there may arise an individual who is capable of entering into the attitudes of the other members of the group. Figures of that

sort become of enormous importance because they make possible communication between groups otherwise completely separated from each other. The sort of capacity we speak of is in
politics the attitude of the statesman who is able to enter into
the attitudes of the group and to mediate between them by making his own experience universal, so that others can enter into
this form of communication through him.

The vast importance of media of communication such as those
involved in journalism is seen at once, since they report situations through which one can enter into the attitude and experience of other persons. The drama has served this function in
presenting what have been felt to be important situations. It
has picked out characters which lie in men's minds from tradition, as the Greeks did in their tragedies, and then expressed
through these characters situations which belong to their own
time but which carry the individuals beyond the actual fixed
walls which have arisen between them, as members of different
classes in the community. The development of this type of communication from the drama into the novel has historically something of the same importance as journalism has for our own
time. The novel presents a situation which lies outside of the
immediate purview of the reader in such form that he enters into
the attitude of the group in the situation. There is a far higher
degree of participation, and consequently of possible communication, under those conditions than otherwise. There is involved, of course, in such a development the existence of common interests. You cannot build up a society out of elements
that lie outside of the individual's life-processes. You have to
presuppose some sort of co-operation within which the individuals are themselves actively involved as the only possible
basis for this participation in communication. You cannot start
to communicate with people in Mars and set up a society where
you have no antecedent relationship. Of course, if there is an
already existing community in Mars of the same character as
your own, then you can possibly carry on communication with
it; but a community that lies entirely outside of your own com-

munity, that has no common interest, no co-operative activity, is one with which you could not communicate.

In human society there have arisen certain universal forms which found their expression in universal religions and also in universal economic processes. These go back, in the case of religion, to such fundamental attitudes of human beings toward each other as kindliness, helpfulness, and assistance. Such attitudes are involved in the life of individuals in the group, and a generalization of them is found back of all universal religions. These processes are such that they carry with them neighborliness and, in so far as we have co-operative activity, assistance to those in trouble and in suffering. The fundamental attitude of helping the other person who is down, who finds himself in sickness or other misfortune, belongs to the very structure of the individuals in a human community. It can be found even under conditions where there is the opposing attitude of complete hostility, as in giving assistance to the wounded enemy in the midst of a battle. The attitude of chivalry, or the mere breaking of bread with another, identifies the individual with the other even if he is an enemy. Those are situations in which the individual finds himself in an attitude of co-operation; and it is out of situations like that, out of universal co-operative activity, that the universal religions have arisen. The development of this fundamental neighborliness is expressed in the parable of the good Samaritan.

On the other hand, we have a fundamental process of exchange on the part of individuals arising from the goods for which they have no immediate need themselves but which can be utilized for obtaining that which they do need. Such exchange can take place wherever individuals who have such surpluses are able to communicate with each other. There is a participation in the attitude of need, each putting himself in the attitude of the other in the recognition of the mutual value which the exchange has for both. It is a highly abstract relationship, for something which one cannot himself use brings him into relationship with anybody else in exchange. It is a situation which is as universal as that to which we have referred in the case of neighborliness. These two attitudes represent the most highly universal, and, for the time being, most highly abstract society. They are attitudes which can transcend the limits of the different social groups organized about their own life-processes, and may appear even in actual hostility between groups. In the process of exchange or assistance persons who would be otherwise hostile can come into an attitude of co-operative activity.

Back of these two attitudes lies that which is involved in any genuine communication. It is more universal in one respect than religious and economic attitudes, and less in another. One has to have something to communicate before communicating. One may seemingly have the symbol of another language, but if he has not any common ideas (and these involve common responses) with those who speak that language, he cannot communicate with them; so that back even of the process of discourse must lie co-operative activity. The process of communication is one which is more universal than that of the universal religion or universal economic process in that it is one that serves them both. Those two activities have been the most universal co-operative activities. The scientific community is one which has come to be perhaps as universal in one sense, but even it cannot be found among people who have no conscious signs or literature. The process of communication is, then, in one sense more universal than these different co-operative processes. It is the medium through which these co-operative activities can be carried on in the self-conscious society. But one must recognize that it is a medium for co-operative activities; there is not any field of thought as such which can simply go on by itself. Thinking is not a field or realm which can be taken outside of possible social uses. There has to be some such field as religion or economics in which there is something to communicate, in which there is a co-operative process, in which what is communicated can be socially utilized. One must assume that sort of a co-operative situation in order to reach what is called the "universe of discourse." Such a universe of discourse is the medium for all these different social processes, and in that sense it is more universal than they; but it is not a process that, so to speak, runs by itself.

It is necessary to emphasize this because philosophy and the dogmas that have gone with it have set up a process of thought and a thinking substance that is the antecedent of these very processes within which thinking goes on. Thinking, however, is nothing but the response of the individual to the attitude of the other in the wide social process in which both are involved, and the directing of one's anticipatory action by these attitudes of the others that one does assume. Since that is what the process of thinking consists in, it cannot simply run by itself.

I have been looking at language as a principle of social organization which has made the distinctively human society possible. Of course, if there are inhabitants in Mars, it is possible for us to enter into communication with them in as far as we can enter into social relations with them. If we can isolate the logical constants which are essential for any process of thinking, presumably those logical constants would put us into a position to carry on communication with the other community. They would constitute a common social process so that one could possibly enter into a social process with any other being in any historical period or spatial position. By means of thought one can project a society into the future or past, but we are always presupposing a social relationship within which this process of communication takes place. The process of communication cannot be set up as something that exists by itself, or as a presupposition of the social process. On the contrary, the social process is presupposed in order to render thought and communication possible.

34. THE COMMUNITY AND THE INSTITUTION[9]

There are what I have termed "generalized social attitudes" which make an organized self possible. In the community there

[9] [See "Natural Rights and the Theory of the Political Institution," *Journal of Philosophy*, XII (1915), 141 ff.]

are certain ways of acting under situations which are essentially identical, and these ways of acting on the part of anyone are those which we excite in others when we take certain steps. If we assert our rights, we are calling for a definite response just because they are rights that are universal—a response which everyone should, and perhaps will, give. Now that response is present in our own nature; in some degree we are ready to take that same attitude toward somebody else if he makes the appeal. When we call out that response in others, we can take the attitude of the other and then adjust our own conduct to it. There are, then, whole series of such common responses in the community in which we live, and such responses are what we term "institutions." The institution represents a common response on the part of all members of the community to a particular situation. This common response is one which, of course, varies with the character of the individual. In the case of theft the response of the sheriff is different from that of the attorney-general, from that of the judge and the jurors, and so forth; and yet they all are responses which maintain property, which involve the recognition of the property right in others. There is a common response in varied forms. And these variations, as illustrated in the different officials, have an organization which gives unity to the variety of the responses. One appeals to the policeman for assistance, one expects the state's attorney to act, expects the court and its various functionaries to carry out the process of the trial of the criminal. One does take the attitude of all of these different officials as involved in the very maintenance of property; all of them as an organized process are in some sense found in our own natures. When we arouse such attitudes, we are taking the attitude of what I have termed a "generalized other." Such organized sets of response are related to each other; if one calls out one such set of responses, he is implicitly calling out others as well.

Thus the institutions of society are organized forms of group or social activity—forms so organized that the individual members of society can act adequately and socially by taking the attitudes of others toward these activities. Oppressive, stereo-typed, and ultra-conservative social institutions—like the church—which by their more or less rigid and inflexible un-progressiveness crush or blot out individuality, or discourage any distinctive or original expressions of thought and behavior in the individual selves or personalities implicated in and sub-jected to them, are undesirable but not necessary outcomes of the general social process of experience and behavior. There is no necessary or inevitable reason why social institutions should be oppressive or rigidly conservative, or why they should not rather be, as many are, flexible and progressive, fostering indi-viduality rather than discouraging it. In any case, without social institutions of some sort, without the organized social attitudes and activities by which social institutions are constituted, there could be no fully mature individual selves or personalities at all; for the individuals involved in the general social life-process of which social institutions are organized manifestations can de-velop and possess fully mature selves or personalities only in so far as each one of them reflects or prehends in his individual ex-perience these organized social attitudes and activities which social institutions embody or represent. Social institutions, like individual selves, are developments within, or particular and formalized manifestations of, the social life-process at its human evolutionary level. As such they are not necessarily subversive of individuality in the individual members; and they do not necessarily represent or uphold narrow definitions of cer-tain fixed and specific patterns of acting which in any given cir-cumstances should characterize the behavior of all intelligent and socially responsible individuals (in opposition to such unin-telligent and socially irresponsible individuals as morons and imbeciles), as members of the given community or social group. On the contrary, they need to define the social, or socially re-sponsible, patterns of individual conduct in only a very broad and general sense, affording plenty of scope for originality, flexibility, and variety of such conduct; and as the main formal-ized functional aspects or phases of the whole organized structure of the social life-process at its human level they properly partake of the dynamic and progressive character of that process.[10]

There are a great number of institutionalized responses which are, we often say, arbitrary, such as the manners of a particular community. Manners in their best sense, of course, cannot be distinguished from morals, and are nothing but the expression of the courtesy of an individual toward people about him. They ought to express the natural courtesy of everyone to everyone else. There should be such an expression, but of course a great many habits for the expression of courtesy are quite arbitrary. The ways to greet people are different in different communities; what is appropriate in one may be an offense in another. The question arises whether a certain manner which expresses a courteous attitude may be what we term "conventional." In answer to this we propose to distinguish between manners and conventions. Conventions are isolated social responses which would not come into, or go to make up, the nature of the community in its essential character as this expresses itself in the social reactions. A source of confusion would lie in identifying manners and morals with conventions, since the former are not arbitrary in the sense that conventions are. Thus conservatives identify what is a pure convention with the essence of a social situation; nothing must be changed. But the very distinction to which I have referred is one which implies that these various institutions, as social responses to situations in which individuals are carrying out social acts, are organically related to each other in a way which conventions are not.

[10] Human society, we have insisted, does not merely stamp the pattern of its organized social behavior upon any one of its individual members, so that this pattern becomes likewise the pattern of the individual's self; it also, at the same time, gives him a mind, as the means or ability of consciously conversing with himself in terms of the social attitudes which constitute the structure of his self and which embody the pattern of human society's organized behavior as reflected in that structure. And his mind enables him in turn to stamp the pattern of his further developing self (further developing through his mental activity) upon the structure or organization of human society, and thus in a degree to reconstruct and modify in terms of his self the general pattern of social or group behavior in terms of which his self was originally constituted.

Such interrelation is one of the points which is brought out, for example, in the economic interpretation of history. It was first presented more or less as a party doctrine by the Marxian socialists, implying a particular economic interpretation. It has now passed over into the historian's technique with a recognition that if he can get hold of the real economic situation, which is, of course, more accessible than most social expressions, he can work out from that to the other expressions and institutions of the community. Medieval economic institutions enable one to interpret the other institutions of the period. One can get at the economic situation directly and, following that out, can find what the other institutions were, or must have been. Institutions, manners, or words, present in a certain sense the life-habits of the community as such; and when an individual acts toward others in, say, economic terms, he is calling out not simply a single response but a whole group of related responses.

The same situation prevails in a physiological organism. If the balance of a person who is standing is disturbed, this calls for a readjustment which is possible only in so far as the affected parts of the nervous system lead to certain definite and inter-connected responses. The different parts of the reaction can be isolated, but the organism has to act as a whole. Now it is true that an individual living in society lives in a certain sort of organism which reacts toward him as a whole, and he calls out by his action this more or less organized response. There is perhaps under his attention only some very minor fraction of this organized response—he considers, say, only the passage of a certain amount of money. But that exchange could not take place without the entire economic organization, and that in turn involves all the other phases of the group life. The individual can go any time from one phase to the others, since he has in his own nature the type of response which his action calls for. In taking any institutionalized attitude he organizes in some degree the whole social process, in proportion as he is a complete self.

The getting of this social response into the individual constitutes the process of education which takes over the cultural media of the community in a more or less abstract way.[11] Education is definitely the process of taking over a certain organized set of responses to one's own stimulation; and until one can respond to himself as the community responds to him, he does not genuinely belong to the community. He may belong to a small community, as the small boy belongs to a gang rather than to the city in which he lives. We all belong to small cliques, and we may remain simply inside of them. The "organized other" present in ourselves is then a community of a narrow diameter. We are struggling now to get a certain amount of international-mindedness. We are realizing ourselves as members of a larger community. The vivid nationalism of the present period should, in the end, call out an international attitude of the larger community. The situation is analogous to that of the boy and the gang; the boy gets a larger self in proportion as he enters into this larger community. In general, the self has answered definitely to that organization of the social response which constitutes the community as such; the degree to which the self is developed depends upon the community, upon the degree to which the individual calls out that institutionalized group of responses in himself. The criminal as such is the individual who lives in a very small group, and then makes depredations upon the larger community of which he is not a member. He is taking the property that belongs to others, but he himself does not belong to the community that recognizes and preserves the rights of property.

There is a certain sort of organized response to our acts which represents the way in which people react toward us in certain situations. Such responses are in our nature because we act as

[11] [Among some eighteen notes, editorials, and articles on education attention may be called to the following: "The Relation of Play to Education," *University of Chicago Record*, I (1896), 140 ff.; "The Teaching of Science in College," *Science*, XXIV (1906), 390 ff.; "Psychology of Social Consciousness Implied in Instruction," *ibid.*, XXXI (1910), 688 ff.; "Industrial Education and Trade Schools," *Elementary School Teacher*, VIII (1908), 402 ff.; "Industrial Education and the Working Man and the School," *ibid.*, IX (1909), 369 ff.; "On the Problem of History in the Elementary School," *ibid.*, 433; "Moral Training in the Schools," *ibid.*, 327 ff.; "Science in the High School," *School Review*, XIV (1906), 237 ff. *See* Bibliography at end of volume.]

members of the community toward others, and what I am emphasizing now is that the organization of these responses makes the community possible.

We are apt to assume that our estimate of the value of the community should depend upon its size. The American worships bigness as over against qualitative social content. A little community such as that of Athens produced some of the greatest spiritual products which the world has ever seen; contrast its achievements with those of the United States, and there is no need to ask whether the mere bigness of the one has any relationship to the qualitative contents of the achievements of the other. I wish to bring out the implicit universality of the highly developed, highly organized community. Now, Athens as the home of Socrates, Plato, and Aristotle, the seat of a great metaphysical development in the same period, the birthplace of political theorists and great dramatists, actually belongs to the whole world. These qualitative achievements which we ascribe to a little community belong to it only in so far as it has the organization that makes it universal. The Athenian community rested upon slave labor and upon a political situation which was narrow and contracted, and that part of its social organization was not universal and could not be made the basis for a large community. The Roman Empire disintegrated very largely because its whole economic structure was laid on the basis of slave labor. It was not organized on a universal basis. From the legal standpoint and administrative organization it was universal, and just as Greek philosophy has come down to us so has Roman law. To the degree that any achievement of organization of a community is successful it is universal, and makes possible a bigger community. In one sense there cannot be a community which is larger than that represented by rationality, and the Greek brought rationality to its self-conscious expression.[12] In that same sense the gospel of Jesus brought definitely

[12] Plato held that the city-state was the best—if not, indeed, the only practicable or feasible—type of state or social organization; and Aristotle agreed. According to Plato, moreover, the complete social isolation of any one city-state from the rest of the world was desirable. Aristotle, on the other hand, did recognize the necessity for social inter-

to expression the attitude of neighborliness to which anyone could appeal, and provided the soil out of which could arise a universal religion. That which is fine and admirable is universal —although it may be true that the actual society in which the universality can get its expression has not arisen.

Politically, America has, in a certain sense, given universality to what we term "self-government." The social organization of the Middle Ages existed under feudalism and craft guilds. The immediate social organizations in which there was self-government were all particular provisional guilds or particular communities. What has happened in America is that we have generalized the principle of self-government so that it is the essential agency of political control of the whole community. If that type of control is made possible there is theoretically no limit to the size of the community. In that sense alone would political bigness become an expression of the achievement of the community itself.

The organization, then, of social responses makes it possible for the individual to call out in himself not simply a single response of the other but the response, so to speak, of the community as a whole. That is what gives to an individual what we term "mind." To do anything now means a certain organized response; and if one has in himself that response, he has what we term "mind." We refer to that response by the symbols which serve as the means by which such responses are called out. To

---

relations among different city-states, or between any one city-state and the rest of the civilized world, but he could not discover a general principle in terms of which those interrelations could be determined without disastrously damaging or vitiating the political and social structure of the city-state itself; and this structure he wished, as did Plato, to preserve. That is to say, he was unable to get hold of a fundamental principle in terms of which the social and political organization of the Greek city-state could be generalized to apply to the interrelations between several such states within a single social whole, like the Alexandrian empire, in which they were all included as units, or to apply to that social whole or empire itself; and especially to apply to such a social whole or empire even if it did not contain city-states as its units. If we are right, this fundamental principle which he was unable to discover was simply the principle of social integration and organization in terms of rational selves, and of their reflection, in their respective organized structures, of the patterns of organized social behavior in which they are involved and to which they owe their existence.

use the terms "government," "property," "family," is to bring out, as we say, the meaning they have. Now, those meanings rest upon certain responses. A person who has in himself the universal response of the community toward that which he does, has in that sense the mind of the community. As a scientist, we will say, one's community consists of all his colleagues, but this community includes anyone who can understand what is said. The same is true of literature. The size of its audience is a functional one; if the achievement of organization is obtained, it may be of any size. Bigness may in this sense be an indication of qualitative achievement. That which is great is always in one sense objective, it is always universal. The mental development of the individual consists in getting in himself these organized responses in their implicated relationships to each other.

The rational phase of it, that which goes with what we term "language," is the symbol; and this is the means, the mechanism, by which the response is carried out. For effective co-operation one has to have the symbols by means of which the responses can be carried out, so that getting a significant language is of first importance. Language implies organized responses; and the value, the implication of these responses, is to be found in the community from which this organization of responses is taken over into the nature of the individual himself. The significant symbol is nothing but that part of the act which serves as a gesture to call out the other part of the process, the response of the other, in the experience of the form that makes the gesture. The use of symbols is then of the highest importance, even when carried to the point attained in mathematics, where one can take the symbols and simply combine them in accordance with the rules of the mathematical community to which they belong without knowing what the symbols mean. In fact, in such fields one has to abstract from the meaning of the symbols; there is here a process of carrying on the rational process of reasoning without knowing what the meaning is. We are dealing with x and y, and how these can be combined with each other; we do not know in advance to what they apply. Although symbols under certain conditions can be handled in such a fashion, we do, after all, bring them to earth and apply them. The symbols as such are simply ways of calling out responses. They are not bare words, but words that do answer to certain responses; and when we combine a certain set of symbols, we inevitably combine a certain set of responses.

This brings up again the problem of the universal. In so far as the individual takes the attitude of the other that symbol is universal, but is it a true universal when it is so limited? Can we get beyond that limitation? The logicians' universe of discourse lays plain the extent of universality. In an earlier stage that universality was supposed to be represented in a set of logical axioms, but the supposed axioms have been found to be not universal. So that, in fact, "universal" discourse to be universal has had to be continually revised. It may represent those rational beings with whom we are in contact, and there is potential universality in such a world as that. Such would be, I suppose, the only universal that is involved in the use of significant symbols. If we can get the set of significant symbols which have in this sense a universal meaning, anyone that can talk in that language intelligently has that universality. Now, there is no limitation except that a person should talk that language, use the symbols which carry those significations; and that gives an absolute universality for anyone who enters into the language. There are, of course, different universes of discourse, but back of all, to the extent that they are potentially comprehensible to each other, lies the logicians' universe of discourse with a set of constants and propositional functions, and anyone using them will belong to that same universe of discourse. It is this which gives a potential universality to the process of communication.[13]

[13] It is in terms of this mechanism of universals (or universally significant gestures or symbols) by means of which thinking operates, that the human individual transcends the local social group to which he immediately belongs, and that this social group accordingly (through its individual members) transcends itself, and relates itself to the whole larger context or environment of organized social relations and interactions which surrounds it and of which it is only one part.

Physiologically, universality of mind in the human social order is fundamentally

I have tried to bring out the position that the society in which we belong represents an organized set of responses to certain situations in which the individual is involved, and that in so far as the individual can take those organized responses over into his own nature, and call them out by means of the symbol in the social response, he has a mind in which mental processes can go on, a mind whose inner structure he has taken from the community to which he belongs.

It is the unity of the whole social process that is the unity of the individual, and social control over the individual lies in this common process which is going on, a process which differentiates the individual in his particular function while at the same time controlling his reaction. It is the ability of the person to put himself in other people's places that gives him his cues as to what he is to do under a specific situation. It is this that gives to the man what we term his character as a member of the community; his citizenship, from a political standpoint; his membership from any one of the different standpoints in which he belongs to the community. It makes him a part of the community, and he recognizes himself as a member of it just because he does take the attitude of those concerned, and does control his own conduct in terms of common attitudes.

Our membership in the society of human beings is something that calls out very little attention on the part of the average individual. He is seldom content to build up a religion on the basis of human society in and of itself with nothing else added—the wider the extent of a religion, the fewer the people who consciously belong to it. We have not taken very seriously our membership in the human society, but it is becoming more real to us. The World War has shaken down a great many values; and we realize that what takes place in India, in Afghanistan, in Mesopotamia, is entering into our lives, so that we are getting what we term "international mindedness." We are reacting in

based on the universality of a similar neural structure in all the individuals belonging to that social order: the type of neural structure, namely, which the social development of mind requires.

a way that answers to the responses of people on the other side of the human group.

The question whether we belong to a larger community is answered in terms of whether our own action calls out a response in this wider community, and whether its response is reflected back into our own conduct. Can we carry on a conversation in international terms?[14] The question is largely a question of social organization. The necessary responses have become more definitely a part of our experience because we are getting closer to other peoples than before. Our economic organization is getting more and more worked out, so that the goods we sell in South America, in India, in China, are definitely affecting our lives. We have to be on good terms with our customers; if we are going to carry on a successful economic policy in South America, we must explain what is the meaning of the Monroe Doctrine, and so on and on.

We are getting to realize more and more the whole society to which we belong because the social organization is such that it brings out the response of the other person to our own act not only in the other person but also in ourselves. Kipling says: "East is East, and West is West, and never the twain shall meet"; but they are meeting. The assumption has been that the response of the East to the West and of the West to the East are not comprehensible to each other. But, in fact, we find that we are awakening, that we are beginning to interchange rôles. A process of organization is going on underneath our conscious experience, and the more this organization is carried out the closer we are brought together. The more we do call out in ourselves the response which our gestures call out in the other, the more we understand him.

There is, of course, back of all this a larger community referred to in religious terms as a "blessed community," the community of a universal religion. But that, too, rests on co-opera-

[14] [See "National-Mindedness and International-Mindedness," *International Journal of Ethics*, XXXIX (1929), 385 ff.; "The Psychological Bases of Internationalism," *Survey*, XXXIII (1914–15), 604 ff.]

tive activities. An illustration is that of the good Samaritan, where Jesus took people and showed that there was distress on the part of one which called out in the other a response which he understood; the distress of the other was a stimulus, and that stimulus called out the response in his own nature. This is the basis of that fundamental relationship which goes under the name of "neighborliness." It is a response which we all make in a certain sense to everybody. The person who is a stranger calls out a helpful attitude in ourselves, and that is anticipated in the other. It makes us all akin. It provides the common human nature on which the universal religions are all built. However, the situations under which that neighborliness may express itself are very narrow; and consequently such religions as are built up on it have to restrict human lives to just a few relationships, such as sympathy in distress, or limit themselves to expressing the emotional sides of human nature. But if the social relation can be carried on further and further then you can conceivably be a neighbor to everybody in your block, in your community, in the world, since you are brought much closer to the attitude of the other when this attitude is also called out in yourself. What is essential is the development of the whole mechanism of social relationship which brings us together, so that we can take the attitude of the other in our various life-processes.

The human individual who possesses a self is always a member of a larger social community, a more extensive social group, than that in which he immediately and directly finds himself, or to which he immediately and directly belongs. In other words, the general pattern of social or group behavior which is reflected in the respective organized attitudes—the respective integrated structures of the selves—of the individuals involved, always has a wider reference, for those individuals, than that of its direct relation to them, namely, a reference beyond itself to a wider social environment or context of social relationships which includes it, and of which it is only a more or less limited part. And their awareness of that reference is a consequence of their being sentient or conscious beings, or of their having minds, and of the activities of reasoning which they hence carry on.[15]

35. THE FUSION OF THE "I" AND THE "ME" IN
SOCIAL ACTIVITIES

In a situation where persons are all trying to save someone from drowning, there is a sense of common effort in which one is stimulated by the others to do the same thing they are doing. In those situations one has a sense of being identified with all because the reaction is essentially an identical reaction. In the case of team work, there is an identification of the individual with the group; but in that case one is doing something different from the others, even though what the others do determines what he is to do. If things move smoothly enough, there may be something of the same exaltation as in the other situation. There is still the sense of directed control. It is where the "I" and the "me" can in some sense fuse that there arises the peculiar sense of exaltation which belongs to the religious and patriotic attitudes in which the reaction which one calls out in others is the response which one is making himself. I now wish to discuss in more detail than previously the fusion of the "I" and the "me" in the attitudes of religion, patriotism, and team work.

[15] It is especially in terms of the logical universe of discourse—the general system of universally significant symbols—which all thought or reasoning presupposes as the field of its activity, and which transcends the bounds of different languages and different racial and national customs, that the individuals belonging to any given social group or community become conscious of this wider social reference of that group or community beyond itself, to the further and larger context of social relations and interactions of human society or civilization as a whole in which, with all other particular human societies or organized social groups, it is implicated. This wider reference or relational implication of the general behavior pattern of any given human social group or community is least evident in the case of primitive man, and is most apparent in the case of highly civilized modern man. In terms of his rational self, or in terms of that organization of social attitudes toward himself and toward others which constitutes the structure of his rational self, and which reflects not only the pattern of behavior of the immediate social group in itself that he belongs to but also the reference of this pattern beyond itself to the whole wider general pattern of human social or group behavior of which it forms only one part, the modern civilized human individual is and feels himself to be a member not only of a certain local community or state or nation, but also of an entire given race or even civilization as a whole.

In the conception of universal neighborliness, there is a certain group of attitudes of kindliness and helpfulness in which the response of one calls out in the other and in himself the same attitude. Hence the fusion of the "I" and the "me" which leads to intense emotional experiences. The wider the social process in which this is involved, the greater is the exaltation, the emotional response, which results. We sit down and play a game of bridge with friends or indulge in some other relaxation in the midst of our daily work. It is something that will last an hour or so, and then we shall take up the grind again. We are, however, involved in the whole life of society; its obligations are upon us; we have to assert ourselves in various situations; those factors are all lying back in the self. But under the situations to which I am now referring that which lies in the background is fused with what we are all doing. This, we feel, is the meaning of life—and one experiences an exalted religious attitude. We get into an attitude in which everyone is at one with each other in so far as all belong to the same community. As long as we can retain that attitude we have for the time being freed ourselves of that sense of control which hangs over us all because of the responsibilities we have to meet in difficult and trying social conditions. Such is the normal situation in our social activity, and we have its problems back in our minds; but in such a situation as this, the religious situation, all seem to be lifted into the attitude of accepting everyone as belonging to the same group. One's interest is the interest of all. There is complete identification of individuals. Within the individual there is a fusion of the "me" with the "I."

The impulse of the "I" in this case is neighborliness, kindliness. One gives bread to the hungry. It is that social tendency which we all have in us that calls out a certain type of response: one wants to give. When one has a limited bank account, one cannot give all he has to the poor. Yet under certain religious situations, in groups with a certain background, he can get the attitude of doing just that. Giving is stimulated by more giving. He may not have much to give, but he is ready to give himself

[274]

completely. There is a fusion of the "I" and the "me." The "me" is not there to control the "I," but the situation has been so constructed that the very attitude aroused in the other stimulates one to do the same thing. The exaltation in the case of patriotism presents an analogous instance of this fusion.

From the emotional standpoint such situations are peculiarly precious. They involve, of course, the successful completion of the social process. I think that the religious attitude involves this relation of the social stimulus to the world at large, the carrying-over of the social attitude to the larger world. I think that that is the definite field within which the religious experience appears. Of course, where one has a clearly marked theology in which there are definite dealings with the deity, with whom one acts as concretely as with another person in the room, then the conduct which takes place is simply of a type which is comparable to the conduct with reference to another social group, and it may be one which is lacking in that peculiar mystical character which we generally ascribe to the religious attitude. It may be a calculating attitude in which a person makes a vow, and carries it out providing the deity gives him a particular favor. Now, that attitude would normally come under the general statement of religion, but in addition it is generally recognized that the attitude has to be one that carries this particular extension of the social attitude to the universe at large. I think it is that which we generally refer to as the religious experience, and that this is the situation out of which the mystical experience of religion arises. The social situation is spread over the entire world.

It may be only on certain days of the week and at certain hours of that day that we can get into that attitude of feeling at one with everybody and everything about us. The day goes around; we have to go into the market to compete with other people and to hold our heads above the water in a difficult economic situation. We cannot keep up the sense of exaltation, but even then we may still say that these demands of life are only a task which is put on us, a duty which we must perform in order to get at particular moments the religious attitude. When the experience is attained, however, it comes with this feeling of complete identification of the self with the other.

It is a different, and perhaps higher, attitude of identification which comes in the form of what I have referred to as "team work." Here one has the sort of satisfaction which comes from working with others in a certain situation. There is, of course, still a sense of control; after all, what one does is determined by what other persons are doing; one has to be keenly aware of the positions of all the others; he knows what the others are going to do. But he has to be constantly awake to the way in which other people are responding in order to do his part in the team work. That situation has its delight, but it is not a situation in which one simply throws himself, so to speak, into the stream where he can get a sense of abandonment. That experience belongs to the religious or patriotic situation. Team work carries, however, a content which the other does not carry. The religious situation is abstract as far as the content is concerned. How one is to help others is a very complicated undertaking. One who undertakes to be a universal help to others is apt to find himself a universal nuisance. There is no more distressing person to have about than one who is constantly seeking to assist everybody else. Fruitful assistance has to be intelligent assistance. But if one can get the situation of a well-organized group doing something as a unit, a sense of the self is attained which is the experience of team work, and this is certainly from an intellectual stand-point higher than mere abstract neighborliness. The sense of team work is found where all are working toward a common end and everyone has a sense of the common end interpenetrating the particular function which he is carrying on.

The frequent attitude of the person in social service who is trying to express a fundamental attitude of neighborliness[16] may be compared with the attitude of the engineer, the organizer, which illustrates in extreme form the attitude of team

[16] ["Philanthropy from the Point of View of Ethics," *Intelligent Philanthropy*, edited by Faris, Lane, and Dodd.]

work. The engineer has the attitudes of all the other individuals in the group, and it is because he has that participation that he is able to direct. When the engineer comes out of the machine shop with the bare blue print, the machine does not yet exist; but he must know what the people are to do, how long it should take them, how to measure the processes involved, and how to eliminate waste. That sort of taking the attitudes of everyone else as fully and completely as possible, entering upon one's own action from the standpoint of such a complete taking of the rôle of the others, we may perhaps refer to as the "attitude of the engineer." It is a highly intelligent attitude; and if it can be formed with a profound interest in social team work, it belongs to the high social processes and to the significant experiences. Here the full concreteness of the "me" depends upon a man's capacity to take the attitude of everybody else in the process which he directs. Here is gained the concrete content not found in the bare emotional identification of one's self with everyone else in the group.

These are the different types of expressions of the "I" in their relationship to the "me" that I wanted to bring out in order to complete the statement of the relation of the "I" and the "me." The self under these circumstances is the action of the "I" in harmony with the taking of the rôle of others in the "me." The self is both the "I" and the "me"; the "me" setting the situation to which the "I" responds. Both the "I" and "me" are involved in the self, and here each supports the other.

I wish now to discuss the fusion of the "I" and the "me" in terms of another approach, namely, through a comparison of the physical object with the self as a social object.

The "me," I have said, presents the situation within which conduct takes place, and the "I" is the actual response to that situation. This twofold separation into situation and response is characteristic of any intelligent act even if it does not involve this social mechanism. There is a definite situation which presents a problem, and then the organism responds to that situation by an organization of the different reactions that are involved. There has to be such an organization of activities in our ordinary movements among different articles in a room, or through a forest, or among automobiles. The stimuli present tend to call out a great variety of responses; but the actual response of the organism is an organization of these tendencies, not a single response which mediates all the others. One does not sit down in a chair, one does not take a book, open a window, or do a great variety of things to which in a certain sense the individual is invited when he enters a room. He does some specific thing; he perhaps goes and takes a sought paper out of a desk and does not do anything else. Yet the objects exist there in the room for him. The chair, the windows, tables, exist as such because of the uses to which he normally puts these objects. The value that the chair has in his perception is the value which belongs to his response; so he moves by a chair and past a table and away from a window. He builds up a landscape there, a scene of objects which make possible his actual movement to the drawer which contains the paper that he is after. This landscape is the means of reaching the goal he is pursuing; and the chair, the table, the window, all enter into it as objects. The physical object is, in a certain sense, what you do not respond to in a consummatory fashion. If, the moment you step into a room, you drop into a chair you hardly do more than direct your attention to the chair; you do not view it as a chair in the same sense as when you just recognize it as a chair and direct your movement toward a distant object. The chair that exists in the latter case is not one you are sitting down in; but it is a something that will receive you after you do drop into it, and that gives it the character of an object as such.

Such physical objects are utilized in building up the field in which the distant object is reached. The same result occurs from a temporal standpoint when one carries out a more distant act by means of some precedent act which must be first carried through. Such organization is going on all the time in intelligent conduct. We organize the field with reference to what we are going to do. There is now, if you like, a fusion of the getting of the paper out of the drawer and the room through which we move to accomplish that end, and it is this sort of fusion that I referred to previously, only in such instances as religious experiences it takes place in the field of social mediation, and the objects in the mechanism are social in their character and so represent a different level of experience. But the process is analogous: we are what we are in our relationship to other individuals through taking the attitude of the other individuals toward ourselves so that we stimulate ourselves by our own gesture, just as a chair is what it is in terms of its invitation to sit down; the chair is something in which we might sit down, a physical "me," if you like. In a social "me" the various attitudes of all the others are expressed in terms of our own gesture, which represents the part we are carrying out in the social co-operative activity. Now the thing we actually do, the words we speak, our expressions, our emotions, those are the "I"; but they are fused with the "me" in the same sense that all the activities involved in the articles of furniture of the room are fused with the path followed toward the drawer and the taking out of the actual paper. The two situations are identical in that sense.

The act itself which I have spoken of as the "I" in the social situation is a source of unity of the whole, while the "me" is the social situation in which this act can express itself. I think that we can look at such conduct from the general standpoint of intelligent conduct; only, as I say, conduct is taking place here in this social field in which a self arises in the social situation in the group, just as the room arises in the activity of an individual in getting to this particular object he is after. I think the same view can be applied to the appearance of the self that applies to the appearance of an object in a field that constitutes in some sense a problem; only the peculiar character of it lies in the fact that it is a social situation and that this social situation involves the appearance of the "me" and the "I" which are essentially social elements. I think it is consistent to recognize this parallelism between what we call the "physical object" over against the organism, and the social object over against the self. The "me" does definitely answer to all the different reactions which the objects about us tend to call out in us. All such objects call out responses in ourselves, and these responses are the meanings or the natures of the objects: the chair is something we sit down in, the window is something that we can open, that gives us light or air. Likewise the "me" is the response which the individual makes to the other individuals in so far as the individual takes the attitude of the other. It is fair to say that the individual takes the attitude of the chair. We are definitely in that sense taking the attitude of the objects about us; while normally this does not get into the attitude of communication in our dealing with inanimate objects, it does take that form when we say that the chair invites us to sit down, or the bed tempts us to lie down. Our attitude under those circumstances is, of course, a social attitude. We have already discussed the social attitude as it appears in the poetry of nature, in myths, rites, and rituals. There we take over the social attitude toward nature itself. In music there is perhaps always some sort of a social situation, in terms of the emotional response involved; and the exaltation of music would have, I suppose, reference to the completeness of the organization of the response that answers to those emotional attitudes. The idea of the fusion of the "I" and the "me" gives a very adequate basis for the explanation of this exaltation. I think behavioristic psychology provides just the opportunity for such development of aesthetic theory. The significance of the response in the aesthetic experience has already been stressed by critics of painting and architecture.

The relationship of the "me" to the "I" is the relationship of a situation to the organism. The situation that presents the problem is intelligible to the organism that responds to it, and fusion takes place in the act. One can approach it from the "I" if one knows definitely what he is going to do. Then one looks at the whole process simply as a set of means for reaching the known end. Or it can be approached from the point of view of the means and the problem appears then as a decision among a set of different ends. The attitude of one individual calls out this response, and the attitude of another individual calls out another response. There are varied tendencies, and the response of the "I" will be one which relates all of these together. Whether looked at from the viewpoint of a problem which has to be solved or from the position of an "I" which in a certain sense determines its field by its conduct, the fusion takes place in the act itself in which the means expresses the end.

36. DEMOCRACY AND UNIVERSALITY IN SOCIETY

There is in human society a universality that expresses itself very early in two different ways—one on the religious side and the other on the economic side. These processes as social processes are universal. They provide ends which any form that makes use of the same medium of communication can enter upon. If a gorilla could bring cocoanuts and exchange them in some sort of market for something he might conceivably want, he would enter into the economic social organization in its widest phase. All that is necessary is that the animal should be able to utilize that method of communication which involves, as we have seen, the existence of a self. On the other hand, any individual that can regard himself as a member of a society in which he is—to use a familiar phrase—a neighbor of the other, also belongs to such a universal group. These religious and economic expressions of universality we find developing in one form or another in the Roman Empire, in India, and in China. In the outgrowth of the Empire into Christianity we find a form of propaganda issuing in the deliberate attempt to organize this sort of universal society.

If evolution is to take place in such a society, it would take place between the different organizations, so to speak, within this larger organism. There would not simply be a competition of different societies with each other, but competition would lie in the relationship of this or that society to the organization of a universal society. In the case of the universal religions we have such forms as that of the Mohammedan, which undertook by the force of the sword to wipe out all other forms of society, and so found itself in opposition to other communities which it undertook either to annihilate or to subordinate to itself. On the other hand, we have the propaganda represented by Christianity and Buddhism, which merely undertook to bring the various individuals into a certain spiritual group in which they would recognize themselves as members of one society. This undertaking inevitably bound itself up with the political structure, especially in the case of Christianity; and back of that lies the assumption, which found its expression in missionary undertakings, that this social principle, this recognition of the brotherhood of men, is the basis for a universal society.

If we look at the economic proceedings, there is no such propaganda as this, no assumption of a single economic society that is undertaking to establish itself. An economic society defines itself in so far as one individual may trade with others; and then the very processes themselves go on integrating, bringing a closer and closer relationship between communities which may be definitely opposed to each other politically. The more complete economic texture appears in the development of trading itself and the development of a financial medium by means of which such trading is carried on, and there is an inevitable adjustment of the production in one community to the needs of the international economic community. There is a development which starts with the lowest sort of universal society and in which the original abstractness gives way to a more and more concrete social organization. From both of these standpoints there is a universal society that includes the whole human race, and into which all can so far enter into relationship with others through the medium of communication. They can recognize others as members, and as brothers.

Such communities are inevitably universal in their character. The processes expressed in the universal religion inevitably carry with them that of the logical community represented by the universe of discourse, a community based simply on the ability of all individuals to converse with each other through use of the same significant symbols. Language provides a universal community which is something like the economic community. It is there in so far as there are common symbols that can be utilized. We see such symbols in the bare signs by means of which savage tribes who do not speak the same language can communicate. They find some common language in the use of the fingers, or in symbolic drawings. They attain some sort of ability to communicate, and such a process of communication has the tendency to bring the different individuals into closer relationship with each other. The linguistic process is in one sense more abstract than the economic process. The economic process, starting off with bare exchange, turns over the surplus of one individual in return for the surplus of another individual. Such processes reflect back at once to the process of production and more or less inevitably stimulate that sort of production which leads to profitable exchange. When we come to bare intercourse on the basis of significant symbols, the process by itself perhaps does not tend to such an integration, but this process of communication will carry or tend to carry with it the very processes in which it has served as a medium.

A person learns a new language and, as we say, gets a new soul. He puts himself into the attitude of those that make use of that language. He cannot read its literature, cannot converse with those that belong to that community, without taking on its peculiar attitudes. He becomes in that sense a different individual. You cannot convey a language as a pure abstraction; you inevitably in some degree convey also the life that lies behind it. And this result builds itself into relationship with the organized attitudes of the individual who gets this language and inevitably brings about a readjustment of views. A community of the Western world with its different nationalities and different languages is a community in which there will be a continued interplay of these different groups with each other. One nation cannot be taken simply by itself, but only in its relationship to the other groups which belong to the larger whole.

The universe of discourse which deals simply with the highest abstractions opens the door for the interrelationship of the different groups in their different characters. The universe of discourse within which people can express themselves makes possible the bringing-together of those organized attitudes which represent the life of these different communities into such relationship that they can lead to a higher organization. The very universality of the processes which belong to human society, whether looked at from the point of view of religion or trading or logical thinking, at least opens the door to a universal society; and, in fact, these tendencies all express themselves where the social development has gone far enough to make it possible.

The political expression of this growth of universality in society is signalized in the dominance of one group over other groups. The earliest expression of this is in the empires of the valleys of the Nile, the Tigris, and the Euphrates. Different communities came in competition with each other, and in such competition is found a condition for the development of the empire. There is not simply the conflict of one tribe with another which undertakes to wipe out the other, but rather that sort of conflict which leads to the dominance of one group over another by the maintenance of the other group. It is of importance to notice this difference when it signalizes the expression of self-consciousness reached through a realization of one's self in others. In a moment of hostility or fierce anger the individual or the community may seek simply to wipe out its enemies. But the dominant expression in terms of the self has been, even on the part of a militaristic society, rather that of subjection, of a realization of the self in its superiority to and exploitation of the other. This attitude of mind is an entirely different attitude from that of the mere wiping-out of one's enemies. There is, from this point of view at least, a definite achievement on the part of the individual of a higher self in his overcoming of the other and holding the other in subjection.

The sense of national prestige is an expression of that self-respect which we tend to preserve in the maintenance of superiority over other people. One does get the sense of one's self by a certain feeling of superiority to others, and that this is fundamental in the development of the self was recognized by Wundt. It is an attitude which passes over, under what we consider higher conditions, into the just recognition of the capacity of the individual in his own fields. The superiority which the person now has is not a superiority over the other, but is grounded in that which he can do in relation to the functions and capacity of others. The development of the expert who is superior in the performance of his functions is of a quite different character from the superiority of the bully who simply realizes himself in his ability to subordinate somebody to himself. The person who is competent in any particular field has a superiority which belongs to that which he himself can do and which perhaps someone else cannot do. It gives him a definite position in which he can realize himself in the community. He does not realize himself in his simple superiority to someone else, but in the function which he can carry out; and in so far as he can carry it out better than anyone else he gets a sense of prestige which we recognize as legitimate, as over against the other form of self-assertion which from the standpoint of our highest sense of social standards is felt to be illegitimate.

Communities may stand in this same kind of relation to each other. There is the sense of pride of the Roman in his administrative capacity as well as in his martial power, in his capacity to subjugate all the people around the Mediterranean world and to administer them. The first attitude was that of subjugation, and then came the administrative attitude which was more of the type to which I have already referred as that of functional superiority. It was that which Virgil expressed in his demand that the Roman should realize that in his ruling he was possessed with the capacity for administration. This capacity made the Roman Empire entirely different from the earlier empires, which carried nothing but brute strength behind them. The passage in that case is from a sense of political superiority and prestige expressed in a power to crush, over into a power to direct a social undertaking in which there is a larger co-operative activity. The political expression starts off with a bare self-assertion, coupled with a military attitude, which leads to the wiping-out of the other, but which leads on, or may lead on, to the development of a higher community, where dominance takes the form of administration. Conceivably, there may appear a larger international community than the empire, organized in terms of function rather than of force.

The bringing-together of the attitude of universal religion on the one hand and the widening political development on the other has been given its widest expression in democracy. There is, of course, a democracy such as that of the Greek cities in which the control is simply the control of the masses in their opposition to certain economically and politically powerful classes. There are, in fact, various forms of democratic government; but democracy, in the sense here relevant, is an attitude which depends upon the type of self which goes with the universal relations of brotherhood, however that be reached. It received its expression in the French Revolution in the conception of fraternity and union. Every individual was to stand on the same level with every other. This conception is one which received its first expression in the universal religions. If carried over into the field of politics, it can get its expression only in such a form as that of democracy; and the doctrine that lies behind it is very largely Rousseau's conception, as found in the *Social Contract*.

The assumption there is of a society in which the individual maintains himself as a citizen only to the degree that he recognizes the rights of everyone else to belong to the same community. With such a universality, such a uniformity of interests, it would be possible for the masses of the community to take the attitude of the sovereign while he also took the attitude of the subjects. If the will of each one was the will of all, then the relationship of subject and sovereign could be embodied in all the different individuals. We get what Rousseau referred to as the "general will of the community" only when as a man is able to realize himself by recognizing others as belonging to the same political organization as himself.[17]

That conception of democracy is in itself as universal as religion, and the appearance of this political movement was essentially religious in so far as it had the gospel of Rousseau behind it. It proceeded also with a sense of propaganda. It undertook to overthrow the old organization of society and substitute its own form of society in its place. In that sense these two factors—one the dominance of the individual or group over other groups, the other the sense of brotherhood and identity of different individuals in the same group—came together in the democratic movement; and together they inevitably imply a universal society, not only in a religious sense, but ultimately in a political sense as well. This gets an expression in the League of Nations, where every community recognizes every other community in the very process of asserting itself. The smallest community is in a position to express itself just because it recognizes the right of every other nation to do the same.

What is involved in the development of a universal society is just such a functional organization as we find in economic development. The economic development is one which starts off on the basis of the exchange. You offer what you do not want in exchange for something which another does not want. That is abstract. But after you find you can produce something you do not want and exchange it for something you want, you stimulate by that action a functional development. You are stimulating one group to produce this and another to produce that; and you are also controlling the economic process, because one will not continue to produce more than can be offered in exchange on the market. The sort of thing ultimately produced

---

[17] If you can make your demand universal, if your right is one that carries with it a corresponding obligation, then you recognize the same right in everyone else, and you can give a law, so to speak, in the terms of all the community. So there can be a general will in terms of the individual because everyone else is expressing the same thing. There then arises a community in which everyone can be both sovereign and subject, sovereign in so far as he asserts his own rights and recognizes them in others, and subject in that he obeys the laws which he himself makes (1927).

will be that which answers to the demand of the customer. In the resulting functional organization one develops an economic personality of a certain sort which has its own sense of superiority but which is used in the carrying-out of its particular function in relation to the others in the group. There can be a self-consciousness based on the ability to manufacture something better than anybody else; but it can maintain its sense of superiority only when it adjusts itself to the community that needs the products in this process of interchange. In such a situation there is a tendency toward functional development, a functional development which may take place even in the political domain.

It might seem that the functional aspect is contradictory to the ends of democracy in so far as it considers the individual in relation to a whole and in that way ignores the individual; and that, accordingly, real democracy must express itself more in the tone of the religious attitude and in making secondary the functional aspect. If we go back to the ideal of democracy as presented in the French Revolution, we do reach just such a sort of conflict. There you have recognition of quality; you demand in yourself what you recognize in others, and that does provide the basis for a social structure. But when you consider the functional expression of that time there is not the same sort of equality. However, equality in a functional sense is possible, and I do not see any reason why it should not carry with it as deep a sense of the realization of the other in one's self as the religious attitude. A physician who through his superior skill can save the life of an individual can realize himself in regard to the person he has benefited. I see no reason why this functional attitude should not express itself in the realization of one's self in the other. The basis of spiritual expression is the ability to realize one's self in the many, and that certainly is reached in the social organization. It seems to me that the apparent conflict under consideration refers to the abstract and preliminary development of the functional organization. Until that functional organization is fully carried out, there is the opportunity for exploitation of the individual; but with the full development of such organization we should get a higher spiritual expression in which the individual realizes himself in others through that which he does as peculiar to himself.[18]

37. FURTHER CONSIDERATION OF RELIGIOUS AND ECONOMIC ATTITUDES

I want to speak again of the organizing nature of these larger and more abstract social relationships which I have been discussing, those of religion and economics. Each of them becomes universal in its working character, not universal because of any philosophical abstraction involved in them. The primitive man who trades or the modern man on the stock exchange is not interested in the form of economic society that is implied in the exchanges he makes; nor is it at all necessary to assume that the individual who in his immediate assistance of another in trouble identifies himself with this other, presents to himself a form of society in which the interest of one is the interest of all. And yet, as I indicated, these two processes are in their nature universal; they can be applied to anyone.

One who can assist any individual whom he finds suffering may extend that universality far beyond man, and put it into the form of allowing no suffering to any sensuous being. The attitude is one which we take toward any other form that actually does, or conceivably may, appeal to us when in distress, or any being to which we can convey immediate satisfaction by our own acts. It finds its expression in a certain attitude of tenderness. It may be generalized in individuals far beyond one's family. Love may show itself toward any young form which excites the parental attitude, even when it is not a human form. Small articles call out a sort of tender attitude. Such facts show how very wide the actual universality of this attitude is; it takes in practically everything, every possible being with whom one can

[18] [For a discussion of pragmatism in relation to the American scene see "The Philosophies of Royce, James, and Dewey in their American Setting," *International Journal of Ethics*, XL (1930), 211 ff.; for historical genesis of pragmatism, see *Movements of Thought in the Nineteenth Century*.]

have a personal relation. It is not always dominant, of course, since sometimes the hostile reactions are more powerful in their expression than any other; but to the extent that it is present it makes possible a universal form of society. The Christian saints represented that sort of society to which every individual could conceivably belong. The ideal received an expression in the religious conception of a world where all are to have absolutely identical interests.

The other process is that of exchange in which one passes over, so to speak, that which he does not need for something which he does need. Relative wants on a basis of communication and common interests make exchange possible. This is a process which does not extend below man, as the other attitude does. One cannot exchange with the ox or the ass, but he may have a kindly feeling for them.

What I want to refer to especially is the organizing power that these two types of attitudes may have, and have had, in the human community. As I have stated, they are primarily attitudes which one may enter into with any actual or ideal human being with whom he can possibly communicate, and in one case at least, with other beings with whom he cannot communicate. We are in social relationships with domestic animals, and our responses assume the identification of the animal with ourselves as much as ourselves with the animal, an assumption which has no ultimate justification. Our own fundamental attitude is a social relationship based on the self; so we treat the acts of domestic animals as if they had selves. We take their attitude, and our conduct in dealing with them implies that they take our attitude; we act as if the dog knew what we wanted. I need not add that our conduct which implies selves in domestic animals has no rational justification.

Such attitudes, then, are attitudes that may lead to a social organization which goes beyond the actual structure in which individuals find themselves involved. It is for this reason that it is possible for these attitudes themselves to work toward, or at least to assist in, the creation of the structure of these larger communities. If we look first of all at the economic attitude where the exchange of one's own surplus with somebody else's surplus puts one in the attitude of production, producing such surpluses for the purpose of exchange (and makes one in particular look toward the ways of exchange, of establishing markets, of setting up means for transportation, of elaborating the media of exchange, of building up banking systems), we recognize that all this may flow from the mere process of exchange providing the value of it is recognized so as to lead sufficiently to the production of the surpluses which are the basis of the original process. Two children can exchange their toys with each other, the one exchanging an old toy with a friend who is willing to part with his; here there is an exchange of surpluses which does not lead to production. But in the case of human beings who can look ahead and see the advantages of exchange, exchange leads to production.

A notable illustration of that is the development of the woolen industry in England. At first the exchange simply took place in England itself, where the wool was spun under feudal conditions; and then came the carrying of this from one locality to another, and the springing-up of an overseas trade. The changes that took place inside of England's communities as a result of this industry are commonly known, as is the very large part that it played in the development of foreign trade, bringing about the gradual change from the agricultural to the industrial life of the community itself. And then as the woolen cloth passed over the nation's boundaries a network of economic organization grew up which has underlain the whole later development of England.

When such an immediate attitude of exchange becomes a principle of social conduct, it carries with it a process of social development in the way of production, of transportation, and of all the media involved in the economic process, that sets up something of the very universal society that this attitude carries with it as a possibility. It is a process, of course, of bringing the man who has the goods to exchange into direct relationship with the person who is willing to exchange for them what he needs. And the process of production and transportation, and of taking the goods received in return, relates the individuals more closely to the others involved in the economic process. It is a slow process of the integration of a society which binds people more and more closely together. It does not bring them spatially and geographically together but unites them in terms of communication. We are familiar with the abstraction in the textbook illustration of three or four men located on the desert island who carry on the process of trading with each other. They are highly abstract figures, but they exist as abstractions in the economic community and as such represent an interrelationship of communication in which the individual in his own process of production is identifying himself with the individual who has something to exchange with him. He has to put himself in the place of the other or he could not produce that which the other wants. If he starts off on that process he is, of course, identifying himself with any possible customer, any possible producer; and if his mechanism is of this very abstract sort, then the web of commerce can go anywhere and the form of society may take in anybody who is willing to enter in this process of communication. Such an attitude in society does tend to build up the structure of a universal social organism.

As taught in economics, money is nothing but a token, a symbol for a certain amount of wealth. It is a symbol for something that is wanted by individuals who are in the attitude of willingness to exchange; and the forms of exchange are then the methods of conversation, and the media of exchange become gestures which enable us to carry out at vast distances this process of passing over something one does not want, to get something he does, by means of bringing himself into the attitude of the other person. The media of these tokens of wealth are, then, in this process of exchange just such gestures or symbols as language is in other fields.

The other universal attitude discussed was neighborliness, which passes over into the principle of religious relationship, the attitude which made religion as such possible. The immediate effect of the attitude may be nothing but sharing one's food with a person who is hungry, giving water to the thirsty, helping the person who is down and out. It may be nothing but surrendering to the impulse to give something to the man who touches you on the street. It may accomplish nothing more than that, just as exchange between two children may not go beyond the process of exchange. But, in fact, the attitude once assumed has proved to have enormous power of social reorganization. It is that attitude which has expressed itself in the universal religions, and which expresses itself in a large part of the social organization of modern society.

Christianity paved the way for the social progress—political, economic, scientific—of the modern world, the social progress which is so dominantly characteristic of that world. For the Christian notion of a rational or abstract universal human society or social order, though originating as a primarily religious and ethical doctrine, gradually lost its purely religious and ethical associations, and expanded to include all the other main aspects of concrete human social life as well; and so became the larger, more complex notion of that many-sided, rationally universal human society to which all the social reconstructions constituting modern social progress involve intellectual reference by the individuals carrying them out.

There is a striking contrast between the ancient—and especially the ancient Greek—world and the modern world relative to the notion of progress. That notion or conception was utterly foreign to, and almost completely absent from, the thought and civilization of the ancient world; whereas it is one of the most characteristic and dominant ideas in the thought and civilization of the modern world. For the world-view of modern culture is essentially a dynamic one—a world-view which allows for, and indeed emphasizes, the reality of genuine creative change and evolution in things; whereas the world-view of ancient culture was essentially a static one—a world-view which did not admit the occurrence or actuality of any genuinely creative change or evolution in the universe at all: a world-view according to which nothing of which the final cause was not already given (and eternally given) in reality could come into existence; i.e., nothing could come into being except as or by the individual realization of a fixed universal type that was already there and always had been there. According to modern thought, there are no fixed or determined ends or goals toward which social progress necessarily moves; and such progress is hence genuinely creative and would not otherwise be progress (indeed, creativeness is essential to the modern idea of progress). But ancient thought, on the contrary, did not recognize the reality or existence or possibility of progress at all, in the modern sense of the term; and the only progress of any sort which it recognized as possible or real was progress toward eternally fixed ends or goals—progress (which modern thought would not consider to be genuine progress at all) toward the realization of given, predetermined types.

The notion of progress was meaningless for Greek society or civilization, by virtue of the distinctive organization of the Greek state, which was wholly impotent to deal effectively with the social conflicts—or conflicts of social interests—that arose within it. But progress is dominantly characteristic of modern society or civilization, by virtue of the distinctive organization of the modern state which is sufficiently flexible to be able to cope, to some extent at least, with the social conflicts among individuals that arise within it; because it lends itself—in a way in which the organization of the Greek state did not—to that more or less abstract intellectual extension of its boundaries, by the minds of the individuals implicated in it, which we have mentioned: an extension whereby these minds are able to envisage a larger social organization or organized social whole environing them, one in which the conflicts of social interests within it are in some degree harmonized or canceled out, and by reference to which, accordingly, these minds are able to bring about the reconstructions within it that are needed to resolve or settle those conflicts.

The economic and religious principles are often put in opposition to each other. There is, on the one hand, the assumption of an economic process which we call "materialistic" in character; and, on the other hand, the identification of people in common interests which we speak of in idealistic terms. Of course, some justification can be found for this view, but it overlooks the importance of the fact that these attitudes have to be continually corrected. It is assumed that the economic process is always a self-centered one in which the individual is simply advancing his own interest over against the other, that one is taking the attitude of the other only to get the better of him. While it has been insisted that free trade, the opportunity to exchange, is something that leads to a recognition of common interests, it has always been assumed that this is the by-product of the economic process, and not involved in the attitude itself, although we do find economic idealism in such a man as James Bryce. On the other hand, religions have been as much sources of warfare in the past as economic competition has been under the present conditions. One of the striking effects of every war is to emphasize the national character of the religion of the people. During the war we had the God of the Germans and the God of the Allies; deity was divided in allegiance. The extent to which the religious life adjusts itself to conflict is frequently illustrated in history; illustrations of the idealistic phases of economic life are not entirely lacking. There is no question but that the economic process is one which has continually brought people into closer relationship with each other and has tended to identify individuals with each other. The outstanding illustration of this is the international character of labor, and the development within the local community of a labor organization as such. There is both the identification of the laborer with his fellow-laborers in the group, and the identification of the laborers in one community with those in another community. In socialism the labor movement has become a religion. The economic process is one which brings groups inevitably closer together through the process of communication which involves participation. It has been the most universal socializing factor in our whole modern society, more universally recognizable than religion.

The religion gathered about the cult of a community becomes very concrete, identifies itself with the immediate history and life of the community, and is more conservative than almost any other institution in the community. The cult has a mysterious value which attaches to it that we cannot fully rationalize, and therefore we preserve it in the form which it always has had, and in its social setting. It tends to fix the character of the religious expression, so that while the religious attitude is one which leads to identification with any other, the cult in which it institutionalizes itself is apt to be specialized almost to the last degree. It is quite possible to understand anybody who comes to you with something of value which you want to get; if he can express himself in commercial terms, you can understand him. If he comes to you, however, with his particular religious cult, the chances are very great that you cannot comprehend him. The missionary movement, which has been so characteristic of different religions, is a movement in which the universal character of the religion has in turn challenged the fixed conservative character of the cult, as such, and has had enormous effects on the character of the religion itself. But even here religion has undertaken to transfer itself as a cult with all its character, its creed and its dogma, so that it has not lent itself so directly as a means of universal communication as has the economic process.

The two attitudes, of course, are attitudes which are quite different from each other. The one attitude identifies the individual with the other only when both are engaged in a trading operation. Exchange is the life-blood of the economic process, and that process abstracts everything from the other individual except what is involved in trading. The religious attitude, on the contrary, takes you into the immediate inner attitude of the other individual; you are identifying yourself with him in so far as you are assisting him, helping him, saving his soul, aiding him in this world or the world to come—your attitude is that of salvation of the individual. That attitude is far more profound in the identification of the individual with others. The economic process is more superficial and therefore is one which perhaps can travel more rapidly and make possible an easier communication. The two processes, however, are always universal in their character, and so far as they get expression they tend to build up in some sense a common community which is as universal as the attitudes themselves. The processes taken simply by themselves, as where one child trades a toy for another child's toy or where one animal helps another, may immediately stop with the exercise of the act; but where one has a group made up of selves as such, individuals that identify themselves with the others, that arouse the attitude of the other as a means of getting their own selves, the processes then go far beyond a mere seizing of something which one can get that the other does not want, or beyond the bare impulse to help the other. In carrying out these activities the individual has set up a process of integration which brings the individuals closer together, creating the mechanism by which a deeper communication with participation is possible.

It is important to recognize this development going on in history; the two processes taken by themselves tend to bring about the larger community even when the persons have not any ideals for its realization. One cannot take the attitude of identifying himself with the other without in some sense tending to set up such communities. It is the particular function of history to enable us to look back and see how far such social reconstruction has taken place—reconstruction that people at the time did not recognize, but which we can recognize because of our advantage of greater distance. And the function of the leader, the individual who is able to grasp such movements and so carry along the community, is to give direction and impetus, with a consciousness of that which is taking place.

It seems to me that such a view of the self as I have presented in detail renders intelligible the accumulation of social growth.

If we can recognize that an individual does achieve himself, his own consciousness, in the identification of himself with the other, then we can say that the economic process must be one in which the individual does identify himself with the possible customers with whom he exchanges things, that he must be continually building up means of communication with these individuals to make this process successful, and that, while the process in itself may be firmly self-centered, it must inevitably lead him to take more and more concretely the attitude of the other. If you are going to carry on the economic process successfully, you have to come into closer and closer relationship with the other individual, identify yourself not simply in the particular matter of exchange, but find out what he wants and why he wants it, what will be the conditions of payment, the particular character of the goods desired, and so on. You have to identify yourself with him more and more. We are rather scornful of the attitude of salesmanship which modern business emphasizes—salesmanship which seems always to carry with it hypocrisy, to advocate putting one's self in the attitude of the other so as to trick him into buying something he does not want. Even if we do not regard this as justifiable, we can at least recognize that even here there is the assumption that the individual has to take the attitude of the other, that the recognition of the interest of the other is essential to a successful trade. The goal of this is seen when we carry the economic process beyond the profit motive over into public-service concerns. The manager of a railroad or public utility has to put himself in the place of the community that he serves, and we can readily see that such public utilities could pass entirely out of the field of gain and become successful economic undertakings simply as a means of communication. The socialist makes out of this possibility a theory for all business.

38. THE NATURE OF SYMPATHY

The term "sympathy" is an ambiguous one, and a difficult one to interpret. I have referred to an immediate attitude of care, the assistance of one individual by another, such as we find especially in the relations among lower forms. Sympathy comes, in the human form, in the arousing in one's self of the attitude of the individual whom one is assisting, the taking the attitude of the other when one is assisting the other. A physician may simply carry through an operation in an objective fashion without any sympathetic attitude toward the patient. But in an attitude which is sympathetic we imply that our attitude calls out in ourselves the attitude of the person we are assisting. We feel with him and we are able so to feel ourselves into the other because we have, by our own attitude, aroused in ourselves the attitude of the person whom we are assisting. It is that which I regard as a proper interpretation of what we ordinarily call "imitation," and "sympathy," in the vague, undefined sense which we find in our psychologies, when they deal with it at all.

Take, for example, the attitude of parents to the child. The child's tone is one of complaint, suffering, and the parent's tone is one that is soothing. The parent is calling out in himself an attitude of the child in accepting that consolation. This illustration indicates as well the limitation of sympathy. There are persons with whom one finds it difficult to sympathize. In order to be in sympathy with someone, there must be a response which answers to the attitude of the other. If there is not a response which so answers, then one cannot arouse sympathy in himself. Not only that, but there must be co-operation, a reply on the part of the person sympathized with, if the individual who sympathizes is to call out in himself this attitude. One does not put himself immediately in the attitude of the person suffering apart from one's own sympathetic attitude toward him. The situation is that of a person assisting the other, and because of that calling out in himself the response that his assistance calls out in the other. If there is no response on the part of the other, there cannot be any sympathy. Of course, one can say that he can recognize what such a person must be suffering if he could only express it. He thereby puts himself in the place of another who is not there but whom he has met in experience, and interprets this individual in view of the former experience. But active sympathy means that the individual does arouse in another the response called out by his assistance and arouses in himself the same response. If there is no response, one cannot sympathize with him. That presents the limitation of sympathy as such; it has to occur in a co-operative process. Nevertheless, it is in the foregoing sense that one person identifies himself with another. I am not referring to an identification in the Hegelian sense of an Ego, but of an individual who perfectly naturally arouses a certain response in himself because his gesture operates on himself as it does on the other.

To take a distinctively human, that is, self-conscious, social attitude toward another individual, or to become aware of him as such, is to identify yourself sympathetically with him, by taking his attitude toward, and his rôle in, the given social situation, and by thus responding to that situation implicitly as he does or is about to do explicitly; in essentially the same way you take his attitude toward yourself in gestural conversation with him, and are thus made self-conscious. Human social activities depend very largely upon social co-operation among the human individuals who carry them on, and such co-operation results from the taking by these individuals of social attitudes toward one another. Human society endows the human individual with a mind; and the very social nature of that mind requires him to put himself to some degree in the experiential places of, or to take the attitudes of, the other individuals belonging to that society and involved with him in the whole social process of experience and behavior which that society represents or carries on.

I wish now to utilize this mechanism in dealing with religion and the economic process. In the economic field the individual is taking the attitude of the other in so far as he is offering something to the other and calling out in reply a response of giving in the individual who has a surplus. There must be a situation in which the individual brings forward his own object as something that is valuable. Now, from his point of view it is not valuable, but he is putting himself in the attitude of the other individual who will give something in return because he can ·find some use for it. He is calling out in himself the attitude of the other in offering something in return for what he offers; and although the object has for the individual no direct value, it becomes valuable from the point of view of the other individual into whose place the first individual is able to put himself.

What makes this process so universal is the fact that it is a dealing with surpluses, dealing with that which is, so to speak, from the point of view of the individual without value. Of course, it gets a value in the market and then one assesses it from the point of view of what one can get for it, but what makes it a universal thing is that it does not pass into the individual's own direct use. Even if he takes something that he can use and trades that, he has to regard it as something he is going to get rid of in order to get something still more valuable; it has to be something he is not going to use. The immediate value of our owning a thing directly is the use to which we put it, its consumption; but in the economic process we are dealing with something that is immediately without value. So we set up a universal sort of a process. The universality is dependent upon this fact that each person is bringing to the market the things he is not going to use. He states them in terms of the abstraction of money by means of which he can get anything else. It is this negative value that gives the universality, for then it can be turned over to anybody who can give something in return which can be used.

In the primitive community where everybody is related to everybody else, a surplus as such has no meaning. The things are distributed in accordance with definite custom; everybody shares the surplus. Wealth does not exist under such conditions at all. There are certain returns given to the artisan, but they are not returns put into the form that can be expended for any goods which he wants to get in return for something he does not want. The setting-up, then, of the media of exchange is something that is highly abstract. It depends upon the ability of the individual to put himself in the place of the other to see that the other needs what he does not himself need, and to see that what he himself does not need is something that another does need. The whole process depends on an identification of one's self with the other, and this cannot take place among living forms in which there is not a capacity for putting one's self in the place of the other through communicating in a system of gestures which constitute language. Here are then two phases in which universal societies, although highly abstract societies, do actually exist, and what I have been presenting is the import from the psychological standpoint of these universal societies and their tendencies to complete themselves. One cannot complete the process of bringing goods into a market except by developing means of communication. The language in which that is expressed is the language of money. The economic process goes right on tending to bring people closer together by setting up more and more economic techniques and the language mechanism necessary to these procedures.

The same is true in a somewhat different sense from the point of view of the universal religions. They tend to define themselves in terms of communities, because they identify themselves with the cult in the community, but break out beyond this in the missionary movement, in the form of propagandists. The religion may be of a relatively primitive sort, as in Mohammedanism, or in the more complex forms of Buddhism and Christianity; but it inevitably undertakes to complete the relations involved in the attitude of saving other people's souls, of helping, assisting, other people. It develops the missionary who is a physician, those who are artisans, those who set up processes in the community which will lead to the attachment to the very things involved in the religious attitude. We see it first of all in the monasteries of Europe, where the monks undertook to set themselves up as the artisans. They illustrate the tendency of religion to complete itself, to complete the community which previously existed in an abstract form. Such is the picture that

I wanted to present as one of the valuable interpretative contributions of such a view of the self as here developed.

39. CONFLICT AND INTEGRATION

I have been emphasizing the continued integration of the social process, and the psychology of the self which underlies and makes possible this process. A word now as to the factors of conflict and disintegration. In the baseball game there are competing individuals who want to get into the limelight, but this can only be attained by playing the game. Those conditions do make a certain sort of action necessary, but inside of them there can be all sorts of jealously competing individuals who may wreck the team. There seems to be abundant opportunity for disorganization in the organization essential to the team. This is so to a much larger degree in the economic process. There has to be distribution, markets, mediums of exchange; but within that field all kinds of competition and disorganizations are possible, since there is an "I" as well as a "me" in every case.

Historical conflicts start, as a rule, with a community which is socially pretty highly organized. Such conflicts have to arise between different groups where there is an attitude of hostility to others involved. But even here a wider social organization is usually the result; there is, for instance, an appearance of the tribe over against the clan. It is a larger, vaguer organization, but still it is there. This is the sort of situation we have at the present time; over against the potential hostility of nations to each other, they recognize themselves as forming some sort of community, as in the League of Nations.

The fundamental socio-physiological impulses or behavior tendencies which are common to all human individuals, which lead those individuals collectively to enter or form themselves into organized societies or social communities, and which constitute the ultimate basis of those societies or social communities, fall, from the social point of view, into two main classes: those which lead to social co-operation, and those which lead to social antagonism among individuals; those which give rise to friendly attitudes and relations, and those which give rise to hostile attitudes and relations, among the human individuals implicated in the social situations. We have used the term "social" in its broadest and strictest sense; but in that quite common narrower sense, in which it bears an ethical connotation, only the fundamental physiological human impulses or behavior tendencies of the former class (those which are friendly, or which make for friendliness and co-operation among the individuals motivated by them) are "social" or lead to "social" conduct; whereas those impulses or behavior tendencies of the latter class (those which are hostile, or which make for hostility and antagonism among the individuals motivated by them) are "anti-social" or lead to "anti-social" conduct. Now it is true that the latter class of fundamental impulses or behavior tendencies in human beings are "anti-social" in so far as they would, by themselves, be destructive of all human social organization, or could not, alone, constitute the basis of any organized human society; yet in the broadest and strictest non-ethical sense they are obviously no less social than are the former class of such impulses or behavior tendencies. They are equally common to, or universal among, all human individuals, and, if anything, are more easily and immediately aroused by the appropriate social stimuli; and as combined or fused with, and in a sense controlled by, the former impulses or behavior tendencies, they are just as basic to all human social organization as are the former, and play a hardly less necessary and significant part in that social organization itself and in the determination of its general character. Consider, for example, from among these "hostile" human impulses or attitudes, the functioning or expression or operation of those of self-protection and self-preservation in the organization and organized activities of any given human society or social community, let us say, of a modern state or nation. Human individuals realize or become aware of themselves as such, almost more easily and readily in terms of the social attitudes connected or associated with these two "hostile" impulses (or in terms of these two impulses as expressed in these attitudes) than they do in terms of any other social attitudes or behavior tendencies as expressed by those attitudes. Within the social organization of a state or nation the "anti-social" effects of these two impulses are curbed and kept under control by the legal system which is one aspect of that organization; these two impulses are made to constitute the fundamental principles in terms of which the economic system, which is another aspect of that organization, operates; as combined and fused with, and organized by means of the "friendly" human impulses—the impulses leading to social co-operation among the individuals involved in that organization—they are prevented from giving rise to the friction and enmity among those individuals which would otherwise be their natural consequence, and which would be fatally detrimental to the existence and well-being of that organization; and having thus been made to enter as integral elements into the foundations of that organization, they are utilized by that organization as fundamental impulsive forces in its own further development, or they serve as a basis for social progress within its relational framework. Ordinarily, their most obvious and concrete expression or manifestation in that organization lies in the attitudes of rivalry and competition which they generate inside the state or nation as a whole, among different socially functional subgroups of individuals—subgroups determined (and especially economically determined) by that organization; and these attitudes serve definite social ends or purposes presupposed by that organization, and constitute the motives of functionally necessary social activities within that organization. But self-protective and self-preservational human impulses also express or manifest themselves indirectly in that organization, by giving rise through their association in that organization with the "friendly" human impulses, to one of the primary constitutive ideals or principles or motives of that organization—namely, the affording of social protection, and the lending of social assistance, to the individual by the state in the conduct of his life; and by enhancing the efficacy, for the purposes of that organization, of the "friendly" human impulses with a sense or realization of the possibility and desirability of such organized social protection and assistance to the individual. Moreover, in any special circumstances in which the state or nation is, as a whole, confronted by some danger common to all its individual members, they become fused with the "friendly" human impulses in those individuals, in such a way as to strengthen and intensify in those individuals the sense of organized social union and co-operative social interrelationship among them in terms of the state; in such circumstances, so far from constituting forces of disintegration or destruction within the social organization of the state or nation, they become, indirectly, the principles of increased social unity, coherence, and co-ordination within that organization. In time of war, for example, the self-protective impulse in all the individual members of the state is unitedly directed against their common enemy and ceases, for the time being, to be directed among themselves; the attitudes of rivalry and competition which that impulse ordinarily generates between the different smaller, socially functional groups of those individuals within the state are temporarily broken down; the usual social barriers between these groups are likewise removed; and the state presents a united front to the given common danger, or is fused into a single unity in terms of the common end shared by, or reflected in, the respective consciousnesses of all its individual members. It is upon these war-time expressions of the self-protective impulse in all the individual members of the state or nation that the general efficacy of national appeals to patriotism is chiefly based.

Further, in those social situations in which the individual self feels dependent for his continuation or continued existence upon the rest of the members of the given social group to which he belongs, it is true that no feeling of superiority on his part toward those other members of that group is necessary to his continuation or continued existence. But in those social situations in which he cannot, for the time being, integrate his social relations with other individual selves into a common, unitary pattern (i.e., into the behavior pattern of the organized society or social community to which he belongs, the social behavior pattern that he reflects in his self-structure and that constitutes this structure), there ensues, temporarily (i.e., until he can so integrate his social relations with other individual selves), an attitude of hostility, of "latent opposition," on his part toward the organized society or social community of which he is a member; and during that time the given individual self must "call in" or rely upon the feeling of superiority toward that society or social community,   ard its other individual members, in order to buoy him   up and "keep himself going" as such. We always present ourselves to ourselves in the most favorable light possible; but since we all have the job of keeping ourselves going, it is quite necessary that if we are to keep ourselves going we should thus present ourselves to ourselves.

A highly developed and organized human society is one in which the individual members are interrelated in a multiplicity of different intricate and complicated ways whereby they all share a number of common social interests,—interests in, or for the betterment of, the society—and yet, on the other hand, are more or less in conflict relative to numerous other interests which they possess only individually, or else share with one another only in small and limited groups. Conflicts among individuals in a highly developed and organized human society are not mere conflicts among their respective primitive impulses but are conflicts among their respective selves or personalities, each with its definite social structure—highly complex and organized and unified—and each with a number of different social facets or aspects, a number of different sets of social attitudes constituting it. Thus, within such a society, conflicts arise between different aspects or phases of the same individual self (conflicts leading to cases of split personality when they are extreme or violent enough to be psychopathological), as well as between different individual selves. And both these types of individual conflict are settled or terminated by reconstructions of the particular social situations, and modifications of the given framework of social relationships, wherein they arise or occur in the general human social life-process—these reconstructions and modifications being performed, as we have said, by the minds of the individuals in whose experience or between whose selves these conflicts take place.

Mind, as constructive or reflective or problem-solving thinking, is the socially acquired means or mechanism or apparatus whereby the human individual solves the various problems of environmental adjustment which arise to confront him in the course of his experience, and which prevent his conduct from proceeding harmoniously on its way, until they have thus been dealt with. And mind or thinking is also—as possessed by the individual members of human society—the means or mechanism or apparatus whereby social reconstruction is effected or accomplished by these individuals. For it is their possession of minds or powers of thinking which enables human individuals to turn back critically, as it were, upon the organized social structure of the society to which they belong (and from their relations to which their minds are in the first instance derived), and to reorganize or reconstruct or modify that social structure to a greater or less degree, as the exigencies of social evolution from time to time require. Any such social reconstruction, if it is to be at all far-reaching, presupposes a basis of common social interests shared by all the individual members of the given human society in which that reconstruction occurs; shared, that is, by all the individuals whose minds must participate in, or whose minds bring about, that reconstruction. And the way in which any such social reconstruction is actually effected by the minds of the individuals involved is by a more or less abstract intellectual extension of the boundaries of the given society to which these individuals all belong, and which is undergoing the reconstruction—an extension resulting in a larger social whole in terms of which the social conflicts that necessitate the reconstruction of the given society are harmonized or reconciled, and by reference to which, accordingly, these conflicts can be solved or eliminated.[19]

The changes that we make in the social order in which we are implicated necessarily involve our also making changes in ourselves. The social conflicts among the individual members of a given organized human society, which, for their removal, necessitate conscious or intelligent reconstructions and modifications of that society by those individuals, also and equally necessitate such reconstructions or modifications by those individuals of their own selves or personalities. Thus the relations between social reconstruction and self or personality reconstruction are reciprocal and internal or organic; social reconstruction by the individual members of any organized human society entails self or personality reconstruction in some degree or other by each of these individuals, and vice versa, for, since their selves or personalities are constituted by their organized social relations to one another, they cannot reconstruct those selves or personalities without also reconstructing, to some extent, the given social order, which is, of course, likewise constituted by their organized social relations to one another. In both types of reconstruction the same fundamental material of organized social relations among human individuals is involved, and is simply treated in different ways, or from different angles or points of view, in the two cases, respectively; or in short, social reconstruction and self or personality reconstruction are the two sides of a single process—the process of human social evolution. Human social progress involves the use by human individuals of their socially derived mechanism of self-consciousness, both in the effecting of such progressive social changes, and also in the development

[19] The reflexive character of self-consciousness enables the individual to contemplate himself as a whole; his ability to take the social attitudes of other individuals and also of the generalized other toward himself, within the given organized society of which he is a member, makes possible his bringing himself, as an objective whole, within his own experiential purview; and thus he can consciously integrate and unify the various aspects of his self, to form a single consistent and coherent and organized personality. Moreover, by the same means, he can undertake and effect intelligent reconstructions of that self or personality in terms of its relations to the given social order, whenever the exigencies of adaptation to his social environment demand such reconstructions.

of their individual selves or personalities in such a way as adaptively to keep pace with such social reconstruction.

Ultimately and fundamentally societies develop in complexity of organization only by means of the progressive achievement of greater and greater degrees of functional, behavioristic differentiation among the individuals who constitute them; these functional, behavioristic differentiations among the individual members implying or presupposing initial oppositions among them of individual needs and ends, oppositions which in terms of social organization, however, are or have been transformed into these differentiations, or into mere specializations of socially functional individual behavior.

The human social ideal—the ideal or ultimate goal of human social progress—is the attainment of a universal human society in which all human individuals would possess a perfected social intelligence, such that all social meanings would each be similarly reflected in their respective individual consciousnesses— such that the meanings of any one individual's acts or gestures (as realized by him and expressed in the structure of his self, through his ability to take the social attitudes of other individuals toward himself and toward their common social ends or purposes) would be the same for any other individual whatever who responded to them.

The interlocking interdependence of human individuals upon one another within the given organized social life-process in which they are all involved is becoming more and more intricate and closely knit and highly organized as human social evolution proceeds on its course. The wide difference, for example, between the feudal civilization of medieval times, with its relatively loose and disintegrated social organization, and the national civilization of modern times, with its relatively tight and integrated social organization (together with its trend of development toward some form of international civilization), exhibits the constant evolution of human social organization in the direction of greater and greater relational unity and complexity, more and more closely knit interlocking and integrated unifying of all the social relations of interdependence which constitute it and which hold among the individuals involved in it.

40. THE FUNCTIONS OF PERSONALITY AND REASON IN SOCIAL ORGANIZATION

Where a society is organized around a monarch, where people within the same state are so separate from each other that they can identify themselves with each other only through being subjects of a common monarch, then, of course, the relationship of the subject to the monarch becomes of supreme importance. It is only through such relationships that such a community can be set up and kept together. This situation is found in the ancient empires of Mesopotamia, where people of different languages and different customs had relationship only through the great kings. It provides the most immediate process of relationship; only so far as the king's authority goes, and this common basis of relationship to the king extends, has this type of society organization.

The importance of the monarch over against the feudal order lay in the fact that the king could set up relationships to the people widely separated except for the relationship with him. The king represented the people in a universal form, where previously they had no relationship to each other except the hostility of feudal communities for each other. There you get the personal relation, the relation of status, which is important in the community. The relation is, of course, that of subject to monarch. It involves the acceptance of an inferior position, but this is an acceptance which is gladly made because of the significance to the community at large which such an order makes possible. The community to which the individual belongs is typified in his relation to the king, and even under a constitutional monarchy the monarch acts to hold it together. Through the feeling of relation to the king one can get a feeling for the vast congeries of communities that do in some way hang together. In this way a situation of status makes possible that wider and larger community. It is possible through personal relationships between a sovereign and subject to constitute a community which could not otherwise be so constituted, and this fact has played a very important part in the development of states.

It is interesting to see how this situation appeared in the Roman Empire. There the relationship of the emperor to the subjects as such was one of absolute power, but it was defined in legal terms which carried over the definitions that belonged to Roman law into the relationship between the emperor and his subjects. This, however, constituted too abstract a relationship to meet the demands of the community, and the deification of the emperor under these conditions was the expression of the necessity of setting up some sort of more personal relation. When the Roman member of the community offered his sacrifice to the emperor he was putting himself into personal relationship with him, and because of that he could feel his connection with all the members in the community. Of course, the conception of the deity under those circumstances was not comparable with the conception that was developed in Christianity, but it was the setting-up of a personal relationship which in a certain sense went beyond the purely legal relations involved in the development of Roman law.

We are all familiar with this function of personality in social organization. We express it in terms of leadership or in the vague term "personality." Where an office force is organized by a good manager, we speak of his personality as playing a part. Where the action of a man in the office is more or less dependent upon his dread of a reprimand or desire for approval from the manager himself, there the element of a personal relationship of selves to each other plays a considerable part, perhaps the dominant part, in the actual social organization. It plays, of course, the dominant part in the relation of children to their parents. It is found in the relation of parents to each other. It frequently plays a part in political organization, where a leader is one whose personality awakens a warm response. It is not necessary to multiply the instances in which this sort of relationship of selves to each other in terms of personality is of importance in social organization.

It is of importance, however, to recognize the difference between that organization and an organization which is founded, we will say, upon a rational basis. If people get together, form a business corporation, look for a competent manager, discuss the candidates from the point of view of their intelligence, of their training, their past experience, and finally settle upon a certain individual; and then while they get him to take technical control, the members of the corporation of directors appointed by the stockholders undertake to determine what the policy shall be, there arises a situation in which this sort of personal relationship is not essential for the organization of this particular community. The officers are depending upon the capacity of the chosen man, and the interests of all involved in the concern, to give the needed control. Just to the degree that people are intelligent in such a situation, they will organize in the recognition of functions which others have to perform, and in the realization of the necessity on the part of each of performing his own functions in order that the whole may succeed. They will look for an expert to carry out the managerial functions.

The managerial form of government is an illustration of the definite advance from an organization which depends very considerably upon personal relations to political leaders, or the devotion of parties to persons in charge, to this sort of rational organization on the basis of what a government ought to do in the community. If we can make the function of the government sufficiently clear; if a considerable portion of the community can be fairly aware of what they want the government to do; if we can get the public problems, public utilities, and so on, sufficiently before the community so that the members can say, "We want just such a sort of government; we know what results are wanted; and we are looking for a man capable of giving us those results," then that would be a rational treatment eliminating all elements of personality which have no bearing upon the function of government. It would avoid the difficulty communities labor under in running their communities by means of parties. If government is by means of parties, it is necessary to organize those parties more or less on personal relations. When a man becomes a good organizer of his ward, what is looked for in such a man is one who gets hold of people (especially those who want to profit by power), awakens their personal relations, and calls forth what is known as "loyalty." Such a situation is made necessary by party organization, and a government conducted on that basis cannot eliminate or rationalize such conditions, except under crises in which some particular issue comes before the country.

I want to indicate this dividing line between an organization depending on what the community wants to accomplish through its government and the direction of the government from the point of view of personal relations. The dependence upon personal relations we have in some sense inherited from the past. They are still essential for our own democracy. We could not get interest enough at the present time to conduct the government without falling back on the personal relations involved in political parties. But it is of interest, I think, to distinguish between these two principles of organization. So far as we have the managerial form of government, it is worth noting that where it has come in, hardly any communities have given it up. This illustrates a situation that has passed beyond personal relationships as the basis for the organization of the community. But as a rule it can be said that our various democratic organizations of society still are dependent upon personal relations for the operation of the community, and especially for the operation of the government.

These personal relations are also of very great importance in the organization of the community itself. If looked at from the functional standpoint, they may seem rather ignoble; and we generally try to cover them up. We may regard them as a way of realizing one's self by some sort of superiority to somebody else. That phase is one which goes back to the situation in which

SOCIETY

a man plumes himself when he gets somebody else in a conflict and emerges victorious. We have very frequently that sense of superiority in what seems relatively unimportant matters. We are able to hold on to ourselves in little things; in the ways in which we feel ourselves to be a little superior. If we find ourselves defeated at some point we take refuge in feeling that somebody else is not as good as we are. Any person can find those little supports for what is called his self-respect. The importance of this phenomenon comes out in the relation of groups to each other. The individual who identifies himself with the group has the sense of an enlarged personality. So the conditions under which this satisfaction can be obtained are the conditions sought for as the basis of all situations in which groups get together and feel themselves in their superiority over other groups. It is on this basis that warfare is carried on. Hate comes back to the sense of superiority of one community over another. It is interesting to see how trivial the basis of that superiority may be; the American may travel abroad and come back with simply a sense of the better hotels in America.

A striking difference is found in the form in which values attached to the self appear in the two forms of social organization we are discussing. In the one case you realize yourself in these personal relations that come back to the superiority of yourself to others, or to the group superiority over other groups; in the other case you come back to the intelligent carrying-out of certain social functions and the realization of yourself in what you do under those circumstances. There may be conceivably as great an enthusiasm in one as in the other case, but we can realize the difference between the actual felt values. In the first case your felt value depends directly or indirectly on the sense of yourself in terms of your superiority which is in a certain sense sublimated; but you come back to a direct feeling of superiority through the identification of yourself with somebody else who is superior. The other sense of the importance of your self is obtained, if you like, through the sense of performing a social function, through fulfilling your duty as commander of the community, finding out what is to be done and going about to do it. In this realization of yourself you do not have to have somebody else who is inferior to you to carry it out. You want other people to fulfil their functions as well. You may feel that you are better than your neighbor who did not do his job, but you regret the fact that he did not do it. You do not feel your self in your superiority to somebody else but in the interrelation necessary in carrying out the more or less common function.

It is the difference between these values that I wanted to call attention to, and, of course, the recognition of the superiority of the second over the first. We cannot ignore the importance of the community based on direct personal relationships, for it has been in a large degree responsible for the organization of large communities which could otherwise not have appeared. It gives a common ground to persons who have no other basis for union; it provides the basis for the ideal communities of great universal religions. We are continually falling back upon that sort of personal relation where it is through opposition that one realizes himself, where a relationship of superiority or inferiority enters directly into the emotional field. We are dependent upon it in many ways even in highly rational organizations, where a man with push gets into a situation and just makes people keep at their jobs. But we always recognize that the sense of the self obtained through the realization of a function in the community is a more effective and for various reasons a higher form of the sense of the self than that which is dependent upon the immediate personal relations in which a relation of superiority and inferiority is involved.

Consider the situation in Europe at the present time. There is an evident desire on the part of national communities to get together in a rational organization of the community in which all the nations exist, and yet there is no desire to dispense with the sense of hostility as a means of preserving national self-consciousness. Nations have to preserve this sense of self; they cannot just go to pieces and disappear. The getting of this national self-consciousness was a distinct step ahead, as was the earlier setting-up of an empire. The communities at Geneva would rather go for one another's throats than give up the self-consciousness that makes their organization possible. Geneva is a stage, or ought to be a stage, on which the communities can get together in a functional relationship, realizing themselves without shaking their fists at one another. If the self cannot be realized in any other way, it is probably better to do it in the latter way. To realize the self is essential, and, if it has to be done by fighting, it may be better to keep at least the threat of a fight; but the realization of the self in the intelligent performance of a social function remains the higher stage in the case of nations as of individuals.

41. OBSTACLES AND PROMISES IN THE DEVELOPMENT OF THE IDEAL SOCIETY

We have presented the self from the side of experience; it arises through co-operative activity; it is made possible through the identical reactions of the self and others. In so far as the individual can call out in his own nature these organized responses and so take the attitude of the other toward himself, he can develop self-consciousness, a reaction of the organism to itself. On the other hand, we have seen that an essential moment in this process is the response of the individual to this reaction which does contain the organized group, that which is common to all, that which is called the "me." If individuals are so distinguished from each other that they cannot identify themselves with each other, if there is not a common basis, then there cannot be a whole self present on either side.

Such a distinction, for example, does lie between the infant and the human society in which he enters. He cannot have the whole self-consciousness of the adult; and the adult finds it difficult, to say the least, to put himself into the attitude of the child. That is not, however, an impossible thing, and our development of modern education rests on this possibility of the adult finding a common basis between himself and the child. Go back into the literature in which children are introduced in the sixteenth, seventeenth, and even eighteenth centuries, and you find children treated as little adults; the whole attitude toward them from the point of view of morals, as well as training, was that they were adults who were somewhat deficient and needed to be disciplined in order to get them into the proper attitude. That which they were to learn was to be brought to them in the form in which an adult makes use of the knowledge. It was not until the last century that there was a definite undertaking on the part of those interested in the education of children to enter into the experience of the child and to regard it with any respect.

Even in the society erected on the basis of castes there are some common attitudes; but they are very restricted in number, and as they are restricted they cut down the possibility of the full development of the self. What is necessary under those circumstances to get such a self is a withdrawal from that caste order. The medieval period in which there was a definite caste organization of society, with serfs, overlords, and ecclesiastical distinctions, presents a situation in which the attainment of membership in the spiritual community required the withdrawal of the individual from the society as ordered in the caste fashion. Such is at least a partial explanation of the cloistered life, and of asceticism. The same thing is revealed in the development of saints in other communities who withdraw from the social order, and get back to some sort of a society in which these castes as such are mediated or absent. The development of the democratic community implies the removal of castes as essential to the personality of the individual; the individual is not to be what he is in his specific caste or group set over against other groups, but his distinctions are to be distinctions of functional difference which put him in relationship with others instead of separating him.[20]

[20] In so far as specialization is normal and helpful, it increases concrete social relations. Differences in occupation do not themselves build up castes. The caste has arisen through the importation of the outsider into the group, just as the animal is brought in, when through the conception of property he can be made useful. The element of hostility toward the person outside the group is essential to the development of the caste. Caste in India arose out of conquest. It always involves the group enemy,

The caste distinction of the early warrior class was one which separated its members from the community. Their characters as soldiers differentiated them from the other members of the community; they were what they were because they were essentially different from others. Their activity separated them from the community. They even preyed upon the community which they were supposed to be defending, and would do so inevitably because their activity was essentially a fighting activity. With the development of the national army which took place at the beginning of the nineteenth century, there was the possibility of everyone's being a warrior, so that the man who was a fighting man was still a person who could identify himself with the other members of the community; he had their attitudes and they had the attitude of the fighting man. Thus the normal relationship between the fighting man and the rest of the community was one which bound people together, integrated the army and the body of the state, instead of separating them. The same progression is found in the other castes, such as the governing as over against the governed, an essential difference which made it impossible for the individual of that particular group to identify himself with the others, or the others to identify themselves with him. The democratic order undertakes to wipe that difference out and to make everyone a sovereign and everyone a subject. One is to be a subject to the degree that he is a sovereign. He is to undertake to administer rights and maintain them only in so far as he recognizes those rights in others. And so one might go on through other caste divisions.

Ethical ideas,[21] within any given human society, arise in the consciousness of the individual members of that society from

when that has been imported into the group; so that I should not myself agree with Cooley that hereditary transmission of differentiated occupation produces castes.

The caste system breaks down as the human relations become more concrete. . . . . Slaves pass over into serfs, peasants, artisans, citizens. In all these stages you have an increase of relations. In the ideal condition separation from the point of view of caste will become social function from the point of view of the group. . . . . Democratic consciousness is generated by differences of functions (1912).

[21] [For the implied ethical position, see Supplementary Essay IV.]

the fact of the common social dependence of all these individuals upon one another (or from the fact of the common social dependence of each one of them upon that society as a whole or upon all the rest of them), and from their awareness or sensing or conscious realization of this fact. But ethical problems arise for individual members of any given human society whenever they are individually confronted with a social situation to which they cannot readily adjust and adapt themselves, or in which they cannot easily realize themselves, or with which they cannot immediately integrate their own behavior; and the feeling in them which is concomitant with their facing and solution of such problems (which are essentially problems of social adjustment and adaptation to the interests and conduct of other individuals) is that of self-superiority and temporary opposition to other individuals. In the case of ethical problems, our social relationships with other individual members of the given human society to which we belong depend upon our opposition to them, rather than, as in the case of the development or formulation of ethical ideals, upon our unity, co-operation, and identification with them. Every human individual must, to behave ethically, integrate himself with the pattern of organized social behavior which, as reflected or prehended in the structure of his self, makes him a self-conscious personality. Wrong, evil, or sinful conduct on the part of the individual runs counter to this pattern of organized social behavior which makes him, as a self, what he is, just as right, good, or virtuous behavior accords with this pattern; and this fact is the basis of the profound ethical feeling of conscience—of "ought" and "ought not"—which we all have, in varying degrees, respecting our conduct in given social situations. The sense which the individual self has of his dependence upon the organized society or social community to which he belongs is the basis and origin, in short, of his sense of duty (and in general of his ethical consciousness); and ethical and unethical behavior can be defined essentially in social terms: the former as behavior which is socially beneficial or conducive to the well-being of society, the latter as behavior which is socially harmful or conducive to the disruption of society. From another point of view, ethical ideals and ethical problems may be considered in terms of the conflict between the social and the asocial (the impersonal and the personal) sides or aspects of the individual self. The social or impersonal aspect of the self integrates it with the social group to which it belongs and to which it owes its existence; and this side of the self is characterized by the individual's feeling of co-operation and equality with the other members of that social group. The asocial or personal aspect of the self (which, nevertheless, is also and equally social, fundamentally in the sense of being socially derived or originated and of existentially involving social relations with other individuals, as much as the impersonal aspect of the self is and does), on the other hand, differentiates it from, or sets it in distinctive and unique opposition to, the other members of the social group to which it belongs; and this side of the self is characterized by the individual's feeling of superiority toward the other members of that group. The "social" aspect of human society—which is simply the social aspect of the selves of all individual members taken collectively—with its concomitant feelings on the parts of all these individuals of co-operation and social interdependence, is the basis for the development and existence of ethical ideals in that society; whereas the "asocial" aspect of human society— which is simply the asocial aspect of the selves of all individual members taken collectively—with its concomitant feelings on the parts of all these individuals of individuality, self-superiority to other individual selves, and social independence, is responsible for the rise of ethical problems in that society. These two basic aspects of each single individual self are, of course, responsible in the same way or at the same time for the development of ethical ideals and the rise of ethical problems in the individual's own experience as opposed to the experience of human society as a whole, which is obviously nothing but the sum-total of the social experiences of all its individual members.

Those social situations in which the individual finds it

easiest to integrate his own behavior with the behavior of the other individual selves are those in which all the individual participants are members of some one of the numerous socially functional groups of individuals (groups organized, respectively, for various special social ends and purposes) within the given human society as a whole; and in which he and they are acting in their respective capacities as members of this particular group. (Every individual member of any given human society, of course, belongs to a large number of such different functional groups.) On the other hand, those social situations in which the individual finds it most difficult to integrate his own behavior with the behavior of others are those in which he and they are acting as members, respectively, of two or more different socially functional groups: groups whose respective social purposes or interests are antagonistic or conflicting or widely separated. In social situations of the former general type each individual's attitude toward the other individuals is essentially social; and the combination of all these social attitudes toward one another of the individuals represents, or tends to realize more or less completely, the ideal of any social situation respecting organization, unification, co-operation, and integration of the behavior of the several individuals involved. In any social situation of this general type the individual realizes himself as such in his relation to all the other members of the given socially functional group and realizes his own particular social function in its relations to the respective functions of all other individuals. He takes or assumes the social attitudes of all these other individuals toward himself and toward one another, and integrates himself with that situation or group by controlling his own behavior or conduct accordingly; so that there is nothing in the least competitive or hostile in his relations with these other individuals. In social situations of the latter general type on the other hand, each individual's attitude toward the other individuals is essentially asocial or hostile (though these attitudes are of course social in the fundamental non-ethical sense, and are socially derived); such situations are so complex that the various individuals involved in any one of them either cannot be brought into common social relations with one another at all or else can be brought into such relations only with great difficulty, after long and tortuous processes of mutual social adjustment; for any such situation lacks a common group or social interest shared by all the individuals—it has no one common social end or purpose characterizing it and serving to unite and co-ordinate and harmoniously interrelate the actions of all those individuals; instead, those individuals are motivated, in that situation, by several different and more or less conflicting social interests or purposes. Examples of social situations of this general type are those involving interactions or relations between capital and labor, i.e., those in which some of the individuals are acting in their socially functional capacity as members of the capitalistic class, which is one economic aspect of modern human social organization; whereas the other individuals are acting in their socially functional capacity as members of the laboring class, which is another (and in social interests directly opposed) economic aspect of that social organization. Other examples of social situations of this general type are those in which the individuals involved stand in the economic relations to each other of producers and consumers, or buyers and sellers, and are acting in their respective socially functional capacities as such. But even the social situations of this general type (involving complex social antagonisms and diversities of social interests among the individuals implicated in any one of them, and respectively lacking the co-ordinating, integrating, unifying influence of common social ends and motives shared by those individuals), even these social situations, as occurring within the general human social process of experience and behavior, are definite aspects of or ingredients in the general relational pattern of that process as a whole.

What is essential to the order of society in its fullest expression on the basis of the theory of the self that we have been discussing is, then, an organization of common attitudes which shall be found in all individuals. It might be supposed that such an organization of attitudes would refer only to that abstract human being which could be found as identical in all members of society, and that that which is peculiar to the personality of the individual would disappear. The term "personality" implies that the individual has certain common rights and values obtained in him and through him; but over and above that sort of social endowment of the individual, there is that which distinguishes him from anybody else, makes him what he is. It is the most precious part of the individual. The question is whether that can be carried over into the social self or whether the social self shall simply embody those reactions which can be common to him in a great community. On the account we have given we are not forced to accept the latter alternative.

When one realizes himself, in that he distinguishes himself, he asserts himself over others in some peculiar situation which justifies him in maintaining himself over against them. If he could not bring that peculiarity of himself into the common community, if it could not be recognized, if others could not take his attitude in some sense, he could not have appreciation in emotional terms, he could not be the very self he is trying to be. The author, the artist, must have his audience; it may be an audience that belongs to posterity, but there must be an audience. One has to find one's self in his own individual creation as appreciated by others; what the individual accomplishes must be something that is in itself social. So far as he is a self, he must be an organic part of the life of the community, and his contribution has to be something that is social. It may be an ideal which he has discovered, but it has its value in the fact that it belongs to society. One may be somewhat ahead of his time, but that which he brings forward must belong to the life of the community to which he belongs. There is, then, a functional difference, but it must be a functional difference which can be entered into in some real sense by the rest of the community. Of course, there are contributions which some make that others cannot make, and there may be contributions which people cannot enter into; but those that go to make up the self are only those which can be shared. To do justice to the recognition of the uniqueness of an individual in social terms, there must be not only the differentiation which we do have in a highly organized society but a differentiation in which the attitudes involved can be taken by other members of the group.

Take, for example, the labor movement. It is essential that the other members of the community shall be able to enter into the attitude of the laborer in his functions. It is the caste organization, of course, which makes it impossible; and the development of the modern labor movement not only brought the situation actually involved before the community but inevitably helped to break down the caste organization itself. The caste organization tended to separate in the selves the essential functions of the individuals so that one could not enter into the other. This does not, of course, shut out the possibility of some sort of social relationship; but any such relationship involves the possibility of the individual's taking the attitude of the other individuals, and functional differentiation does not make that impossible. A member of the community is not necessarily like other individuals because he is able to identify himself with them. He may be different. There can be a common content, common experience, without there being an identity of function. A difference of functions does not preclude a common experience; it is possible for the individual to put himself in the place of the other although his function is different from the other. It is that sort of functionally differentiated personality that I wanted to refer to as over against that which is simply common to all members of a community.

There is, of course, a certain common set of reactions which belong to all, which are not differentiated on the social side but which get their expression in rights, uniformities, the common methods of action which characterize members of different communities, manners of speech, and so on. Distinguishable from those is the identity which is compatible with the difference of social functions of the individuals, illustrated by the capacity of the individual to take the part of the others whom he is affecting, the warrior putting himself in the place of those whom he is proceeding against, the teacher putting himself in the position of the child whom he is undertaking to instruct. That capacity allows for exhibiting one's own peculiarities, and at the same time taking the attitude of the others whom he is himself affecting. It is possible for the individual to develop his own peculiarities, that which individualizes him, and still be a member of a community, provided that he is able to take the attitude of those whom he affects. Of course, the degree to which that takes place varies tremendously, but a certain amount of it is essential to citizenship in the community.

One may say that the attainment of that functional differentiation and social participation in the full degree is a sort of ideal which lies before the human community. The present stage of it is presented in the ideal of democracy. It is often assumed that democracy is an order of society in which those personalities which are sharply differentiated will be eliminated, that everything will be ironed down to a situation where everyone will be, as far as possible, like everyone else. But of course that is not the implication of democracy: the implication of democracy is rather that the individual can be as highly developed as lies within the possibilities of his own inheritance, and still can enter into the attitudes of the others whom he affects. There can still be leaders, and the community can rejoice in their attitudes just in so far as these superior individuals can themselves enter into the attitudes of the community which they undertake to lead.

How far individuals can take the rôles of other individuals in the community is dependent upon a number of factors. The community may in its size transcend the social organization, may go beyond the social organization which makes such identification possible. The most striking illustration of that is the economic community. This includes everybody with whom one can trade in any circumstances, but it represents a whole in which it would be next to impossible for all to enter into the attitudes of the others. The ideal communities of the universal religions are communities which to some extent may be said to exist, but they imply a degree of identification which the actual organization of the community cannot realize. We often find the existence of castes in a community which make it impossible for persons to enter into the attitude of other people although they are actually affecting and are affected by these other people. The ideal of human society is one which does bring people so closely together in their interrelationships, so fully develops the necessary system of communication, that the individuals who exercise their own peculiar functions can take the attitude of those whom they affect. The development of communication is not simply a matter of abstract ideas, but is a process of putting one's self in the place of the other person's attitude, communicating through significant symbols. Remember that what is essential to a significant symbol is that the gesture which affects others should affect the individual himself in the same way. It is only when the stimulus which one gives another arouses in himself the same or like response that the symbol is a significant symbol. Human communication takes place through such significant symbols, and the problem is one of organizing a community which makes this possible. If that system of communication could be made theoretically perfect, the individual would affect himself as he affects others in every way. That would be the ideal of communication, an ideal attained in logical discourse wherever it is understood. The meaning of that which is said is here the same to one as it is to everybody else. Universal discourse is then the formal ideal of communication. If communication can be carried through and made perfect, then there would exist the kind of democracy to which we have referred, in which each individual would carry just the response in himself that he knows he calls out in the community. That is what makes communication in the significant sense the organizing process in the community. It is not simply a process of transferring abstract symbols; it is always a gesture in a social act which calls out in the individual himself the tendency to the same act that is called out in others.

What we call the ideal of a human society is approached in some sense by the economic society on the one side and by the universal religions on the other side, but it is not by any means fully realized. Those abstractions can be put together in a single community of the democratic type. As democracy now exists, there is not this development of communication so that individuals can put themselves into the attitudes of those whom they affect. There is a consequent leveling-down, and an undue recognition of that which is not only common but identical. The ideal of human society cannot exist as long as it is impossible for individuals to enter into the attitudes of those whom they are affecting in the performance of their own peculiar functions.

42. SUMMARY AND CONCLUSION

We have approached psychology from the standpoint of behaviorism; that is, we have undertaken to consider the conduct of the organism and to locate what is termed "intelligence," and in particular, "self-conscious intelligence," within this conduct. This position implies organisms which are in relationship to environments, and environments that are in some sense determined by the selection of the sensitivity of the form of the organism. It is the sensitivity of the organism that determines what its environment shall be, and in that sense we can speak of a form as determining its environment. The stimulus as such as found in the environment is that which sets free an impulse, a tendency to act in a certain fashion. We speak of this conduct as intelligent just in so far as it maintains or advances the interests of the form or the species to which it belongs. Intelligence is, then, a function of the relation of the form and its environment. The conduct that we study is always the action of the form in its commerce with the environment. Such intelligence we may find in plants or animals when the form in its reaction to the environment sets free its impulses through the stimuli that come from the environment.

Earlier psychologists—and many psychologists of the present time, for that matter—assume that at a certain point in the development of the organism consciousness as such arises. It is supposed to appear first of all in affective states, those of pleasure and pain; and it is assumed that through pleasure and pain the form controls its conduct. It is assumed that later consciousness finds its expression in the sensation of the antecedent stimulus process in the environment itself. But these sensations, from the point of view of our study, involve the statement of the environment itself; that is, we cannot state the environment in any other way than in terms of our sensations, if we accept such a definition of sensation as a consciousness that simply arises. If we try to define the environment within which sensation does arise, it is in terms of that which we see and feel and that which our observation assumes to be present. The suggestion I have made is that consciousness, as such, does not represent a separate substance or a separate something that is superinduced upon a form, but rather that the term "consciousness" (in one of its basic usages) represents a certain sort of an environment in its relation to sensitive organisms.

Such a statement brings together two philosophic concepts, one of emergence and one of relativity. We may assume that certain types of characters arise at certain stages in the course of development. This may extend, of course, far below the range to which we are referring. Water, for example, arises out of a combination of hydrogen and oxygen; it is something over and above the atoms that make it up. When we speak, then, of such characters as sensations arising, emerging, we are really asking no more than when we ask the character of any organic compound. Anything that as a whole is more than the mere form of its parts has a nature that belongs to it that is not to be found in the elements out of which it is made.

Consciousness, in the widest sense, is not simply an emergent at a certain point, but a set of characters that is dependent upon the relationship of a thing to an organism. Color, for instance, may be conceived of as arising in relationship to an organism that has an organ of vision. In that case, there is a certain environment that belongs to a certain form and arises in relationship to that form. If we accept those two concepts of emergence and relativity, all I want to point out is that they do answer to what we term "consciousness," namely, a certain environment that exists in its relationship to the organism, and in which new characters can arise in virtue of the organism. I have not undertaken here[22] to defend this as a philosophic view, but simply to point out that it does answer to certain conscious characteristics which have been given to forms at certain points in evolution. On this view the characters do not belong to organisms as such but only in the relationship of the organism to its environment. They are characteristics of objects in the environment of the form. The objects are colored, odorous, pleasant or painful, hideous or beautiful, in their relationship to the organism. I have suggested that in the development of forms with environments that answer to them and that are regulated by the forms themselves there appear or emerge characters that are dependent on this relation between the form and its environment. In one sense of the term, such characters constitute the field of consciousness.

This is a conception which at times we use without any hesitancy. When an animal form appears, certain objects become food; and we recognize that those objects have become food because the animal has a certain sort of digestive apparatus. There are certain micro-organisms that are dangerous to human beings, but they would not be dangerous unless there were individuals susceptible to the attack of these germs. We do constantly refer to certain objects in the environment as existing there because of the relationship between the form and the environment. There are certain objects that are beautiful but that would not be beautiful if there were not individuals that have an appreciation of them. It is in that organic relation that beauty arises. In general, then, we do recognize that there are

[22] [See *The Philosophy of the Present* and *The Philosophy of the Act* for such a defense.]

objective fields in the world dependent upon the relation of the environment to certain forms. I am suggesting the extension of that recognition to the field of consciousness. All that I aim to point out here is that with such a conception we have hold of what we term "consciousness," as such; we do not have to endow the form with consciousness as a certain spiritual substance if we utilize these conceptions, and, as I said, we do utilize them when we speak of such a thing as food emerging in the environment because of the relationship of an object with the form. We might just as well speak of color, sound, and so on, in the same way.

The psychical in that case answers to the peculiar character which the environment has for a particular organism. It comes back to the distinction which we made between the self in its universal character and in its individual character. The self is universal, it identifies itself with a universal "me." We put ourselves in the attitude of all, and that which we all see is that which is expressed in universal terms; but each has a different sensitivity, and one color is different to me from what it is to you. These are differences which are due to the peculiar character of the organism as over against that which answers to universality.

I want to keep in the field of psychological analysis; but it does seem to me that it is important to recognize the possibility of such a treatment of consciousness, because it takes us into a field where the psychologists have been working. It is important to determine whether experienced characters are states of consciousness or whether they belong to the surrounding world. If they are states of consciousness, a different orientation results than if so-called "conscious states" are recognized as the characters of the world in its relation to the individual. All I am asking is that we should make use of that conception as we do use it in other connections. It opens the door to a treatment of the conscious self in terms of a behaviorism which has been regarded as inadequate at that point. It avoids, for example, the criticism made by the configuration psychologists, that psychologists have to come back to certain conscious states which people have.

The "I" is of importance, and I have treated it in so far as it has relation to the definite field of psychology, without undertaking to consider or defend what metaphysical assumptions may be involved. That limitation is justified, for the psychologist does not undertake to maintain a metaphysics as such. When he deals with the world about him, he just accepts it as it is. Of course, this attitude is shot through and through with metaphysical problems, but the approach is scientifically legitimate.

Further, what we term "mental images" (the last resort of consciousness as a substance) can exist in their relation to the organism without being lodged in a substantial consciousness. The mental image is a memory image. Such images which, as symbols, play so large a part in thinking, belong to the environment.[23] The passage we read is made up from memory images, and the people we see about us we see very largely by the help of memory images. Very frequently we find that the thing we see and that we suppose answers to the character of an object is not really there; it was an image. The image is there in its relation to the individual who not only has sense organs but who also has certain past experiences. It is the organism that has had such experiences that has such imagery. In saying this we are taking an attitude which we are constantly using when we say we have read a certain thing; the memory image is there in its relationship to a certain organism with certain past experiences, with certain values also definitely there in relation to that particular environment as remembered.

Consciousness as such refers to both the organism and its environment and cannot be located simply in either. If we free the field in this sense, then we can proceed with a behavioristic treatment without having the difficulties in which Watson found himself in dealing with mental images. He denied there was

[23] [Supplementary Essay I deals further with the topic of imagery.]

any such thing, and then had to admit it, and then tried to minimize it. Of course, the same difficulty lies in dealing with experience regarded as states of consciousness. If we recognize that these characters of things do exist in relation to the organism, then we are free to approach the organism from the standpoint of behaviorism.

I do not regard consciousness as having selective power, in one current sense of "selection." What we term "consciousness" is just that relation of organism and environment in which selection takes place. Consciousness arises from the interrelation of the form and the environment, and it involves both of them. Hunger does not create food, nor is an object a food object without relation to hunger. When there is that relation between form and environment, then objects can appear which would not have been there otherwise; but the animal does not create the food in the sense that he makes an object out of nothing. Rather, when the form is put into such relation with the environment, then there emerges such a thing as food. Wheat becomes food; just as water arises in the relation of hydrogen and oxygen. It is not simply cutting something out and holding it by itself (as the term "selection" seems to suggest), but in this process there appears or emerges something that was not there before. There is not, I say, anything about this view that impresses us as involving any sort of magic when we take it in the form of the evolution of certain other characters, and I want to insist that this conception does cover just that field which is referred to as consciousness.

Of course, when one goes back to such a conception of consciousness as early psychologists used, and everything experienced is lodged in consciousness, then one has to create another world outside and say that there is something out there answering to these experiences. I want to insist that it is possible to take the behavioristic view of the world without being troubled or tripped up by the conception of consciousness; there are certainly no more serious difficulties involved in such a view as

has been proposed than there are in a conception of consciousness as a something that arises at a certain point in the history
of physical forms and runs parallel in some way with specific
nervous states. Try to state that conception in a form applicable to the work of the psychologist and you find yourself in
all sorts of difficulties that are far greater than those in the conceptions of emergence and relativity. If you are willing to approach the world from the standpoint of these conceptions,
then you can approach psychology from the behaviorist's point
of view.

The other conception that I have brought out concerns the
particular sort of intelligence that we ascribe to the human
animal, so-called "rational intelligence," or consciousness in another sense of the term. If consciousness is a substance, it can
be said that this consciousness is rational per se; and just by
definition the problem of the appearance of what we call rationality is avoided. What I have attempted to do is to bring rationality back to a certain type of conduct, the type of conduct
in which the individual puts himself in the attitude of the whole
group to which he belongs. This implies that the whole group
is involved in some organized activity and that in this organized activity the action of one calls for the action of all the
others. What we term "reason" arises when one of the organisms takes into its own response the attitude of the other organisms involved. It is possible for the organism so to assume the
attitudes of the group that are involved in its own act within this
whole co-operative process. When it does so, it is what we term
"a rational being." If its conduct has such universality, it has
also necessity, that is, the sort of necessity involved in the
whole act—if one acts in one way the others must act in another
way. Now, if the individual can take the attitude of the others
and control his action by these attitudes, and control their action through his own, then we have what we can term "rationality." Rationality is as large as the group which is involved;
and that group could be, of course, functionally, potentially, as

large as you like. It may include all beings speaking the same language.

Language as such is simply a process by means of which the individual who is engaged in co-operative activity can get the attitude of others involved in the same activity. Through gestures, that is, through the part of his act which calls out the response of others, he can arouse in himself the attitude of the others. Language as a set of significant symbols is simply the set of gestures which the organism employs in calling out the response of others. Those gestures primarily are nothing but parts of the act which do naturally stimulate others engaged in the co-operative process to carry out their parts. Rationality then can be stated in terms of such behavior if we recognize that the gesture can affect the individual as it affects others so as to call out the response which belongs to the other. Mind or reason presupposes social organization and co-operative activity in this social organization. Thinking is simply the reasoning of the individual, the carrying-on of a conversation between what I have termed the "I" and the "me."

In taking the attitude of the group, one has stimulated himself to respond in a certain fashion. His response, the "I," is the way in which he acts. If he acts in that way he is, so to speak, putting something up to the group, and changing the group. His gesture calls out then a gesture which will be slightly different. The self thus arises in the development of the behavior of the social form that is capable of taking the attitude of others involved in the same co-operative activity. The pre-condition of such behavior is the development of the nervous system which enables the individual to take the attitude of the others. He could not, of course, take the indefinite number of attitudes of others, even if all the nerve paths were present, if there were not an organized social activity going on such that the action of one may reproduce the action of an indefinite number of others doing the same thing. Given, however, such an organized activity, one can take the attitude of anyone in the group.

Such are the two conceptions of consciousness that I wanted to bring out, since they seem to me to make possible a development of behaviorism beyond the limits to which it has been carried, and to make it a very suitable approach to the objects of social psychology. With those key concepts one does not have to come back to certain conscious fields lodged inside the individual; one is dealing throughout with the relation of the conduct of the individual to the environment.

SUPPLEMENTARY ESSAYS

I

THE FUNCTION OF IMAGERY
IN CONDUCT[1]

a) Human behavior, or conduct, like the behavior of lower animal forms, springs from impulses. An impulse is a congenital tendency to react in a specific manner to a certain sort of stimulus, under certain organic conditions. Hunger and anger are illustrations of such impulses. They are best termed "impulses," and not "instincts," because they are subject to extensive modifications in the life-history of individuals, and these modifications are so much more extensive than those to which the instincts of lower animal forms are subject that the use of the term "instinct" in describing the behavior of normal adult human individuals is seriously inexact.

It is of importance to emphasize the sensitivity to the appropriate stimuli which call out the impulses. This sensitivity is otherwise referred to as the "selective character of attention," and attention on its active motor side connotes hardly anything beyond this relationship of a preformed tendency to act to the stimulus which sets the impulse free. It is questionable whether there is such a thing as passive attention. Even the dependence of sensory attention upon the intensity of stimuli implies general attitudes of escape or protection which are mediated through such stimuli or through the pain stimuli which attend intense stimulation. Where through the modification arising out of experience—e.g., the indifference to loud noises which workmen attain in factories—the response of the individual to these intense stimuli lapses, it is at least not unreasonable to assume that the absence of power to hold so-called "passive attention"

[1] [See also "Image or Sensation," *Journal of Philosophy*, I (1904), 604 ff.]

is due to the dissociation of these stimuli from the attitudes of reflexive avoidance and flight.

There is another procedure by which the organism selects the appropriate stimulus, where an impulse is seeking expression. This is found in the relation to imagery. It is most frequently the image which enables the individual to pick out the appropriate stimulus for the impulse which is seeking expression. This imagery is dependent on past experience. It can be studied only in man, since the image as a stimulus or a part of the stimulus can only be identified by the individual, or through his account of it given in social conduct. But in this experience of the individual or of a group of individuals, the object to which the image refers, in the same sense in which a sensory process refers to an object, can be identified, either as existing beyond the immediate range of sensory experience or as having existed in what is called the "past." In other words, the image is never without such reference to an object. This fact is embodied in the assertion that all our imagery arises out of previous experience. Thus, when one recalls the face of one whom he has met in the past, and identifies it through actual vision of the face, his attitude is identical with that of a man who identifies an object seen uncertainly at a distance. The image is private or psychical only in the situation in which the sensory process may be private or psychical. This situation is that in which readjustment of the individual organism and its environment is involved in the carrying-out of the living process. The private or psychical phase of the experience is that content which fails to function as the direct stimulus for the setting-free of the impulse. In so far as the contents from past experience enter into the stimulus, filling it out and fitting it to the demands of the act, they become a part of the object, though the result of the reaction may lead us to recognize that it failed, when our judgment is that what looked hard or soft or near or far proves to be quite otherwise. In this case we describe the content so estimated as private or psychical. Thus contents which refer to objects not present in the field of stimulation and which do not enter into the object, i.e., images of distant objects in time and space which are not integral parts of the physical surroundings as they extend beyond the range of immediate perception, nor of the memory field which constitutes the background of the self in its social structure, are psychical.

This definition of the private and psychical stands, therefore, on an entirely different basis from that which identifies the private or psychical with the experience of the individual, as his own, for in so far as the individual is an object to himself in the same sense as that in which others are objects to him, his experiences do not become private and psychical. On the contrary, he recognizes the common characters in them all, and even that which attaches to the experience of one individual as distinguished from others is felt to represent a contribution which he makes to a common experience of all. Thus what one man alone, through keener vision, detects would not be regarded as psychical in its character. It is that experience which falls short of the objective value which it claims that is private and psychical. There are, of course, experiences which are necessarily confined to a particular individual, and which cannot in their individual character be shared by others; e.g., those which arise from one's own organism, and affective experiences —feelings—which are vague and incapable of reference to an object, and which cannot be made common property of the community to which one belongs (such mystical experiences are in part responsible for the assumption of a spiritual being—a God—who can enter into and comprehend these emotional states). But these states either have, or are assumed to have, objective reference. The toothache from which a man suffers is no less objective because it is something that cannot be shared, coming as it does from his own organism. One's moods may helplessly reach out toward something that cannot be attained, leaving him merely with the feelings and a reference which is not achieved; but there is still an implication of something that has objective reality. The psychical is that which fails to secure its reference and remains therefore the experience

simply of the individual. Even then it invites reconstruction
and interpretation, so that its objective character may be discovered; but until this has been secured, it has no habitat except the experience of the individual and no description except
in terms of his subjective life. Here belong the illusions, the
errors of perception, the emotions that stand for frustrated
values, the observations which record genuine exceptions to
accepted laws and meanings. From this standpoint the image,
in so far as it has objective reference, is not private or psychical. Thus the extended landscape reaching beyond our visual
horizon, bounded perhaps by nearby trees or buildings; the immediate past that is subject to no question—these stand out as
real as do the objects of perception, as real as the distance of
neighboring houses, or the polished cool surface of a marble
table, or the line of the printed page on which the eye in its ap-
perceptive leaps rests but two or three times. In all these experiences sensuous contents which we call "imagery" (because
the objects to which they refer are not the immediate occasions
of their appearance) are involved, and are only rendered private
or psychical by having their objectivity questioned in the same
manner in which the sensuous contents which answer to immediate excitements of end-organs may be questioned. As the
perceptual sensuous experience is an expression of the adjustment of the organism to the stimulation of objects temporally
and spatially present, so the images are adjustments of the
organism to objects which have been present but are now
spatially and temporally absent. These may merge into immediate perceptions, giving the organism the benefit of past experience in filling out the object of perception; or they may
serve to extend the field of experience beyond the range of immediate perception, in space or time or both; or they may appear without such reference, although they always imply a
possible reference, i.e., we hold that they could always be
referred to the experiences out of which they arose if their whole
context could be developed.

In the latter case the images are spoken of as existing in the mind. It is important to recognize that the location of the imagery in the mind is not due to the stuff of the imagery, for the same stuff goes into our perceptions and into the objects beyond immediate perception, which exist beyond our spatial and temporal horizons. It is due rather to the control over the appearance of the imagery in the mental processes which are commonly called those of "association," especially in the process of thinking in which we readjust our habits and reconstruct our objects.

The laws of association are now generally recognized as simple processes of redintegration, in which the imagery tends to complete itself in its temporal, spatial, or functional (similarity) phases. It has been found most convenient to deal with these tendencies as expressions of neural co-ordinations. The association of ideas has been superseded by associations of nerve elements. Thus the sight of a room recalls an individual whom one has met there. The area of the central nervous system affected on the occasion of the encounter being partially affected by the sight of the room on the later occasion is aroused by this stimulation and the image of the acquaintance appears. As a piece of mechanism this is not different from the perception of distance or solidity which accompanies our visual experiences through the imagery of past contacts filling out the immediate visual experience, except that the image of the acquaintance does not fit into the visual experience so as to become a part of the perception. In the case of a hallucination this does take place, and only the attempt to establish contact with the acquaintance proves that one is dealing with an image instead of a perceptual fact. What is still unexplained in such a statement of association is the fact that one image appears rather than countless others which have also been a part of the experience of the room. The customary explanation derived from frequency and vividness and contrast proves inadequate, and we must fall back upon the impulses seeking expression, in other words, upon interest, or in still other terms, upon attention. The so-called "selective nature" of consciousness is as necessary for the explanation of association as for that of attention and shows itself in our sensitivity to the stimuli which set free impulses seeking expression, when those stimuli arise from objects in the immediate field of perception or from imagery. The former answer to adjustment of the organism to objects present in space and time, the latter to those which are no longer so present but which are still reflected in the nervous structure of the organism. The sensitizing of the organism holds for both classes of stimulation. Imagery thus far considered no more exists in a mind than do the objects of external sense perception. It constitutes a part of the field of stimulation to which our attitudes or impulses seeking expression sensitize us. The image of the stimulus we need is more vivid than others. It serves to organize the perceptual attitude toward the object which we need to recognize, as embodied in Herbart's phrase, "apperception-mass." The sensuous content of the imagery may be relatively slight, so slight that many psychologists have taught that much of our thinking is imageless; but though the adjustment of the organism to the carrying-out of the response involved in the whole act may be the most readily recognized, and thus this part of the imagery be regarded as the most important, there is no reason to question the presence of the sensuous content which serves as stimulation.

The dominant part which the doctrine of association of ideas has played in explaining conduct finds its ground in the control over the imagery which thought exercises. In thinking, we indicate to ourselves imagery which we may use in reconstructing our perceptual field, a process which will be the subject of later discussion. What I wish to point out here is that imagery so controlled has been regarded as subject to the same principles of redintegration as those by which we bring it into the process of thought. The latter principles are the relations of the significant vocal gestures or signs to that which they signify. We speak of words as associated with things, and carry over this relation to the connections of images with each other, together with the reactions they help to mediate. The principle of the association of words and things is in large measure that of habit-forming. It has no import for the explanation of the sort of habit to be formed. It has no relation to the structure of experience through which we adjust ourselves to changing conditions. The child makes habits of applying certain names to certain things. This does not explain the relations of things in the child's experience or the type of his reactions to them, but this is just what the associational psychologist assumes. A habit fixes a certain response, but its habitual character does not explain either the inception of the reaction or the ordering of the world within which the reaction takes place. In this preliminary account of mind we recognize, first, contents which are not objective, that is, do not go to constitute the immediate perceptual world to which we react—which are then termed "subjective imagery"; and, second, the thought-process and its contents, arising through the social process of conversation with the self as another, whose function in behavior we have to investigate later. It is important to recognize that the self, as one among other individuals, is not subjective, nor are its experiences as such subjective. This account is introduced to free imagery as such from an all inclusive predicate of subjectivity. Certain images are there just as are other perceptual contents, and our sensitivity to them serves the same function as does our sensitivity to other perceptual stimulations, namely, that of selecting and building out the objects which will give expression to the impulses [MS].

b) Of imagery the only thing that can be said is that it does not take its place among our distant stimuli which build up the surrounding world that is the extension of the manipulatory area. Probably Hume's distinction of vividness is legitimate here, though the better statement is to be found in its efficiency in carrying out the function of calling forth the movement toward the distant object and receiving the confirmation of contact experience. It is true that characters in the distance experience presumably come in from imagery and do call out the response. Thus the contours of a familiar face may be filled in by imagery, and lead to approach to the individual and the grasp of the hand, which ultimately assures us of his real existence in the present experience. Hallucinations and illusions also call out these responses and lead to the results which correct the first impression. If we find that we have met a stranger instead of the supposed friend, we identify, perhaps, the part of the distance experience which was imagery as distinct from what is called "sensation." We speak of imagery as "psychically present." What do we mean by this? The simplest answer would be that the imagery is the experience of the individual organism that is the percipient event in the perspective. If by this we mean that there is an experience in the central nervous system which is the condition of the appearance of the imagery, the statement has a certain meaning. But it is confessed that the disturbance in the central nervous system is not what we term the "imagery," unless we place some inner psychical content in the molecules of the brain, and then we are not talking about the central nervous system which is a possible object in the field [of perception].

Imagery is, of course, not confined to memory. Whatever may be said about its origin in past experience, its reference to the future is as genuine as to the past. Indeed, it is fair to say that it only refers to the past in so far as it has a future reference in some real sense. It may be there without immediate reference to either future or to past. We may be quite unable to place the image. The location of imagery in a psychical field implies the self as existent and cannot be made the account of its locus in a theory which undertakes to show how the self arises in an experience within which imagery must be assumed as antecedent to the self. Here we are thrown back on the vividness as a reason for the organism not responding to it as it does to the distant stimulus which we do not call imagery. Perhaps there is some other character which is not expressed in the term "vividness." But it is evident that if the imagery had the quality which belongs to the so-called "sensuous experience" we should react to it, and its entrance into sensuous experience as above noted indicates that it is not excluded by its quality. In our own sophisticated experience the controlling factor seems to be its failure to fit into the complex of the environment as a continuous texture. Where as filling or as hallucination it does so enter, there is no hesitancy on the part of the organism in reacting to it as to sensuous stimuli, and it is there in the same sense in which the normal stimuli are there, i.e., the individual acts to reach or avoid the contacts which the images imply. It is then its failure to become a part of the distance environment which is responsible for its exclusion. That it is not the imagery of hardness that constitutes the stuff of what we see, I have already insisted. Here again it is the functional attitude of the organism in using the resistance which the distance stimulus is responsible for, that constitutes the stuff of the distant object, and the image does not call out this attitude. Imagery has to be accepted as there but as not a part of the field to which we respond in the sense in which we respond to the distance stimuli of sense experience, and the immediate reason for not so responding seems to lie in its failure to fall into the structure of the field except as filling, when it is indistinguishable. The light that we get upon its character comes from the evidence that its contents have always been in former experiences, and from the part which the central nervous system seems to play in its appearance. But the part played by the central nervous system is largely inference from the function which memory and anticipation have in experience. The present includes what is disappearing and what is emerging. Toward that which is emerging our action takes us, and what is disappearing provides the conditions of that action. Imagery then comes in to build out both stretches. We look before and after, and sigh for what is not. This building-out process is already in operation in building up the present, in so far as the organism endows its field with present existence [MS].

c) Imagery is an experience that takes place within the individual, being by its nature divorced from the objects that would give it a place in the perceptual world; but it has representational reference to such objects. This representational reference is found in the relation of the attitudes that answer to the symbols of the completion of the act to the varied stimuli that initiate the acts. The bringing of these different attitudes into harmonious relation takes place through the reorganization of the contents of the stimuli. Into this reorganization enter the so-called "images" of the completion of the act. The content of this imagery is varied. It may be of vision and contact or of the other senses. It is apt to be of the nature of the vocal gestures. It serves as a preliminary testing of the success of the reorganized object. Other imagery is located at the beginning of the act, as in the case of a memory image of an absent friend that initiates an act of meeting him at an agreed rendezvous. Imagery may be found at any place in the act, playing the same part that is played by objects and their characteristics. It is not to be distinguished, then, by its function.

What does characterize it is its appearance in the absence of the objects to which it refers. Its recognized dependence upon past experience, i.e., its relation to objects that were present, in some sense removes this difference; but it brings out the nature of the image as the continued presence of the content of an object which is no longer present. It evidently belongs to that phase of the object which is dependent upon the individual in the situation within which the object appears [MS].

II

THE BIOLOGIC INDIVIDUAL

The distinction of greatest importance between types of conduct in human behavior is that lying between what I will term the conduct of the "biologic individual" and the conduct of the "socially self-conscious individual." The distinction answers roughly to that drawn between conduct which does not involve conscious reasoning and that which does, between the conduct of the more intelligent of the lower animals and that of man. While these types of conduct can be clearly distinguished from each other in human behavior, they are not on separate planes, but play back and forth into each other, and constitute, under most conditions, an experience which appears to be cut by no lines of cleavage. The skill with which one plays a fast game of tennis and that by which he plans a house or a business undertaking seem to belong to the organic equipment of the same individual, living in the same world and subject to the same rational control. For the tennis-player criticizes his game at times and learns to place the ball differently over against different opponents; while in the sophisticated undertakings of planning, he depends confidently on his flair for conditions and men. And yet the distinction is of real and profound importance, for it marks the distinction between our biologic inheritance from lower life and the peculiar control which the human social animal exercises over his environment and himself.

It would be a mistake to assume that a man is a biologic individual plus a reason, if we mean by this definition that he leads two separable lives, one of impulse or instinct, and another of reason—especially if we assume that the control exercised by reason proceeds by means of ideas considered as mental contents which do not arise within the impulsive life and form a real part thereof. On the contrary, the whole drift of modern psychology has been toward an undertaking to bring will and reason within the impulsive life. The undertaking may not have been fully successful, but it has been impossible to avoid the attempt to bring reason within the scope of evolution; and if this attempt is successful, rational conduct must grow out of impulsive conduct. My own attempt will be to show that it is in the social behavior of the human animal that this evolution takes place. On the other hand, it is true that reasoning conduct appears where impulsive conduct breaks down. Where the act fails to realize its function, when the impulsive effort to get food does not bring the food—and, more especially, where conflicting impulses thwart and inhibit each other—here reasoning may come in with a new procedure that is not at the disposal of the biologic individual. The characteristic result of the reasoning procedure is that the individual secures a different set of objects to which to respond, a different field of stimulation. There has been discrimination, analysis, and a rebuilding of the things that called out the conflicting impulses and that now call out a response in which the conflicting impulses have been adjusted to each other. The individual who was divided within himself is unified again in his reaction. So far, however, as we react directly toward things about us without the necessity of finding different objects from those which meet our immediate vision and hearing and contact, so far are we acting impulsively; and we act accordingly as biologic individuals, individuals made up of impulses sensitizing us to stimuli, and answering directly to this stimulation.

What are the great groups of impulses making up this biologic individual? The answer for the purposes of this discussion need only be a rough answer. There are, first of all, the adjustments by which the individual maintains his position and balance in motion or at rest; (2) the organization of responses toward distant objects, leading to movement toward or from them; (3) the adjustment of the surfaces of the body to contacts with objects which we have reached by movement, and especially the manipulations of these objects by the hand; (4) attack on, and defense from, hostile forms of prey, involving specialized organization of the general impulses just noted; (5) flight and escape from dangerous objects; (6) movements toward, or away from, individuals of the opposite sex, and the sexual process; (7) securing and ingesting food; (8) nourishment and care of child forms, and suckling and adjustment of the body of the child to parental care; (9) withdrawals from heat, cold, and danger, and the relaxations of rest and sleep; and (10) the formation of various sorts of habitats, serving the functions of protection and of parental care.

While this is but a roughly fashioned catalogue of primitive human impulses, it does cover them, for there is no primitive reaction which is not found in the list, or is not a possible combination of them, if we except the debatable field of the herding instinct. There seem to be in the last analysis two factors in this so-called "instinct"; first, a tendency of the member of the group that herds to move in the direction of, and at the same rate as, other members of the group; second, the carrying-out of all the life-processes more normally and with less excitability in the group than outside it. The latter is evidently a highly composite factor, and seems to point to a heightened sensitivity to the stimuli to withdrawal and escape in the absence of the group. I have referred to this especially because the vagueness and lack of definition of this group of impulses have led many to use this instinct to explain phenomena of social conduct that lie on an entirely different level of behavior.

It is customary to speak of the instincts in the human individual as subject to almost indefinite modification, differing in this from the instincts in the lower animal forms. Instincts in the latter sense can hardly be identified in man, with the exception of that of suckling and perhaps certain of the immediate reactions of anger which very young infants exhibit, together with a few others which are too undeveloped to deserve the term. The life of the child in human society subjects these and all the impulses with which human nature is endowed to a pressure which carries them beyond possible comparison with the animal instincts, even though we have discovered that the instincts in lower animals are subject to gradual changes through long-continued experience of shifting conditions. This pressure is, of course, only possible through the rational character that finds its explanation, if I am correct, in the social behavior into which the child is able to enter.

This material of instinct or impulse in the lower animals is highly organized. It represents the adjustment of the animal to a very definite and restricted world. The stimuli to which the animal is sensitive and which lie in its habitat constitute that world and answer to the possible reactions of the animal. The two fit into each other and mutually determine each other, for it is the instinct-seeking-expression that determines the sensitivity of the animal to the stimulus, and it is the presence of the stimulus which sets the instinct free. The organization represents not only the balance of attitude and the rhythm of movement but the succession of acts upon each other, the whole unified structure of the life of the form and the species. In any known human community, even of the most primitive type, we find neither such a unified world nor such a unified individual. There is present in the human world a past and an uncertain future, a future which may be influenced by the conduct of the individuals of the group. The individual projects himself into varied possible situations and by implements and social attitudes undertakes to make a different situation exist, which would give expression to different impulses.

From the point of view of instinctive behavior in the lower animals, or of the immediate human response to a perceptual world (in other words, from the standpoint of the unfractured relation between the impulses and the objects which give them expression), past and future are not there; and yet they are represented in the situation. They are represented by facility of adjustment through the selection of certain elements both in the direct sensuous stimulation through the excitement of the end-organs, and in the imagery. What represents past and what represents future are not distinguishable as contents. The surrogate of the past is the actual adjustment of the impulse to the object as stimulus. The surrogate of the future is the control which the changing field of experience during the act maintains over its execution.

The flow of experience is not differentiated into a past and future over against an immediate now until reflection affects certain parts of the experience with these characters, with the perfection of adjustment on the one hand, and with the shifting control on the other. The biologic individual lives in an undifferentiated now; the social reflective individual takes this up into a flow of experience within which stands a fixed past and a more or less uncertain future. The now of experience is represented primarily by the body of impulses listed above, our inherited adjustment to a physical and social world, continuously reconstituted by social reflective processes; but this reconstitution takes place by analysis and selection in the field of stimulation, not by immediate direction and recombination of the impulses. The control exercised over the impulses is always through selection of stimulations conditioned by the sensitizing influence of various other impulses seeking expression. The immediacy of the now is never lost, and the biologic individual stands as the unquestioned reality in the minds of differently constructed pasts and projected futures. It has been the work of scientific reflection to isolate certain of these fixed adjustments (in terms of our balanced postures, our movements toward objects, our contacts with and manipulations of objects) as a physical world, answering to the biologic individual with its intricate nervous system.

The physical world, which has arisen thus in experience, answers not only to our postures and movements with reference to distant objects and our manipulations of these objects, but also to the biological mechanism, especially its complex nervous co-ordinations by which these reactions are carried out. As it is in this physical world that we attain our most perfect controls, the tendency toward placing the individual, as a mechanism, in this physical world is very strong. Just in so far as we present ourselves as biological mechanisms are we better able to control a correspondingly greater field of conditions which determine conduct. On the other hand, this statement in mechanical terms abstracts from all purposes and all ends of conduct. If these appear in the statement of the individual, they must be placed in mind, as an expression of the self—placed, in other words, in a world of selves, that is, in a social world. I do not wish to enter the subtle problems involved in these distinctions—the problems of mechanism and teleology, of body and mind, the psychological problem of parallelism or interaction. I desire simply to indicate the logical motive which carries the mechanical statement of behavior into the physical field and the statement of ends and purposes into the mental world, as these terms are generally used. While these two emphases which have been recognized above in the distinction between the past and the future are of capital importance, it is necessary to underscore the return which modern scientific method (and this is but an elaborate form of reflection) inevitably makes to unsophisticated immediate experience in the use of experiment as the test of reality. Modern science brings its most abstract and subtle hypotheses ultimately into the field of the "now" to evidence their reliability and their truth.

This immediate experience which is reality, and which is the final test of the reality of scientific hypotheses as well as the test of the truth of all our ideas and suppositions, is the experience of what I have called the "biologic individual." The term refers to the individual in an attitude and at a moment in which the impulses sustain an unfractured relation with the objects around him. The final registering of the pointer on a pair of scales, of the coincidence of the star with the hair line of a telescope, of the presence of an individual in a room, of the actual consummation of a business deal—these occurrences which may confirm any hypothesis or supposition are not themselves subject to analysis. What is sought is a coincidence of an anticipated result with the actual event. I have termed it "biologic" because the term lays emphasis on the living reality which may be distinguished from reflection. A later reflection turns back upon it and endeavors to present the complete interrelationship between the world and the individual in terms of physical stimuli and biological mechanism; the actual experience did not take place in this form but in the form of unsophisticated reality [MS].

III

THE SELF AND THE PROCESS OF REFLECTION

It is in social behavior that the process of reflection itself arises. This process should first of all be stated in its simplest appearance. It implies, as I have already stated, some defeat of the act, especially one due to mutually inhibiting impulses. The impulse to advance toward food or water is checked by an impulse to hold back or withdraw through the evidence of danger or a sign forbidding trespass. The attitude of the animal lower than man under these conditions is that of advancing and retreating—a process which may of itself lead to some solution without reflection. Thus the cats in the trick box by continuous erratic movements find at last the spring that sets them free; but the solution thus found is not a reflective solution, though continuous repetition may at last stamp this reaction in, so that the experienced cat will at once release the spring when placed again in the puzzle box. A very large part of human skill gained in playing games, or musical instruments, or in attaining in general muscular adjustments to new situations, is acquired by this trial-and-error procedure.

In this procedure one of the opposing impulses after the other is dominant, gaining expression up to the point at which it is definitively checked by the opposing impulse or impulses. Thus a dog approaching a stranger who offers it meat may almost reach him, and then under the summation of the stimuli of the strangeness of the man suddenly dart away barking and snarling. Such a seesaw between opposing impulses may continue for some time, until, after exhausting each other, they leave the door open to other impulses and their stimuli entirely outside the present field. Or this approach and retreat many bring into play still other characters in the objects, arousing other impulses which may thus solve the problem. A closer approach to the stranger may reveal a familiar odor from the man and banish the stimulus which has set free the impulse of flight and hostility. In the other instance cited—that of the cats in the box—one impulsive act after another finally leads by chance to the setting-off of the spring. The bungling, awkward, hesitating play of the beginner at tennis or on the violin is an instance of the same thing in human conduct; and here we are able to record the player himself as saying that he learns without knowing how he learns. He finds that a new situation appears to him that he has not recognized in the past. The position of his opponent and the angle of the approaching ball suddenly become important to him. These objective situations had not existed for him in the past. He has not built them up on any theory. They are simply there, whereas in the past they had not been in his experience; and introspection shows that he recognizes them by a readiness to a new sort of response. His attention is called to them by his own motor attitudes. He is getting what he calls "form." In fact, "form" is a feel for those motor attitudes by which we sensitize ourselves to the stimuli that call out the responses seeking expression. The whole is an unreflective process in which the impulses and their corresponding objects are there or are not there. The reorganization of the objective field and of conflicting impulses does take place in experience. When it has taken place it is registered in new objects and new attitudes, and for the time being we may postpone the manner in which the reorganization takes place. Current explanations in terms of trial and error, stamping-in of successful reactions and elimination of unsuccessful reactions, and the selective power of the pleasure attending success and the pain attending upon failure have not proved satisfying, but the processes lie outside the field of reflection and need not detain us at present.

As an example of simple reflection we may take the opening of a drawer that refuses to give way to repeated pulls of ever increasing energy. Instead of surrendering one's self to the effort to expend all his strength until he may have pulled off the handles themselves, the individual exercises his intelligence by locating, if possible, the resistance, identifying a little give on this side or that, and using his strength at the point where the resistance is greatest, or attending to the imagery of the contents of the drawer and removing the drawer above so that he may take out the obstacle that has defeated his efforts. In this procedure the striking difference from that unreflective method which we have just been considering is found in the analysis of the object. The drawer has ceased for the time being to be a mere something to be pulled. It is a wooden thing of different parts, some of which may have swollen more than others. It is also a crowded receptacle of objects which may have projected themselves against the containing frame. This analysis, however, does not take us out of the field of the impulses. The man is operating with two hands. A sense of greater resistance on one side rather than on the other leads to added effort where the resistance is the greatest. The imagery of the contents of the drawer answers to a tendency to drag away the offending hindrance. The mechanism of ordinary perception, in which the person's tendencies to act lead him to remark the objects which will give the tendencies free play, is quite competent to deal with the problem, if he can only secure a field of behavior within which the parts of the unitary object may answer to the parts of the organized reaction. Such a field is not that of overt action, for the different suggestions appear as competing hypotheses of the best plan of attack, and must be related to each other so as to be parts of some sort of a new whole.

Mere inhibition of conflicting impulses does not provide such a field. This may leave us with objects that simply negate each other—a drawer that is not a drawer, since it cannot be drawn, an individual that is both an enemy and a friend, or a road that is a no-thoroughfare; and we may simply bow to the inevitable, while the attention shifts to other fields of action. Nor are we at liberty to predicate a mind, as a locus for reflection—a mind that at a certain stage in evolution is there, a heaven-given inner endowment ready to equip man with a new technique of life. Our undertaking is to discover the development of mind within behavior that took no thought to itself, and belonged entirely to a world of immediate things and immediate reactions to things. If it is to be an evolution within behavior, it must be statable in the way we have conceived behavior to take place in living forms, i.e., every step of the process must be an act in which an impulse finds expression through an object in a perceptual field. It may be necessary again to utter a warning against the easy assumption that experiences originating from under the skin provide an inner world within which in some obscure manner reflection may arise, and against the assumption that the body of the individual as a perceptual object provides a center to which experiences may be attached, thus creating a private and psychical field that has in it the germ of representation and so of reflection. Neither a colic nor a stubbed toe can give birth to reflection, nor do pleasures or pains, emotions or moods, constitute inner psychical contents, inevitably referred to a self, thus forming an inner world within which autochthonous thought can spring up. Reflection as it appears in the instance cited above involves two attitudes at least: one of indicating a novel feature of the object which gives rise to conflicting impulses (analysis); and the other of so organizing the reaction toward the object, thus perceived, that one indicates the reaction to himself as he might to another (representation). The direct activities out of which thought grows are social acts, and presumably find their earliest expression in primitive social responses. It will be well, then, to consider first the simplest forms of social conduct and return to reflection when we learn whether such conduct provides a field and method for reflection.

The social conduct of any individual may be defined as that conduct arising out of impulses whose specific stimuli are found in other individuals belonging to the same biologic group. These stimuli may appeal to any of the sense organs, but there is a class of such stimuli which needs to be especially noted and emphasized. These are the motor attitudes and early stages in the movements of other individuals which govern the reactions of the individual in question. They have been largely overlooked by comparative psychologists; or when discussed, as they have been, by Darwin, Piderit, and Wundt, they have been treated as affecting other individuals not directly but through their expression of emotion, of intention, or idea; that is, they have not been recognized as specific stimuli but as secondary and derived stimuli. But anyone who studies what may be called the "conversation of attitudes" of dogs preparing for a fight, or the adjustments of infants and their mothers, or the mutual movements of herding animals will recognize that the beginnings of social acts call out instinctive or impulsive responses as immediately as do the animal forms, odors, contacts, or cries. Wundt has done a great service in bringing these stimuli under the general term of gestures, thus placing the uttered sounds which develop into articulate significant speech in man in this class, as vocal gestures. Another comment should be made upon the conception of social conduct. It must not be confined to mutual reactions of individuals whose conduct accepts, conserves, and serves the others. It must include the animal enemies as well. For the purposes of social conduct, the tiger is as much a part of the jungle society as the buffalo or the deer. In the development of the group more narrowly conceived, the instincts or impulses of hostility and flight, together with the gestures that represent their early stages, play most important rôles, not only in the protection of the mutually supporting forms, but in the conduct of these forms toward each other. Nor is it amiss to point out that in the evolution of animal forms within the life-process the hunter and the hunted, the eater and the eaten, are as closely interwoven as are the mother and the child or the individuals of the two sexes.

Among the lower forms, social conduct is implicated in the instincts of attack and flight, of sex, parenthood and childhood, in those of the herding animals (though these are somewhat vague in their outline), and probably in the construction of habitats. In all these processes the forms themselves, their movements, especially the early stages of these movements—for in adjustment to the action of another animal the earliest indication of the oncoming reaction is of greatest importance—and the sounds they utter serve as specific stimuli to social impulses. The responses are as immediate and objective in their character as are the responses to non-social physical stimuli. However complex and intricate this conduct may become, as in the life of the bee and the ant, or in building such habitats as those of the beaver, no convincing evidence has been gained by competent animal observers that one animal gives to another an indication of an object or action which is registered in what we have termed a "mind"; in other words, there is no evidence that one form is able to convey information by significant gestures to another form. The beast that responds directly to external objects, and presumably to imagery also, has no past or future, has no self as an object—in a word, has no mind as above described, is capable of no reflection, nor of "rational conduct" as that term is currently used.

We find among birds a curious phenomenon. The birds make an extensive use of the vocal gesture in their sexual and parental conduct. The vocal gesture has in a peculiar degree the character of possibly affecting directly the animal that uses it, as it does the other form. It does not of course follow that this effect will be realized; whether it is realized or not depends upon the presence of impulses requiring the stimulus to set them free. In the common social life of animals the impulse of one form would not be to do what it is stimulating the other form to do, so that even if the stimulus were of such a character as to affect the sense organ of the individual itself as it does the other, this stimulus would normally have no direct effect upon his conduct. There is, however, some evidence that this does take place in the case of birds. It is difficult to believe that the bird does not stimulate itself to sing by its own notes.

If bird *a* by its note calls out a response in bird *b*, and bird *b* not only responds by a note which calls out a response in bird *a* but has in its own organism an attitude finding expression in the same note as that which bird *a* has uttered, bird *b* will have stimulated itself to utter the same note as that which it has called out in bird *a*. This implies like attitudes seeking expression in the two birds and like notes expressing these attitudes. If this were the case and one bird sang frequently in the hearing of the other, there might result common notes and common songs. It is important to recognize that such a process is not what is commonly called "imitation." The bird *b* does not find in the note of bird *a* a stimulus to utter the same note. On the contrary, the supposition here is that its reply to bird *a* stimulates itself to utter the same note that bird *a* utters. There is little or no convincing evidence that any phase of the conduct of one animal is a direct stimulus to another to act in the same fashion. One animal stimulating itself to the same expression as that which it calls out in the other is not imitating in this sense at least, though it accounts for a great deal that passes as such imitation. It could only take place under the condition which I have emphasized: that the stimulus should act upon the animal itself in the same manner as that in which it acts upon the other animal, and this condition does obtain in the case of the vocal gesture. Certain birds, such as the mocking bird, do thus reproduce the connected notes of other birds; and a sparrow placed in the cage with a canary may reproduce the canary's song. The instance of this reproduction of vocal gesture with which we are most familiar is that of the accomplishments of talking birds. In these cases the combinations of phonetic elements, which we call words, are reproduced by the birds, as the sparrow reproduces the canary's song. It is a process of interest for the light it may throw on a child's learning of the language heard about it. It emphasizes the importance of the vocal gesture, as possibly stimulating the individual to respond to itself. While it is essential to recognize that response of the animal to its own stimulation can only take place where there are impulses seeking expression which this stimulation sets free, the importance of the vocal gesture as a social act which is addressed to the individual itself, as well as to other individuals, will be found to be very great.

Here in the field of behavior we reach a situation in which the individual may affect itself as it affects other individuals, and may therefore respond to this stimulation as it would respond to the stimulation of other individuals; in other words, a situation arises here in which the individual may become an object in its own field of behavior. This would meet the first condition of the appearance of mind. But this response will not take place unless there are reactions answering to these self-stimulations which will advance and reinforce the individual's conduct. So far as the vocal gestures in the wooing of birds of both sexes are alike, the excitement which they arouse will give expression to other notes that again will increase excitement. An animal that is aroused to attack by the roar of its rival may give out a like roar that stimulates the hostile attitude of the first. This roar, however, may act back upon the animal itself and arouse a renewed battle excitement that calls out a still louder roar. The cock that answers the crow of another cock, can stimulate itself to answer its own crow. The dog that bays at the moon would not probably continue its baying if it did not stimulate itself by its own howls. It has been noted that parent pigeons excite each other in the care of the young by their cooings. So far as these notes affect the other birds they have the tendency to affect the bird that utters them in the same fashion. Here we find social situations in which the preparation for the sexual act, for the hostile encounter, and for the care of the young, is advanced by vocal gestures that play back upon the animal that utters them, producing the same effect of readiness for social activity that they produce upon the individuals to which they are immediately addressed. If, on the other hand, the vocal gesture calls out a different reaction in the other form, which finds expression in a different vocal gesture, there would be no such immediate reinforcement of the vocal gesture. The parental note which calls out the note of the child form, unless it called out in the parent the response of the child to stimulate again the parental note, would not stimulate the parent to repeat its own vocal gesture. This complication does arise in the case of human parents, but presumably not in the relations of parent and offspring in forms lower than man.

In these instances we recognize social situations in which the conduct of one form affects that of another in carrying out acts in which both are engaged. They are acts in which the gestures and corresponding attitudes are so alike that one form stimulates itself to the gesture and attitude of the other and thus restimulates itself. In some degree the animal takes the rôle of the other and thus emphasizes the expression of its own rôle. In the forms we have cited this is possible only where the rôles are, up to a certain stage of preparation for the social act, more or less identical. This action does not, however, belong to the type of inhibition out of which reflection springs (though in all adjustment of individuals to each other's action there must be some inhibition), nor does it involve such variety of attitudes as is essential to analysis and representation. Nor is this lack of variety in attitude (by "attitude" I refer to the adjustment of the organism involved in an impulse ready for expression) due to lack of complexity in conduct. Many of the acts of these lower forms are as highly complex as many human acts which are reflectively controlled. The distinction is that which I have expressed in the distinction between the instinct and the impulse. The instinct may be highly complex, e.g., the preparation of the wasp for the larval life that will come from the egg which is laid in its fabricated cell; but the different elements of the whole complex process are so firmly organized together that a check at any point frustrates the whole undertaking. It does not leave the parts of the whole free for recombination in other forms. Human impulses, however, are generally susceptible to just such analysis and recombination in the presence of obstacles and inhibitions.

There is a circumstance that is not unconnected, I think, with this separable character of the human act. I refer to the contact experiences which come to man through his hands. The contact experiences of most of the vertebrate forms lower than man represent the completion of their acts. In fighting, the food process, sex, most of the activities of parenthood or childhood, attack, flight to a place of security, search for protection against heat and cold, choice of a place for sleep, contact is coincident with the goal of the instinct; while man's hand provides an intermediate contact that is vastly richer in content than that of the jaws or the animal's paws. Man's implements are elaborations and extensions of his hands. They provide still other and vastly more varied contacts which lie between the beginnings and the ends of his undertakings. And the hand, of course, includes in this consideration not only the member itself but its indefinite co-ordination through the central nervous system with the other parts of the organism. This is of peculiar importance for the consideration of the separability of the parts of the act, because our perceptions include the imagery of the contacts which vision or some other distance sense promises. We see things hard or soft, rough or smooth, big or little in measurement with ourselves, hot or cold, and wet or dry. It is this imaged contact that makes the seen thing an actual thing. These imaged contacts are therefore of vast import in controlling conduct. Varied contact imagery may mean varied things, and varied things mean varied responses. Again I must emphasize the fact that this variety will exist in experience only if there are impulses answering to this variety of stimuli and seeking expression. However, man's manual contacts, intermediate between the beginnings and the ends of his acts, provide a multitude of different stimuli to a multitude of different ways of doing things, and thus invite alternative impulses to express themselves in the accomplishment of his acts, when obstacles and hindrances arise. Man's hands have served greatly to break up fixed instincts by giving him a world full of a number of things.

Returning now to the vocal gesture, let me note another feature of the human species that has been of great importance in the development of man's peculiar intelligence—his long period of infancy. I do not refer to the advantage insisted upon by Fiske, the opportunities which come with a later maturity, but to the part which the vocal gesture plays in the care of the child by the parent, especially by the mother. The phonetic elements, out of which later articulate speech is constructed, belong to the social attitudes which call out answering attitudes in others together with their vocal gestures. The child's cry of fear belongs to the tendency to flight toward the parent, and the parent's encouraging tone is part of the movement toward protection. This vocal gesture of fear calls out the corresponding gesture of protection.

There are two interesting human types of conduct that seemingly arise out of this relationship of child and parent. On the one hand we find what has been called the imitation of the child, and on the other the sympathetic response of the parent. The basis of each of these types of conduct is to be found in the individual stimulating himself to respond in the same fashion as that in which the other responds to him. As we have seen, this is possible if two conditions are fulfilled. The individual must be affected by the stimulus which affects the other, and affected through the same sense channel. This is the case with the vocal gesture. The sound which is uttered strikes on the ear of the individual uttering it in the same physiological fashion as that in which it strikes on the ear of the person addressed. The other condition is that there should be an impulse seeking expression in the individual who utters the sound, which is functionally of the same sort as that to which the stimulus answers in the other individual who hears the sound. The illustration most familiar to us is that of a child crying and then uttering the soothing sound which belongs to the parental attitude of protection. This childish type of conduct runs out later into the countless forms of play in which the child assumes the rôles of the adults about him. The very universal habit of playing with dolls indicates how ready for expression, in the child, is the parental attitude, or perhaps one should say, certain of the parental attitudes. The long period of dependence of the human infant during which his interest centers in his relations to those who care for him gives a remarkable opportunity for the play back and forth of this sort of taking of the rôles of others.

Where the young animal of lower forms very quickly finds itself responding directly to the appropriate stimuli for the conduct of the adult of its species, with instinctive activities that are early matured, the child for a considerable period directs his attention toward the social environment provided by the primitive family, seeking support and nourishment and warmth and protection through his gestures—especially his vocal gestures. These gestures inevitably must call out in himself the parental response which is so markedly ready for expression very early in the child's nature, and this response will include the parent's corresponding vocal gesture. The child will stimulate himself to make the sounds which he stimulates the parent to make. In so far as the social situation within which the child reacts is determined by his social environment, that environment will determine what sounds he makes and therefore what responses he stimulates both in others and himself. The life about him will indirectly determine what parental responses he produces in his conduct, but the direct stimulation to adult response will be inevitably found in his own childish appeal. To the adult stimulation he responds as a child. There is nothing in these stimulations to call out an adult response. But in so far as he gives attention to his own childish appeals it will be the adult response that will appear—but will appear only in case that some phases of these adult impulses are ready in him for expression. It is, of course, the incompleteness and relative immaturity of these adult responses that gives to the child's conduct one of the peculiar characters which attach to play. The other is that the child can stimulate himself to this activity. In the play of young children, even when they play together, there is abundant evidence of the child's taking different rôles in the process; and a solitary child will keep up the process of stimulating himself by his vocal gestures to act in different rôles almost indefinitely. The play of the young animal of other species lacks this self-stimulating character and exhibits far more maturity of instinctive response than is found in the early play of children. It is evident that out of just such conduct as this, out of addressing one's self and responding with the appropriate response of another, "self-consciousness" arises. The child during this period of infancy creates a forum within which he assumes various rôles, and the child's self is gradually integrated out of these socially different attitudes, always retaining the capacity of addressing itself and responding to that address with a reaction that belongs in a certain sense to another. He comes into the adult period with the mechanism of a mind.

The attitude that we characterize as that of sympathy in the adult springs from this same capacity to take the rôle of the other person with whom one is socially implicated. It is not included in the direct response of help, support, and protection. This is a direct impulse, or in lower forms, a direct instinct, which is not at all incompatible with the exercise on occasion of the opposite instincts. The parent forms that on occasion act in the most ordinary parental fashion may, with seeming heartlessness, destroy and consume their offspring. Sympathy always implies that one stimulates himself to his assistance and consideration of others by taking in some degree the attitude of the person whom one is assisting. The common term for this is "putting yourself in his place." It is presumably an exclusively human type of conduct, marked by this involution of stimulating one's self to an action by responding as the other responds. As we shall see, this control of one's conduct, through responding as the other responds, is not confined to kindly conduct. We tend to reserve the term "sympathetic," however, for those kindly acts and attitudes which are the essential binding-cords in the life of any human group. Whether we agree with McDougall or not in his contention that the fundamental character of tenderness which goes out into whatever we denominate as humane, or human in the sense of humane, has its source in the parental impulses, there can be no doubt that the fundamental attitude of giving assistance in varied ways to others gets its striking exercise in relation to children. Helplessness in any form reduces us to children, and arouses the parental response in the other members of the community to which we belong. Every advance in the recognition of a wider social grouping is like the kingdom of heaven; we can enter it only as little children. The human adult has already come into society through the door of childhood with a self of some sort, a self that has arisen through assuming various rôles; he turns to his or her own children therefore with what we term "sympathy"; but the mother and the father exercise this attitude most constantly in their parental responses. More than in any other sense, psychologically society has developed out of the family. The parental attitudes, like the infantile attitudes, serve first of all the purpose of the self-stimulation which we have noted in birds, and thus emphasize valuable responses, but secondarily they provide the mechanism of mind.

The most important activity of mind that can be identified in behavior is that of so adjusting conflicting impulses that they can express themselves harmoniously. Recalling the illustration already used, when the impulse to go ahead toward food or rest is checked by an impulse to draw back from a sharp declivity, mind so organizes these mutually defeating tendencies that the individual advances by a detour, both going ahead and escaping the danger of the descent. This is not accomplished through a direct reorganization of motor processes. The mental process is not one of readjusting a mechanism from the inside, a rearrangement of springs and levers. Control over impulse lies only in the shift of attention which brings other objects into the field of stimulation, setting free other impulses, or in such a resetting of the objects that the impulses express themselves on a different time schedule or with additions and subtractions. This shift of attention again finds its explanation in the coming into play of tendencies that before were not immediately in action. These tendencies render us sensitive to stimuli which are not in the field of stimulation. Even sudden powerful stimuli act upon us because there are in our make-up responses of sudden withdrawal or attack in the presence of such stimulation. As I have already stated, in the conduct of lower forms such conflicts lead to the switching from one type of reaction to another. In these animals the impulses are so firmly organized in fixed instincts that alternatives of reaction lie only between one congenital habit and others. Stated in other terms, the instinctive individual cannot break up his objects and reconstruct his conduct through the adjustment to a new field of stimulation, because its organized reactions cannot be separated to come together again in new combinations. The mechanical problem of mind, then, is in securing a type of conduct coming on top of that of the biologic individual that will dissociate the elements of our organized responses. Such a dismemberment of organized habits will bring into the field of perception all the objects that answer to the different impulses that made up the fixed habits.

It is from this standpoint that I wish to consider the social conduct into which the self has entered as an integral factor. So far as it merely emphasizes certain reactions through self-stimulation, as in the case of the wooing of birds, it introduces no new principle of action. For in these cases the self is not present as an object toward which an attitude is assumed as toward other objects, and which is subject to the effects of conduct. When the self does become such an object to be changed and directed as other objects are affected, there appears over and above the immediate impulsive responses a manner of conduct which can conceivably both analyze the act through an attention shifting where our various tendencies to act direct it, and can allow representation, by holding out the imagery of the results of the various reactions, instead of allowing it to simply enter into the presentation or perception of the objects. Such reflective direction of activity is not the form in which intelligence first appears, nor is this its primitive function. Its earliest function, in the instance of the infant, is effective adjustment to the little society upon which it has so long to depend. The child is for a long time dependent upon moods and emotional attitudes. How quickly he adjusts himself to this is a continual surprise. He responds to facial expressions earlier than to most stimuli and answers with appropriate expressions of his own, before he makes responses that we consider significant. He comes into the world highly sensitive to this so-called "mimic gesture," and he exercises his earliest intelligence in his adaptation to his social environment. If he is congenitally deprived of the vocal gesture that affects himself as it does others, and the loss is not early made good, in part through other means of communication which in principle follow the same procedure as that of vocal communication, he is confined to this instinctive means of adjustment to those about him, and lives a life hardly above that of the lower animals—indeed, lower than theirs because of his lack of their varied instinctive reactions to the physical and social world about them. As we have seen, in the normal child the vocal gesture arouses in himself the responses of his elders, through their stimulation of his own parental impulse and later of other impulses which in their childish form are beginning to ripen in his central nervous system. These impulses find their expression first of all in tones of voice and later in combinations of phonetic elements which become articulate speech as they do in the vocal gesture of the talking birds. The child has become, through his own impulses, a parent to himself. The same selective process which leads him to use the phonetic elements of the speech about him leads him to use the general types of attitudes of those about him, not by direct imitation, but through his tending to call out in himself in any situation the same reaction which he calls out in others. The society which determines these situations will, of course, determine not only his direct replies but also those adult responses within himself which his replies arouse. In so far as he gives expression to these, at first in voice and later in play, he is taking many rôles and addressing himself in all of them. He is of course fitting himself in his play to take up the adult activities later, and among primitive people this is practically all the training he receives. But he is doing far more than this: he is gradually building up a definite self that becomes the most important object in his world. As an object, it is at first the reflection of the attitudes of others toward it. Indeed, the child in this early period often refers to his own self in the third person. He is a composite of all the individuals he addresses when he takes the rôles of those about him. It is only gradually that this takes clear enough form to become identified with the biologic individual and endow him with a clear-cut personality that we call self-conscious. When this has taken place he has put himself in the position of commenting on what he is doing and what he intends to do from the standpoint of any of the rôles that this so-called "imaginative conduct" finds him carrying. In so far as these rôles differ, the undertaking has a different aspect, and different elements in the field of objects about him stand out, answering to his own different impulses. If he cannot yet be said to be thinking, he has at least the mechanism of thought.

It is necessary to emphasize the wide stretch between the direct immediate life of the child and this self growing in his conduct. The latter is almost imposed from without. He may passively accept the individual that the group about him assigns to him as himself. This is very different from the passionate assertive biologic individual, that loves and hates and embraces and strikes. *He* is never an object; *his* is a life of direct suffering and action. In the meantime, the self that is growing up has as much reality and as little as the rôles the child plays. Interesting documents on this early self are to be found in the so-called "imaginary companions" with which many children confessedly, all children implicitly, provide themselves. They are, of course, the imperfectly personified responses in the child to his own social stimulation, but which have more intimate and lasting import in his play life than others of the shadowy clan. As the child completes the circle of the social world to which he responds and whose actions he stimulates himself to produce, he has completed in some fashion his own self toward which all these play activities can be directed. It is an accomplishment that announces itself in the passage from the earlier form of play into that of games, either the competitive or the more or less dramatic games, in which the child enters as a definite personality that maintains itself throughout. His interest passes from the story, the fairy tale, the folk tale, to the connected accounts in which he can sustain a sympathetic identity with the hero or the heroine in the rush of events. This not only involves a more or less definitely organized self seen from the standpoints of those about him whose attitudes he takes, but it involves, further, a functional interrelationship of this object-self with the biologic individual in his conduct. His reactions now are not simply the direct responses to the social and physical things about him, but are also to this self which has become an object of continually increasing moment. It is made up of social responses to others regarded primarily through their eyes as he takes their parts. Thus a child comes to regard himself as a playmate who must share his toys with other children if he is to keep them as playmates. This compels him to see other characters in the playthings beside their immediate attraction to his play impulse and to that of possession. The plaything becomes a composite object; it is not only that which gives expression to his own impulse but something that keeps with him his cherished friends. His habits of response are reconstructed and he becomes a rational animal. The reconstruction takes place unwittingly as he recognizes the different features in the objects about him which force themselves upon his attention as a self. But as the self becomes effectively organized, it provides the technique that helps the child out of as many situations as it creates. A smooth interplay results between the biologic individual and the self. All conduct that presents difficulties passes into this reflective form. The subject is the biologic individual— never on the scene, and this self adjusted to its social environment, and through this to the world at large, is the object. It is true that the subject in the conversation between the two takes now this rôle and now that. We are familiar with this in thought-processes which we carry on in the form of a discussion with another individual. One not infrequently puts the arguments which he wishes to meet into the mouth of some advocate of the idea. It is the argument which this supporter of the doctrine offers which appears in thought; and when one has replied to that, it is the reply which he would make that calls out the next answer. But though the voice is the voice of another, the source of it all is one's self—the organized group of impulses which I have called the biologic individual. It is this individual in action, with his attention on the object. He does not come into the field of his own vision. But in so far as he can address himself, and call out a response, that self and its response does become an object, as we have seen.

It is necessary to make another distinction here, for the experience is subtle in the extreme. At the stage which we are considering, that of the young child, the rôle of the other which he assumes is taken without recognition. The child is aware of his response to the rôle, not of the rôle he is taking. It is only the later sophisticated inner experience that is aware of the character under which the invisible "I" enters the scene, and then only through a setting which must be later presented. The medium of interaction between the subject and object is the vocal gesture with the imagery which gathers about it, but this vocal gesture is but part of a social act. It represents the adjustment to an environment, in the attitude of some overt action. The action is, however, indicated to the self by the gesture, and the self as another social being through its gestures takes the attitude of varying responses—the conversation of gestures which I have already described in the conduct of animals. To this attitude and its gesture the biologic individual, the subject, again replies; but his reply is to the self, while the responses of the self are not directed toward the subject but toward the social situation involved in the attitude which has called it out. Expressed in our adult thought, this is the distinction between the idea that comes into our heads (the idea that occurs to us), and its relation to the world, of which as objects we are a part. It is what the child is preparing to do and the attitudes which he will take in consequence. He starts to do something and finds himself in the early stage of the process objecting and taking some other tack. In a sense he is trying out this undertaking through the medium of communication with a self. Thus the biologic individual becomes essentially interrelated with the self, and the two go to make up the personality of the child. It is this conversation that constitutes the earliest mechanism of mind. Into it comes the material of perception and imagery which are involved in the actions which these gestures initiate. In particular the imagery of the results of the actions presaged by the gestures becomes of peculiar interest. As we have seen, this imagery goes directly into the object under conditions of direct action. In the presence of alternative activities, in some sense competing with each other, this imagery of the result of the acts is, for the time being, dissociated from the objects and serves to check and call for readjustments.

I have noted two standpoints from which imagery may be regarded. It is *there*, as percepts are *there*; and like percepts, imagery can be stated in terms of its relation to the physiological organism; but while percepts are dominantly an expression of an immediate relation between the organism and its field of objects, imagery represents an adjustment between an organism and an environment that is not there. In case that the imagery is fused with the other contents of the percept, it extends and fills out the field of objects. In so far as it does not enter into the immediate environment, it presents material for which an instinctive form can have little or no use. It may serve it as it does us, to pick out objects which cannot be at once detected; but as the objects that enter into the field of perception answer to organized habits, and since an instinctive form cannot reconstruct its congenital habits, images can hardly serve the function which they do in man's mind of reconstructing both objects and habits. This latter function is a development of the function of the image in filling out the object, by putting into that which comes through the distance senses—such as vision and hearing —the content of the contact which actual approach to the object will reveal. Its primal function in reflection is that of determining what course of action shall be pursued, by the presentation of the results of different courses. It is a function that inevitably emphasizes the content of imagery, as the reaction becomes dependent upon the imaged outcome of the process.

And yet this emphasis presupposes something beyond this distinction and its function. It implies a definite location and identification of imagery apart from its fusion with other contents in the object. We have seen that this takes place in the formation of past and future, and in the extension, through these dimensions, of the immediate environment beyond the range of sense perception. However, before this location can take place, the imagery hangs unoriented; and especially as past and future take on more definiteness, the imagery, which does not at once fall into place, needs a local habitation and is placed in the mind.

In terms of a behavioristic psychology the problem of stating reflection is that of showing how in immediate conduct, shifting attention, springing from varied impulses, may lead to reorganization of objects so that conflicts between organized impulses may be overcome. We have just seen that imagery which goes into the structure of objects, and which represents the adjustment of the organism to environments which are not there, may serve toward the reconstruction of the objective field. It is important to present more fully the part which the social activity of the individual mediated through vocal gesture plays in this process. Social acts of this type proceed co-operatively, and the gestures serve to adjust the attitudes of the different individuals within the whole act to each other's attitudes and actions. The child's cry directs the attention of the mother toward the location of the child and the character of his need. The mother's response directs the child toward the mother and the assistance he is prepared to accept. The challenging calls of rival animals, and the wooing notes of birds, serve analogous purposes. These gestures and the immediate responses to them are preparations for a mutual activity that is to take place later. The human individual, through his gesture and his own response to it, finds himself in the rôle of another. He thus places himself in the attitude of the individual with whom he is to co-operate. The conduct of little children, which is so largely directed, can only go on in combination with that of their elders; and this early facility in playing the rôles of others gives them the adjustment necessary for this interrelated activity. The prohibitions, the taboos, involve conflicting tendencies which appear in terms of personal commands. It is these that recur as imagery when the impulse again arises to do the forbidden thing. Where an animal would only slink back from a forbidden spot, the child repeats the prohibition in the rôle of the parent. What simply enters into the object to render it dangerous for the animal builds up for the child an imaginary scene, since his own social attitude summons up that of the other in his own response. What was part of an unbroken flow becomes now an event which precedes breaking of the law or compliance with it.

What the assumption of the different attitudes makes possible is the analysis of the object. In the rôle of the child the thing is the object of an immediate want. It is simply desirable. That which occupies the attention is this answer to the impulse to seize and devour. In the rôle of the parent the object is taboo, reserved for other times and people, the taking of which calls out retribution. The child's capacity for being the other puts both of these characters of the object before him in their disparateness. The object does not simply lead him on and drive him away, as it does the well-mannered dog. It is with this material that the child sets out upon his creations of imagination: the mother relents and removes the taboo, or when the object is eaten the child escapes attention, or a thousand things may happen in the activities of the different characters on the scene so that the desirable thing is his and its character as taboo, while recognized, fails to bring the dreaded consequences. Or the more matter-of-fact child may take and eat and face the consequence of the whipping as worth the while, thus affecting the union of the conflicting characters in a heroic fashion, but still with the lingering hope that the unexpected may happen that will hide the deed, or change the law or its enforcement. In a word, the sympathetic assumption of the attitude of the other brings into play varying impulses which direct the attention to features of the object which are ignored in the attitude of direct response. And the very diverse attitudes assumed furnish the material for a reconstruction of the objective field in which and through which the co-operative social act may take place, giving satisfactory expression to all the rôles involved. It is this analysis and reconstruction which is rendered possible by the apparatus of the vocal gesture, with its related organic equipment. It is in this field that the continuous flow breaks up in ordered series, in the relation of alternative steps leading up to some event. Time with its distinguishable moments enters, so to speak, with the intervals necessary to shift the scene and change the costumes. One cannot be another and yet himself except from the standpoint of a time which is composed of entirely independent elements.

It is important to recognize how entirely social the mechanism of young children's reflective conduct is. The explanation lies both in the long period of infancy, necessitating dependency upon the social conduct of the family group, and in the vocal gesture, stimulating the child to act toward himself as others act toward him, and thus putting him in the position of facing his problems from the standpoints, as far as he can assume them, of all who are involved therein. One should not, however, assume that these social attitudes of the child imply the existence in his conduct of the full personalities of those whose attitudes he is taking. On the contrary, the full personality with which he finds himself ultimately endowed and which he finds in others is the combination of the self and the others. As social objects, the others with whom the child plays are uncertain in their outlines and shadowy in their structure. What is clear and definite in the child's attitude is the *reaction* in either rôle, that of the self or the other. The child's earliest life is that of social activities, including this reflexive stimulation and response, in a field in which neither social nor merely physical objects have arisen with definiteness. It is a great mistake to overlook the social character of these processes, for in the human animal this social factor carries with it the complication of possible self-stimulation as well. The reaction of the human animal toward another, in which a gesture plays a part that can affect the first individual as it does the other, has a value which cannot attach to the direct instinctive or impulsive responses to objects, whether they be other living forms or mere physical things.

Such a reaction, even with its self-reflection only implicitly there, must be still more sharply distinguished from our reactions to physical things in terms of our modern scientific attitude. Such a physical world did not exist in the earlier and less sophisticated experience of man. It is a product of modern scientific method. It is not found in the unsophisticated child or in the unsophisticated man, and yet most psychologies treat the experience of the child's reactions to the so-called "physical objects" about him as if these objects were for him what they are for the adult. There is most interesting evidence of this difference in the attitude of primitive man toward his environment. The primitive man has the mind of the child— indeed, of the young child. He approaches his problems in terms of social conduct—the social conduct in which there is this self-reflection which has just been the subject of discussion. The child gets his solutions of what from our standpoint are entirely physical problems, such as those of transportation, movement of things, and the like, through his social reaction to those about him. This is not simply because he is dependent, and must look to those about him for assistance during the early period of infancy, but, more important still, because his primitive process of reflection is one of mediation through vocal gestures of a co-operative social process. The human individual thinks first of all entirely in social terms. This means, as I have emphasized above, not that nature and natural objects are personalized, but that the child's reactions to nature and its objects are social reactions, and that his responses imply that the actions of natural objects are social reactions. In other words, in so far as the young child acts reflectively toward his physical environment, he acts as if it were helping or hindering him, and his responses are accompanied with friendliness or anger. It is an attitude of which there are more than vestiges in our sophisticated experi-

[377]

ence. It is perhaps most evident in the irritations against the total depravity of inanimate things, in our affection for familiar objects of constant employment, and in the aesthetic attitude toward nature which is the source of all nature poetry. The distinction between this attitude and that of personification is that between the primitive cult attitude and the later attitude of the myth, between the period of the Mana, of magic in its primitive form, and the period of the gods. The essence of the reflective process at this stage is that through friendly or hostile attitudes difficulties are overcome . . . . [MS].

IV

FRAGMENTS ON ETHICS[1]

1. It is possible to build up an ethical theory on a social basis, in terms of our social theory of the origin, development, nature, and structure of the self. Thus, for example, Kant's categorical imperative may be socially stated or formulated or interpreted in these terms, that is, given its social equivalent.

Man is a rational being because he is a social being. The universality of our judgments, upon which Kant places so much stress, is a universality that arises from the fact that we take the attitude of the entire community, of all rational beings. We are what we are through our relationship to others. Inevitably, then, our end must be a social end, both from the standpoint of its content (that which would answer to primitive impulses) and also from the point of view of form. Sociality gives the universality of ethical judgments and lies back of the popular statement that the voice of all is the universal voice; that is, everyone who can rationally appreciate the situation agrees. The very form of our judgment is therefore social, so that the end, both content and form, is necessarily a social end. Kant approached that universality from the assumption of the rationality of the individual, and said that if his ends, or the form of his acts, were universal, then society could arise. He conceived of the individual first of all as rational and as a condition for society. However, we recognize that not only the form of the judgment is universal but the content also—that the end itself can

[1] [Cf. "Suggestions toward a Theory of the Philosophical Disciplines," *Philosophical Review*, IX (1900), 1 ff.; "The Social Self," *Journal of Philosophy*, X (1913), 374 ff.; "The Social Settlement: Its Basis and Function," *University of Chicago Record*, XII (1908), 108 ff. "The Philosophical Basis of Ethics," *International Journal of Ethics*, XVIII (1908), 311 ff.; "Scientific Method and the Moral Sciences," *ibid.*, XXXIII (1923), 229 ff.; "Philanthropy from the Point of View of Ethics," in *Intelligent Philanthropy*, ed. by Ellsworth Faris *et al.* (1930).]

be universalized. Kant said we could only universalize the form. However, we do universalize the end itself. If we recognize that we can universalize the end itself, then a social order can arise from such social, universal ends.

2. We can agree with Kant that the "ought" does involve universality. As he points out, that is true in the case of the Golden Rule. Wherever the element of the "ought" comes in, wherever one's conscience speaks, it always takes on this universal form.

Only a rational being could give universal form to his act. The lower animals simply follow inclinations; they go after particular ends, but they could not give a universal form to acts. Only a rational being would be able so to generalize his act and the maxim of his act, and the human being has such rationality. When he acts in a certain way he is willing that everyone should act in the same way, under the same conditions. Is not that the statement we generally make in justifying ourselves? When a person has done something that is questionable, is not the statement that is first made, "That is what anyone would have done in my place"? Such is the way in which one does justify his conduct if it is brought into question at all; that it should be a universal law is the justifiable support that one gives to a questioned act. This is quite apart from the content of the act, as one can be sure that what he is doing is what he wants everyone else to do under the same circumstances. Do unto others as you would have them do unto you; that is, act toward other people as you want them to act toward you under the same conditions.

3. In general, when you are taking advantage of other people, the universalizing of the principle of the act would take away the very value of the act itself. You want to be able to steal things and yet keep them as your own property; but if everyone stole, there would not be any such thing as property. Just generalize the principle of your act and see what would follow with reference to the very thing you are trying to do. This Kantian test is not a test of feeling but a rational test that does

meet a very large number of acts which we recognize as moral. It is valuable in its way. We try to decide whether we are making ourselves exceptions or whether we should be willing to have everyone else act as we are doing.

If a man will set up as a maxim for his conduct the principle that everybody else should be honest with him while he would be dishonest with everybody else, there could not be a factual basis for his attitude. He is commanding the honesty of other people, and he is in no position to command it if he is dishonest. The rights one recognizes in others one can demand in others; but we cannot demand from others what we refuse to respect. It is a practical impossibility.

Any constructive act is, however, something that lies outside of the scope of Kant's principle. From Kant's standpoint you assume that the standard is there; and then if you slip around it yourself while expecting other people to live up to it, Kant's principle will find you out. But where you have no standard, it does not help you to decide. Where you have to get a restatement, a readjustment, you get a new situation in which to act; the simple generalizing of the principle of your act does not help. It is at that point that Kant's principle breaks down.

What Kant's principle does is to tell you that an act is immoral under certain conditions, but it does not tell you what is the moral act. Kant's categorical imperative assumes that there is just one way of acting. If that is the case, then there is only one course that can be universalized; then the respect for law would be the motive for acting in that fashion. But if you assume that there are alternative ways of acting, then you cannot utilize Kant's motive as a means of determining what is right.

4. Both Kant and the Utilitarians wish to universalize, to make universal that in which morality lies. The Utilitarian says it must be the greatest good of the greatest number; Kant says that the attitude of the act must be one which takes on the form of a universal law. I want to point out this common attitude of these two schools which are so opposed to each other in

other ways: they both feel that an act which is moral must have in some way a universal character. If you state morality in terms of the result of the act, then you state the results in terms of the whole community; if in the attitude of the act, it must be in the respect for law, and the attitude must take on the form of a universal law, a universal rule. Both recognize that morality involves universality, that the moral act is not simply a private affair. A thing that is good from a moral standpoint must be a good for everyone under the same conditions. This demand for universality is found in both the Utilitarian and Kantian doctrines.

5. If the categorical imperative is obeyed as Kant wishes, everyone will make a universal law of his act, and then a combination of such individuals will be one that is harmonious, so that a society made up out of beings who recognize the moral law would be a moral society. In that way Kant gets a content in his act; his statement is that there is no content, but by setting the human being up as an end in himself, and so society as a higher end, he introduces content.

This picture of a kingdom of ends is hardly to be distinguished from Mill's doctrine, since both set up society as an end. Each of them has to get to some sort of an end that can be universal. The Utilitarian reaches that in the general good, the general happiness of the whole community; Kant finds it in an organization of rational human beings, who apply rationality to the form of their acts. Neither of them is able to state the end in terms of the object of desire of the individual.

Actually, what you have to universalize is the object toward which desire is directed, that upon which your attention must be centered if you are going to succeed. You have to universalize not the mere form of the act but the content of the act.

If you assume that what you want is just pleasure, you have a particular event, a feeling which you experience under certain conditions. But if you desire the object itself, you desire that which can be given a universal form; if you desire such an object, the motive itself can be as moral as the end. The break which the act puts between the motive and the intended end then disappears.

6. There is the question of the relation of endeavor and achievement to will, the question as to whether the result is something that can have anything to do with the morality of the act. You do have to bring the end into your intention, into your attitude. You can, at every stage of the act, be acting with reference to the end; and you can embody the end in the steps that you are immediately taking.

That is the difference between meaning well and having the right intention. Of course, you cannot have the final result in your early steps of the act, but you can at least state that act in terms of the conditions which you are meeting.

If you are going to be successful, you have to be interested in an end in terms of the steps which are necessary to carry it out. In that sense the result is present in the act. A person who is taking all the steps to bring about a result sees the result in the steps. It is that which makes one moral or immoral, and distinguishes between a man who really means to do what he says he is going to do, and one who merely "means well."

7. All of our impulses are possible sources of happiness; and in so far as they get their natural expression they lead up to happiness. In the moral act there will be pleasure in our satisfactions; but the end is in the objects, and the motives are in the impulses which are directed toward these objects. When a person, for example, becomes extremely interested in some undertaking, then he has impulses that are directed toward certain ends, and such impulses become the motives of his conduct. We distinguish such impulses from the motive that the Utilitarian recognizes. He recognizes only one motive: the feeling of pleasure that will arise when the desire is satisfied. In place of that we put the impulse which is directed toward the end itself and maintain that such impulses are the motives of moral conduct.

The question then becomes the determination of the sort of ends toward which our action should be directed. What sort of a standard can we set up? Our ends should, first of all, be ends which are desirable in themselves, that is, which do lead to the expression and satisfaction of the impulses. Now there are some impulses which lead simply to disintegration, which are not desirable in themselves. There are certain of our impulses which find their expression, for example, in cruelty. Taken by themselves they are not desirable because the results which they bring are narrowing, depressing, and deprive us of social relations. They also lead, so far as others are concerned, to injury to other individuals.

In Dewey's terms, the moral impulses should be those "which reinforce and expand not only the motives from which they directly spring but also the other tendencies and attitudes which are sources of happiness."[2] If a person becomes interested in other persons, he finds the interest which he has does lead to reinforcing that motive and to expanding other motives. The more we become interested in persons the more we become interested in general in life. The whole situation within which the individual finds himself takes on new interest. Similarly, to get an intellectual motive is one of the greatest boons which one may have, because it expands interest so widely. We recognize such ends as particularly important.

So, looking at happiness from the point of view of impulses themselves, we can set up a standard in this fashion: the end should be one which reinforces the motive, one which will reinforce the impulse and expand other impulses or motives. That would be the standard proposed.

We are free now from the restrictions of the Utilitarian and Kantian if we recognize that desire is directed toward the object instead of toward pleasure. Both Kant and the Utilitarian are fundamentally hedonists, assuming that our inclinations are toward our own subjective states—the pleasure that comes from satisfaction. If that is the end, then of course our motives are all subjective affairs. From Kant's standpoint they are bad, and from the Utilitarian's standpoint they are the same for all

[2] [Dewey and Tufts, *Ethics* (1st ed.), p. 284.]

actions and so neutral. But on the present view, if the object itself is better, then the motive is better. The motive can be tested by the end, in terms of whether the end does reinforce the very impulse itself.

Impulses will be good to the degree that they reinforce themselves and expand and give expression to other impulses as well.

8. All the things worth while are shared experiences. Even when a person is by himself, he knows that the experience he has in nature, in the enjoyment of a book, experiences which we might think of as purely individual, would be greatly accentuated if they could be shared with others. Even when a person seems to retire into himself to live among his own ideas, he is living really with the others who have thought what he is thinking. He is reading books, recalling the experiences which he has had, projecting conditions under which he might live. The content is always of a social character. Or it may pass into those mystical experiences in religious life—communion with God. The conception of the religious life is itself a social conception; it gathers about the idea of the community.

It is only in so far as you can identify your own motive and the actual end you are pursuing with the common good that you reach the moral end and so get moral happiness. As human nature is essentially social in character, moral ends must be also social in their nature.

9. If we look at the individual from the point of view of his impulses, we can see that those desires which reinforce themselves, or continue on in their expression, and which awaken other impulses, will be good; whereas those which do not reinforce themselves lead to undesirable results, and those which weaken the other motives are in themselves evil. If we look now toward the end of the action rather than toward the impulse itself, we find that those ends are good which lead to the realization of the self as a social being. Our morality gathers about our social conduct. It is as social beings that we are moral beings. On the one side stands the society which makes the self possible, and on the other side stands the self that makes a highly or-

ganized society possible. The two answer to each other in moral conduct.

In our reflective conduct we are always reconstructing the immediate society to which we belong. We are taking certain definite attitudes which involve relationship with others. In so far as those relationships are changed, the society itself is changed. We are continually reconstructing. When it comes to the problem of reconstruction there is one essential demand—that all of the interests that are involved should be taken into account. One should act with reference to all of the interests that are involved: that is what we could call a "categorical imperative."

We are definitely identified with our own interests. One is constituted out of his own interests; and when those interests are frustrated, what is called for then is in some sense a sacrifice of this narrow self. This should lead to the development of a larger self which can be identified with the interests of others. I think all of us feel that one must be ready to recognize the interests of others even when they run counter to our own, but that the person who does that does not really sacrifice himself, but becomes a larger self.

10. The group advances from old standards toward another standard; and what is important from the standpoint of morality is that this advance takes place through the individual, through a new type of individual—one who conceives himself as individuals have not conceived themselves in the past. The illustrations are those of the Prophets among the Hebrews and the Sophists among the Greeks. The point that I want to emphasize is that this new individual appears as the representative of a different social order. He does not appear simply as a particular individual; he conceives of himself as belonging to another social order which ought to take the place of the old one. He is a member of a new, a higher, order. Of course, there have been evolutionary changes that took place without individual reaction. But moral changes are those that take place through

the action of the individual as such. He becomes the instrument, the means, of changing the old into a new order.

What is right arises in the experience of the individual: he comes to change the social order; he is the instrument by which custom itself may be changed. The prophet becomes highly important for this reason, since he represents the sort of consciousness in which one decides to change the conception of what is right. By asking what is right, we are in that same situation, and we are helping in this way toward the development of the moral consciousness of the community. Values come into conflict with each other in the experiences of the individual; it is his function to give expression to the different values and help to formulate more satisfactory standards than have existed.

11. When we reach the question of what is right, I have said that the only test we can set up is whether we have taken into account every interest involved. What is essential is that every interest in a man's nature which is involved should be considered. He can consider only the interests which come into his problem. The scientist has to consider all of the facts, but he considers only those facts involved in the immediate problem. A scientist trying to find out whether acquired characteristics can be inherited does not have to take into account the facts of relativity, but only those facts which apply to his problem. The moral problem is one which involves certain conflicting interests. All of those interests which are involved in conflict must be considered.

In moral judgments we have to work out a social hypothesis, and one never can do it simply from his own point of view. We have to look at it from the point of view of a social situation. The hypothesis is one that we present, just as the Prophets presented the conception of a community in which all men were brothers. Now, if we ask what is the best hypothesis, the only answer we can make is that it must take into account all of the interests that are involved. Our temptation is to ignore certain interests that run contrary to our own interests, and emphasize those with which we have been identified.

You cannot lay down in advance fixed rules as to just what should be done. You can find out what are the values involved in the actual problem and act rationally with reference to them. That is what we ask, and all we ask, of anyone. When we object to a person's conduct, we say that he has failed to recognize the values, or that in recognizing them he does not act rationally with reference to them. That is the only method that an ethics can present. Science cannot possibly tell what the facts are going to be, but can give a method for approach: recognize all the facts that belong to the problem, so that the hypothesis will be a consistent, rational one. You cannot tell a person what must be the form of his act any more than you can tell a scientist what his facts are going to be. The moral act must take into account all the values involved, and it must be rational—that is all that can be said.

12. The only rule that an ethics can present is that an individual should rationally deal with all the values that are found in a specific problem. That does not mean that one has to spread before him all the social values when he approaches a problem. The problem itself defines the values. It is a specific problem and there are certain interests that are definitely involved; the individual should take into account all of those interests and then make out a plan of action which will rationally deal with those interests. That is the only method that ethics can bring to the individual. It is of the greatest importance that one should define what those interests are in the particular situation. The great need is that one should be able to regard them impartially. We feel that persons are apt to take what we call a selfish attitude with reference to them. I have pointed out that the matter of selfishness is the setting-up of a narrow self over against a larger self. Our society is built up out of our social interests. Our social relations go to constitute the self. But when the immediate interests come in conflict with others we had not recognized, we tend to ignore the others and take into account only those which are immediate. The difficulty is to make ourselves recognize the other and wider interests, and then to bring

them into some sort of rational relationship with the more immediate ones. There is room for mistakes, but mistakes are not sins.

13. A man has to keep his self-respect, and it may be that he has to fly in the face of the whole community in preserving this self-respect. But he does it from the point of view of what he considers a higher and better society than that which exists. Both of these are essential to moral conduct: that there should be a social organization and that the individual should maintain himself. The method for taking into account all of those interests which make up society on the one hand and the individual on the other is the method of morality.

BIBLIOGRAPHY OF THE WRITINGS OF
GEORGE H. MEAD

CHRONOLOGICALLY ARRANGED

1. Review of K. Lasswitz, *Die moderne Energetik in ihrer Bedeutung für Erkenntniskritik*, in *Psychological Review*, I (1894), 210–13.
2. Abstract. "Herr Lasswitz on Energy and Epistemology," *ibid.*, pp. 172–75.
3. Review of C. L. Morgan, *An Introduction to Comparative Psychology*, in *Psychological Review*, II (1895), 399–402.
4. Abstract. "A Theory of Emotions from the Physiological Standpoint," *ibid.*, pp. 162–64.
5. Abstract. "Some Aspects of Greek Philosophy," *University of Chicago Record*, I (1896–97), 42.
6. "The Relation of Play to Education," *ibid.*, pp. 140–45.
7. Review of Le Bon, *Psychology of Socialism*, in *American Journal of Sociology*, V (1899), 404–12.
8. "The Working Hypothesis in Social Reform," *ibid.*, pp. 367–71.
9. "Suggestions toward a Theory of the Philosophical Disciplines," *Philosophical Review*, IX (1900), 1–17.
10. "The Definition of the Psychical," *Decennial Publications, University of Chicago*, III (1903), 77–112.
11. "The Basis for a Parents' Association," *Elementary School Teacher*, IV (1903–4), 337–46.
12. "Image or Sensation," *Journal of Philosophy*, I (1904), 604–7.
13. "The Relations of Psychology and Philology," *Psychological Bulletin*, I (1904), 375–91.
14. Reviews of D. Draghicesco, *Du rôle de l'individu dans le déterminisme social*, and *Le probleme du déterminisme, déterminisme biologique et déterminisme social*, in *Psychological Bulletin*, II (1905), 399–405.
15. "The Teaching of Science in College," *Science*, XXIV (1906), 390–97.
16. "The Imagination in Wundt's Treatment of Myth and Religion," *Psychological Bulletin*, III (1906), 393–99.
17. "Science in the High School," *School Review*, XIV (1906), 237–49.
18. "Editorial Notes," *ibid.*, XV (1907), 160, 164.
19. Review of Jane Addams, *The Newer Ideal of Peace*, in *American Journal of Sociology*, XIII (1907), 121–28.
20. "Concerning Animal Perception," *Psychological Review*, XIV (1907), 383–90.
21. Abstract. "The Relation of Imitation to the Theory of Animal Perception," *Psychological Bulletin*, IV (1907), 210–11.
22. "On the Educational Situation in the Chicago Public Schools," *City Club Bulletin*, I (1907–8), 131–38.
23. "Industrial Education and Trade Schools," *Elementary School Teacher*, VIII (1907–8), 402–6.

BIBLIOGRAPHY

24. "Policy of the *Elementary School Teacher*," *ibid.*, pp. 281–84.
25. "The Philosophical Basis of Ethics," *International Journal of Ethics*, XVIII (1908), 311–23.
26. "The Social Settlement: Its Basis and Function," *University of Chicago Record*, XII (1908), 108–10.
27. "Educational Aspects of Trade Schools," *Union Labor Advocate*, VIII, No. 7 (1908), 19–20.
28. "Industrial Education and the Working Man and the School," *Elementary School Teacher*, IX (1908–9), 369–83.
29. "On the Problem of History in the Elementary School," *ibid.*, p. 433.
30. "Moral Training in the Schools," *ibid.*, pp. 327–28.
31. "Social Psychology as Counterpart to Physiological Psychology," *Psychological Bulletin*, VI (1909), 401–8.
32. "What Social Objects Must Psychology Presuppose?" *Journal of Philosophy*, VII (1910), 174–80.
33. "Social Consciousness and the Consciousness of Meaning," *Psychological Bulletin*, VII (1910), 397–405.
34. "Psychology of Social Consciousness Implied in Instruction," *Science*, XXXI (1910), 688–93.
35. Review of B. M. Anderson, Jr., *Social Value, a Study in Economic Theory*, in *Psychological Bulletin*, VIII (1911), 432–36.
36. Review of Warner Fite, *Individualism: Four Lectures on the Significance of Consciousness for Social Relations*, in *Psychological Bulletin*, VIII (1911), 323–28.
37. "Remarks on Labor Night," *City Club Bulletin*, V (1912), 214–15.
38. "Exhibit of City Club Committee on Public Education," *ibid.*, p. 9.
39. "The Mechanism of Social Consciousness," *Journal of Philosophy*, IX (1912), 401–6.
40. *A Report on Vocational Training in Chicago and in Other Cities*, by a committee of the City Club, George H. Mead, Chairman. (Chicago: City Club of Chicago, 1912), pp. 315. Reviewed by Judd, *Elementary School Teacher*, XIII (1912–13), 248–49.
41. "The Social Self," *Journal of Philosophy*, X (1913), 374–80.
42. "A Heckling School Board and an Educational Stateswoman," *Survey*, XXXI (1913–14), 443–44.
43. "The Psychological Bases of Internationalism," *ibid.*, XXXIII (1914–15), 604–7.
44. "Natural Rights and the Theory of the Political Institution," *Journal of Philosophy*, XII (1915), 141–55.
45. "Madison—The Passage of the University through the State Political Agitation of 1914; the Survey by Wm. H. Allen and His Staff and the Legislative Fight of 1915, with Indications these offer of the Place the State University Holds in the Community," *Survey*, XXXV (1915–16), 349–51, 354–61.
46. "Smashing the Looking Glass, Rejoinder," *ibid.*, pp. 607, 610.
47. "Professor Hoxie and the Community," *University of Chicago Magazine*, IX (1916–17), 114–17.

48. *The Conscientious Objector*, Pamphlet No. 33, "Patriotism through Education Series," issued by National Security League, New York City, 1917.

49. "Josiah Royce—A Personal Impression," *International Journal of Ethics*, XXVII (1917), 168–70.

50. "Scientific Method and Individual Thinker," *Creative Intelligence* (New York: Henry Holt & Co., 1917), pp. 176–227.

51. Review of Edith Abbott and Sophonisba P. Breckinridge, *Truancy and Non-Attendance in the Chicago Public Schools*, in *Survey*, XXXVIII (1917), 369–70.

52. "The Psychology of Punitive Justice," *American Journal of Sociology*, XXIII (1917–18), 577–602.

53. "Retiring President's Address," *City Club Bulletin*, XIII (1920), 94.

54. "A Behavioristic Account of the Significant Symbol," *Journal of Philosophy*, XIX (1922), 157–63.

55. "Scientific Method and the Moral Sciences," *International Journal of Ethics*, XXXIII (1923), 229–47.

56. "The Genesis of the Self and Social Control," *ibid.*, XXXV (1924–25), 251–77.

57. "The Objective Reality of Perspectives," *Proceedings of the Sixth International Congress of Philosophy* (1926), pp. 75–85. Reprinted in *The Philosophy of the Present* (Chicago, 1932); *see* No. 67.

58. "The Nature of Aesthetic Experience," *International Journal of Ethics*, XXXVI (1926), 382–92.

59. "A Pragmatic Theory of Truth," *Studies in the Nature of Truth, University of California Publications in Philosophy*, XI (1929), 65–88.

60. "The Nature of the Past," *Essays in Honor of John Dewey* (New York: Henry Holt & Co., 1929), pp. 235–42.

61. "National-Mindedness and International-Mindedness," *International Journal of Ethics*, XXXIX (1929), 385–407.

62. "Bishop Berkeley and His Message," *Journal of Philosophy*, XXVI (1929), 421–30.

63. "Cooley's Contribution to American Social Thought," *American Journal of Sociology*, XXXV (1929–30), 693–706.

64. "The Philosophies of Royce, James, and Dewey, in their American Setting," *International Journal of Ethics*, XL (1930), 211–31. Also in the co-operative volume, *John Dewey: The Man and His Philosophy* (Cambridge, Massachusetts: Harvard University Press, 1930), pp. 75–105.

65. "Philanthropy from the Point of View of Ethics," *Intelligent Philanthropy*, edited by Faris, Lane, and Dodd (Chicago: University of Chicago Press, 1930), pp. 133–48.

66. "Dr. A. W. Moore's Philosophy," *University of Chicago Record*, N.S., XVII (1931), 47–49.

67. *The Philosophy of the Present*, The Paul Carus Foundation Lectures, III (Chicago: Open Court Publ. Co., 1932), with an Introduction by Arthur E. Murphy and Prefatory Remarks by John Dewey. Pp. xl+195.

68. "The Philosophy of John Dewey," to be published in *International Journal of Ethics*, XLVI (1936).

INDEX

Abstraction, due to conflict and inhibition, 83 n.

Act
as fundamental datum for psychology, 8
as involving a natural teleology, 6 n.
consummation of, vs. physical thing, 184–85
defined, 6 n.
inner and outer aspects of, 5–6
its organization in terms of attitudes, 11
social, defined, 7
stress by comparative psychology on wholeness of, 8 n.

Action
co-operative, possible without language, 55–56
unified, due to organization of acts, 23–24

Aesthetic experience, in relation to the symbol, 147–49

Aesthetic response, its nature, 86–87

Aesthetic theory, significance of behaviorism for, 280

America, as universalizing self-government, 267

Analysis, as characteristic of reason, 94–95

Analysis of object, made possible by rôle-taking, 375–76

Animals. See Man and animals.
compared to men, 354–55
lack personality, 182–83

Aristotle, 266

Art, relation to the unconventional, 209–10

Association, laws of, as processes of redintegration, 341–43

Associational psychology, as static, 18

Attention, 25–26; 95–96
its relation to impulse, 337–38

Attitude of the engineer, 276–77

Attitudes. See Economic attitude; Religious attitude.
relation to act, 5, 362
significance for behaviorism, 8–13
social, and the physical world. 178–86

Attributes, relation to substance, 125–26

Baldwin, J. M., 64 n.

Beauty, as objectively relative character of objects, 330

Behavior. See Response.
place of mind in, 367–68

Behaviorism
and parallelism, 105, 109–17
its account of reflection, 100–109
its general position, 2, 328
practical nature of its program, 33–41
significance for aesthetic theory, 280
summary of its treatment of consciousness, 328–36
use of term, in contrast to Watson's narrower usage, 2

Bergson, H., 7 n., 22 n.

Biologic individual, in relation to self, 347–53, 370–73

Birds, song of, 61–65, 359–60

Body, relation to mind, 186 n.

Brain, 237 n.
consciousness not in brain, 112

Bryce, J., 295

Buddha, 217

Buddhism, 282, 302

Bully, explanation of, as coward, 66

Burrows, 250

Caste, 318–19

Categorical imperative
a proposed formulation, 386
inadequate for constructive moral behavior, 381
socially interpreted, 379–82

Cause, 126

Censor, 255 n.

Child. See Education.
and adult, 317–18
origin of its self in social conduct, 368–73
social nature of its reflection, 376–78

Choice, dependent on temporal dimension of nervous system, 98–100

City-state, as ideal social organization for Greeks, 266 n.

Clan, as generalization of the family, 229

Christianity, 281–82, 302
  as factor in social progress, 293
Communication, 327–28
  difference in man and in animals, 253–55
  importance of media of, 257–58
  its ideal as universal discourse, 327
  makes possible the self-conscious self, 138–39, 142, 242–44
  provides material of mind, 97
  relation to religious and economic universality, 259–60
  relation to thought and significant symbol, 68–75
  rôle in development of self, 242–44
  social foundations and functions of, 253–60
Community, and the institution, 260–73
Conditioned reflex, 9
  inadequate as explanation of thought, 106–7
  contrasted to symbol, 122 n.
Conduct
  function of imagery in, 337–44
  impulsive, 210
  intelligent, contrasted to reflective, 73–74
  social, 357–59
Conflict
  place in social integration, 303–11
  resolution through reflective thought, 308–9
Consciousness
  ambiguity of term, 27–33, 111–12, 165–73
  as corresponding only to sensory processes, 22
  as emergent in social act, 17–18
  as experience, contrasted to consciousness as rational intelligence, 30–31, 111–12, 328–36
  as experience, stated in terms of environment, 329–34
  as functional, not substantive, 112
  as reflective intelligence, 334–35
  failure of Watson's denial of, 10–11
  James's use of term, 3–4
  relation to psychology, 3–4
Consummation of act, 184–85
Contract theory of society, 233
Control
  human control of evolution, 251–52

method of controlling experience, 112–17
  of earlier phases of act by later phases, 117–18
  social, expressed in terms of self-criticism, 255
Conventions, contrasted to manners, 263
Conversation of gestures, 14, 63, 253–54
  relation to development of self, 167
  value of importation into the individual, 179
Conversion, social nature of, 219
Cooley, C. H., 173, 224 n., 318–19 n.
Co-operation, linguistic vs. non-linguistic, 55–56
Cortex, 236. See Nervous system.
Creativity of the self, 214–22
Criminal, 265
Cult, and religious conservatism, 296, 302

Darwin, 19, 358
  and the expression of the emotions, 15–18
  and Wundt, 42–44
Delayed reaction, necessary to intelligent conduct, 99–100
Democracy
  and social universality, 281–89
  implies removal of castes, 318
  its ideal as functional realization of self, 326–28
  relation to religious attitude of universal brotherhood, 286–87
Dewey, J., 79, 384
  on emotion, 21 n.
  on ethical standards, 384
  on universality as social, 88
Double
  conception of, in primitive people, 149–50
  relation to imaginary companions of the child, 150–51
Drama, social function of, 257

Economic attitudes, compared to religious attitudes, 289–98
Economic interpretation of history, 264
Economic process of exchange, its nature, 258–59, 282, 300–302
Education, 159–60, 264–65
  and the child, 317–18
  and the kindergarten, 153

Education—*Continued*
and the parental relation, 241
its task in bridging the mind-body dualism, 187 n.
Einstein, A., 202
Emergence
and consciousness, 329–34
and novelty, 198
Empire, social significance of, 284
Emotion
expression of, according to Darwin, 15–18
relation to symbol, 147–49
Ends, moral
are social in nature, 385
directed on objects, 383
Environment
as determined by individual and social organisms, 125–34, 215, 245–52
as element in the generalized other, 154 n.
its relation to consciousness as experience, 329–31
Ethical ideals and ethical problems, 319–21
Ethics, fragments on, 379–89
Evolution
appearance of mind in, 134
Darwinian, theoretically transcended by man, 250–52
mechanism and freedom in, 251–52
Exclamatory cry, 66–67
Experience
aesthetic, in relation to symbols, 147–49
and physical world, 131 n., 377–78
and science, 351–53
as environment relative to individual or social organism, 111–12
common experience compatible with differences of social function, 325–26
contact experience and things, 362–63
distance experience, 246–47
individual and social aspects of, 1–2, 33–34, 133
method of control of, 112–17
nature of the private or psychical phase of, 338–41
not necessarily of a self, 135–36
of biologic vs. social reflective individual, 351–53
of self, involves experience of others, 195

relation between private and public phases of, 41 n.
social, 89 n., 222–23
shared experience and morality, 385
subjective vs. objective contents of, 225–26
subjectivistic consequences of individualistic theory of, 224 n.

Family, 229, 238–40
Final cause and progress, 294
Fiske, J., 363
Foresight, dependent on temporal dimension of nervous system, 98–100
Freud, S., 255 n.
Freudian psychology, 211
Functional differentiation and democracy, 288–89
Functional realization of self, 323–28
Functional superiority, 285–86

Game, in relation to play, 151–63
Generalized other
as attitude of community, 154
as giving social control of individual, 155
its attitude taken in abstract thought, 155–56
relation to play and the game, 152–63
General will, 287 n.
Genius, 216–18
Gestalt psychology, an objection answered, 331–32
Gesture. *See* Conversation of gestures.
basic mechanism of social process, 13 n.
defined as part of social acts, 42–51, 53, 69 n.
relation to meaning, 145–46
self-stimulation through vocal gesture, 360–62, 364–67
significant vs. non-significant, 81
significance for behaviorism, 13–18
vocal, and significant symbol, 61–68
vocal, in birds, 61–65, 359–60
vocal, central importance of, 65–68, 69–70
Groups, social, 321–23

Hand
and the physical thing, 184–85, 248–49, 362–63
and speech in the development of the self, 237

Hallucination, 341
Helmholtz, H., 34
Herd instinct, 58, 238–39, 349
History, social importance of, 256, 297
Hume, D., 18, 343

"I." *See* "Me"; Self.
  and "me" as components of the self,
    173–78, 192–200
  appears in experience only in memory,
    173–75, 196
  as response of biologic individual to
    the "me," 175–76, 371–73
  contributions of the "I" and the "me,"
    209–13
  fusion with "me" in social activities,
    273–81
  its unpredictable nature, 176–78, 203–4
  its variable importance relative to the
    "me," 199
Idea. *See* Thought; Mind.
  as organization of attitudes, 12–13
  as reply to a social demand, 180–81
  distinction between getting and having
    an idea, 107
  getting an idea as a social process,
    72 n., 107–9
  relation to control of behavior in terms
    of future consequences, 99, 118
Ideal of human society, 310
Imagery, 113–14
  and vividness, 343–44
  as dependent upon individual, 345–46
  as objectively relative character of
    things, 332–33
  conditions for exclusion from environ-
    ment, 344–45
  its function in conduct, 337–44
  its relation to the psychical, 340–41, 343
  place in past and future reference, 344–
    45
  relation to mind, 340–43
  relation to percept, 373–74
  supposed difficulty of imagery for be-
    haviorism, 9
Imaginary companions, 370
Imitation
  does not serve as explanation of origin
    of language, 51–61
  impossible as a primitive process, 58, 60
Imperative, categorical. *See* Categorical
  imperative

Implication, a relation of responses, 126 n.
Impulses
  catalogue of, in biologic individual,
    348–49
  division into friendly and hostile, social
    and anti-social, 303–7
  function of imagery in relation to, 338
  moral, nature of, 384–85
  relation to happiness, 383–84
  relation to stimulus, 6 n.; 337–38
Individual. *See* Self.
  arises in a social process, 188–89
  as center of moral advance, 386–89
  biologic, in relation to self, 347–53,
    370, 373
  integration of, in social situations,
    321–23
  vs. institutional pole of social differen-
    tiation, 229–30
Individuality
  and democracy, 288–89
  in primitive and civilized society, 221–
    22
  not crushed by social control, 255
  not incompatible with social nature of
    the self, 201–3
  relation to social institutions, 262–63
Infancy, importance for development of
  self, 363–67
Insect society, compared to human society, 227–37
Instinct, 337, 349–50
Institution
  and the community, 260–73
  defined in terms of socially common re
    sponses, 167, 211, 261
  relation to individuality, 262–63
Institutional and individual poles of social
  differentiation, 229–30
Integration of society in relation to social
  conflict, 303–11
Intelligence
  a function of relation of form and en-
    vironment, 328
  as problem-solving, 254 n.
  human vs. animal, 92–97
  rational, as symbolic indication of
    stimulus, 93–95
  rational, summary of view presented,
    334–35
Intention, considered in relation to
  achievement, 383

Internationalism, 271–72
Introspection
    and psychology, 4
    as formulated by Watson in terms of
        language, 2, 3, 8

James, W., 3–4, 20, 28, 86, 173, 204
Jesus, 217, 266, 272
Journalism, its social function, 257

Kant, I., 379, 380, 381, 382, 384
Keller, H., 149
Kindergarten, its utilization of play in
    building the self, 153
Köhler, W., 37 n.

Labor movement, 295, 323, 325
Language, 190 n., 283, 335. See Commu-
    nication; Symbol.
    a part of social co-operative behavior,
        13–15, 74–75
    a process of self-conditioning, 108–9
    and the constitution of objects of ex-
        perience, 78
    as approached by philologist, 14
    as making analysis possible, 97
    criticism of Wundt's theory of, 48–51
    gives control of organization of the act,
        13
    gives mechanism for reflective intelli-
        gence, 124
    involves significant symbols, 45–46
    involves socially common symbols,
        54–55
    its early stages are prior to emergence
        of mind, 192
    origin not explained by imitation, 51–61
    provides field for emergence of mind,
        133
    provides mechanism for rôle-taking,
        160–61
    relation to thought, 74 n.
    rôle at the level of the developed self,
        242–44
Laughter, social nature of, 206–7
Leader, social function of, 216–18, 256–
    57
League of Nations, 209, 287
Logic. See Universe of discourse
    dependent on a field of social inter-
        course, 90 n.
    of multiple relations, 202

implication a relation of responses,
    126 n.
Logical constants, 260

Magic and science, 186
Managerial form of government, 313–14
Man and animals
    difference in social organization, 227–45
    difference in types of intelligence, 119–
        20, 347–48
    distinguished in regard to self-condi-
        tioning, 108
Manners vs. conventions, 263
Mathematics, symbols in, 268–69
McDougall, W., 366
"Me." See "I"; Self.
    and "I" as components of the self,
        173–78, 192–200
    as censor, 210
    as organized set of social attitudes in
        the individual, 175
Meaning, 125, 145–46. See Gesture; Lan-
    guage; Symbol
    and the nervous system, 104
    and the significant symbol, 72
    as involving participation and com-
        municability, 81 n.
    as socially objective, 76, 82
    does not necessarily involve conscious-
        ness of meaning, 77–81
    its definition within the social act, 75–
        82
    relation to symbols, 122 n.
    requires responses, 67
Mentality, behavioristically stated, 132–
    33
Mill, J. S., 212, 382
Mind, 131, 356–57
    and imagery, 340–43
    and the symbol, 117–25
    as a social emergent, 132–34
    as basis of resolution of social conflicts,
        308–9
    complete vs. partial social account of,
        223–25
    functional and not substantive explana-
        tion of, 223 n.
    genesis of mind-body problem, 186 n.
    involves importation of social process
        by the individual, 109, 117–25; 186–
        92
    its place in behavior, 367–68

Mind—*Continued*
its unity contrasted with the unity of
the self, 144 n.
not intra-epidermal, 223 n.
relation to human and animal intelligence, 118-19
relation to response and to environment, 125-34
relation to response and to symbol,
189-90
subjective experiences provide no explanation of, 357
Missionary movements, 296, 302
Mob, 213, 218
Mohammedanism, 281, 302
Monarch, as method of social integration,
311-12
Money, as method of economic conversation, 292
Morality
as involving rational consideration of
all conflicting interests, 386, 387-89
as method of social reconstruction, 388-
89
Morley, John, 85
Motive, moral, as impulse directed to
moral end, 383
Müller, M., 74 n.
Multiple personality, 170
Münsterberg, H., 28
Music, 280
Musical instruments, 241-42
Mystical experience, 275
Myth, 152-53, 192-93

Nature
relation to experience, 131 n.
sense in which it is intelligent, 185
Neighborliness, 272, 292-93
Nervous system
and parallelism, 115-17
as providing mechanism for recognition, 83
gives physiological basis for society,
240-42
relation to objects and to ideas, 70-71
temporal dimension of, 85, 98-100,
117-18
Novel, social function of, 257

Objects, relation of, to response, 77-80,
129-30. *See* Physical object.

Organism
social and individual, as determining
environment, 215, 245-52
relation to self, 135-44
Organization, social, through religious
and economic attitudes, 290-93, 295-
98

Parallelism, psychophysical
a practical and not metaphysical distinction, 33-41, 109-17
and behaviorism, 105, 109-17
bases of doctrine, 110-11
fundamental defect of, 42 n.
its rise in psychology, 18-33
Parental relation, 241, 364-67
Particular, in relation to universal, 84-85
Past
its character in instinctive and rational
behavior, 350-51
its relation to the present and to nervous processes, 116-17
Patriotism, 207, 306
Paul, 220
Perception, dependent on response, 114
Personality. *See* Individual; Self.
dependent on language for existence,
182-83
multiple, and dissociation, 142-44
not lost in a social theory of the self,
323-28
vs. reason as principle of social organization, 311-17
Perspectives, and meaning, 89
Philologist, his customary approach to
language, 6 n., 14
Physical object
and the hand, 248-49, 362-63
as abstraction from social process, 184
as element in the generalized other,
154 n.
as universal, 184-85
compared to self as social object, 277-81
Physical World
and experience, 377-78
relation to rôle-taking, 178-86
Physiological processes. *See* Nervous
system.
as basic to mind, found only in men,
236 n., 237 n.
social aspect of, 139 n., 227-30

INDEX

Physiological processes—*Continued*
  differentiation of, as characteristic of
    insects, 230–33
Piderit, Th., 358
Plato, 266
Play
  compared to myth, 152–53
  contrasted to game, 150–64
  relation to rôle-taking, 364–65
Poetry, nature, and rôle-taking, 183–84
Political parties
  defects of, 314
  social function of, 220
Pragmatism, 289 n.
Property, 161–62
Psychical, as a phase of experience, 331,
  338–41
Psychology. *See* Behaviorism.
  and states of consciousness, 329–34
  comparative, 8 n.
  concerned with the conditions of ex-
    perience, 35, 39, 40
  Gestalt, 37–38
  has tended to neglect the self, 200 n.
  individual, contrasted to social psy-
    chology, 1–2, 40–41
  its attempt to state reason in terms of
    conduct, 347–48
  its historical transformations, 21–22
  physiological, 20, 22–23, 27–33
  relation to consciousness, 3–4
Purpose, as factor in behavior, 100

Quality vs. quantity in social achievement, 266–68

Rationality, 334–35
Reason vs. personality as principle of
  social organization, 311–17
Recognition
  as involved in universality, 82–85
  criteria of, not normally identified,
    91–92
Reconstruction, complementary character of individual and social, 309–10
Reflection. *See* Reflective intelligence.
  involves analysis and representation
  process of, in relation to self, 354–78
Reflective intelligence
  its nature, 90–100
  behavioristic account of, 100–109

Reflexiveness, essential condition for development of mind, 134
Relativity, and consciousness, 329–34
Religious attitude
  as factor in social organization, 290–93,
    295–98
  compared to economic attitude, 289–98
  involves a social relation to world, 275
Religion, universal, 281–82
Response
  aesthetic, 86–87
  as determining environment, 77, 125–
    34
  delayed, essential to human intelli-
    gence, 254 n.
  relation to symbol, 189–90
  socially common responses define the
    institution, 261
  stimuli as means for, 6 n.
Right, moral, 387–89
Rôle-taking, 254, 360–62, 364–67, 368–73
  as condition for analysis of object, 375–
    76
  as essential to human intelligence,
    141 n.
  dependent upon language, 160–61
  factors which limit the process of, 326–
    28
  in economic process, 302
  in the play and games of children, 150–
    52
  varying degrees of the process of, 256–
    57
Rousseau, J. J., 286–87
Russell, B., 40, 111, 112

Science
  and experience, 351–53
  relation to magic, 186
Selection and consciousness, 333
Self. *See* "I"; "Me"; Mind.
  and organism, 135–44
  and process of reflection, 354–78
  and the subjective, 164–73
  as involving organization of social atti-
    tudes, 162–64
  as social object, compared to physical
    object, 277–81
  content vs. structure of, 230 n.
  factors in its genesis, 144–52
  genesis of self in social conduct, 140–
    41, 152–64, 167, 368–73

Self—*Continued*
  identified with interests, 386
  individualistic and social theories of, compared, 222–26
  its characteristic of being an object to itself, 136–37
  its importance in social reconstruction, 192, 214–22 .
  its individuality not incompatible with its social nature, 201–3, 323–28
  its realization through performing a social function, 200–209, 315–16
  its unity as social, 144
  two stages in the development of, 158
Self-consciousness
  distinguished from consciousness, 163, 165–73
  in nations, 316–17
Self-conditioning, characteristic of human intelligence, 108–9
Self-criticism, as social criticism, 255
Self-expression, in relation to convention, 212–13
Self-feeling, provides no explanation of self, 173
Sex impulse, 228
Signals, relation to significant symbols, 190–91
Significant speech, a process of self-conditioning, 108–9
Significant symbol, 71–72, 181, 268–69, 335. *See* Language; Symbol.
  and universe of discourse, 89–90
  in relation to signals of animals, 190–91
  influences the self as it influences others, 67
  not found in animal world, 358
  place in the origin of the self, 138–39
  relation to thought and communication, 68–75
  relation to vocal gesture, 61–68
"Social," wider and narrower uses of, 304
Social act
  defined, 7
  possible without consciousness, 18
Social control
  expressed in terms of self-criticism, 255
  gained through the "me" 210–11
Social evolution, two poles of the process of, 229–30; 309–10
Social groups, 157–58, 321–23

Social organization, function of personality and reason in, 311–17
Social process
  its unity analyzable but irreducible, 118 n.
  various degrees of internalization, 256 –57
Social progress, idea of, in Greek and modern world, 293–94
Social psychology
  characterized, 1, 6–8
  relation to behaviorism, 1–8
Social sciences, and psychology, 36–37
Society
  bases of human, 227–44
  human and insect, 227–37
  human and vertebrate, 238–44
  human, as end of process of organic evolution, 252
  ideal, obstacles and promises in the development of, 317–28
  primitive vs. civilized in respect to individuality, 221–22
Socrates, 217
Soul, 150
Spearman, C. E., 150
Specious present, 176
Spencer, H., 25
Standard, moral, expressed in terms of impulses, 383–85
Stimulus, as occasion for release of impulse, 6 n.
Subjective
  degree to which mind is subjectivization of social process, 188
  its relation to the self, 164–73
Substance, relation to attributes, 125–26
Superiority, sense of
  functional and assertive forms distinguished, 208–9, 285–86, 315–17
  its place in the realization of the self, 204–9
Symbol. *See* Significant symbol.
  and mind, 117–25
  as giving mechanism for reflective intelligence, 120–22
  intellectual vs. emotive character of, 75, 147–49
  involved in all thinking, 146
  involved in constituting objects, 78
  limitation of arbitrariness of, 74–75

INDEX

Symbol—*Continued*
  money as symbol, 292
  nature of, 122 n.
  relation to response, 189–90
  universal character of, 146–47
  vocal, as matrix for development of other forms of symbolism, 67–68
Sympathy, nature of, in terms of rôle-taking, 298, 366–67

Tarde, G., 53
Team work, 276
Thought
  abstract, involves generalized other, 155–56
  and the conditioned reflex, 101–2
  as elaboration of perceptual interpretation, 114–15
  as taking place by means of universals, 88
  necessarily requires symbols, 146
  not feeling, but thought, as core of the self, 173
  relation to conduct, 93 n.
  relation to significant symbol and to communication, 68–75
  social nature and function of, 141–42, 181–82, 259–60
  Watson's view of, 69
Tolstoi, L., 137

Universe of discourse
  as system of socially common meanings, 89–90, 156, 157–58, 195, 202, 269
  social significance of, 273 n., 284
Universal religions, 258, 271–72
Universality. *See* Universals.
  biological aspect of, 82–88

in society, and democracy, 281–89
  ethical, rationality a precondition of, 380
  general theory of, 82–90
  of discourse, as ideal of communication, 327
  social aspect of, 88–90, 146–47
Universals
  and particulars, 88, 125
  and universe of discourse, 269
  relation to response, 83–85
Utilitarianism, 381–82, 384

Value
  as future character of object determining response, 5 n.
  ethical, defined by the problematic situation, 388
Vertebrates and man, 238–44
Virgil, 285

War, and patriotism, 306
Watson, J. B., 2, 101, 103, 104, 106, 107, 332
  failure of his denial of consciousness, 10–11
  neglect of attitudinal phase of act, 6
  on introspection, 3, 8
  on thinking as vocalization, 69
  theory of thought and reflection inadequate, 100–109
Wordsworth, 183
Wundt, W., 19, 31–32, 53, 56, 192, 285, 358
  and the gesture, 42–51
  criticism of his theory of language, 48–51